2017.

My
iPhone® for Seniors

THIRD EDITION

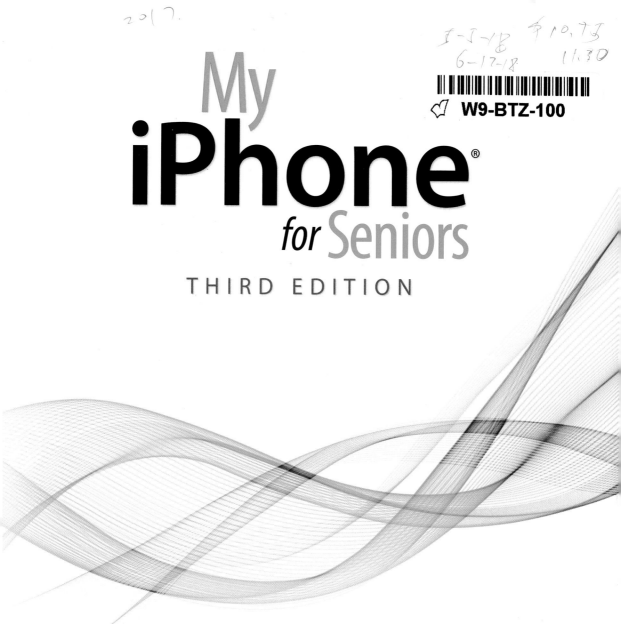

que®

800 East 96th Street,
Indianapolis, Indiana 46240 USA

My iPhone® for Seniors, Third Edition

Copyright © 2017 by Pearson Education, Inc.

ISBN-13: 978-0-7897-5817-0
ISBN-10: 0-7897-5817-2

Library of Congress Control Number: 2016955448

1 17

Trademarks

Warning and Disclaimer

Special Sales

Editor-in-Chief
Greg Wiegand

Senior Acquisitions Editor
Laura Norman

Marketing
Stephane Nakib

Director, AARP Books
Jodi Lipson

Development Editor
Charlotte Kughen

Managing Editor
Sandra Schroeder

Project Editor
Mandie Frank

Copy Editor
Charlotte Kughen

Indexer
Ken Johnson

Proofreader
The Wordsmithery LLC

Editorial Assistant
Cindy Teeters

Designer
Chuti Prasertsith

Compositor
TnT Design, Inc.

Contents at a Glance

Find the online chapters and other helpful information on this book's website at quepublishing.com/title/9780789758170.

Table of Contents

3 Connecting Your iPhone to the Internet, Bluetooth Devices, and iPhones/iPods/iPads   101

177.178.196—202—208

About the Author

Brad Miser has written extensively about technology, with his favorite topics being the amazing "i" devices, especially the iPhone, that make it possible to take our lives with us while we are on the move. In addition to *My iPhone for Seniors*, Third Edition, Brad has written many other books, including *My iPhone*, Tenth Edition; and *My Pages, Keynote, and Numbers*. He has also been an author, development editor, or technical editor for more than 50 other titles.

Brad is or has been a sales support specialist, the director of product and customer services, and the manager of education and support services for several software development companies. Previously, he was the lead proposal specialist for an aircraft engine manufacturer, a development editor for a computer book publisher, and a civilian aviation test officer/engineer for the U.S. Army. Brad holds a bachelor of science degree in mechanical engineering from California Polytechnic State University at San Luis Obispo and has received advanced education in maintainability engineering, business, and other topics.

Brad would love to hear about your experiences with this book (the good, the bad, and the ugly). You can write to him at bradmiser@icloud.com.

About AARP and AARP TEK

AARP is a nonprofit, nonpartisan organization, with a membership of nearly 38 million, that helps people turn their goals and dreams into real possibilities™, strengthens communities, and fights for the issues that matter most to families such as healthcare, employment and income security, retirement planning, affordable utilities, and protection from financial abuse. Learn more at aarp.org.

The AARP TEK (Technology Education & Knowledge) program aims to accelerate AARP's mission of turning dreams into real possibilities™ by providing step-by-step lessons in a variety of formats to accommodate different learning styles, levels of experience, and interests. Expertly guided hands-on workshops delivered in communities nationwide help instill confidence and enrich lives of people 50+ by equipping them with skills for staying connected to the people and passions in their lives. Lessons are taught on touchscreen tablets and smartphones—common tools for connection, education, entertainment, and productivity. For self-paced lessons, videos, articles, and other resources, visit aarptek.org.

Dedication

To those who have given the last full measure of devotion so that the rest of us can be free.

Acknowledgments

To the following people on the *My iPhone* project team, my sincere appreciation for your hard work on this book:

Laura Norman, my acquisitions editor, who envisioned the original concept for *My iPhone for Seniors* and works very difficult and long hours to ensure the success of each edition. Laura and I have worked on many books together, and I appreciate her professional and effective approach to these projects. Thanks for putting up with me yet one more time! Frankly, I have no idea how she does all the things she does and manages to be so great to work with given the incredible work and pressure books like this one involve!

Charlotte Kughen, my development and copy editor, who helped craft this book so that it provides useful information delivered in a comprehensible way. Thanks for your work on this book!

Mandie Frank, my project editor, who skillfully managed the hundreds of files and production process that it took to make this book. Imagine keeping dozens of plates spinning on top of poles and you get a glimpse into Mandie's daily life! (And no plates have been broken in the production of this book!)

Cindy Teeters, who handles the administrative tasks associated with my books. Cindy does her job extremely well and with a great attitude. Thank you!

Chuti Prasertsith for the cover of the book.

Que's production and sales team for printing the book and getting it into your hands.

We Want to Hear from You!

As the reader of this book, *you* are our most important critic and commentator. We value your opinion and want to know what we're doing right, what we could do better, what areas you'd like to see us publish in, and any other words of wisdom you're willing to pass our way.

We welcome your comments. You can email or write to let us know what you did or didn't like about this book—as well as what we can do to make our books better.

Please note that we cannot help you with technical problems related to the topic of this book.

When you write, please be sure to include this book's title and author as well as your name and email address. We will carefully review your comments and share them with the author and editors who worked on the book.

Email: feedback@quepublishing.com

Mail: Que Publishing
ATTN: Reader Feedback
800 East 96th Street
Indianapolis, IN 46240 USA

Reader Services

Register your copy of *My iPhone for Seniors* at quepublishing.com for convenient access to downloads, updates, and corrections as they become available. To start the registration process, go to quepublishing.com/register and log in or create an account*. Enter the product ISBN, 9780789758170, and click Submit. Once the process is complete, you will find any available bonus content under Registered Products.

*Be sure to check the box that you would like to hear from us in order to receive exclusive discounts on future editions of this product.

Using This Book

This book has been designed to help you transform an iPhone into *your* iPhone by helping you learn to use it easily and quickly. As you can tell, the book relies heavily on pictures to show you how an iPhone works. It is also task-focused so that you can quickly learn the specific steps to follow to do lots of cool things with your iPhone.

Using an iPhone involves lots of touching its screen with your fingers. When you need to tap part of the screen, such as a button or keyboard, you see a callout with the step number pointing to where you need to tap. When you need to swipe your finger along the screen, such as to browse lists, you see the following icons:

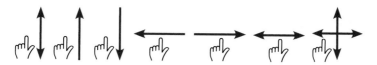

The directions in which you should slide your finger on the screen are indicated with arrows. When the arrow points both ways, you can move your finger in either direction. When the arrows point in all four directions, you can move your finger in any direction on the screen.

To zoom in or zoom out on screens, you unpinch or pinch, respectively, your fingers on the screen. These motions are indicated by the following icons:

When you need to tap once or twice, such as to zoom out or in, you see the following icons matching the number of times you need to tap:

If you use an iPhone 6s/6s Plus or later model, you can use pressure on the screen to activate certain functions. The following icons indicate when you should apply some pressure (called a peek) or slightly more pressure (called a pop):

When you can rotate your iPhone, you see this icon:

As you can see on its cover, this book provides information about iPhone models that can run iOS 10, which are the iPhone 5, iPhone 5s, iPhone 5c, iPhone SE, iPhone 6, iPhone 6 Plus, iPhone 6s, iPhone 6s Plus, iPhone 7, and iPhone 7 Plus. Each of these models has specific features and capabilities that vary slightly from the others. Additionally, they have different screen sizes with the SE being the smallest and the iPhone Plus models being the largest.

Because of the variations between the models, the figures you see in this book might be slightly different than the screens you see on your iPhone. For example, the iPhone 7 has settings that aren't on the iPhone 5s, whereas the 5s and later models support Touch ID (fingerprint recognition), although the 5 doesn't. In most cases, you can follow the steps as they are written with any of these models even if there are minor differences between the figures and your screens.

When the model you are using doesn't support a feature being described, such as the Display Zoom that is on the iPhone 6 and later but not on earlier models, you can skip that information or read it to help you decide if you want to upgrade to a newer model.

Although there are many changes in iOS 10 that you will notice, some are significant and still others are entirely new. In the case of those features that have changed significantly, or are completely new, we have added an indicator to the text and table of contents to help you easily locate them. When you see **New!** be sure to check out those tasks to quickly get up to speed on what's new in iOS 10.

Getting Started

Learning to use new technology can be intimidating. Don't worry; with this book as your guide, you'll be working with your iPhone like you've been using it all your life in no time at all.

There are several ways you can purchase an iPhone, such as from an Apple Store, from a provider's store (such as AT&T or Verizon), or from a website. And, you may be upgrading from a previous iPhone or other type of cell phone, in which case, you are using the same phone number, or you might be starting with a completely new phone and phone number. However you received your new phone, you need to turn it on, perform the basic setup (the iPhone leads you through this step-by-step), and activate the phone.

If you purchased your phone in a physical store, you probably received help with these tasks and you are ready to start learning how to use your iPhone. If you purchased your iPhone from an online store, it came with basic instructions that explain how you need to activate your phone; follow those instructions to get your iPhone ready for action.

For this book, I've assumed you have an iPhone in your hands, you have turned it on, followed the initial setup process it led you through, and activated it.

With your iPhone activated and initial setup complete, you are ready to learn how to use it. This book is designed for you to read and do at the same time. The tasks explained in this book contain step-by-step instructions that guide you; to get the most benefit from the information, perform the steps as you read them. This book helps you learn by doing!

As you can see, this book has quite a few chapters. However, there are only a few that you definitely should read as a group as you get started. You can read the rest of them as the topics are of interest to you. Most of the chapters are designed so that they can be read individually as you move into new areas of your iPhone.

After you've finished reading this front matter, I recommend you read and work through Chapter 1, "Getting Started with Your iPhone;" Chapter 2, "Using Your iPhone's Core Features," Chapter 3, "Connecting Your iPhone to the Internet, Bluetooth Devices, and iPhones/iPods/iPads;" and Chapter 4, "Setting Up and Using iCloud and Other Online Accounts" in their entirety. These chapters give you a good overview of your iPhone and help you set up the basics you use throughout the rest of the book.

From there, read the parts of Chapter 5, "Customizing How Your iPhone Works," and Chapter 6, "Customizing How Your iPhone Looks and Sounds," that are of interest to you (for example, in Chapter 6, you find out how to change the wallpaper image that you see in the background of the Home and Lock screens). Tasks covering how to protect your iPhone with a passcode and how to have your iPhone recognize your fingerprints to unlock it and to make purchases from the iTunes Store (tasks that are covered in Chapter 5) should be high on your priority list. Chapters 5 and 6 are good references whenever you need to make changes to how your iPhone is configured.

After you've finished these core chapters, you're ready to explore the rest of the book in any order you'd like. For example, when you want to learn how to use your iPhone's camera and work with the photos you take, see Chapter 14, "Taking Photos and Video with Your iPhone," and Chapter 15, "Viewing and Editing Photos and Video with the Photos App."

You'll soon wonder how you ever got along without one!

In this chapter, you get introduced to the amazing iPhone! Topics include the following:

→ Getting to know your iPhone's external features
→ Getting to know your iPhone's software

1

Getting Started with Your iPhone

Your iPhone is one of the most amazing handheld devices ever because of how well it is designed. It has only a few external features you need to understand. For most of the things you do, you just use your fingers on your iPhone's screen (which just seems natural), and the iPhone's consistent interface enables you to accomplish most tasks with similar steps.

Getting to Know Your iPhone's External Features

Take a quick look at the iPhone's physical attributes. It doesn't have many physical buttons or controls because you mostly use software to control it.

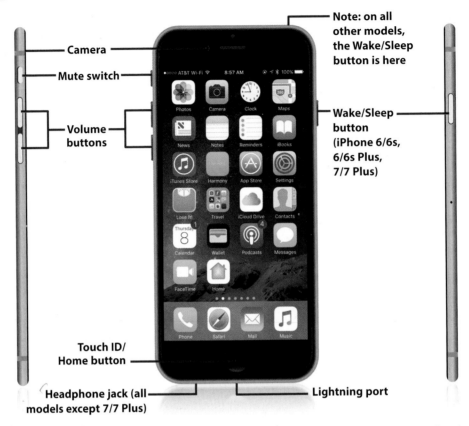

Note: on all other models, the Wake/Sleep button is here

Camera

Mute switch

Volume buttons

Wake/Sleep button (iPhone 6/6s, 6/6s Plus, 7/7 Plus)

Touch ID/ Home button

Headphone jack (all models except 7/7 Plus)

Lightning port

- **Cameras**—One of the iPhone's camera lenses is located on its backside near the top-left corner (the iPhone 7 Plus has two lenses here); the other is on the front at the top near the center of the phone. When you take photos or video, you can choose either camera to use. All iPhone models have a flash located near the camera on the backside. The iPhone 6s/6s Plus and 7/7 Plus also have a flash on the front that comes from the screen; for all earlier models, there is no flash when you use the camera on the front.

- **Wake/Sleep button**—Press this to lock the iPhone's screen and put it to sleep. Press it again to wake the iPhone from Sleep mode. You also use this button to shut down the iPhone and to power it up.

- **Mute switch**—This switch determines whether the iPhone makes sounds, such as ringing when a call comes in or making the alert noise for notifications, such as for an event on a calendar. Slide it toward the front of the iPhone to hear sounds. Slide it toward the back of the iPhone to mute all sound. When muted, you see orange in the switch.

- **Volume**—Press the upper button to increase volume; press the lower button to decrease volume. These buttons are contextual; for example, when you are listening to music, they control the music's volume, but when you aren't, they control the ringer volume. When you are using the Camera app, pressing either button takes a photo.

- **Lightning port**—Use this port, located on the bottom side of the iPhone, to plug in the Lightning headphones (iPhone 7/7 Plus) or connect it to a computer or power adapter using the included USB cable. There are also accessories that connect to this port. The Lightning port accepts Lightning plugs that are flat, thin, rectangular plugs. It doesn't matter which side is up when you plug something into this port.

  The iPhone 7/7 Plus come with an adapter that enables you to plug devices that have a 3.5 mm plug (such as prior versions of the EarPods) into the Lightning port.

- **Headphone jack (all models except the 7/7 Plus)**—This standard 3.5 mm jack can be used for headphones (such as the older EarPods) and powered speakers.

- **Touch ID/Home button (all iOS 10 compatible models except the 5/5c)**—This serves two functions. The Touch ID sensor recognizes your fingerprint, so you can simply touch it to unlock your iPhone, sign in to the iTunes Store, use Apple Pay, and enter your password in Touch ID-enabled apps. On the iPhone 7/7 Plus, it isn't technically a button, rather it is a sensor only (though it still works like a button because you press it). On all models, it also functions just like the Home button described in the following bullet.

- **Home button (iPhone 5c and 5)**—When the iPhone is asleep, press it to wake up the iPhone; press it again to unlock the phone. When the iPhone is awake and unlocked, press this button to move to the all-important Home screens; press it twice quickly to open the App Switcher. Press and hold the Home button to activate Siri to speak to your iPhone. You can also configure it so you can use it to perform other actions, such as pressing it three times to open the Magnifier.

Apple Does It Again

Apple has a history of being the first company to remove aging, but widely used, technology from its devices (for example, it was first to stop including floppy disk and CD drives on Mac computers). The iPhone 7 and 7 Plus don't have a traditional 3.5 mm headphone jack that all previous models have used to connect EarPods or external speakers. Instead, the new EarPods connect to the Lightning port. Apple includes a Lightning-to-3.5 mm headphone jack adapter that enables you to use devices that have the 3.5 mm pin connector, such as older versions of the EarPods. All other models have a 3.5 mm headphone jack in addition to the Lightning port.

One reason Apple removed the 3.5 mm jack is that the headphone jack is more susceptible to liquid penetration. Another reason is that wireless headphones are becoming more common; Apple released its own wireless AirPods shortly after the iPhone 7/7 Plus were available.

So Many iPhones, So Few Pages

The iPhone is now in its tenth generation of software that runs on multiple generations of hardware. Each successive generation has added features and capabilities to the previous version. All iPhone hardware runs the iOS operating system. However, this book is based on the current version of this operating system, iOS 10. Only the iPhone 5 and newer can run this version of the software. If you have an older version of the iPhone, this book helps you see why it is time to upgrade, but most of the information contained herein won't apply to your iPhone until you do.

There are also differences even among the models of iPhones that can run iOS 10. For example, the iPhone 5s, 6, 6 Plus, 6s, 6s Plus, 7, and 7 Plus models have Touch ID that uses your fingerprint to unlock your iPhone, to sign in to your Apple ID, and for other purposes (such as Apple Pay). The iPhone 5 and 5c do not have this capability.

This book is primarily based on the latest generation of iPhones, the iPhone 7 and 7 Plus. If you use one of the other models that can run iOS 10, there might be some differences between the details you read in this book and your phone. Those differences aren't significant and shouldn't stop you from accomplishing the tasks as described in this book.

Getting to Know Your iPhone's Software

You might not suspect it based on the iPhone's simple and elegant exterior, but this powerhouse runs very sophisticated software that enables you to do all sorts of great things. The beauty of the iPhone's software is that it is both very powerful and also easy to use—once you get used to its user interface (UI for the more technical among you). The iPhone's UI is so well designed that after a few minutes, you might wish everything worked so well and was so easy to use.

Using Your Fingers to Control Your iPhone

Apple designed the iPhone to be touched. Most of the time, you control your iPhone by using your fingers on its screen to tap buttons, select items, swipe on the screen, zoom, type text, and so on. If you want to get technical, this method of interacting with software is called the multi-touch interface.

Going Home

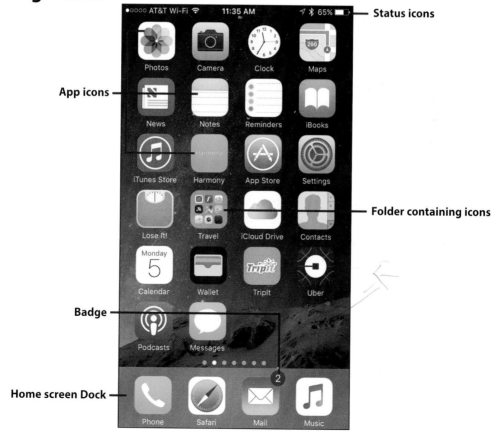

Almost all iPhone activities start at the Home screen, or Home screens, to be more accurate, because the Home screen consists of multiple pages. When your iPhone is unlocked and you are using an app, you get to the Home screen by pressing the Touch ID/Home button once. You move to the Home screen automatically any time you restart your iPhone and unlock it. Along the bottom of the Home screen (or along the side on an iPhone 6 Plus/6s Plus/7 Plus held horizontally) is the Dock, which is always visible on the Home screen. This gives you easy access to the icons it contains; up to four icons can be placed on this Dock. Above the Dock are apps that do all sorts of cool things. As you install apps, the number of icons on the Home screens increases. To manage these icons, you can organize the pages of the Home screens in any way you like, and you can place icons into folders to keep your Home screens tidy. At the top of the screen are status icons that provide you with important information, such as whether you are connected to a Wi-Fi network and the current charge of your iPhone's battery.

Touching the iPhone's Screen

The following figures highlight the major ways you control an iPhone:

- **Tap**—Briefly touch a finger to the iPhone's screen and then lift your finger again. When you tap, you don't need to apply pressure to the screen, simply touch your finger to it. For example, to open an app, you tap its icon.

Tap an app's icon to launch it

- **Double-tap**—Tap twice. You double-tap to zoom in on something; for example, you can double-tap on a webpage to view something at a larger size.

- **Swipe**—Touch the screen at any location and slide your finger (you don't need to apply pressure, just touching the screen is enough). You use the swipe motion in many places, such as to browse a list of options or to move among Home page screens.

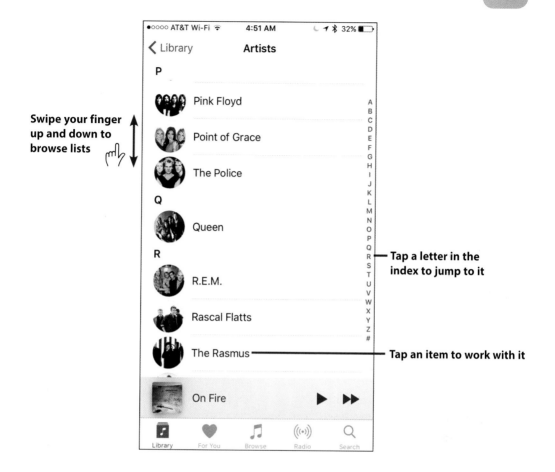

Swipe your finger up and down to browse lists

Tap a letter in the index to jump to it

Tap an item to work with it

- **Drag**—Tap and hold an object and move your finger across the screen without lifting it up; the faster you move your finger, the faster the resulting action happens. (Again, you don't need to apply pressure, just make contact.) For example, you can drag icons around the Home screens to rearrange them.

- **Pinch or unpinch**—Place two fingers on the screen and drag them together or move them apart; the faster and more you pinch or unpinch, the "more" the action happens (such as a zoom in). When you are viewing photos, you can unpinch to zoom in on them or pinch to zoom out again.

Swipe your finger up, down, left, and right to scroll

Unpinch your fingers or tap twice to zoom in

Pinch your fingers or tap twice to zoom out

Tap a link to move to it

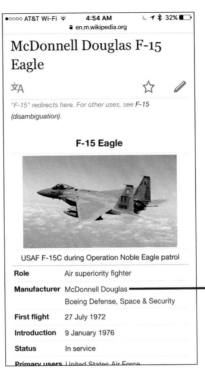

Swipe your finger to the right to move to the previous screen

Swipe your finger to the left to move to the next screen

Tap the screen to show/hide toolbars

Tap controls to activate them

- **Rotate**—Rotate the iPhone to change the screen's orientation.

Rotate the iPhone to change the screen's orientation

- **Peek**—On an iPhone that supports 3D Touch (iPhone 6s, 6s Plus, 7, and 7 Plus), you can take action by applying pressure to the screen. When you are looking at a preview of something, such as an email, tap and put a small amount of pressure on the screen to perform a Peek. A Peek causes a window to open that shows a preview of the object. You can look at the preview of the object in the Peek window; if you swipe up on a Peek, you get a menu of commands related to the object. For example, when you perform a Peek on an email and then swipe up on the Peek, you can tap Reply to reply to the email.

Tap and press on something to perform a Peek

When you see the upward-facing arrow, you can swipe up on a Peek to reveal menus with actions you can select to perform them

A Peek is a quick way to look at something without actually opening it

When you swipe up on a Peek, you get a menu; tap an action to perform it

- **Pop**—When you are looking at a Peek, apply slightly more pressure on the screen to perform a Pop, which opens the object in its app. For example, you can perform a Peek on a photo's thumbnail to preview it. Apply a bit more pressure (a Pop) on the preview to "pop" it open in the Photos app.

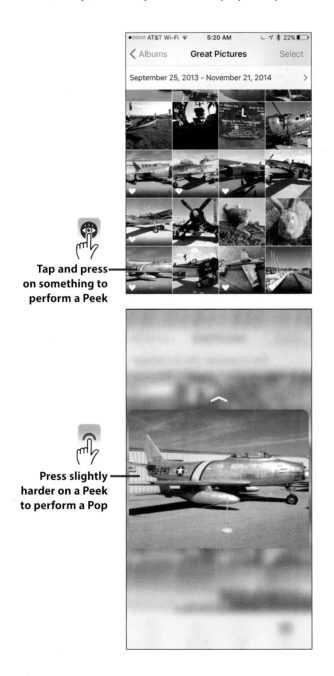

Tap and press on something to perform a Peek

Press slightly harder on a Peek to perform a Pop

When you perform a Pop, the object opens in the associated app

Working with iPhone Apps

When you tap an app's icon, it opens and fills the iPhone's screen

One of the best things about an iPhone is that it can run all sorts of applications, or in iPhone lingo, *apps*. It includes a number of preinstalled apps, such as Mail, Safari, and so on, but you can download and use thousands of other apps through the App Store. You learn about many of the iPhone's preinstalled apps as you read through this book. And, as you learned earlier, to launch an app, you simply tap its icon. The app opens and fills the iPhone's screen. You can then use the app to do whatever it does.

Pressing on an app's icon pops open the Quick Actions menu ⟶

Tap a Quick Action to perform it ⟶

On an iPhone that supports 3D Touch (iPhone 6s, 6s Plus, 7, and 7 Plus), you can press on an app's icon to open its Quick Actions menu; tap an action to take it. For example, when you open the Quick Actions menu for the Phone app, you can place calls to people you have designated as favorites.

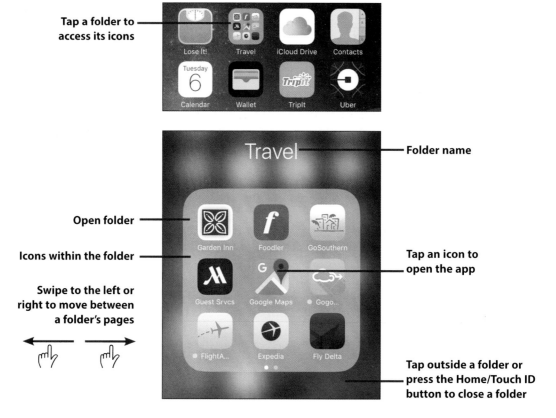

Tap a folder to access its icons

Folder name

Open folder

Icons within the folder

Tap an icon to open the app

Swipe to the left or right to move between a folder's pages

Tap outside a folder or press the Home/Touch ID button to close a folder

In Chapter 6, "Customizing How Your iPhone Looks and Sounds," you learn how you can organize icons in folders to keep your Home screens tidy and make getting to icons faster and easier. To access an icon that is in a folder, tap the folder. It opens and takes over the screen. Under its name is a box showing the apps it contains. Like the Home screens, folders can have multiple pages. To move between a folder's pages, swipe to the left to move to the next screen or to the right to move to the previous one. Each time you "flip" a page, you see another set of icons. You can close a folder without opening an app by tapping outside its borders or by pressing the Home/Touch ID button.

To open an app within a folder, tap its icon.

When you are done using an app, press the Home/Touch ID button. You return to the Home screen you were most recently using.

When you move out of an app by pressing the Home/Touch ID button, the app moves into the background but doesn't stop running (you can control whether or not apps are allowed to work in the background, as you learn in a later section).

So, if the app has a task to complete, such as uploading photos or playing audio, it continues to work behind the scenes. In some cases, most notably games, the app becomes suspended at the point you move it into the background by switching to a different app or moving to a Home screen. In addition to the benefit of completing tasks when you move into another app, the iPhone's capability to multitask means that you can run multiple apps at the same time. For example, you can run an Internet radio app to listen to music while you switch over to the Mail app to work on your email.

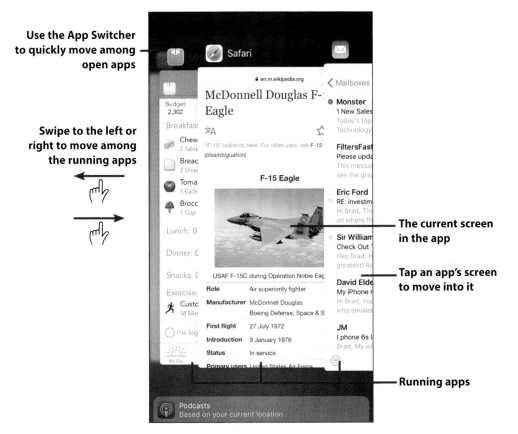

Use the App Switcher to quickly move among open apps

Swipe to the left or right to move among the running apps

The current screen in the app

Tap an app's screen to move into it

Running apps

You can control apps by using the App Switcher. To see this, quickly press the Touch ID/Home button twice. The App Switcher appears.

At the top of the App Switcher, you see icons for apps you have used recently. Under each app's icon, you see a thumbnail of that app's screen. You can swipe to the left or right to move among the apps you see. You can tap an app's screen to move into it. That app takes over the screen, and you can work with it, picking up right where you left off the last time you used it.

When you open the App Switcher, the app you were using most recently comes to the center to make it easy to return to. This enables you to toggle between two apps easily. For example, suppose you need to enter a confirmation number from one app into another app. Open the app into which you want to enter the number. Then open the app containing the number you need to enter. Open the App Switcher and tap the previous app to return to it quickly so that you can enter the number.

To close the App Switcher without moving into a different app, press the Home/Touch ID button once. You move back into the app or Home screen you were most recently using.

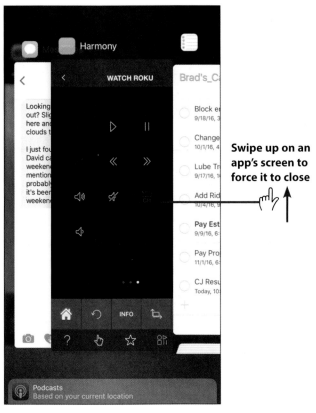

Swipe up on an app's screen to force it to close

In some cases, you might want to force an app to quit, such as when it's using up your battery too quickly or it has stopped responding to you. To do this, open the App Switcher by quickly pressing the Touch ID/Home button twice. Swipe up on the app you want to stop. The app is forced to quit, its icon and screen disappear, and you remain in the App Switcher. You should be careful about this, though, because if the app has unsaved data, that data is lost when you force the app to quit. The app is not deleted from the iPhone—it is just shut down until you open it again (which you can do by returning to the Home screen and tapping the app's icon).

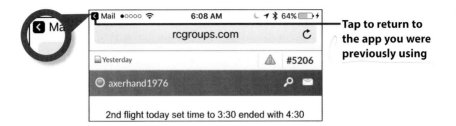

Tap to return to the app you were previously using

Sometimes, a link in one app takes you into a different app. When this happens, you see a left-facing arrow with the name of the app you were using in the upper-left corner of the screen. You can tap this button to return to the app you came from. For example, you can tap a link in a Mail email message to open the associated web page in Safari. To return to the email you were reading in the Mail app, tap the Mail button in the upper-left corner of the screen.

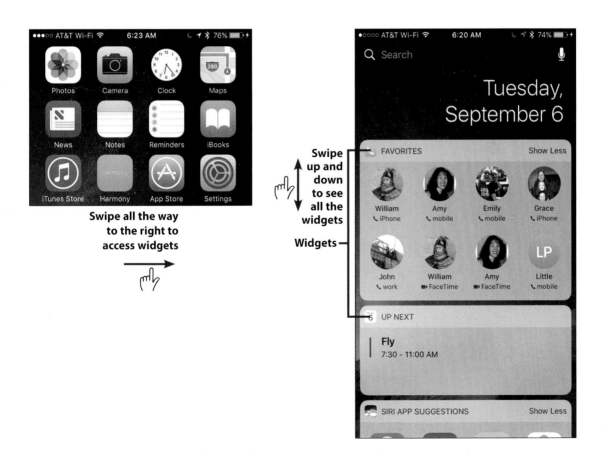

Swipe all the way to the right to access widgets

Swipe up and down to see all the widgets

Widgets

Music widget — MUSIC — Show Less — Tap to show less

Tap an album to play it

Mail widget — MAIL — Show More — Tap to show more

Tap a VIP to read email from him

Laura No...   Edward   Pappy   The Bruce

New! Apps can provide widgets, which make it easy to work with those apps from the Widget Center. To access these widgets, swipe all the way to the right from a Home screen or from the Lock screen (more on this later). You see widgets for various apps. Swipe up or down the screen to browse all the widgets available to you. Tap Show Less to collapse a widget or tap Show More to expand it. Tap something inside a widget to use that app. For example, tapping an album in the Music widget plays it. You learn more about how to use and configure widgets in Chapter 2, "Using Your iPhone's Core Features."

Using the Home Screens

Previously in this chapter, you read that the Home screen is the jumping-off point for many of the things you do with your iPhone because that is where you access the icons you tap to launch things such as apps you've saved there.

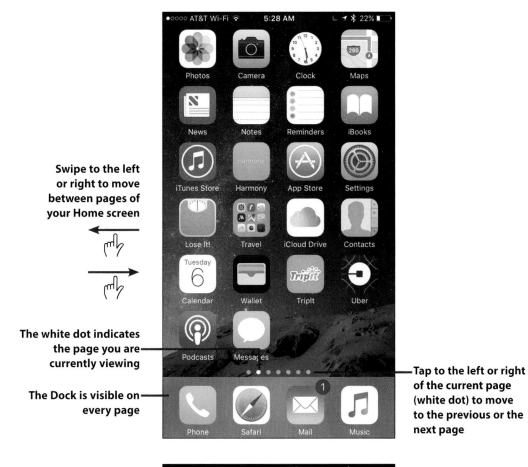

Swipe to the left or right to move between pages of your Home screen

The white dot indicates the page you are currently viewing

The Dock is visible on every page

Tap to the left or right of the current page (white dot) to move to the previous or the next page

When you move to a different page, you see a different set of icons and folders

The Home screen has multiple pages. To change the page you are viewing, swipe to the left to move to later pages or to the right to move to earlier pages. The dots above the Dock represent the pages of the Home screen. The white dot represents the page being displayed. You can also change the page by tapping to the left of the white dot to move to the previous page or to the right of it to move to the next page.

Using the iPhone Plus' Split-Screen

When you hold an iPhone 6 Plus/6s Plus/7 Plus in the horizontal orientation, you can take advantage of the Split-screen feature in many apps (not all apps support this). In Split-screen mode, the screen has two panes. The left pane is for navigation, whereas the right pane shows the content selected in the left pane. The two panes are independent, so you can swipe up and down on one side without affecting the other. In most apps that support this functionality, there is a button you can use to open or close the split screen. This button changes depending on the app you are using. For example, when you are using Safari to browse the Web, tap the Bookmark button to open the left pane and tap it again to close the left pane (while the left pane is open, you can select bookmarks on that pane and see the associated web pages in the right pane). As another example, in the Mail app, you tap the Full Screen button (two arrows pointing diagonally away from each other) to open or close the left pane.

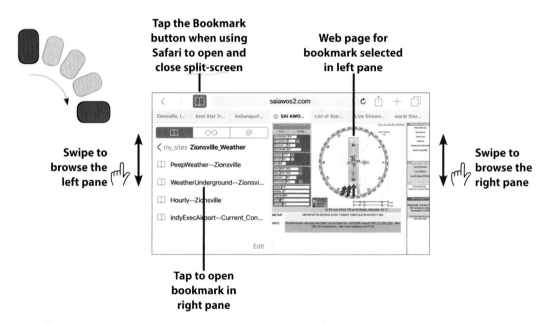

Tap the Bookmark button when using Safari to open and close split-screen

Web page for bookmark selected in left pane

Swipe to browse the left pane

Swipe to browse the right pane

Tap to open bookmark in right pane

Apps that support this functionality include Settings, Mail, Safari, and Messages; you see examples showing how Split-screen works in those apps later in this book. You should hold the iPhone 6 Plus/6s Plus/7 Plus horizontally when using your favorite apps to see if they support this feature.

Home screen pages   Dock

When you hold the 6 Plus/6s Plus/7 Plus horizontally and move to the Home screen, the Dock moves to the right side of the screen and you see the Home screen's pages in the left part of the window. Though this looks a bit different, it works the same as when you hold an iPhone vertically.

Working with the Control Center

On the Home screen or when you are using apps, swipe up from the bottom of the screen to open the Control Center

On the Lock screen, swipe up from the bottom of the screen to open the Control Center

On some app screens, where you swipe up to open the Control Center is indicated by an upward-facing arrow

Picked one of these up used today! Great deal too.

The Control Center provides quick access to a number of very useful controls. To access it, swipe up from the bottom of the screen. If your iPhone is asleep/locked, press the Sleep/Wake or Touch ID/Home button to wake up the phone and then swipe up from the bottom of the screen. Sometimes when you are using an app, the place where you swipe up is marked with an upward-pointing arrow. Regardless of the screen you are on, when you swipe up, the Control Center opens and gives you quick access to a number of controls.

Control Center Tip

Some apps have their own Dock at the bottom of the screen. When you are using such an app, make sure you don't touch a button on the Dock when you are trying to open the Control Center because you'll do whatever the button is for instead. Just swipe up on an empty area of the app's Dock and the Control Center opens.

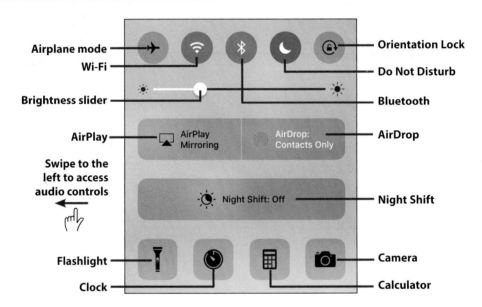

At the top of the Control Center are buttons you can use to turn on or turn off important functions. To activate a function, tap the button, which changes color to show the function is active. To disable a function, tap the button so that it becomes gray to show you it is inactive. For example, to lock the orientation of the iPhone's screen in its current position, tap the Orientation Lock button so it becomes red. Your iPhone screen's orientation no longer changes when you rotate the phone. To make the orientation change when you rotate the phone again, turn off the Orientation Lock button. You learn about Airplane mode later in this chapter and Do Not Disturb in Chapter 2. Wi-Fi and Bluetooth are explained in Chapter 3, "Connecting Your iPhone to the Internet, Bluetooth Devices, and iPhones/iPods/iPads."

Below the top function buttons is the Brightness slider. Drag the slider to the right to make the screen brighter or to the left to make it dimmer.

The AirDrop button enables you to share content with other iOS devices and Mac users in the same vicinity; this is covered in Chapter 3. The AirPlay button enables you to stream your iPhone's music, podcasts, photos, and video onto other devices, such as a TV to which an Apple TV is connected.

The Night Shift button turns this feature off or on; Night Shift is covered in Chapter 6.

At the bottom of the Control Center are four app icons; tap an icon to open the app, just as you do on the Home screens. The Flashlight app uses your iPhone's flash as a flashlight. The Clock app provides you with a number of time-related functions, which are world clocks, alarms, bedtime clock, stopwatch, and timer; when you open this app from the Control Center, it opens in the timer, but you can use its other functions by tapping the function you want to use. The Calculator does just what it sounds like it does; when you hold the iPhone vertically, you see a simple calculator, whereas if you rotate the iPhone to horizontal, the calculator becomes more powerful. The Camera app enables you to capture photos and video (this is covered in Chapter 14, "Taking Photos and Video with Your iPhone").

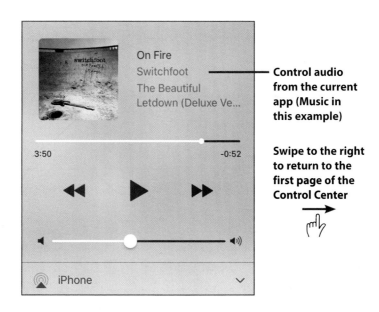

On Fire
Switchfoot
The Beautiful
Letdown (Deluxe Ve...

Control audio from the current app (Music in this example)

3:50   -0:52

Swipe to the right to return to the first page of the Control Center

iPhone

New! If you swipe to the left on the Control Center, you see controls you can use to play audio in the app you are currently using or recently used. For example, if you listen to music with the Music app, you can use the controls on the Control Center to play or pause music, change the volume, and so on. If you are listening to a podcast using the Podcasts app, you see its controls there instead. Swipe to the right to return to the first page of the Control Center.

Control Center Options

By default, the Control Center is available when you are on the Lock screen and when you are using apps. If you don't want it to be available in these locations, open the Settings app (you learn more about this app in Chapter 2) and tap Control Center. To prevent the Control Center from being used on the Lock screen, set the Access on Lock Screen switch to off (white). To prevent the Control Center from being used while an app is on the screen, set the Access Within Apps switch to off (white); you can still open the Control Center by first moving back to a Home screen.

Working with the Notification Center

Your iPhone has a lot of activity going on, from new emails to reminders to calendar events. The iOS notification system keeps you informed of these happenings through a number of means. Visual notifications include alerts, banners, and badges. Alert sounds can also let you know something has happened, and vibrations make you feel the new activity. There are a variety of notification options for each app. You learn how to work with and customize the notifications your iPhone uses in Chapter 2.

Swipe down from the top of the screen to open the Notification Center

Individual notifications (onscreen alerts, sounds, or vibrations) arrive with the events with which they are associated such as new emails, messages, and updated information from apps. For example, you can have banner notifications and a sound when you receive new emails.

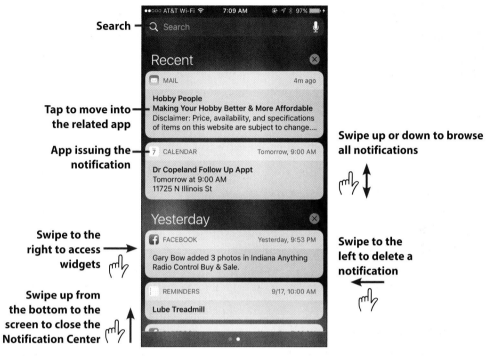

Search

Tap to move into the related app

App issuing the notification

Swipe up or down to browse all notifications

Swipe to the right to access widgets

Swipe to the left to delete a notification

Swipe up from the bottom to the screen to close the Notification Center

You can also access groups of notifications on the Notification Center, which you open by swiping down from the top of the screen. The Notification Center opens and displays notifications grouped by day and the app from which they come. You can read the notifications by swiping up and down the screen. On an iPhone with 3D Touch, touch a notification to pop it open to read more of it or to take action on it; press a little harder to open the associated app. On iPhones without 3D Touch, tap a notification to move into the associated app.

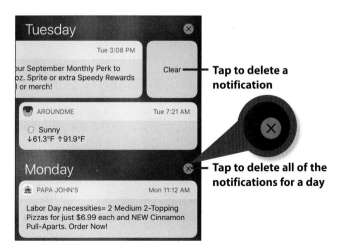

Tap to delete a notification

Tap to delete all of the notifications for a day

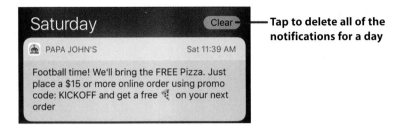

Tap to delete all of the
notifications for a day

You can delete an individual notification by swiping to the left on it and tapping Clear.

You can remove all the notifications for a day by tapping its delete (x) button and then tapping Clear.

If you swipe to the right on the Notification Center, you access app widgets, which are also explained in more detail in Chapter 2.

To close the Notification Center, swipe up from the bottom of the screen.

I've Been Searching for You

At the top of the Notification Center and SIRI SUGGESTIONS screen, you see the Search bar. You can use this to search your iPhone. This feature is explained in Chapter 2.

Using Siri Suggestions

Swipe down
from about ¾
up the screen
to open SIRI
SUGGESTIONS

Tap to show
fewer apps

Tap an app
to open it

Tap to close SIRI
SUGGESTIONS

Earlier, you learned how to access apps from the Home page and App Switcher. Your iPhone can make recommendations about apps that you might want to use based on those you have most recently used, your current activity, and even your location. You can see these suggestions by swiping down from about ¾ up the screen (if you swipe down from the top, you open the Notification Center instead). In the SIRI SUGGESTIONS panel, you see the apps being suggested. Tap an app to open it. You can show more apps by tapping Show More, or if the panel is already expanded, tap Show Less to show fewer apps. If you don't want to use any of the apps shown, tap outside the SIRI SUGGESTIONS area to close it.

Using the Do Not Disturb Mode

All the notifications your iPhone uses to communicate with you are useful, but at times, they can be annoying or distracting. When you put your iPhone in Do Not Disturb mode, its visual, audible, and vibration notifications are disabled so that they won't bother you. For example, the phone won't ring if someone calls you unless you specify certain contacts whose calls you do want to receive while your phone is in this mode.

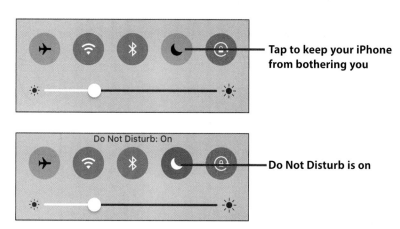

Tap to keep your iPhone from bothering you

Do Not Disturb is on

To put your iPhone in Do Not Disturb mode, open the Control Center and tap the Do Not Disturb button. It becomes purple and the Do Not Disturb: On status appears at the top of the Control Center. Your iPhone stops notifications. To make your notifications active again, tap the Do Not Disturb button so it is gray; your iPhone resumes trying to get your attention when it is needed.

In Chapter 2, you learn how to set a schedule for Do Not Disturb so that your iPhone goes into this mode automatically at certain times, such as from 10 p.m. to 6 a.m. You can also configure certain exceptions, including whose calls come in even when your iPhone is in Do Not Disturb mode.

Using Airplane Mode

Although there's a debate about whether cellular devices such as iPhones pose any real danger to the operation of aircraft, there's no reason to run any risk by using your iPhone's cellular functions while you are on an airplane. (Besides, not following crew instructions on airplanes can lead you to less-than-desirable interactions with the flight crew.) When you place your iPhone in Airplane mode, its transmitting and receiving functions are disabled, so it poses no threat to the operation of the aircraft. While it is in Airplane mode, you can't use the phone, the Web, Siri, or any other functions that require communication between your iPhone and other devices or networks.

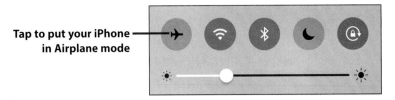

Tap to put your iPhone in Airplane mode

To put your iPhone in Airplane mode, swipe up from the bottom of the screen to open the Control Center and tap the Airplane mode button. All connections to the Internet and the cell network stop, and your iPhone goes into quiet mode in which it doesn't broadcast or receive any signals. The Airplane mode button becomes orange, the Wi-Fi and Bluetooth buttons are set to off, and you see the Airplane mode icon at the top of the screen.

In Airplane mode, you can use apps that don't require an Internet connection, such as iBooks, Music, Videos, Photos, and so on.

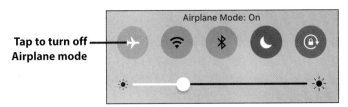

Tap to turn off Airplane mode

To turn off Airplane mode, open the Control Center and tap the Airplane mode button; it becomes gray again and the Airplane mode icon disappears. The iPhone resumes transmitting and receiving signals, and all the functions that require a connection start working again.

 Wi-Fi in Airplane Mode

Many airplanes support Wi-Fi on board. To access a Wi-Fi network without violating the requirement not to use a cell network, put the iPhone in Airplane mode, which turns off Wi-Fi. On the Control Center, tap the Wi-Fi button to turn Wi-Fi back on. Wi-Fi starts up and you can select the network you want to join (see Chapter 3). You can use this configuration at other times, too, such as when you want to access the Internet but don't want to be bothered with phone calls. When your iPhone is in Airplane mode and Wi-Fi is on, all your calls (including Wi-Fi calls) go straight to voicemail but you can use your Internet-related apps. (I would never do this, you understand.)

Meeting Siri

Siri is the iPhone's voice-recognition and control software. This feature enables you to accomplish many tasks by speaking. For example, you can create and send text messages, reply to emails, make phone calls, get directions, and much more. (Using Siri is explained in detail in Chapter 12, "Working with Siri.")

When you perform actions, Siri uses the related apps to accomplish what you've asked it to do. For example, when you create a meeting, Siri uses the Calendar app.

Siri is a great way to control your iPhone, especially when you are working in handsfree mode.

Your iPhone has to be connected to the Internet for Siri to work. That's because the words you speak are sent over the Internet, transcribed into text, and then sent back to your iPhone. If your iPhone isn't connected to the Internet, this can't happen and Siri reports that it can't connect to the network or simply that it can't do what you ask right now.

Using Siri is pretty simple because it follows a consistent pattern and prompts you for input and direction.

Activate Siri by pressing and holding down the Touch ID/Home button or pressing and holding down the center part of the buttons on the right EarPod wire until you hear the Siri chime. If so configured (see Chapter 12), you can say "Hey Siri" to activate it, too. This puts Siri in "listening" mode and the "What can I help you with?" text appears on the screen. This indicates Siri is ready for your command.

Siri is ready to do your bidding

This line shows what Siri is hearing

What Siri heard you say

Siri is going to call Robert and needs to know which number to call

Tell Siri which phone number to use by saying "iPhone"

Speak your command or ask a question. When you stop speaking, Siri goes into processing mode. After Siri interprets what you've said, it provides two kinds of feedback to confirm what it heard: It displays what it heard on the screen and provides audible feedback to you. Siri then tries to do what it thinks you've asked and shows you what it is doing. If it needs more input from you, you're prompted to provide it and Siri moves into "listening" mode automatically.

If Siri requests that you confirm what it is doing or to make a selection, do so. Siri completes the action and displays what it has done; it also audibly confirms the result.

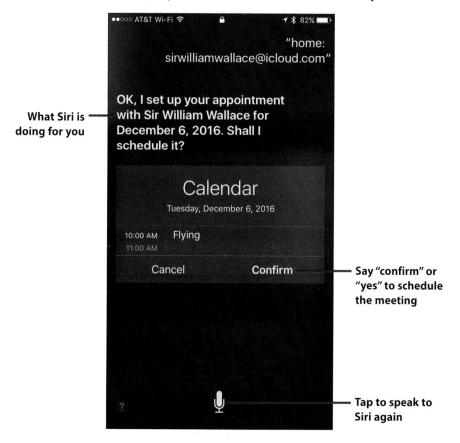

What Siri is doing for you

Say "confirm" or "yes" to schedule the meeting

Tap to speak to Siri again

Siri isn't quite like using the computer on the Starship Enterprise on *Star Trek*, but it's pretty darn close. Mostly, you can just speak to Siri as you would talk to someone else, and it is able to do what you want or asks you the information it needs to do what you want.

Understanding iPhone Status Icons

At the top of the screen is the Status bar with various icons that provide you with information, such as if you are in Airplane mode, whether you are connected to a Wi-Fi or cellular data network, the time, whether the iPhone's orientation is locked, the state of the iPhone's battery, and so on. Keep an eye on this area as you use your iPhone. The following table provides a guide to the most common of these icons.

iPhone Status Icons

Icon	Description	Where to Learn More
●●○○○	Signal Strength—Indicates how strong the cellular signal is.	Chapter 3
AT&T	Provider name—The provider of the current cellular network.	Chapter 3
LTE	Cellular data network—Indicates which cellular network your iPhone is using to connect to the Internet.	Chapter 3
📶	Wi-Fi—Indicates your phone is connected to a Wi-Fi network.	Chapter 3
Wi-Fi 📶	Wi-Fi calling—Indicates your phone can make voice calls over a Wi-Fi network.	Chapter 3
🌙	Do Not Disturb—Your iPhone's notifications and ringer are silenced.	Chapters 1, 2
❋	Bluetooth—Indicates if Bluetooth is turned on or off and if your phone is connected to a device.	Chapter 3
15%	Battery percentage—Percentage of charge remaining in the battery.	Chapter 17
🔋	Battery status—Relative level of charge of the battery.	Chapter 17
🔋	Low Battery status—The battery has less than 20% power remaining.	Chapter 17
🔋	Low Power mode—The iPhone is operating in Low Power mode.	Chapter 17
🔒	Orientation Lock—Your iPhone's screen won't change when you rotate your iPhone.	Chapter 1
⚡	Charging—The battery in the iPhone is being charged.	Chapter 17
➤	Location Services—An app is using the Location Services feature to track your iPhone's location.	Chapter 4
✈	Airplane mode—The transmit and receive functions are disabled.	Chapter 1

Turning Your iPhone Off or On

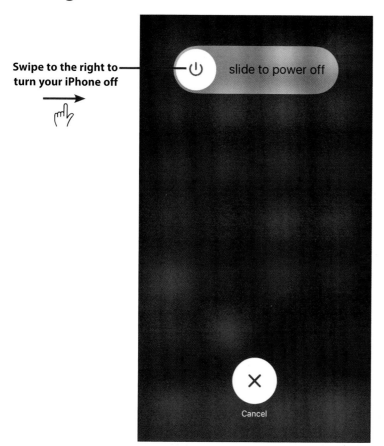

Swipe to the right to turn your iPhone off

You seldom need to turn your iPhone off, but when you do, press and hold the Wake/Sleep button until the slider appears at the top of the screen. Swipe the slider to the right to shut down the iPhone. The iPhone shuts down.

To restart your iPhone, press and hold the Wake/Sleep button until the Apple logo appears on the screen, and then let go of the button.

After it starts up, and you have a passcode, you see the Enter Passcode screen. Enter your passcode to start using your phone; once your passcode is entered correctly, you move to the Home screen. (Even if you have Touch ID enabled to unlock your phone, you must enter your passcode the first time you unlock it after a restart.)

If you don't have a passcode configured, you move directly to the Home screen when the phone starts and it's ready for you to use. Keep in mind, if you do not have a passcode configured, your phone is vulnerable to anyone who gets hold of it. (See Chapter 5 for more information about configuring passcodes and Touch ID.)

Sleeping/Locking and Waking/Unlocking Your iPhone

When your iPhone sleeps, it goes into a low power mode to extend battery life. Some processes keep working, such as playing music, whereas others stop until your iPhone wakes up. Almost all of the time, you'll put your iPhone to sleep rather than turning it off because it's much faster to wake up than to turn on. Because it uses so little power when it's asleep, there's not much reason to shut it down.

Also, when you put your iPhone to sleep, much of its functionality can't be used until it is unlocked; you can do a number of tasks, such as use widgets and view notifications while the iPhone is awake, but locked. If you set your iPhone to require a passcode to unlock, this also protects your information. Even when the iPhone is asleep, you can receive and work with notifications, such as when you receive emails or text messages. (See Chapter 2 to configure which notifications you see on the Lock screen and how you can interact with them.)

To put your iPhone to sleep and lock it, press the Wake/Sleep button. The screen goes dark.

When an iPhone is asleep/locked, you need to wake it up to use it. You can do this in several ways: touch the Home/Touch ID button, press the Wake/Sleep button, or simply raise the iPhone (on models that support the Raise to Wake feature). The Lock screen appears.

If you want to use app widgets (swipe to the right), access the Notification Center (swipe down from the top of the screen), open the Control Center (swipe up from the bottom of the screen), take photos or video (swipe to the left), or control audio playback (when audio is playing the controls appear on the Lock screen), you can do so directly on the Lock screen.

When you are ready to use apps or access your Home screens, you need to unlock your iPhone.

Swipe down to open the Notification Center

This iPhone is awake and locked

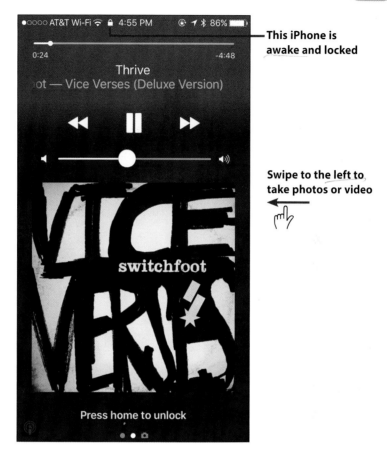

Swipe to the right to access widgets

Swipe to the left to take photos or video

Swipe up to open the Control Center

If you have an iPhone 5s or later model, and have configured it to recognize your fingerprint to unlock it, wake up the iPhone using any of the options described earlier and then press the Home/Touch ID button with a finger whose fingerprint has been stored for use; if you are using an iPhone 7 or 7 Plus, you don't need to press the Home/Touch ID button and can simply touch it instead. When your fingerprint is recognized, your iPhone unlocks and you can start using it.

Be Recognized

To use the Touch ID, you need to train your iPhone to recognize the fingerprints you want to use. You were prompted to configure one fingerprint when you started your iPhone for the first time. You can change or add fingerprints for Touch ID at any time; see Chapter 5 for the details of configuring Touch ID.

If you have an iPhone 5 or 5c, or you don't have Touch ID configured to unlock your phone, wake up the phone and then press the Touch ID/Home button. Enter your passcode to unlock the phone.

However you unlock the phone, when it unlocks, you move to the last screen you were using before it was locked.

The Time Is Always Handy

If you use your iPhone as a watch the way I do, just wake it up. The current time and date appear; if you don't unlock it, the iPhone goes back to sleep after a few seconds.

Enter your passcode to start using your iPhone ———

If you don't use your iPhone for a while, it automatically goes to sleep and locks according to the preferences you have set for it (these are covered in Chapters 5 and 6).

Signing In to Your Apple ID

As you learn throughout this book, an Apple ID is useful in many situations, such as to access iCloud services; purchase music, movies, and other content from the iTunes Store; download apps from the App Store; and so on. If you have an iPhone 5s or later, you can quickly sign in to your Apple ID by using the iPhone's Touch ID/Home button. (As referenced in the prior note, you need to configure your iPhone to recognize your fingerprint to use Touch ID and to enable where it can be used; see Chapter 5 for details.)

When you need to sign in to your Apple ID, you see a prompt. Simply touch your finger to the Touch ID/Home button. When your fingerprint is recognized, you sign in to your Apple ID and can complete whatever you were doing, such as downloading music from the iTunes Store.

If you have an iPhone that doesn't support Touch ID or you don't have the settings configured to enable you to use Touch ID with your Apple ID, you need to provide your Apple ID password to sign in by typing it and tapping OK. Whatever action you were performing is completed.

Setting the Volume

Setting the ringer volume

To change the iPhone's volume, press the up or down Volume button on the side of the iPhone. When you change the volume, your change affects the current activity. For example, if you are on a phone call, the call volume changes, or if you are listening to music, the music's volume changes. If you aren't on a screen that shows a Volume slider, an icon pops up to show you the relative volume you are setting and the type, such as setting the ringer's volume. When the volume is right, release the Volume button.

Drag to the left or right to change the volume level

When you are using an audio app, such as the Music app, you can also drag the volume slider in that app or on the Control Center to increase or decrease the volume. Drag the slider to the left to lower volume or to the right to increase it.

When you use the iPhone's EarPods, you can change the volume by pressing the upper part of the switch on the right EarPod's wire to increase volume or the lower part to decrease it.

To mute your phone's sounds, slide the Mute switch, located on the left side of the phone, toward the back of the phone. You see an on-screen indicator that the phone is muted and notification and other sounds won't play; you also see orange within the Mute switch on the side of the iPhone. To restore normal sound, slide the switch toward the front of the phone.

Unintentional Muting

If your phone suddenly stops ringing when calls come in or doesn't play notification sounds that you think it should, always check the Mute switch to ensure it hasn't been activated accidentally or that you forgot that you had muted your iPhone.

- **Text**—You enter text on your iPhone for many different purposes, including sending messages and emails and searching. You can type text to enter it and you can also dictate text. The iPhone's Predictive Text feature even suggests text you might want to enter so you can do so with a tap.

- **Search**—Your iPhone has a lot of information on it. This includes apps, emails, music, and much more. The iPhone's Search tool enables you to find what you want to work with quickly and easily.

- **Siri Suggestions**—You frequently want to "go back" to something you were using recently, such as an app or a search. The Siri Suggestions tool presents these recent items to you so that you can return to them with a single tap.

- **Notifications**—The iPhone's notification system keeps you informed about activity in which you may be interested, such as new emails, events, app updates, and so on. There are a number of types of these notifications that you experience. Visual notifications include alerts, banners, and badges. Alert sounds can also let you know something has happened, and vibrations make you feel the new activity.

- **Do Not Disturb**—Notifications are great, but at times, you may want your iPhone to keep quiet. As mentioned in Chapter 1, you can put your iPhone in Do Not Disturb mode so that its notifications are silenced and your iPhone doesn't disturb you. In this chapter, you learn how to set an automatic Do Not Disturb schedule; for example, you might want your iPhone to enter this mode automatically during your normal sleeping hours.

- **Print**—The paperless world has never become a reality—and probably never will. Fortunately, you can print emails, documents, and other content directly from your iPhone.

- **Wallet app and Apple Pay**—The Wallet app manages all sorts of information that you need, including boarding passes, membership cards, and gift cards. Instead of using paper or plastic to conduct transactions, you can simply have your iPhone's screen scanned. Apple Pay securely stores credit and debit cards so that you can pay for things by scanning your iPhone's screen; as you learn later in this chapter, this is actually safer than using a plastic card.

Introducing the Settings App

Tap to open the Settings app

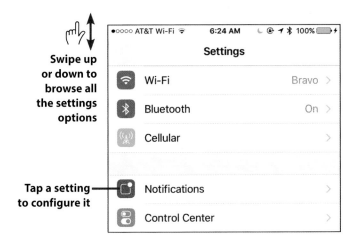

Swipe up or down to browse all the settings options

Tap a setting to configure it

To use the Settings app, tap Settings on the Home screen. The app opens. Swipe up and down the screen to browse the various settings tools. Tap an item to configure its settings. For example, to configure your notifications, tap Notifications (using these settings is covered in detail in "Working with Notifications" later in this chapter). The settings that you use to configure notifications appear and you can make changes to the notifications your iPhone uses to communicate with you.

Using and Configuring Widgets

New! In this section, you find out how to open the Widget Center and use the apps you see there. You also see how to configure the Widget Center so it is fast and easy to find the widgets you use most often.

Accessing Widgets

You can open the Widget Center in a number of ways:

Quickly access widgets by swiping to the right on the Lock screen

- Wake your iPhone and swipe to the right.
- Move to a Home page and swipe to the right.
- Swipe down the screen to open the Notification Center and then swipe to the right.

At the top of the Widget Center, you see the Search tool (more on this later) and the current time and date if you have opened it from the Lock screen; you see just the current date if you open it another way. Beneath that, you see widgets for apps installed on your iPhone (as you'll see, you can choose which widgets you see and what order they are in). Swipe up and down the screen to browse your widgets.

Each widget provides information or functions based on its app. For example, you can use the FAVORITES widget to place phone calls using the Phone app or to make FaceTime calls to your contacts you've designated as Favorites (you learn how to do this in Chapter 8, "Communicating with the Phone and FaceTime Apps"). You can see your daily calendar in the CALENDAR widget, get news in the NEWS widget, or listen to music in the MUSIC widget.

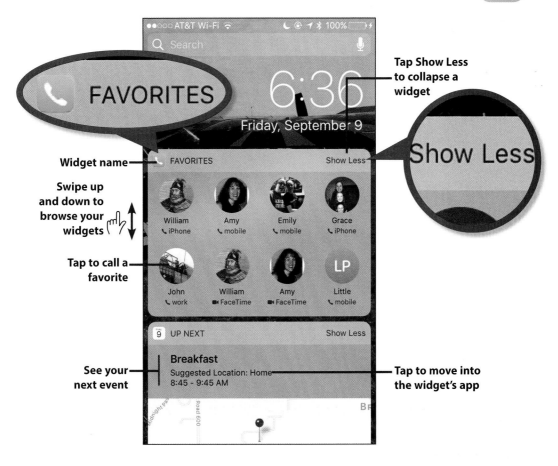

You can expand a widget to show all of its information or tools by tapping the Show More command or collapse it to a more minimal state by tapping the Show Less command.

You can interact with widgets in several ways. Some widgets provide information that you can view within the widget, such as CALENDAR, STOCKS, or UP NEXT. Some apps provide buttons you can tap to perform specific actions, these include FAVORITES and MUSIC. When you tap something within a widget, the associated app opens and either performs the task you indicated or shows more information about what you selected.

Some apps even have multiple widgets. For example, the Calendar app has the UP NEXT widget that shows you the next event on your calendar and the CALENDAR widget that shows the events on the current date.

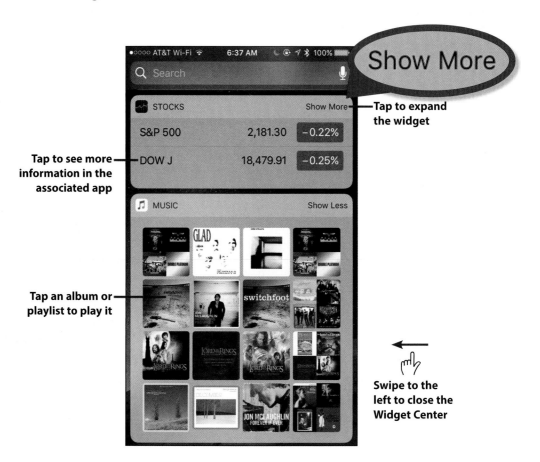

Tap to expand the widget

Tap to see more information in the associated app

Tap an album or playlist to play it

Swipe to the left to close the Widget Center

If you don't move into an app from a widget, you can close the Widget Center by swiping to the left. You move back to the screen you came from, such as a Home screen. If you do move into an app from a widget, you work with that app just as if you moved into it from a Home screen.

Configuring the Widget Center

You can determine which widgets are shown in the Widget Center and the order in which those widgets appear on the screen; for example, you might want your most frequently used widgets to be at the top of the screen.

Swipe all the way up the Widget Center to configure it

Tap to configure the Widget Center

Edit

To configure the Widget Center, swipe all the way up the screen and tap Edit. You see the Add Widgets screen.

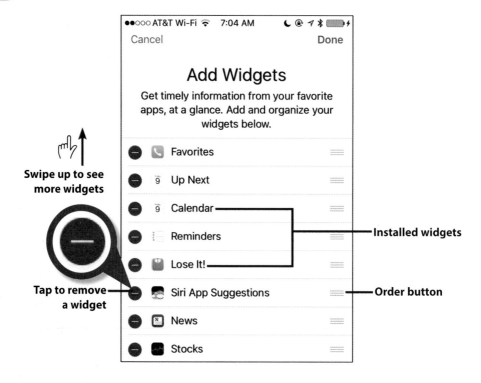

This screen has two sections. At the top are the widgets currently installed; installed widgets have the remove buttons (red circle with a – in its center) next to their icons. Toward the bottom of the screen, you see the MORE WIDGETS section that shows you available widgets that aren't currently on your Widget Center. Along the right side of the screen are the order buttons that you can use to change the order in which the widgets appear on the screen.

To remove a widget, tap the remove button (red circle with a –); then tap Remove. The widget is removed from the Widget Center but remains available to you should you want to add it again.

To change where a widget appears on the Widget Center, drag its order button up or down the screen. When it is in the position you want, take your finger off the screen and the widget is placed there.

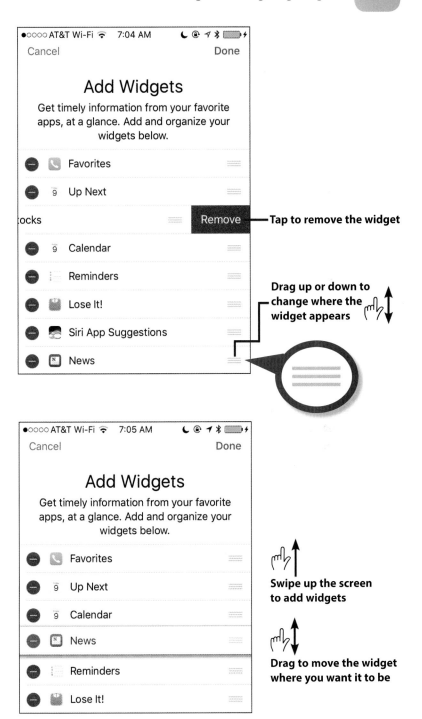

Tap to remove the widget

Drag up or down to change where the widget appears

Swipe up the screen to add widgets

Drag to move the widget where you want it to be

To add widgets, swipe up the screen until you see the MORE WIDGETS section. In this section, you see the widgets not currently installed in the Widget Center. These are marked with the Add button (a green circle with a +).

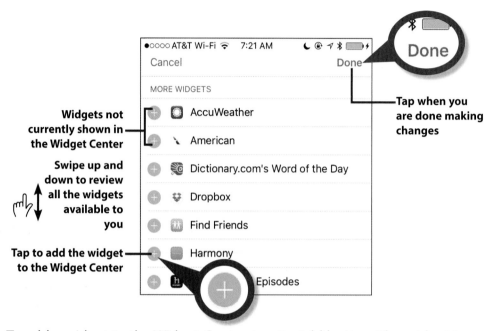

To add a widget to the Widget Center, tap its Add button. The widget jumps up the screen to become the last widget on the installed list (you can drag it up the list to reposition the widget on the Widget Center).

When you're done making changes to the Widget Center, tap Done. You return to the Widget Center and see the results of the changes you've made.

New Widgets

When new widgets become available, you see a message under the Edit button on the Widget Center screen. Tap this to move into Edit mode so you can see the new widgets and add them to the Widget Center.

Working with Text

You can do lots of things with an iPhone that require you to provide text input. There are a couple of ways you can do this, the most obvious of which is by typing. Whenever you need the iPhone's keyboard, whether it's for emailing, messaging, entering a website URL, performing a search, or any other typing function, it pops up automatically.

Tap to dictate to your iPhone

Tap to change keyboards

Tap and hold to open the Keyboard menu

Tap to use the Emoji keyboard

Tap to enter Predictive Text

Use the iPhone's virtual keyboard to type

To type, just tap the keys. As you tap each key, you hear audio feedback (you can disable this sound if you want to) and the key you tapped pops up in a magnified view on the screen. The keyboard includes all the standard keys, plus a few for special uses. To change from letters to numbers and special characters, just tap the 123 key. Tap the #+= key to see more special characters. Tap the 123 key to move back to the numbers and special characters or the ABC key to return to letters. The keyboard also has contextual keys that appear when you need them. For example, when you enter a website address, the .com key appears so you can enter these four characters with a single tap.

Working with Predictive Text

You can also use Predictive Text, which is the feature that tries to predict text you want to enter based on the context of what you are currently typing and what you have typed before. Predictive Text appears in the bar between the text and the keyboard and presents you with three options. If one of those is what you want to enter, tap it and it is added to the text at the current location of the cursor. If you don't see an option you want to enter, keep typing and the options change as the text changes. You can tap an option at any time to enter it. The nice thing about Predictive Text is that it gets better at predicting your text needs over time. In other words, the more you use it, the better it gets at predicting what you want to type. You can also enable or disable Predictive Text, as you see shortly.

Predictive Text Need Not Apply

When you are entering text where Predictive Text doesn't apply, such as when you are typing email addresses, the Predictive Text bar is hidden and can't be enabled. This makes sense because there's no way text in things such as email addresses can be predicted. When you move back into an area where it does apply, Predictive Text becomes active again.

Working with Keyboards

A virtual keyboard like the one the iPhone has can change to reflect the language or symbols you want to type. As you learn in Chapter 5, "Customizing How Your iPhone Works," you can install multiple keyboards, such as one for your primary language and more for your secondary languages. You can also install third-party keyboards to take advantage of their features (this is also covered in Chapter 5).

By default, two keyboards are available for you to use. One is for the primary language configured for your iPhone (for example, mine is U.S. English). The other is the Emoji keyboard (more on this shortly). How you change the keyboard you are using depends on whether you have installed additional keyboards and the orientation of the iPhone.

If you haven't installed additional keyboards, you can change keyboards by tapping the Emoji key, which has a smiley face on it.

If you have installed other keyboards, you change keyboards by tapping the Globe key.

Each time you tap this key (Globe if available, Emoji if there isn't a Globe), the keyboard changes to be the next keyboard installed; along with the available keys changing, you briefly see the name of the current keyboard in the Space bar. When you have cycled through all the keyboards, you return to the one where you started.

The Keys, They Are A-Changin'

The keys on the keyboard can change depending on the orientation of the iPhone. For example, when you have more than one keyboard installed and hold the iPhone vertically, the Emoji key disappears and you see only the Globe key. Not to worry though, you can still get to the Emoji keyboard by tapping the Globe key until the Emoji keyboard appears, or by opening the Keyboard menu and tapping Emoji. When you have installed additional keyboards and hold the iPhone horizontally, you see both the Globe and Emoji keys. Tap the Emoji key to switch to that keyboard or the Globe key to cycle through all the keyboards.

Tap to enable/disable Predictive Text

Tap a keyboard to use it

You can also select the specific keyboard you want to use and enable/disable Predictive Text by tapping and holding on the Globe key (or the Emoji key, if you don't see the Globe key). The Keyboard menu appears. Tap a keyboard to switch to it. Tap the Predictive Text switch to enable or disable it. When the switch is green, Predictive Text is enabled; when the switch is white, it is disabled.

Using Emojis

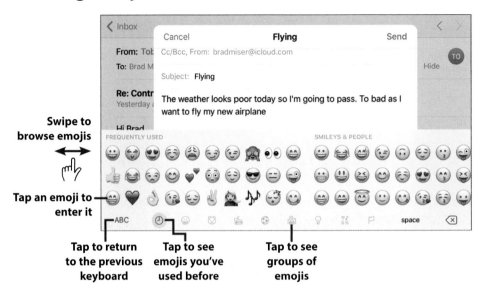

Swipe to browse emojis

Tap an emoji to enter it

Tap to return to the previous keyboard

Tap to see emojis you've used before

Tap to see groups of emojis

Emojis are icons you insert into your text to liven things up, communicate your feelings, or just to have some fun. If you don't have this keyboard installed, see Chapter 5. You can open this keyboard by tapping its key (the smiley face) or by tapping it on the Keyboard menu. You see a palette containing many emojis, organized into groups. You can change the groups of emojis you are browsing by tapping the buttons at the bottom of the screen. Swipe to the left or right on the emojis to browse the emojis in the current group. Tap an emoji to enter it at the cursor's location in your message, email, or other type of document. To use an emoji you've used before, tap the Clock button to see the emojis you've used recently; you'll probably find that you use this recent set of emojis regularly so this can save a lot of time. To return to the mundane world of letters and symbols, tap the ABC key.

The Predictive text feature also suggests emojis when you type certain words; just tap the emoji to replace the word with it.

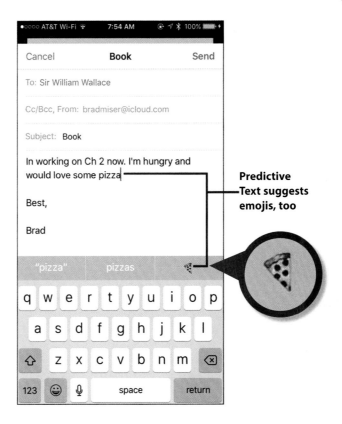

Predictive Text suggests emojis, too

Emoji Options

If you tap and hold on some emojis, you see options. For example, if you tap and hold on the thumbs-up emoji, you see a menu with the emoji in different flesh tones. Slide your finger over the menu and tap the version you want to use. The version you select becomes the new default for that emoji. You can go back to a previous version by opening the menu and selecting it.

What's Your Typing Orientation?

Like many other tasks, you can rotate the iPhone to change the screen's orientation while you type. When the iPhone is in the horizontal orientation, the keyboard is wider, making it easier to tap individual keys. When the iPhone is in vertical orientation, the keyboard is narrower, but you can see more of the typing area. So, try both to see which mode is most effective for you.

Correcting Spelling as You Type

If you type a word that the iPhone doesn't recognize, that word is flagged as a possible mistake and suggestions are made to help you correct it. How this happens depends on whether or not Predictive Text is enabled.

If you tap the space key, the suspicious word is replaced with this one

Tap to keep the suspicious word

Suspicious word

Tap to replace the suspicious word with this one

If Predictive Text is enabled, potential replacements for suspicious words appear in the Predictive Text bar. When you tap the space key, the suspicious word is replaced with the word in the center of the Predictive Text bar. Tap the word on the far left to keep what you've typed (because it isn't a mistake) or tap the word on the right end of the bar to enter it instead of what you've typed.

Suspicious word

Tap X to reject the suggestion

If Predictive Text isn't enabled, a suspicious word is highlighted and a suggestion about what it thinks is the correct word appears in a pop-up box. To accept the suggestion, tap the space key. To reject the suggestion, tap the pop-up box to close it and keep what you typed. You can also use this feature for shorthand typing. For example, to type "I've" you can simply type "Ive" and iPhone suggests "I've," which you can accept by tapping the space key.

Another Reason It's Called a Plus

When you rotate an iPhone 6Plus/6s Plus/7 Plus to the horizontal position, the keyboard gains some extra keys. These include Cut (scissors), Copy (two squares), Paste (paper and clipboard), Format (**B**/U), and Undo (curved arrow).

Typing Tricks

Many keys, especially symbols and punctuation, have additional characters. To see a character's options, tap it and hold down. If it has options, a menu pops up after a second or so. To enter one of the optional characters, drag over the menu until the one you want to enter is highlighted, and then lift your finger off the screen. The optional character you selected is entered. For example, if you tap and hold on the period, you can select .com, .edu, and so on, which is very helpful when you are typing a website or email address.

By default, the iPhone attempts to correct the capitalization of what you type. It also automatically selects the Shift key when you start a new sentence, start a new paragraph, or in other places where its best guess is that you need a capital letter. If you don't want to enter a capital character, simply tap the Shift key before you type. You can enable the Caps Lock key by tapping the Shift key twice. When the key is highlighted (the upward-facing arrow is black), everything you type is in uppercase letters.

Editing Text

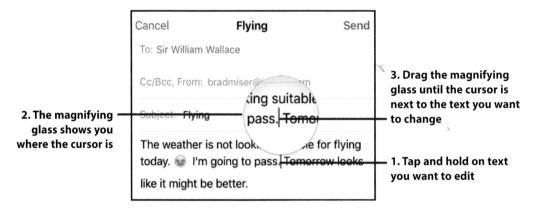

2. The magnifying glass shows you where the cursor is

3. Drag the magnifying glass until the cursor is next to the text you want to change

1. Tap and hold on text you want to edit

To edit text you've typed, touch and hold on the area containing the text you want to edit. A magnifying glass icon appears on the screen, and within it you see a magnified view of the location of the cursor. Drag the magnifying glass to where you want to make changes (to position the cursor where you want to start making changes), and then lift your finger from the screen. The cursor remains in that location, and you can use the keyboard to make changes to the text or to add text at that location.

Using 3D Touch with Text

When you are using an iPhone that supports 3D Touch (6s and later models), you can apply slight pressure when you touch the screen to have the closest word selected automatically; it is highlighted in blue to show you that it is selected. To place the cursor without selecting words that are near your finger, just touch the screen without applying any pressure.

Your Own Text Replacements

You can create your own text shortcuts so you can type something like "eadd" and it is automatically replaced with your email address. See Chapter 5 for the details.

Selecting, Copying, Cutting, or Pasting Text

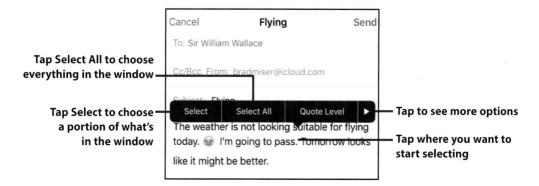

Tap Select All to choose everything in the window

Tap Select to choose a portion of what's in the window

Tap to see more options

Tap where you want to start selecting

You can also select text or images to copy and paste the selected content into a new location or to replace that content. Touch and hold down briefly where you want to start the selection until the magnifying glass icon appears; then lift your finger off the screen. The Select menu appears. Tap Select to select part of the content on the screen, or tap Select All to select everything in the current window.

More Commands

Some menus that appear when you are making selections and performing actions have a right-facing arrow at the right end. Tap this to see a new menu that contains additional commands. These commands are contextual, meaning that you see different commands depending on what you are doing at that specific time. You can tap the left-facing arrow to move back to a previous menu.

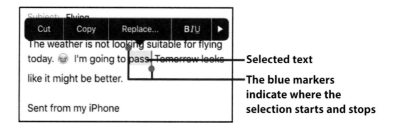

Selected text

The blue markers indicate where the selection starts and stops

You see markers indicating where the selection starts and stops. (The iPhone attempts to select something logical, such as the word or sentence.) New commands appear on the menu; these provide actions for the text currently selected.

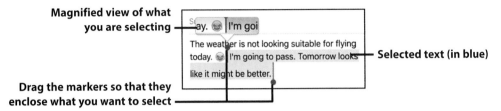

Magnified view of what you are selecting

Selected text (in blue)

Drag the markers so that they enclose what you want to select

Drag the two markers so that the content you want to select is between them; the selected portion is highlighted in blue. As you drag, you see a magnified view of where the selection marker is, which helps you place it more accurately. When the selection markers are located correctly, lift your finger from the screen. (If you tapped the Select All command, you don't need to do this because the content you want is already selected.)

Use the Menu Luke!

When you select text, a menu of commands appears, such as the select commands you see in these figures. These commands are contextual, meaning they change based on what you have selected, and you can see different commands in the menu depending on the app you are using. For example, when you have a word selected, one of the suggestions might be Define, which looks up the selected word in the Dictionary (tap Done to return to where you came from). As you select text, explore this menu by tapping the left- and right-facing arrows to see all the available commands because you'll find some very useful options.

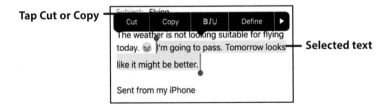

Tap Cut or Copy

Selected text

Tap Cut to remove the content from the current window, or tap Copy to just copy it.

Format It!

If you tap the **B/U** button, you can tap Bold, Italics, or Underline to apply those formatting options to the selected text. You also can tap multiple format options to apply them at the same time. You might need to tap the right-facing arrow at the end of the menu to see this command, depending on how many commands are on the menu.

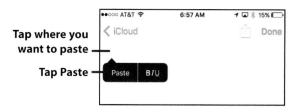

Tap where you
want to paste

Tap Paste

Move to where you want to paste the content you selected; for example, use the
App Switcher to change to a different app. Tap where you want the content to be
pasted. (For a more precise location, tap and hold and then use the magnifying
glass icon to move to a specific location.) Lift your finger off the screen and the
menu appears. Then tap Paste.

Pasted content

The content you copied or cut appears where you placed the cursor.

Correcting Spelling After You've Typed

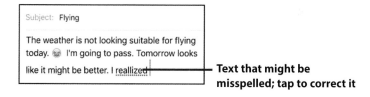

Text that might be
misspelled; tap to correct it

The iPhone also has a spell-checking feature that comes into play after you have
entered text (as opposed to the Predictive Text and autocorrect/suggestions
features that change text as you type it). When you've entered text the iPhone
doesn't recognize, it is underlined in red.

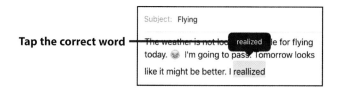

Tap the correct word

Tap the underlined word. It is shaded in red to show you what is being checked, and a menu appears with one or more replacements that might be the correct spelling. If one of the options is the one you want, tap it. The incorrect word is replaced with the one you tapped.

Contextual Menus and You

In some apps, tapping a word causes a menu with other kinds of actions to appear; you can tap an action to make it happen. For example, in the iBooks app, when you tap a word, the resulting menu enables you to look up the word in a dictionary. Other apps support different kinds of actions, so it's a good idea to try tapping words in apps that involve text to see which commands are available.

Undo

The iPhone has a somewhat hidden undo command. To undo what you've just done, such as typing text, gently shake your phone back and forth a couple of times. An Undo Typing prompt appears on the screen. Tap Undo to undo the last thing you did or tap Cancel if you activated the undo command accidentally.

Dictating Text

You can also enter text by dictating it, which can be much faster and easier than typing it. Dictation is available almost anywhere you need to enter text. (Exceptions are passcodes and passwords, such as for your Apple ID.)

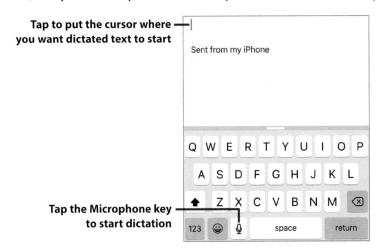

Tap to put the cursor where you want dictated text to start

Tap the Microphone key to start dictation

To start dictating, tap the Microphone key. The iPhone goes into Dictation mode. A gray bar appears at the bottom of the window. As the iPhone "hears" you, the line oscillates.

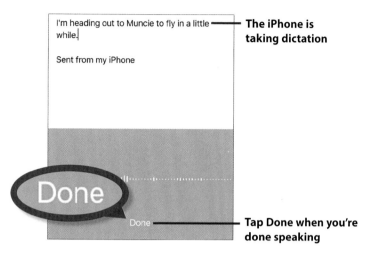

I'm heading out to Muncie to fly in a little while. ——— **The iPhone is taking dictation**

Sent from my iPhone

Done ——— **Tap Done when you're done speaking**

Start speaking the text you want the iPhone to type. As you speak, the text is entered starting from the location of the cursor. Speak punctuation when you want to enter it. For example, when you reach the end of a sentence, say "period" or to enter a colon, say "colon." To start a new paragraph, say "new paragraph."

I'm heading out to Muncie to fly in a little while. ——— **The text you spoke**

Sent from my iPhone

When you've finished dictating, tap Done. The keyboard reappears and you see the text you spoke. This feature is amazingly accurate and can be a much faster and more convenient way to enter text than typing it.

You can edit the text you dictated just like text you typed using the keyboard.

Searching on Your iPhone

You can use the Spotlight Search tool to search your iPhone. There are a number of ways you can start a search:

Swipe down from the center part of the screen to open the Spotlight search tool

- Swipe down from the top of the screen to open the Notification Center. The Search bar is at the top of the screen. (Note that if you use this option when your phone is locked, you must unlock your phone to see all the results of the search).

- Swipe to the right to open the Widgets Center. The Search bar is at the top of the screen.

- On a Home screen, swipe down from the center of the screen to open just the Search tool.

Type what you want to search for

Current results

When you're done entering your search term, tap Search

To perform a search, tap in the Search bar and type the search term using the onscreen keyboard. As you type, items that meet your search are shown on the list below the Search bar. When you finish typing the search term, tap Search.

The results are organized into sections, such as TOP HIT, APPLICATIONS, MAPS, MUSIC, and so on. Swipe up and down the screen to browse all of the results. To work with an item you find, such as to view a location you found, tap it; you move to a screen showing more information or into the associated app and see the search result that you tapped.

Search results

Location related to the search term

To work with a result, tap it

Swipe up and down to browse all of the results

Music related to your search term

Tap to play

Tap to go back to your search

Back

Search

Tap to go back to your search

The results remain in the Spotlight Search tool as you work with them. To move back to the search results, tap the Back button in the upper-left corner of the screen or tap Search (which you see depends on the result you tapped on).

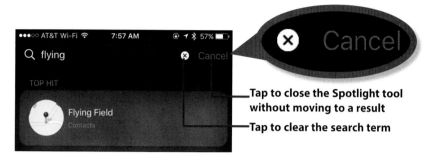

Tap to close the Spotlight tool without moving to a result

Tap to clear the search term

The results of the most recent search are still listed. To clear the search term, tap the Clear button (x). To close the Spotlight tool without going to one of the results, tap Cancel.

Tell Me More

If one of the categories you find in a search has a lot of entries, you see the Show More command. Tap this to show more of the results for that category. Tap Show Less to collapse the category again. When you can search within an app, you see the Search in App text on the right side of the screen aligned with the results section; tap this to open the app and perform the search within that app.

Working with Siri Suggestions

Siri Suggestions can make it easy to get back to apps, searches, or other items you've used recently.

Swipe down from the center part of the screen to open Siri Suggestions

Tap to repeat a search

Tap to open an app

To access Siri Suggestions, swipe down from the center of a Home screen. You see the SIRI SUGGESTIONS page. This page shows you apps you use and searches you've recently performed. Tap an app to open it or tap a search to perform it again.

You can use the SIRI APP SUGGESTIONS widget to open apps you've used recently or that are suggested based on what you are currently doing or where you are located (for example, the Starbucks app may be suggested when you are near a Starbucks location).

To see these suggestions, swipe to the right to open the Widgets Center and locate the SIRI APP SUGGESTIONS widget. Tap an app to open it.

Swipe to the right to open the Widgets Center

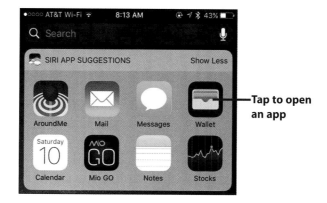

Tap to open an app

Working with Notifications

Notifications are the way your iPhone communicates with you when "something" happens; "something" can include new email or text messages, appointments, new alerts, or just about any other activity that you manage with your iPhone. Notifications can be visual, which means the notification appears on the screen; auditory, meaning you hear the notification; or vibratory, which causes your iPhone to vibrate in various ways.

You can determine which types of notifications are used for specific activity on your iPhone. This might be one of the most important areas to configure because you want to make sure you are aware of activity that is important to you, but too many notifications can be disruptive and annoying. So, you want to strike a good balance between being aware and being annoyed.

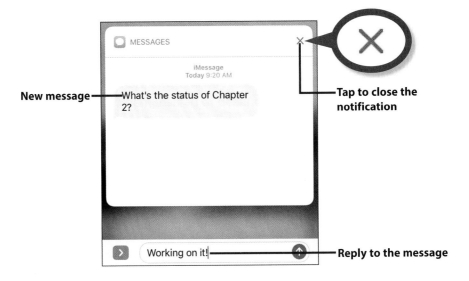

New message —— What's the status of Chapter 2?

Tap to close the notification

Working on it! —— Reply to the message

Banner notifications can also appear on the Lock screen, which is really convenient because you can read and take action on them without unlocking your phone. To respond to the notification or take other action on it, press it to open it (3D Touch iPhones) or swipe to the right (non-3D Touch iPhones) and then take action, such as replying to a message.

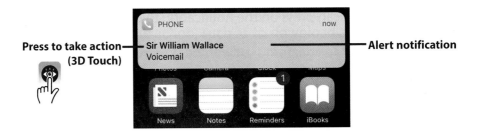

Press to take action (3D Touch)

Sir William Wallace
Voicemail

Alert notification

Though they look like banner notifications, when an alert notification appears, you must take action on the notification—such as listening to a voice message—before it goes off the screen. When the alert appears, you won't be able to do anything until you at least open the notification. Once opened (press on it on a 3D Touch iPhone or swipe to the right on older models), you can take action on the notification or close it to dismiss it from the screen. You should use alerts for extremely important notifications, such as event notifications from the Calendar app, so that you are sure they will get your attention.

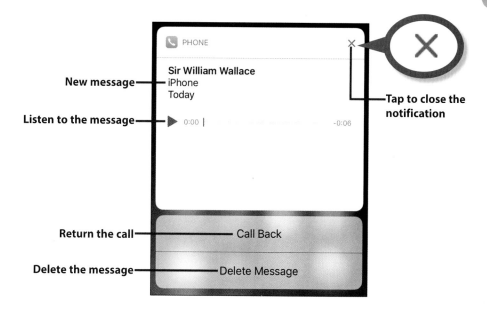

Notifications on the Lock Screen

Banner and alert notifications can appear on the Lock screen. This is useful because you can see them when your iPhone is locked. If your phone is asleep, the notifications appear briefly on the screen and then it goes dark again; you can press the Wake/Sleep button or the Touch/ID Home button or raise your phone to see your notifications without unlocking the iPhone. You can swipe up or down the screen to browse the notifications on the Lock screen, and take action on them as described in this section. In some cases, you might need to unlock your phone to complete an action associated with a notification.

You can also disable visual notifications by selecting the None option, in which case no visual notifications are issued.

Working with Other Types of Notifications

Sounds are audible indicators that something has happened. For example, you can be alerted to a new email message by a specific sound. You can choose global sound notifications, such as a general ringtone, and specific ones, such as a specific ringtone when someone in your contacts calls you.

Vibrations are a physical indicator that something has happened. Like sounds, you can configure general vibrations, and you can also configure an app's vibration pattern for its notifications.

Configuring Your Notifications

You can configure how apps can provide notifications and, if you allow notifications, which type. You can also configure other aspects of notifications, such as whether an app displays in the Notification Center or whether its notifications appear on the Lock screen. Not all apps support all notification options. Some apps, such as Mail, support notification configuration by account (for example, you can set a different alert sound for new mail in each account). You can follow the same general steps to configure notifications for each app; you should explore the options for the apps you use most often to ensure they work the best for you.

The steps in this task show how to configure Mail's notifications, which is a good example because it supports a lot of notification features; other apps might have fewer features or might be organized slightly differently. But configuring the notifications for any app follows a similar pattern as exemplified by the steps for Mail's notification settings.

Stop Bothering Me!

As you learned in Chapter 1, you can use the Do Not Disturb mode to disable all or most of your iPhone's notifications. In the next section, you learn how to configure an automatic Do Not Disturb period.

Configuring an App's Notifications

To configure notifications from the Mail app, perform the following steps:

1. Tap Settings on the Home screen.

2. Tap Notifications. On this screen, you see all the apps installed on your phone. Along with the app name and icon, you see the current status of its notifications.

3. Swipe up and down to locate the app whose notifications you want to configure. (The apps are listed in alphabetical order.)

4. Tap the app whose notifications you want to configure.

5. If you want the app to provide notifications, set the Allow Notifications switch to on (green) and move to step 6. If you don't want notifications from the app, set the Allow Notifications switch to off (white) and skip to step 18.

6. Tap the account for which you want to configure notifications; if the app doesn't support accounts, skip this step.

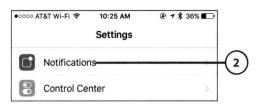

Types of notifications being used

No notifications are allowed

7 To show notifications from the app/account in the Notification Center, set the Show in Notification Center switch to on (green); if you set this to off (white), notifications from the app/account are not shown in the Notification Center.

8 Tap Sounds.

9 Use the resulting Sounds screen to choose the alert sound and vibration for new email messages to the account (see Chapter 6 for the details about configuring sounds and vibrations).

10 Tap the back button located in the upper-left corner of the screen (how it is labeled depends on what you are working with).

11 To display the app's badge, set the Badge App Icon switch to on (green).

12 If you want the notifications to appear on the Lock screen, slide the Show on Lock Screen switch to on (green).

13 Choose the type of visual notification you want by tapping None, Banners, or Alerts. You know which alert type is currently selected because its name appears in an oblong button.

14 If you don't want a preview to appear in the app's notifications, slide the Show Previews switch

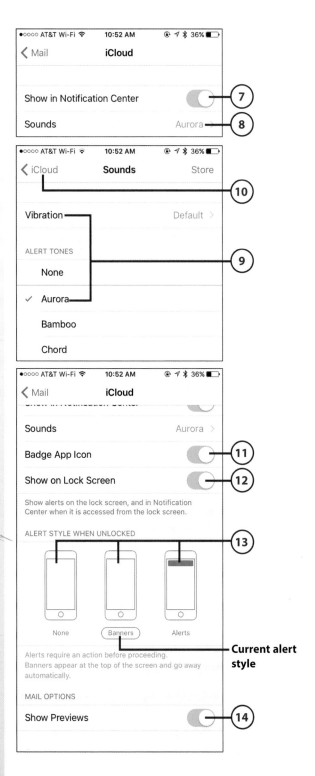

to off (white). For example, you might want to keep some types of messages private when you receive a notification; to do so, disable the Show Previews option by setting its switch to off (white).

15. Tap the back button, which is located in the upper-left corner of the window.

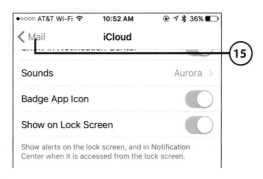

16. Configure notifications for the other accounts used in the app.

17. Configure notifications for VIP email and threads.

18. Tap Notifications.

19. Repeat these steps for each app shown on the Notification Center screen. Certain apps might not have all the options shown in these steps, but the process to configure their notifications is similar.

More Options

Some apps provide notifications for the types of activity they manage. For example, the Calendar app allows you to configure notifications for upcoming events, invitations, and so on. Open the Notification Settings screens for the apps you use frequently to explore the notification options they offer.

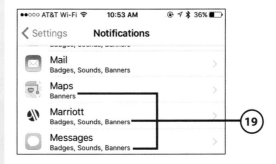

>>>Go Further

NOTIFY THIS

Here are some other hopefully useful notification tidbits for your consideration:

- **VIPS**—Mail supports VIPs, which are people from whom email messages are treated specially, such as having a dedicated mailbox in the Mail app. You can apply specific notification settings to VIP messages using the VIP notification option. These override the notification settings for the email account to which messages from VIPs are sent.

- **Threads**—Mail can keep related messages together as threads. Like VIP messages, you can override Mail's notifications for messages that are part of threads using the Thread Notifications option.

- **Special sounds and vibrations for contacts**—You can override some app's sounds and vibration notification settings for individuals in your Contacts app. For example, you can configure a specific ringtone, new text tone, and vibrations for calls or texts from a contact. You do this using the contact information screen as explained in Chapter 7, "Managing Contacts."

- **Installed app not shown**—You must have opened an app at least once for it to appear on the Notifications screen.

- **Initial notification prompt**—The first time you open many apps, you are prompted to allow that app to send you notifications. If you allow this, the app is able to send notifications about its activity. If you deny this, the app isn't able to send notifications. You can always configure the app's notifications using the steps in this task regardless of your initial decision.

- **Special notifications**—At the bottom of the Notifications screen, you might see some special alerts in the GOVERNMENT ALERTS section. What you see here depends on the country or region your phone is associated with. For example, where I live in the United States, there are two notifications. Amber alerts are issued when a child is missing and presumed abducted, while Emergency alerts are issued for things such as national crises, local weather, and so on. You can use the switches to enable (green) or prevent (white) these types of alerts, but you can't choose the types of notifications you receive for these events.

Configuring the Do Not Disturb Mode

As you learned in Chapter 1, the Do Not Disturb feature enables you to temporarily silence notifications; you can also configure quiet times during which notifications are automatically silenced.

You can set an automatic Do Not Disturb schedule by performing the following steps:

1. Open the Settings app and tap Do Not Disturb.

2. To activate Do Not Disturb manually, set the Manual switch to on (green). (This does the same thing as activating it from the Control Center as explained in Chapter 1.)

3. To configure Do Not Disturb to activate automatically on a schedule, set the Scheduled switch to on (green).

4. Tap the From and To box.

5 Tap From.

6 Swipe on the time selection wheels to select the hour and minute (AM or PM) when you want the Do Not Disturb period to start.

7 Tap To.

8 Swipe on the time selection wheels to set the hour and minute (AM or PM) when you want the Do Not Disturb period to end.

9 Tap Do Not Disturb.

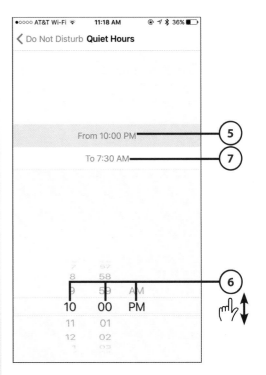

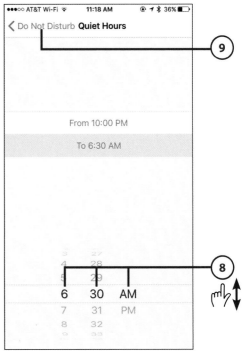

10 Tap Allow Calls From.

11 Tap the option for whose calls should be allowed during the Do Not Disturb period. The options are Everyone, which doesn't prevent any calls; No One, which sends all calls to voicemail; Favorites, which allows calls from people on your Favorites lists to come through but all others go to voicemail; or one of your contact groups, which allows calls from anyone in the selected group to come through while all others go to voicemail.

12 Tap Do Not Disturb.

When you are in the app from which you want to print, tap the Share button. Tap Print on the resulting menu. You might need to swipe to the right to expose the Print command. (If you don't see the Share button or the Print command, the app you are using doesn't support printing.)

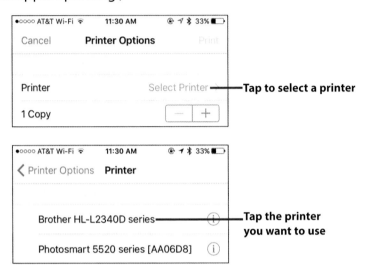

Tap to select a printer

Tap the printer you want to use

The first time you print, you need to select the printer you want to use. On the Printer Options screen, tap Select Printer. Then tap the printer you want to use. You move back to the Printer Options screen and see the printer you selected.

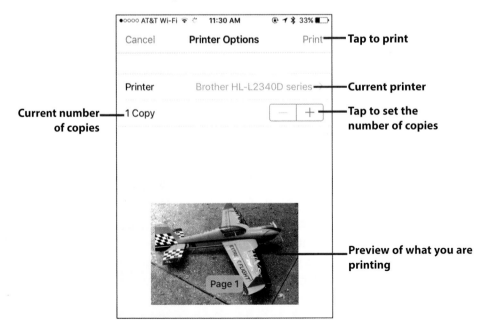

Tap to print

Current printer

Current number of copies

Tap to set the number of copies

Preview of what you are printing

Tap the − or + to set the number of copies; the current number of copies is shown to the left of the buttons. Tap Print to print the document.

The next time you print, if you want to use the same printer, you can skip the printer selection process because the iPhone remembers the last printer you used. To change the printer, tap Printer and tap the printer you want to use.

Working with the Wallet App and Apple Pay

The Wallet app provides instant access to many different kinds of information, including airline boarding passes, retail gift cards, and membership cards. When you need to access these items, you simply open your Wallet and scan the information.

You also use the Wallet app to access your Apple Pay information to make payments when you are in a physical location, such as a store or hotel (Apple Pay is covered in detail in "Working with Apple Pay" later in this chapter). You can also use Apple Pay when you make purchases online using some apps on your iPhone.

Working with the Wallet App

You can store a wide variety of cards in your wallet so that it is easily accessible, including boarding passes, membership cards (to a gym for example), store cards (such as Starbucks if you are an addict like I am), and loyalty or discount cards (things like loyalty cards for grocery stores or gas stations). The Wallet app eliminates the need to carry physical cards or paper for each of these; instead, your information is available to you digitally, and you can enter it as needed by scanning the iPhone's screen.

Tap to open your Wallet

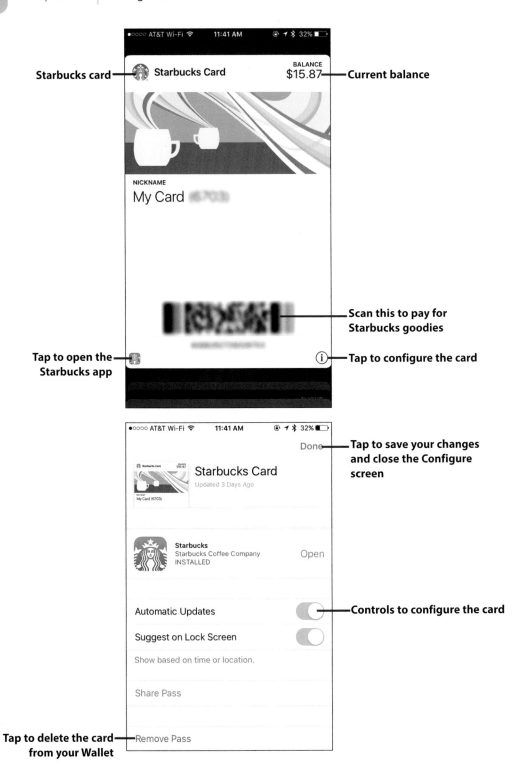

Starbucks card — Starbucks Card

Current balance — BALANCE $15.87

Scan this to pay for Starbucks goodies

Tap to open the Starbucks app

Tap to configure the card

Tap to save your changes and close the Configure screen — Done

Controls to configure the card

Tap to delete the card from your Wallet — Remove Pass

To delete a card from your Wallet (such as a boarding pass when the flight is finished), tap its Info button (i), tap Delete or Remove Pass, and then confirm that you want to delete or remove it. The pass or card is removed from your Wallet.

When you're done configuring a card, tap Done. The Configure screen closes and you return to the card you were configuring.

There are a couple of ways to add cards to your Wallet. The most frequent way to add a card is by using the Add to Wallet command in the app associated with the card. In some cases, you might be able to scan the code on a card to add it.

Adding Passes or Cards to Your Wallet Using an App

If you are a frequent patron of a particular business (perhaps you are addicted to Starbucks coffee like I am) that has an iPhone app, check to see if it also supports the Wallet app. For example, when you use the Starbucks app configured with your account, you can add a Starbucks card to your Wallet as follows:

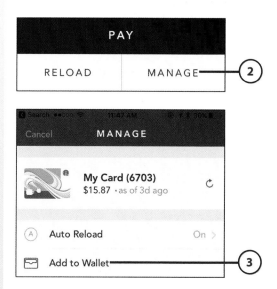

1. Open the app for which you want to add a pass or card to your Wallet.

2. Tap the app's command to manage its information; this command can be labeled with different names in different apps (it is the MANAGE command in the Starbucks app), or it might be accessed with an icon or menu.

3. Tap Add to Wallet.

4 Tap Add. The card or pass is added to your Wallet and is ready to use. (You might be prompted to do some additional configuration of the card, such as to indicate favorite locations.)

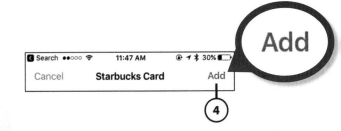

Finding Apps that Support the Wallet

You can search for apps that support the Wallet by opening your Wallet, tapping the Add button (+) in the Passes section, and tapping Find Apps for Wallet. This takes you into the App Store app and you see apps that support the Wallet. You can then download and install apps you want to use as described in Chapter 5.

Adding Passes or Cards to Your Wallet by Scanning Their Codes

In some cases, you can add a card or pass to the Wallet by scanning its code. To do so, follow these steps:

1 Open the Wallet app and tap the Add button (+) in the Passes section.

2 Tap Scan Code to Add a Pass.

3 Use the iPhone's camera to scan the bar code on the card by positioning the phone so that the white box encloses the bar code on the card. If the bar code is recognized and is available for the Wallet, the pass or card is added to the Wallet and is ready for use. If the bar code isn't recognized or doesn't support the Wallet, you see an error and you need to find an associated app for the card to use it with the Wallet.

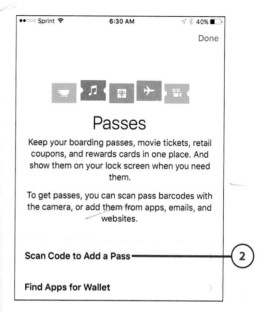

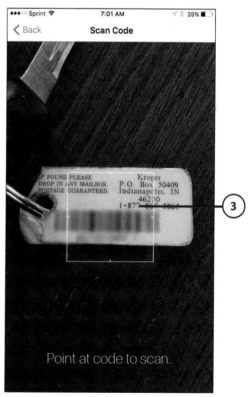

Working with Apple Pay

With Apple Pay, you can store your cards in the Wallet app, and they are instantly and automatically available to make purchases.

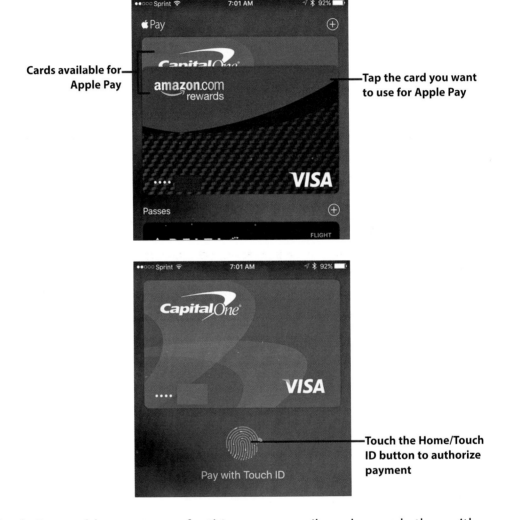

Cards available for Apple Pay

Tap the card you want to use for Apple Pay

Touch the Home/Touch ID button to authorize payment

Apple Pay enables you to pay for things more easily and securely than with physical credit or debit cards. (Note that Apple Pay requires an iPhone 6 or later.) When you are making a purchase in a physical store, you can simply hold your iPhone up to a contactless reader connected to the cash register and tap your finger on the Touch ID button. The iPhone communicates the information required to complete the purchase.

When you are making a transaction in an app that supports Apple Pay, tap this to pay

Apple Pay also simplifies purchases made in online stores. When you use an app or a website that supports Apple Pay, you can tap the Buy with Apple Pay button to complete the purchase.

Apple Pay is actually more secure than using a credit or debit card because your card information is not passed to the device; instead, a unique code is passed that ties back to your card, but that can't be used again. And, you never present your card so the number is not visible to anyone, either visually or digitally.

Apple Pay Support

In addition to requiring an iPhone 6 or later model, a credit or debit card must support Apple Pay for it to work with that card. The easiest way to figure out if your cards support it is to try to add a card to Apple Pay. If you can do so, the card is supported and you can use it. If not, you can check with the credit or debit card company to see when support for Apple Pay will be added so you can use it.

Adding Credit or Debit Cards to Apple Pay

To start using Apple Pay, add a credit or debit card to it:

1 Open your Wallet by tapping its icon on the Home screen.

2 Tap the Add button (+) in the Apple Pay section at the top of the screen.

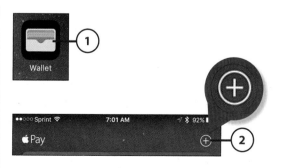

③ Tap Next.

④ Position the iPhone so that the card is inside the white box. The app captures information from the card, which is highlighted in white on the screen. When it has captured all the information it can, you move to the Card Details screen.

Prefer to Type?

If you don't want to use the camera option, or if that option doesn't capture the information correctly, you can also type your card's information directly into the fields. To do this, perform step 3, and then tap Enter Card Details Manually, which is at the bottom of the screen. You can use the resulting Card Details screens to manually enter the card's information.

⑤ Use the keyboard or keypad to enter any information that wasn't captured or to correct any information that wasn't captured correctly.

⑥ Tap Next. The information for the card is verified. If it can't be verified, you see an error message. For example, if the card doesn't support Apple Pay, you see a message saying so. If this happens, tap OK to close the message and then wait for your card to support Apple Pay or enter a different card's information. When the card is verified, you see the Terms and Conditions screen.

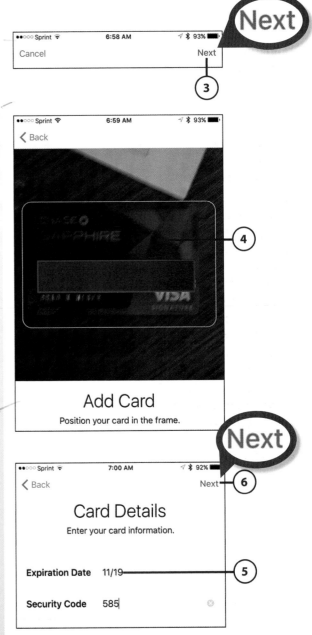

7 Tap Agree.

8 Tap Agree at the prompt. The card's verification is complete and you see it in your Wallet. You are ready to use Apple Pay.

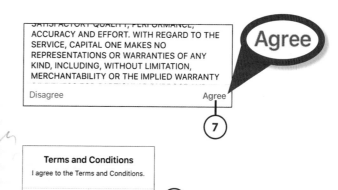

More Verification Required

In some cases, there might be an additional verification step after you tap Agree in step 8. When this is the case, the Complete Verification screen appears. Tap how you want to receive the verification code, such as via Email or Text Message, and then tap Next. The card configuration completes. You should receive a verification code. When you have the code, open the Settings app and tap Wallet & Apple Pay. Tap the card you need to verify, and then tap Enter Code. Enter the verification code you received; when you enter the correct code, the card is verified and becomes available for Apple Pay.

Managing Apple Pay

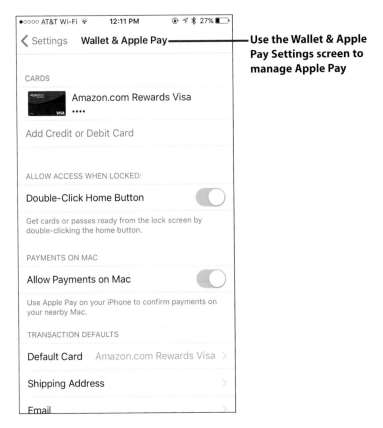

Use the Wallet & Apple Pay Settings screen to manage Apple Pay

To manage Apple Pay, open the Settings app and tap Wallet & Apple Pay. On the resulting screen, you can:

- Tap a card to configure it, such as to determine if notifications related to it are sent. You also see a list of recent transactions for the card.

- Add a new credit or debit card.

- Use the Double-Click Home Button switch to determine whether you can access the cards in your Wallet by pressing the Home/Touch ID button twice when the phone is locked. This makes using your Wallet even easier because you press the Home button twice and your cards appear; tap a card to use it or touch the Home/Touch ID button to pay for something with Apple Pay.

- Set the Allow Payments on a Mac switch to on (green) if you use a Mac computer and want to be able to use Apple Pay for online transactions.

- Set your default Apple Pay card. The default card is used automatically; you have to manually select other cards in the Wallet app to use one of them instead.

- Update your shipping address, email addresses, and phone numbers.

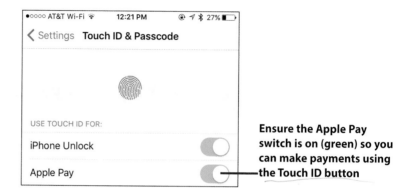

Ensure the Apple Pay switch is on (green) so you can make payments using the Touch ID button

You should also make sure Apple Pay is set to use Touch ID because this makes it much easier and faster than having to type your password. Open the Settings app, tap Touch ID & Passcode, and then enter your passcode. Ensure that the Apple Pay switch is on (green). This enables you to complete Apple Pay transactions by touching the Home/Touch ID button. (See Chapter 5 for the steps to help you configure Touch ID.)

Connect to the Internet via Wi-Fi or a cellular network

Use AirDrop to share content with other nearby iOS devices

Tap here to join Wi-Fi networks to connect to the Internet and configure Bluetooth to connect to other devices

Take advantage of an Internet connection in many different apps

In this chapter, you explore how to connect your iPhone to the Internet; Bluetooth devices; and other iPhones, iPod touches, and iPads. You also learn how to use AirDrop to share content among various nearby Apple devices. Topics include the following:

→ Getting started
→ Securing your iPhone
→ Using Wi-Fi networks to connect to the Internet
→ Using cellular data networks to connect to the Internet
→ Using Bluetooth to connect to other devices
→ Connecting your iPhone to other iPhones, iPod touches, or iPads

Connecting Your iPhone to the Internet, Bluetooth Devices, and iPhones/iPods/iPads

Your iPhone has many functions that rely on an Internet connection. Fortunately, you can connect your iPhone to the Internet by connecting it to a Wi-Fi network that provides Internet access. You can also connect to the Internet through a cellular data network operated by your cell phone provider.

Using Bluetooth, you can wirelessly connect your iPhone to other devices, including speakers, keyboards, headsets, and headphones.

There are a number of ways to connect your iPhone to other iPhones, iPod touches, iPads, and Macintosh computers. This is useful to use collaborative apps, play games, and share information. For example, using AirDrop, you can quickly and easily share photos and other content with other people nearby using iOS devices and Macintosh computers.

Getting Started

The bad news is that there are lots of complex-sounding terms that you hear and see when you are connecting your iPhone to the Internet and other devices. The good news is that you don't need to understand these terms in-depth to be able to connect your iPhone to the Internet and other devices because the iPhone manages the complexity for you. You just need to make a few simple settings, and you'll be connected in no time. Here's a quick guide to the most important concepts you encounter in this chapter:

- **Wi-Fi**—This acronym stands for Wireless Fidelity and encompasses a whole slew of technical specifications around connecting devices together without using cables or wires. Wi-Fi networks have a relatively short range and are used to create a Local Area Network (LAN). The most important thing to know is that you can use Wi-Fi networks to connect your iPhone to the Internet. This is great because Wi-Fi networks are available in many places you go. You probably have a Wi-Fi network available in your home, too. (If you connect your computers to the Internet without a cable from your computer to a modem or network hub, you are using a Wi-Fi network.) You can connect your iPhone to your home's Wi-Fi network, too.

- **Cellular data network**—In addition to your voice, your iPhone can transmit and receive data over the cellular network to which it is connected. This enables you to connect your iPhone to the Internet just about anywhere you are. You use the cellular network provided by your cell phone company. There are many different cell phone providers that support iPhones. In the United States, these include AT&T, Sprint, T-Mobile, and Verizon. You don't need to configure your iPhone to use the cellular data network, as it is set up from the start to do so.

- **3G/4G/LTE**—The speed of the connection you have when using a cellular data network varies, which means the things you do on the Internet (such as browsing a web page) are faster or slower depending on the current connection speed. Depending on the cellular provider you use, you may see these networks called by other names. Each type of network, regardless of its name, has a different speed. LTE networks are currently the fastest type. You usually don't choose which type of network you use because the iPhone connects to the fastest one available automatically.

- **Data plan**—When you use your iPhone on the Internet (for web browsing, email, and apps), data is transmitted to your iPhone and the iPhone transmits data back to the Internet. Your cellular account includes a data plan that defines how much data you can send/receive during a specific time period (usually per month) based on how much you pay per month. It's important to know the size of your data plan so that you can be aware of how much of it you are using per month.

- **Overage charge**—If you use more data than is allowed under your data plan, you can be charged a fee. These fees can be quite expensive so you need to be aware of how much data you are using so that you can avoid overage charges.

- **Roaming charge**—Your cellular provider's network covers a defined geographic area. When you leave your provider's network coverage area, your iPhone automatically connects to another provider's network when one is available. When your iPhone is connected to a different provider's network, this is called roaming. You need to be aware when you are roaming because you can incur additional fees while using the roaming network.

- **Bluetooth**—This is the name of a technology that is used to wirelessly connect devices together. It is widely used for many different kinds of devices. Your iPhone can use Bluetooth to connect to speakers, the audio system in your car, keyboards, and headphones.

- **AirDrop**—This is Apple's technology for connecting iPhones, iPads, iPod touches, and Macintosh computers together to share information. AirDrop is a short-range technology—typically, the devices need to be in the same room or area for it to work. For example, you can use AirDrop to send photos from your iPhone to someone's iPad. The nice thing about AirDrop is that it requires very little setup and is quite easy to use, as you will see in this chapter.

Securing Your iPhone

Even though you won't often be connecting a cable to it, an iPhone is a connected device, meaning that it sends information to and receives information from other devices, either directly or via the Internet, during many different activities. Some are obvious, such as sending text messages or browsing the Web, whereas others might not be so easy to spot, such as when an app is determining

when you aren't home) for sensitive transactions, such as accessing bank accounts or other financial information.

- Never accept a request to share information from someone you don't know. Later in this chapter, you learn about AirDrop, which enables you to easily share photos and lots of other things with other people using iOS devices. If you receive an AirDrop request from someone you don't recognize, always decline it. In fact, if you have any doubt, decline such requests. It's much easier for someone legitimate to confirm with you and resend a request than it is for you to recover from damage that can be done if you inadvertently accept a request from someone you don't know.

- Only download apps through Apple's App Store through the App Store app on your iPhone. Fortunately, the way the iPhone is set up, you have to do something very unusual to install apps outside of the App Store. As long as you download apps only as described in this book, you are free of apps that can harm your information because Apple has strict controls over the apps that make it into the App Store. (Downloading apps is explained in Chapter 5.

Reality Check

Internet security is a complex topic, and it can be troublesome to think about. It's best to keep in mind the relative level of risk when you use your iPhone compared to other risks in the physical world that most of us don't think twice about. For example, every time you hand your credit card to someone, there is a chance that that person will record the number and use it without your knowledge or permission. Even when you swipe a credit card in a reader, such as at a gas station, that information is communicated across multiple networks and can be intercepted. (For example, there have been numerous compromises of credit card information at a number of well-known retailers.) If you take basic precautions like those described here, the risks to you when you are using your iPhone are similar to the other risks we all face in everyday life. My recommendation is to take the basic precautions, and then don't worry about it overly much. It might be a good idea to have identity theft insurance (try to find a company that assigns someone to do the work of recovering for you should your identity be stolen).

Using Wi-Fi Networks to Connect to the Internet

Almost all Wi-Fi networks broadcast their information so that you can easily see them with your iPhone; these are called *open networks* because anyone who is in range can attempt to join one since they appear on Wi-Fi devices automatically. The Wi-Fi networks you can see on your iPhone in public places (such as airports and hotels) are all open. Likewise, any Wi-Fi networks in your home or office are very likely to be open as well. To connect your iPhone to an open network, you tap its name and then enter its password (if required).

By default, when you access one of your iPhone's Internet functions, such as Safari, your iPhone automatically searches for Wi-Fi networks to join if you aren't already connected to one. A prompt appears showing the networks available to your iPhone. You can select and join one of these networks by tapping its name on the list of networks and entering its password (if required).

Connecting to Open Wi-Fi Networks

To connect your iPhone to a Wi-Fi network, perform the following steps:

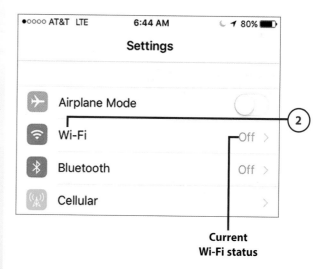

(1) On the Home screen, tap Settings. Next to Wi-Fi, you see the status of your Wi-Fi connection. It is Off if Wi-Fi is turned off, Not Connected if Wi-Fi is turned on and your phone isn't currently connected to Wi-Fi, or the name of the Wi-Fi network to which your iPhone is connected.

(2) Tap Wi-Fi.

Current Wi-Fi status

(3) If Wi-Fi isn't enabled already, slide the Wi-Fi switch to on (green) and your iPhone searches for available networks. A list of available networks is displayed in the CHOOSE A NETWORK section (it can take a moment for all the networks available in the area to be shown). Along with each network's name, icons indicating whether it requires a password (the padlock icon) to join and the current signal strength (the radio waves icon) are displayed.

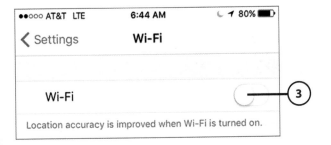

(4) Tap the network you want to join. Of course, when a network requires a password, you must know that password to be able to join it. Another consideration should be signal strength; the more waves in the network's signal strength icon, the stronger the connection.

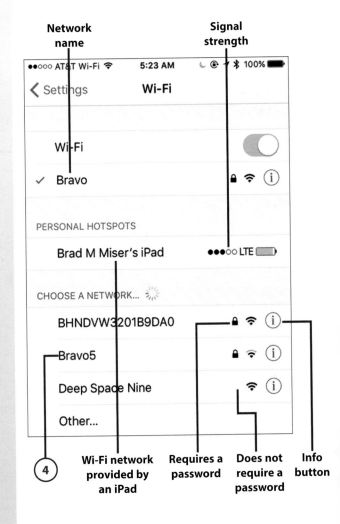

Network name

Signal strength

Wi-Fi network provided by an iPad

Requires a password

Does not require a password

Info button

5 At the prompt, enter the password for the network you selected. If you aren't prompted for a password, skip to step 7. (You're likely to find networks that don't require a password in public places; see the next section for information on these types of networks.)

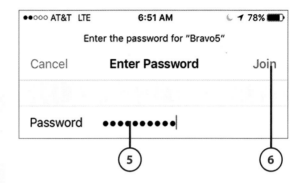

6 Tap Join. If you provided the correct password, your iPhone connects to the network and gets the information it needs to connect to the Internet. If not, you're prompted to enter the password again. After you successfully connect to the network, you return to the Wi-Fi screen.

7 Review the network information. The network to which you are connected appears just below the Wi-Fi switch and is marked with a check mark. You also see the signal strength for that network.

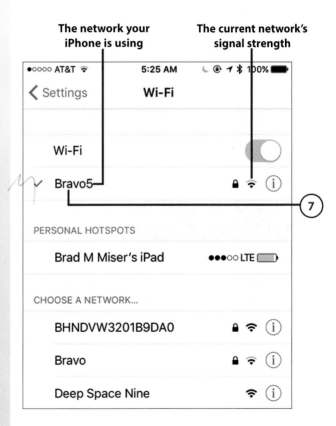

The network your iPhone is using

The current network's signal strength

8 Try to move to a web page, such as www.wunderground.com, to test your Wi-Fi connection (not shown). (See Chapter 13, "Surfing the Web," for details.) If the web page opens, you are ready to use the Internet on your phone. If you are taken to a login web page for a Wi-Fi provider rather than the page you were trying to access, see the next task. If you see a message saying the Internet is not available, there is a problem with the network you joined. Go back to step 4 to select a different network.

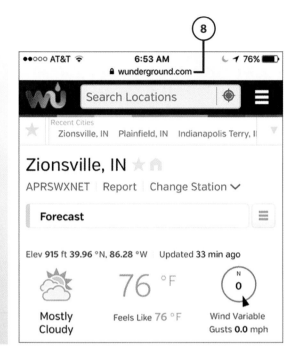

>>>Go Further
CONNECTING TO WI-FI NETWORKS

As you connect to Wi-Fi networks, consider the following:

- **Typing passwords**—As you type a password, each character is hidden by a dot in the Password field except for the last character you entered, which is displayed on the screen for a moment. Keep an eye on characters as you enter them because you can fix a mistake as soon as you make it rather than finding out after you've entered the entire password and having to start over.

- **Changing networks**—You can use these same steps to change the Wi-Fi network you are using at any time. For example, if you have to pay to use one network but a different one is free, simply choose the free network in step 4.

- **Be known**—After your iPhone connects to a Wi-Fi network successfully, it becomes a known network. This means that your iPhone remembers its information so you don't have to enter it again. Your iPhone automatically connects to known networks when it needs to access the Internet. So unless you tell your iPhone to forget a network, you need to enter its password only the first time you connect to it.

- **Forget it**—If you no longer want your iPhone to automatically connect to a network, you can have your iPhone forget that network. For example, you might have used a network in an airport that you pay for, and no longer want to use that network. To forget a network, move to the Wi-Fi screen, tap the network's Info button (i), tap Forget This Network, and then tap Forget at the prompt. Your iPhone no longer connects to the network automatically. You can re-connect to the network using the steps in the preceding task; when you do, it gets remembered again.

- **Automatic prompting**—When your iPhone isn't connected to a network and you try to access the Internet, you're prompted to join an available network (if you've connected to a network in that area before and haven't forgotten it, this doesn't happen because your iPhone connects to that network automatically). This can sometimes be annoying if you return to a location and don't want to use the network about which you are prompted. If you want to disable these automatic prompts, move to the Wi-Fi screen and set the Ask to Join Networks switch to off (white). You'll have to manually select a network to join if none of your known networks are available.

- **Security recommendation**—If you are connected to a network that doesn't use what Apple considers being the strongest security, you see the words "Security Recommendation" under the network's name. If you tap that network, you see its Info screen. At the top of that screen, you see the type of security the network is using and a recommendation about the type of security it should use. If the Wi-Fi network comes from a router or modem you own or rent, contact your Internet service provider, such as a cable company, to learn how the security provided by that router or modem can be reconfigured to be more secure. If the network is in a public place or business, you just have to use it as is (unless you can contact the administrator of that network to see if better security is available).

- **Personal hotspots**—iPhones and iPads can share their cellular Internet connection with other devices by providing a Wi-Fi network to which you can connect your iPhone. The icons for these networks are a bit different, being two connected loops that indicate the network is from a hotspot. You can select and use these networks just like the other types of networks being described in this chapter. The speed of your access is determined mostly by the speed of the device's cellular data connection. Also, the data you use while connected to the hotspot's network counts against the data plan for the device to which you are connected.

Connecting to Public Wi-Fi Networks

Many Wi-Fi networks in public places, such as hotels or airports, require that you pay a fee or provide other information to access the Internet through that network; even if access is free, you usually have to accept terms and conditions for the network to be able to use it.

When you connect to one of these public networks, you're prompted to provide whatever information is required. This can involve different details for different networks, but the general steps are the same. You're prompted to provide whatever information is required. Then, follow the instructions that appear.

Following are the general steps to connect to many types of public Wi-Fi networks:

1. Use the steps in the previous task to move to and tap the public network you want to join. The iPhone connects to the network, and you see the Log In screen for that network.

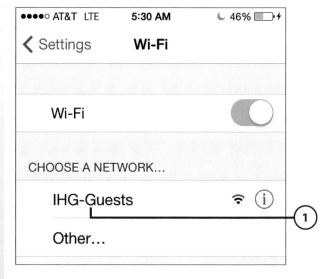

2 If prompted to do so, provide the information required to join the network, such as a last name and room number. If a fee is required, you have to provide payment information. In almost all cases, you at least have to indicate that you accept the terms and conditions for using the network, which you typically do by checking a check box.

3 Tap the button to join the network. This button can have different labels depending on the type of access, such as Authenticate, Done, Free Access, Login, and so on.

4 Try to move to a web page, such as www.wikipedia.org, to test your Wi-Fi connection (this is not shown in a figure). (See Chapter 13 for details.) If the web page opens, you are ready to use the Internet on your phone. If you are taken to a login web page for the Wi-Fi network's provider, you need to provide the required information to be able to use the Internet. For example, when access is free, as it is at most airports, you usually just have to indicate you accept the terms of use for that network.

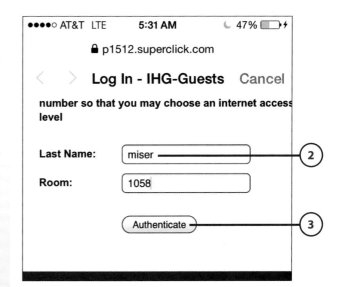

No Prompt?

Not all public networks prompt you to log in as these steps explain. Sometimes, you use the network's website to log in instead. After you join the network (step 1), your iPhone is connected to the network without any prompts. When you try to move to a web page as explained in step 4, you're prompted to log in to or create an account with the network's provider on the web page that appears.

Cell Phone Provider Wi-Fi Networks

Many cell phone providers also provide other services, particularly public Wi-Fi networks. In some cases, you can access that provider's Internet service through a Wi-Fi network that it provides; often, you can do this at no additional charge. So, you can take advantage of the speed a Wi-Fi connection provides without paying more for it. You connect to these networks just like any other by selecting them on the network list. What happens next depends on the specific network. In some cases, you need to enter your mobile phone number and then respond to a text message to that phone number. Check your provider's website to find out whether it offers this service and where and how you can access it.

Using Cellular Data Networks to Connect to the Internet

The provider for your iPhone also provides a cellular data connection your iPhone uses to connect to the Internet automatically when a Wi-Fi connection isn't available. (Your iPhone tries to connect to an available Wi-Fi network before connecting to a cellular data connection, because Wi-Fi is typically less expensive and faster to use.) These networks cover large geographic areas and the connection to them is automatic; your iPhone chooses and connects to the best cellular network currently available. Access to these networks is part of your monthly account fee; you choose from among various amounts of data per month for different monthly fees.

Most providers have multiple cellular data networks, such as a low-speed network that is available widely and one or more higher-speed networks that have a more limited coverage area. Your iPhone chooses the best connection available automatically.

The cellular data networks you can use are determined based on your provider, your data plan, the model of iPhone you are using, and your location within your provider's networks or the roaming networks available, when you are outside of your provider's coverage area. The iPhone automatically uses the fastest connection available to it at any given time (assuming you haven't disabled that option, as explained later).

In the United States, the major iPhone providers are AT&T, Sprint, T-Mobile, and Verizon. There are also other smaller providers, such as Boost Mobile, Metro PCS, Union Wireless, and Virgin Mobile. All these companies offer high-speed Long Term Evolution (LTE) cellular networks (these are also referred to as *true 4G networks*) along with the slower 4G and 3G networks. In other locations, the names and speeds of the networks available might be different.

The following information is focused on LTE networks because I happen to live in the United States, use an iPhone 7 and 6 Plus, and use AT&T and Sprint as my cell phone providers. If you use another provider or a different iPhone model, you are able to access your provider's networks similarly, though your details might be different. For example, the icon on the Home screen reflects the name of your provider's network, which might or might not be LTE.

**This iPhone is connected to a
high-speed LTE cellular network**

LTE high-speed wireless networks provide very fast Internet access from many locations. (Note: LTE networks might not be available everywhere, but you can usually access them near populated areas.) To connect to the LTE network, you don't need to do anything. If you aren't connected to a Wi-Fi network, you haven't turned off LTE, and your iPhone isn't in Airplane mode, the iPhone automatically connects to the LTE network when available. When you are connected to the LTE network, you see the LTE indicator at the top of the iPhone's screen. If you can't access the LTE network, such as when you aren't in its coverage area, the iPhone automatically connects to the next fastest network available, such as 4G. If that

Configuring Cellular Data Use

The following steps show configuring cellular data use on an iPhone 7 using AT&T in the United States; you can use similar steps to configure these options on an iPhone from a different provider:

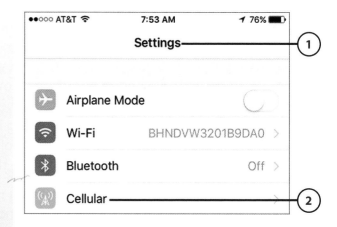

(1) Open the Settings app.

(2) Tap Cellular.

(3) To use a cellular Internet connection, set the Cellular Data switch to on (green) and move to step 4; if you don't want to use a cellular Internet connection, set this switch to off (white) and skip the rest of these steps. To use the Internet when the Cellular Data switch is off, you have to connect to a Wi-Fi network that provides Internet access.

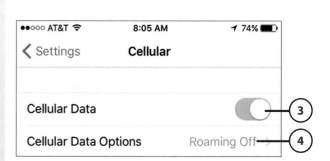

(4) Tap Cellular Data Options.

(5) To configure the high-speed network, tap Enable *high-speed network*, where *high-speed network* is the network's name. With some providers, this is a switch that enables or disables the high-speed network; set the switch to be on or off and skip to step 8 (if you set the switch to off, the iPhone can't use the higher-speed network but can still use slower networks).

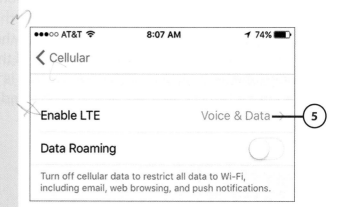

6 To disable the high-speed network, tap Off; to use it for both voice and data, tap Voice & Data; or to use it only for data, tap Data Only. (When you enable the high-speed network for voice, the quality of the sound of your calls may be better.)

7 Tap the back button.

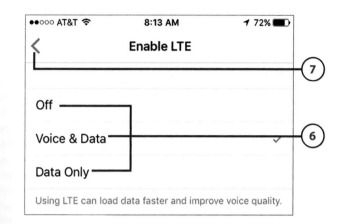

8 If you want to allow data roaming, slide the Data Roaming switch to the on (green) position. With some providers, Roaming is an option instead of a switch; tap Roaming and use the resulting switches to enable or disable roaming for voice or data and then tap the back button.

9 Tap Cellular.

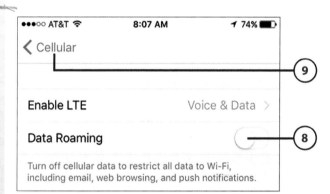

10 Swipe up the screen until you see the USE CELLULAR DATA FOR section. This section enables you to allow or prevent individual apps from accessing a cellular data network. To limit the amount of data you use, it's a good idea to review this list and allow only those apps that you rely on to use the cellular data network. (Of course, if you are fortunate enough to have an unlimited cellular data plan, you can leave all the apps enabled.)

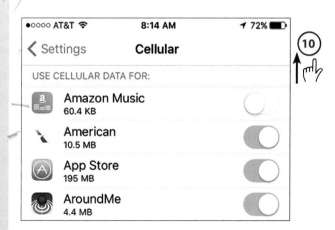

- **Apps' cellular data use**—Just under each app's name in the USE CELLULAR DATA FOR section, you see how much data the app has used since the counter was reset. This number can help you determine how much data a particular app uses. For example, if an app's use is shown in megabytes (MB), it's used a lot more data than an app whose use is shown in kilobytes (KB).

- **Cellular data use reset**—You can reset all of the statistics on the Cellular screen by swiping up until you reach the bottom of the screen and tapping Reset Statistics. Tap Reset Statistics again.

Using Bluetooth to Connect to Other Devices

The iPhone includes built-in Bluetooth support so you can use this wireless technology to connect to other Bluetooth-capable devices. The most likely devices to connect to iPhone in this way are Bluetooth headphones, speakers, headsets, or car audio/entertainment/information systems, but you can also use Bluetooth to connect to other kinds of devices, most notably keyboards, headphones, computers, iPod touches, iPads, and other iPhones.

To connect Bluetooth devices together, you *pair* them. In Bluetooth, pairing enables two Bluetooth devices to communicate with each other. The one constant requirement is that the devices can communicate with each other via Bluetooth. For devices to find and identify each other so they can communicate, one or both must be *discoverable*, which means they broadcast a Bluetooth signal other devices can detect and connect to.

There is also a "sometimes" requirement, which is a pairing code passkey, or PIN. All those terms refer to the same thing, which is a series of numbers, letters, or both, entered on one or both devices being paired. Sometimes you enter this code on both devices, whereas for other devices you enter the first device's code on the second device. Some devices, such as speakers, don't require a pairing code at all.

When you have to pair devices, you're prompted to do so, and you have to complete the actions required by the prompts to communicate via Bluetooth. This might be just tapping Connect, or you might have to enter a passcode on one or both devices to connect them.

Connecting to Bluetooth Devices

This task demonstrates pairing an iPhone with a Bluetooth keyboard; you can pair it with other devices similarly.

(1) Move to the Settings screen. The current status of Bluetooth on your iPhone is shown.

(2) Tap Bluetooth.

(3) If Bluetooth isn't on (green), tap the Bluetooth switch to turn it on. If it isn't running already, Bluetooth starts up. The iPhone immediately begins searching for Bluetooth devices. You also see the status Now Discoverable, which means other Bluetooth devices can discover the iPhone. In the MY DEVICES section, you see devices to which you've previously paired your iPhone; their current status is either Connected, meaning the device is currently communicating with your iPhone, or Not Connected, meaning the device is paired with your iPhone, but is not currently connected to it. In the OTHER DEVICES section, you see the devices that are discoverable to your iPhone but that are not paired with it.

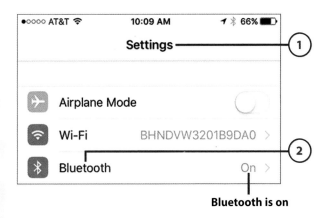

Bluetooth is on

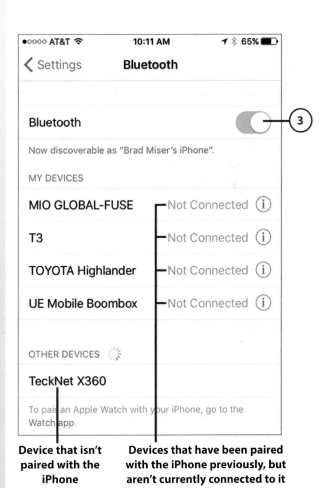

Device that isn't paired with the iPhone

Devices that have been paired with the iPhone previously, but aren't currently connected to it

4 If the device you want to use isn't shown in the OTHER DEVICES section, put it into Discoverable mode. (Not shown; see the instructions provided with the device.) When it is discoverable, it appears in the OTHER DEVICES section.

5 Tap the device to which you want to connect. If the device isn't currently paired with your iPhone, you might need to provide a passkey. If a passkey is required, you see a prompt to enter it on the device with which you are pairing; perform step 6. If no passkey is required, skip to step 7. If the device is currently paired with your iPhone (it is shown on the MY DEVICES list), but not currently connected, tapping the device causes it to be reconnected, its status becomes Connected, and you can skip the rest of these steps.

6 If it is required, input the pairing code, passkey, or PIN on the device, such as typing the passkey on a keyboard if you are pairing your iPhone with a Bluetooth keyboard.

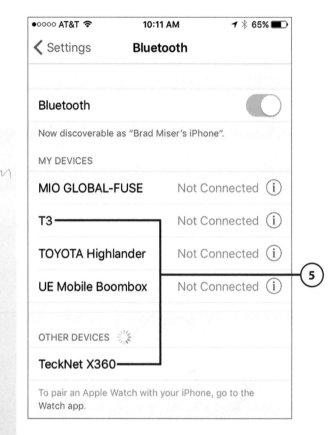

7) If required, tap Connect (not shown in the figures)—some devices connect as soon as you enter the passkey and you won't need to do this. If a passkey isn't required, such as with a Bluetooth speaker, you tap Connect instead. You see the device to which the iPhone is connected in the MY DEVICES section of the Bluetooth screen, and its status is Connected, indicating that your iPhone can communicate with and use the device.

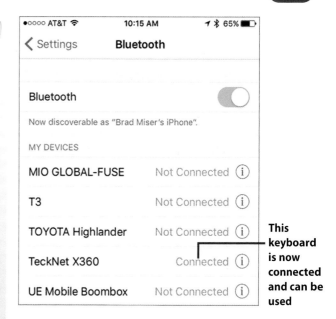

●○○○○ AT&T 📶   10:15 AM   ✈ ∗ 65% 🔋

❮ Settings   **Bluetooth**

Bluetooth

Now discoverable as "Brad Miser's iPhone".

MY DEVICES

MIO GLOBAL-FUSE   Not Connected ⓘ

T3   Not Connected ⓘ

TOYOTA Highlander   Not Connected ⓘ

TeckNet X360   Connected ⓘ

UE Mobile Boombox   Not Connected ⓘ

This keyboard is now connected and can be used

>>>Go Further

MANAGING BLUETOOTH

Following are a few pointers for using Bluetooth with other devices:

- Like other connections you make, the iPhone remembers Bluetooth devices to which you've connected before and reconnects to them automatically, which is convenient— most of the time anyway. If you don't want your iPhone to keep connecting to a device, move to the Bluetooth screen and tap the device's Info (i) button. Tap the Forget this Device button and then tap Forget Device. The pairing is removed. Of course, you can always pair the devices again at any time. If you just want to stop using the device, but keep the pairing in place, you can tap Disconnect instead.

- If a device is already paired but has the Not Connected status, you need to connect it to use it. Move to the Bluetooth screen and tap the device to connect it to your iPhone. Once its status becomes Connected, your iPhone can communicate with the device again.

- You can use multiple Bluetooth devices with your iPhone at the same time. For example, you might want to be connected to a Bluetooth speaker and a keyboard at the same time.

Connecting Your iPhone to Other iPhones, iPod touches, or iPads

The iPhone (and other devices that run the iOS software, including iPod touches and iPads) supports peer-to-peer connectivity, which is the technical way of saying that these devices can communicate with one another directly via a Wi-Fi network or Bluetooth. This capability is used in a number of apps, especially multiplayer gaming, for information sharing, and for other collaborative purposes.

If the app you want to use communicates over a Wi-Fi network, such as a network you use to access the Internet, all the devices with which you want to communicate must be on that same network. If the application uses Bluetooth, you must enable Bluetooth on each device and pair them (as described in the previous task) so they can communicate with one another.

The specific steps you use to connect to other iOS devices using a collaborative app depend on the specific app you are using. The general steps are typically as follows:

1. Ensure the devices can communicate with each other. If the app uses Wi-Fi, each device must be on the same Wi-Fi network. If the app uses Bluetooth, the devices must be paired.

2. Each person opens the app on his device.

3. Use the app's controls to select the devices with which you'll be collaborating. Usually, this involves a confirmation process in which one person selects another person's device and that person confirms that the connection should be allowed.

4. Use the app's features to collaborate. For example, if the app is a game, each person can interact with the group members. Or, you can directly collaborate on a document with all parties providing input into the document.

---

iPhone and Apple Watch

The Apple Watch is designed to be a perfect partner device for your iPhone and can work with it in many ways. For detailed information about the Apple Watch, see the book *My Apple Watch* by Craig James Johnston (Que Publishing).

Using AirDrop to Share Content with Other iPhones, iPod touches, iPads, or a Mac

You can use the iOS AirDrop feature to share content directly with people using a Mac running OS X Yosemite or later, or using a device running iOS 7 or later. For example, if you capture a great photo on your iPhone, you can use AirDrop to instantly share that photo with iOS device and Mac users near you.

AirDrop can use Wi-Fi or Bluetooth to share, but the nice thing about AirDrop is that it manages the details for you. You simply open the Share menu—which is available in most apps—tap AirDrop, and tap the people with whom you want to share.

When you activate AirDrop, you can select Everyone, which means you see anyone who has a Mac running OS X Yosemite or later, or an iOS device running version iOS 7 or newer and is on the same Wi-Fi network as you (or has a paired Bluetooth device); those people can see you, too. Or, you can select Contacts Only, which means only people who are in your Contacts app are able to use AirDrop to communicate with you. In most cases, you should choose the Contacts Only option so you have more control over who uses AirDrop with you.

Is AirDrop Safe?

Anything you share with AirDrop is encrypted, so the chances of someone else being able to intercept and use what you share are quite low. Likewise, you don't have to worry about someone using AirDrop to access your information or to add information to your device without your permission. However, like any networking technology, there's always some chance—quite small in this case—that someone will figure out how to use this technology for nefarious purposes. The best thing you can do is to be wary of any requests you receive to share information and ensure they are from people you know and trust before you accept them.

Enabling AirDrop

To use AirDrop, you must enable it on your iPhone.

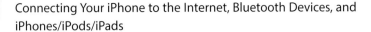

1. Swipe up from the bottom of the screen to open the Control Center.

2. If AirDrop is not active—indicated by the AirDrop icon showing AirDrop: Receiving Off—tap AirDrop. If it is active, the AirDrop icon and text is in white and you see its status (Everyone or Contacts Only); if it is already active, skip the next two steps.

3. Tap Contacts Only to allow only people in your Contacts app to communicate with you via AirDrop, or tap Everyone to allow anyone using a device running iOS 7 or later or a Mac running OS X Yosemite or later in your area to do so.

Current AirDrop status (disabled)

You can be discoverable in AirDrop to receive from everyone or only people in your contacts.

Receiving Off

Contacts Only — 3

Everyone

Cancel

(4) Swipe down from the top of the Control Center to close it. You're ready to use AirDrop to share.

Share and Share Alike?

You should disable AirDrop when you aren't using it, especially if you use the Everyone option. By disabling it, you avoid having people in your area be able to try to communicate with you without you wanting them to do so. Generally, you should enable AirDrop only when you are actively using it and disable it when you aren't. To disable AirDrop, open the Control Center, tap AirDrop, and then tap Receiving Off.

People in your Contacts app can use AirDrop to share content with you

Using AirDrop to Share Your Content

To use AirDrop to share your content, do the following:

(1) Open the content you want to share. This example shows sharing a photo using the Photos app (this app is covered in detail in Chapter 15, "Viewing and Editing Photos and Video with the Photos App"). The steps to share content from any other app are quite similar.

(2) Tap the Share button.

3 Tap AirDrop (not shown on the figure) or just wait a couple of seconds. The AirDrop button is replaced with icons for each person in your area who has AirDrop enabled that you have permission to access (such as being in her Contacts app if she is using the Contacts Only option).

4 Swipe to the left or right to browse all the people with whom you can share.

5 Tap the people with whom you want to share the content. A sharing request is sent to those people's devices. Under their icons, the Waiting status is displayed. When a recipient accepts your content, the status changes to Sent. If a recipient rejects your content, the status changes to Declined.

Photo selected to share

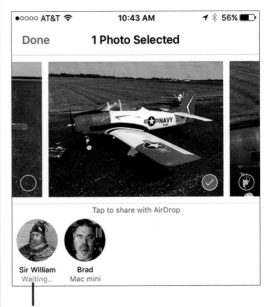

Waiting for the recipient to accept or decline your sharing

6 If the app supports it, browse and select more content to share.

7 Tap the people with whom you want to share the content.

8 When you're done sharing, tap Done.

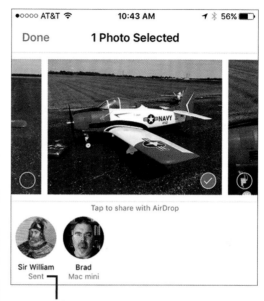

Recipient has accepted your content

Use iCloud and other accounts to store the data your apps use on the cloud

Go here to configure and manage iCloud and your other online accounts

Store files on the cloud

In this chapter, you learn how to connect your iPhone to various types of accounts, such as iCloud and Google, so that apps on your iPhone can access your data stored on the Internet cloud. Topics include the following:

→ Getting started
→ Configuring and using iCloud
→ Setting up other types of built-in online accounts on your iPhone
→ Configuring other types of online accounts
→ Setting how and when your accounts are updated

Setting Up and Using iCloud and Other Online Accounts

No iPhone is an island. Connecting your iPhone to the Internet enables you to share and sync a wide variety of content using popular online accounts such as iCloud and Google. Using iCloud, you can put your email, contacts, calendars, photos, and more on the Internet so that multiple devices—most importantly your iPhone—can connect to and use that information. (There's a lot more you can do with iCloud, too, as you learn throughout this book.) There are lots of other online accounts you might also want to use, such as Google for email, calendars, and contacts as well as Facebook for accessing social networks.

You need to configure these accounts on your iPhone to be able to use them; in this chapter you'll find sections for several different online accounts you might want to use. Of course, you need to refer only to the sections related to the accounts you actually use. You will also find out how you can determine how and when your information is updated along with tasks you might find valuable as you manage the various accounts on your iPhone.

- **Wallet**—The Wallet app stores coupons, tickets, boarding passes, and other documents so you can access them quickly and easily. With iCloud, you can ensure that these documents are available on any iCloud-enabled device.

- **Keychain**—The Keychain securely stores sensitive data, such as passwords, so that you can easily use that data without having to remember it.

- **Backup**—You can back up your iPhone to the cloud so that you can recover your data and your phone's configuration should something ever happen to it.

- **Find My iPhone**—This service enables you to locate and secure your iPhone and other devices.

You learn about iCloud's many useful features throughout this book (such as using iCloud with your photos, which is covered in Chapter 15, "Viewing and Editing Photos and Video with the Photos App"). The tasks in this chapter show you how to set up and configure the iCloud features you want to use.

Obtaining an iCloud Account

Of course, to use iCloud on your iPhone, you need to have an iCloud account. The good news is that you probably already have one. The other good news is that even if you don't, obtaining one is simple and free.

If you have any of the following accounts, you already have an iCloud account and are ready to start using iCloud and can skip ahead to the next section:

- **iTunes Store**—If you've ever shopped at the iTunes Store, you created an account with an Apple ID and password. You can use that Apple ID and password to access iCloud.

- **Apple Online Store**—As with the iTunes Store, if you made purchases from Apple's online store, you created an account with an Apple ID and password that also enables you to use iCloud.

- **Find My iPhone**—If you obtained a free Find My iPhone account, you can log in to iCloud using that Apple ID.

During the initial iPhone startup process, you were prompted to sign in to or create an iCloud account. If you created one at that time, you are also good to go and can move to the next task.

If you don't have an iCloud account, you can use your iPhone to create one by performing the following steps:

(1) On the Home screen, tap Settings.

(2) Swipe up the screen and tap iCloud.

(3) Tap Create a New Apple ID.

(4) Provide the information required on the following screens; tap Next to move to the next screen after you've entered the required information. You start by entering your birthday.

During the process, you're prompted to use an existing email address or to create a free iCloud email account. You can choose either option. The email address you use becomes your Apple ID that you use to sign in to iCloud. If you create a new email account, you can use that account from any email app on any device, just like other email accounts you have.

You also create a password, set up security questions, enter a rescue email address (optional), choose email updates you want to receive, and agree to license terms. When your account has been created, you're prompted to enter your password.

After you successfully create your password, you are logged in to your iCloud account and might be prompted to merge information already stored on your iPhone, such as Safari bookmarks, onto iCloud. Tap Merge to copy the information that currently is stored on your iPhone to the cloud or Don't Merge to keep it out of the cloud.

When you've worked through merging your information, you see that iCloud will track the location of your iPhone through the Find My iPhone feature.

5 Tap OK. You are ready to complete the configuration of your iCloud account, which is covered in the next section.

Find My iPhone Enabled

This allows you to locate, lock, or erase your iPhone. Your Apple ID and password will be required to reactivate your iPhone.

OK ——————— **5**

Multiple iCloud Accounts

You can have more than one iCloud account; although, you can be signed in to only one iCloud account on your iPhone at a time.

Signing In To Your iCloud Account

To be able to use an iCloud account on your iPhone, you need to first sign in to your account and then enable the services you want to use and disable those that you don't want to use. After iCloud is set up on your iPhone, you rarely need to change your account settings. If you restore your iPhone at some point, you might need to revisit these steps to ensure iCloud remains set up as you want it.

To get started, sign in to your iCloud account—if you created your iCloud account on your iPhone, you don't need to perform these steps because you signed in when you created the account; in that case, skip to the next task.

1. On the Home screen, tap Settings.

2. Swipe up the screen and tap iCloud.

3. Enter your Apple ID. If you see account information instead of the Apple ID field, an iCloud account is already signed in to on the iPhone. If it is your account, skip to the next task. If it isn't your account, swipe up the screen and tap Sign Out; tap Delete to delete various data from your iPhone at the prompts and continue with these steps.

4. Enter your Apple ID password.

5. Tap Sign In. You are logged in to your iCloud account.

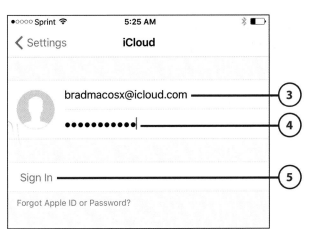

(6) If prompted to do so, tap Merge to merge existing data, such as Safari bookmarks, already stored on the iPhone onto the cloud or tap Don't Merge if you don't want the information on your iPhone combined with the information stored in your iCloud account.

(7) At the prompt, tap OK to indicate that you realize Find My iPhone is enabled. You're ready to configure the rest of iCloud's services.

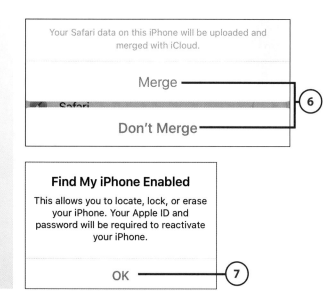

> Your Safari data on this iPhone will be uploaded and merged with iCloud.
>
> Merge —— (6)
> Safari
> Don't Merge——

> **Find My iPhone Enabled**
> This allows you to locate, lock, or erase your iPhone. Your Apple ID and password will be required to reactivate your iPhone.
>
> OK —— (7)

Enabling iCloud to Store Your Information on the Cloud

One of the best things about iCloud is that it stores email, contacts, calendars, reminders, bookmarks, notes, photos, and other data on the cloud so that all your iCloud-enabled devices can access the same information. You can choose the types of data stored on the cloud by performing the following steps:

(1) Move to the iCloud screen by tapping Settings, iCloud. Just below the Storage information are the iCloud data options. Some of these have a right-facing arrow that you tap to configure options, and others have a two-position switch. When a switch is green, it means that switch is turned on and the related data is stored to your iCloud account and kept in sync with the information on the iPhone.

(2) If you don't want a specific type of data to be stored on the cloud and synced to your iPhone, tap its switch to turn that data off (the switch becomes white instead of green). The types of data that have switches are Mail, Contacts, Calendars, Reminders, Safari, Home, Notes, News, and Wallet.

When you turn off a switch because you don't want that information stored on the cloud any more, you might be prompted to keep the associated information on your iPhone or delete it.

If you choose Keep on My iPhone, the information remains on your iPhone but is no longer connected to the cloud; this means any changes you make exist only on the iPhone. If you choose Delete from My iPhone, the information is erased from your iPhone. Whether you choose to keep or delete the information, any information of that type that was previously stored on the cloud remains available there; the delete action only affects the information stored on the iPhone.

After you've configured each data switch on the iCloud screen, you're ready to configure the rest of the data options, which are explained in the following tasks.

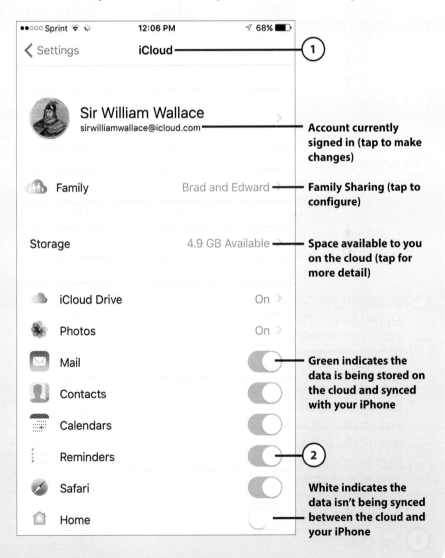

the cloud; should something happen to your iPhone, you can easily get to your photos again.

(**3**) If you enable the iCloud Photo Library feature, tap Optimize iPhone Storage to keep lower resolution versions of photos and videos on your iPhone (this means the file sizes are smaller so that you can store more of them on your phone) or Download and Keep Originals if you want to keep the full-resolution photos on your iPhone. In most cases, you should choose the Optimize option so that you don't use as much of your iPhone's storage space for photos.

(**4**) Ensure the Upload to My Photo Stream switch is on (green) (if you aren't using the iCloud Photo Library, this switch is called My Photo Stream); if you disabled this, skip to step 6. Any photos you take with the iPhone's camera are copied onto iCloud, and from there they are copied to your other devices on which the Photo Stream is enabled. Note that Photo Stream only affects photos that you take with the iPhone from the time you enable it, while the iCloud Photo Library feature uploads all of your photos, those you took in the past and will take in the future.

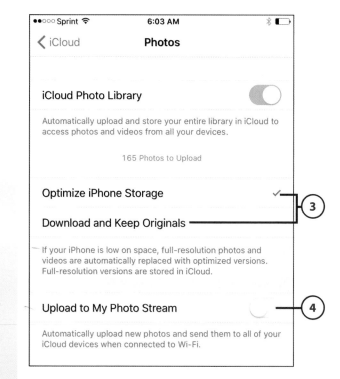

5 If you want all of your burst photos to be uploaded to iCloud, set the Upload Burst Photos switch to on (green). In most cases, you should leave this off (white) because you typically don't want to keep all the photos in a burst. When you review and select photos to keep, the ones you keep are uploaded.

6 To be able to share your photos and to share other people's photos, set the iCloud Photo Sharing switch to on (green).

7 Tap iCloud.

Need More Storage?

A free iCloud account includes 5 GB of storage space, which is enough to get started and use iCloud for a while. Over time, you may need to add storage, especially if you have a lot of photos and video. When your space starts to get full, you see warning messages. To add more space, open the Settings app, tap iCloud, and tap Storage. You can use the controls on the resulting Storage screen to change the amount of space you can use (adding more space requires an additional fee).

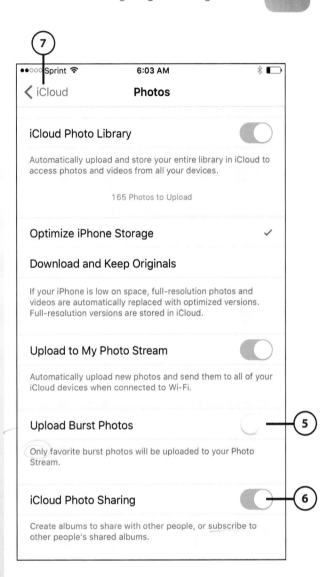

Configuring Your iCloud Backup

It is important to back up your iPhone's data so that you can recover should something bad happen to your iPhone. You can back up your iPhone's data and settings to iCloud, which is really useful because that means you can recover the backed-up data using a different device, such as a replacement iPhone. Configure your iCloud backup with the following steps:

(1) On the iCloud screen, tap Backup.

(2) Set the iCloud Backup switch to on (green). Your iPhone's data and settings are backed up to the cloud automatically.

(3) Tap iCloud.

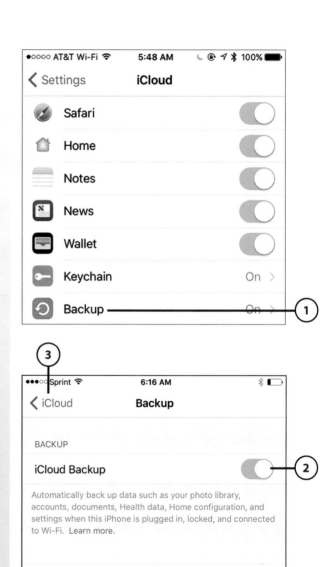

Back Me Up on This

You can manually back up your iPhone's data and settings at any time by tapping Back Up Now on the Backup screen. This can be useful to ensure recent data or settings changes are captured in your backup. For example, if you know you are going to be without a Wi-Fi connection to the Internet for a while, back up your phone to ensure that your current data is saved in the backup.

Configuring Your iCloud Keychain

A keychain can be used to store user-names, passwords, and credit cards so you can access this information without retyping it every time you need it. Enabling keychain syncing through iCloud makes this information available on multiple devices. For example, if you've configured a website's password on your keychain on a Mac, that password is available in the Safari app if the keychain is synced via iCloud. Follow these steps to enable keychain syncing through iCloud:

1. On the iCloud screen, tap Keychain.

2. If prompted to do so, enter your Apple ID password and tap OK.

3. Set the iCloud Keychain switch to on (green). You need to verify you want the keychain to be enabled on the device. You can do this by entering your security code or approving on another device that has access to your keychain. When you enable the keychain, approval requests are sent to the other devices that have access to your keychain. You can enter your Apple ID password at the prompt on those devices to approve the keychain on your iPhone or continue with these steps to use your security code to do so.

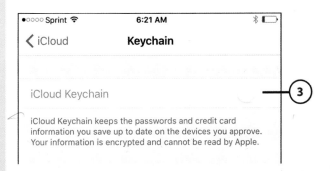

④ Tap Approve with Security Code.

Assumptions

These steps assume you have a keychain already configured for iCloud syncing on another device, such as a Mac or iPad, and that you know your security code. If not, your steps might be slightly different than those shown here. For example, you create a security code if this is the first time you set up keychain syncing.

⑤ Enter your security code. You're prompted to enter a verification code, which you receive via text to your phone.

⑥ Enter the verification code you receive via text. Your keychain syncing starts and your keychain information is stored on the cloud and synced onto your iPhone.

Advanced Keychain Syncing

When keychain syncing has been enabled, Advanced appears on the Keychain screen. Tap this to access additional Keychain commands. Use the Approve with Security Code switch to determine if your code can be used to set up keychain syncing on other devices. Tap Change Security Code to change your security code. Use the controls in the VERIFICATION NUMBER section to see or change the phone number to which the verification code is texted.

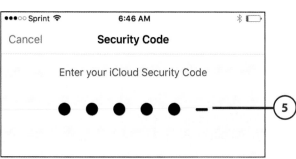

>>>Go Further
PROCEED WITH CAUTION

If you store a lot of sensitive information in your keychain on a Mac, such as usernames and passwords to websites, credit cards, and such, be careful about enabling keychain syncing. When you enable this iCloud feature, all this data becomes available on your iPhone and can be used by anyone who can use your phone. Assuming you have a passcode to the phone, you are protected from someone using your phone without you knowing it, but if you let someone use your phone, she can also use your sensitive information. You may choose to leave keychain syncing off and just keep a minimum amount of sensitive information on your phone.

>>>Go Further
CONFIGURING FIND MY IPHONE

Find My iPhone enables you to locate and secure your iPhone if you lose it. This feature is enabled by default when you sign in to your iCloud account. There are a couple of configuration tasks you can do for Find My iPhone:

- To disable Find My iPhone, open Settings and tap the iCloud option, and then tap Find My iPhone. Set the Find My iPhone switch to off (white) and enter your Apple ID password at the prompt. You can no longer access your iPhone via the Find My iPhone feature.

- To send the last known location of the iPhone to Apple when power is critically low, open the Find My iPhone screen and set the Send Last Location switch to on (green). When your iPhone is nearly out of power, its location is sent to Apple. You can contact Apple to try to locate your iPhone should it run out of power while it isn't in your possession.

Setting Up Other Types of Built-In Online Accounts on Your iPhone

Many types of online accounts provide different services, including email, calendars, contacts, social networking, and so on. To use these accounts, you need to configure them on your iPhone. The process you use for most types of accounts is similar to the steps you used to set up your iCloud account. In this section, you learn how to configure a Google account.

Configuring a Google Account

A Google account provides email, contacts, calendar, and note syncing that is similar to iCloud. To set up a Google account on your iPhone, do the following:

(1) On the Home screen, tap Settings.

(2) Tap Mail.

(3) Tap Accounts.

(4) Tap Add Account.

(5) Tap Google.

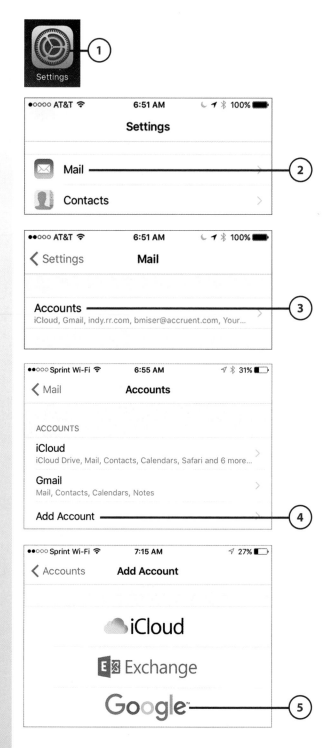

6 Enter your Google email address.

7 Tap Next.

8 Enter your Google account password.

9 Tap Next.

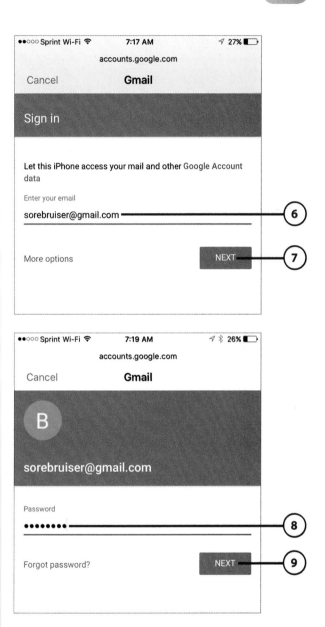

(10) Enable the features of the account you want to access on the iPhone, which are Mail, Contacts, Calendars, and Notes by setting the switch to on (green) for the types of data you do want to use or to off (white) for the types of data you don't want to use.

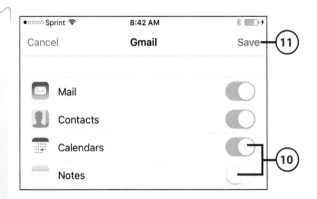

(11) Tap Save. The account is saved, and the data you enabled becomes available on your iPhone.

Configuring Other Types of Built-In Online Accounts on Your iPhone

The iPhone supports a number of other types of built-in online accounts, which are Aol.com, Exchange, Outlook.com, and Yahoo!. You can configure any of these accounts very similarly to how you set up a Google account. Move to the Add Account screen (steps 1 through 4 in the previous task). Then tap the type of account you want to configure, such as Yahoo!. Follow the onscreen prompts to enter that account's information and determine the type of data you want to use (for example, Mail to access that account's email). When you're done, you'll be able to use that account with apps on the iPhone. For example, when you configure a Yahoo! account and enable Mail data, you can receive email sent to your Yahoo! email address in the Mail app on your iPhone.

Configuring Other Types of Online Accounts

There are other types of online accounts you might want to use. An email account included with an Internet access account, such as one from a cable Internet provider, is one example. Support for these accounts isn't built in to the iOS, but you can usually set up such accounts on your iPhone fairly easily.

If you use Facebook, you can configure your account on your iPhone so that you can use the Facebook app and access Facebook for other purposes, such as to share photos on your Facebook page.

Setting Up an Online Account that Isn't Built-in

When you obtain an account, such as email accounts that are part of your cable Internet service, you should receive all the information you need to configure those accounts on your iPhone. If you don't have this information, visit the provider's website and look for information on configuring the account in an email application. You need to have this information to configure the account on the iPhone.

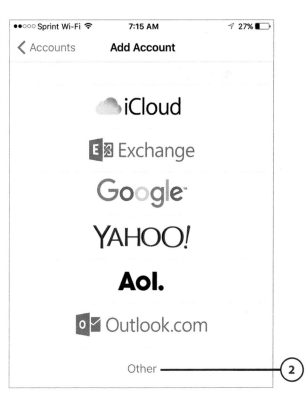

With the configuration information for the account you want to use on your iPhone in hand, you're ready to set it up:

1. In the Settings app, move to the Mail screen, tap Accounts, and tap Add Account.

2. Tap Other.

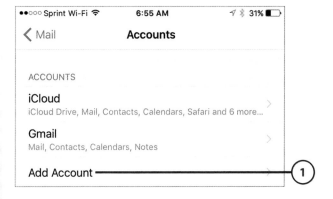

3 Tap the type of account you want to add. For example, to set up an email account, tap Add Mail Account.

4 Enter the information by filling in the fields you see; various types of information are required for different kinds of accounts. You just need to enter the information you received from the account's provider.

5 Tap Next. If the iPhone can set up the account automatically, its information is verified and it is ready for you to use (if the account supports multiple types of information, you can enable or disable the types with which you want to work on your iPhone). If the iPhone can't set up the account automatically, you're prompted to enter additional information to complete the account configuration. When you're done, the account appears on the list of accounts and is ready for you to use.

6 Configure the switches for the data sync options you see. For example, to use the account for email, set the Mail switch to on (green).

7 Tap Save. The account you configured is available in the related app, such as Mail if you set up an email account.

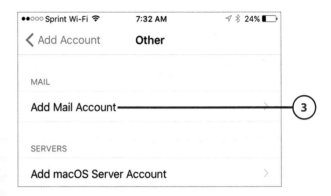

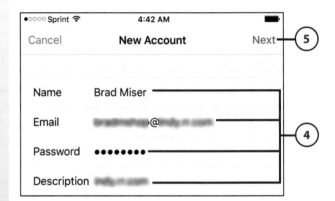

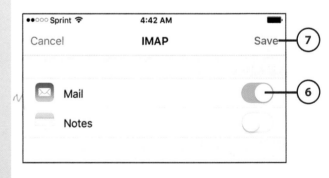

Multiple Accounts

There is no limit (that I have found so far) on the number of online accounts even of the same type, such as Gmail, that you can access on your iPhone. You can only have one iCloud account configured on your iPhone at the same time.

Configuring a Facebook Account

Facebook is one of the most popular social media channels you can use to keep informed about other people and inform them about you. Facebook is integrated into the iOS so you can use your Facebook page to share photos, messages, and such from the associated iPhone apps (for example, you can share photos from the Photos app), and you can also use the Facebook app itself.

To configure Facebook, perform the following steps:

(1) Move to the Home screen and tap Settings.

(2) Swipe up the screen and tap Facebook. If you see INSTALLED at the top of the screen, the Facebook app is installed on your iPhone and you can get right into your account. If not, tap INSTALL to install the app (downloading and installing apps is covered in Chapter 5, "Customizing How Your iPhone Works"); when the app is done installing, move back to the Facebook screen in the Settings app and continue with these steps.

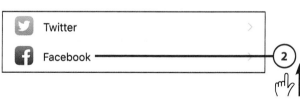

No Facebook Account?

If don't have a Facebook account, tap Create New Account and follow the onscreen instructions to create one. When you are done creating the new account, you're signed in to it automatically.

(3) Type your Facebook username.

(4) Type your Facebook password.

(5) Tap Sign In. Your account information is verified and you are signed in to your account.

(6) Tap Sign In at the prompt.

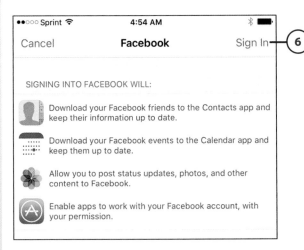

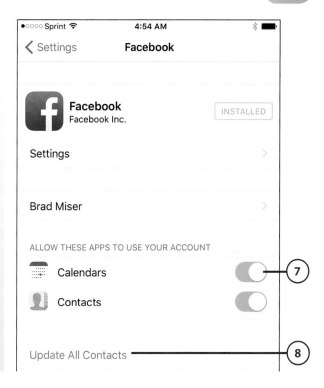

7. To prevent apps from accessing your Facebook information, slide their switches to the off position (white).

8. Tap Update All Contacts. Facebook attempts to match as much of your contact information with your Facebook friends as it can. When the process is complete, you are ready to access your Facebook account within the Facebook app or in any number of other apps.

Setting How and When Your Accounts Are Updated

The great thing about online accounts is that their information can be updated any time your iPhone can connect to the Internet. This means you have access to the latest information, such as new emails, changes to your calendars, and so on. There are three basic ways information gets updated:

- **Push**—When information is updated via Push, the server pushes (thus the name) updated information onto your iPhone whenever that information changes. For example, when you receive a new email, that email is immediately sent (or pushed) to your iPhone. Push provides you with the most current information all the time but uses a lot more battery than the other options.

- **Fetch**—When information is updated via Fetch, your iPhone connects to the account and retrieves the updated information according to a schedule, such as every 15 minutes. Fetch doesn't keep your information quite as current as Push does, but it uses much less battery than Push does.

• **Manual**—You can cause an app's information to be updated manually. This happens whenever you open or move into an app or by a manual refresh. For example, you can get new email by moving onto the Inboxes screen in the Mail app and swiping down from the top of the screen.

You can configure the update method that is used globally, and you can set the method for specific accounts. Some account types, such as iCloud, support all three options whereas others might support only Fetch and Manual. The global option for updating is used unless you override it for individual accounts. For example, you might want your personal account to be updated via Push so your information there is always current, but configuring Fetch on a club email account might be frequent enough.

Configuring How New Data Is Retrieved for Your Accounts

To configure how your information is updated, perform the following steps:

1. Move to the Mail screen of the Settings app and tap Accounts to move to the Accounts screen.

2. Tap Fetch New Data.

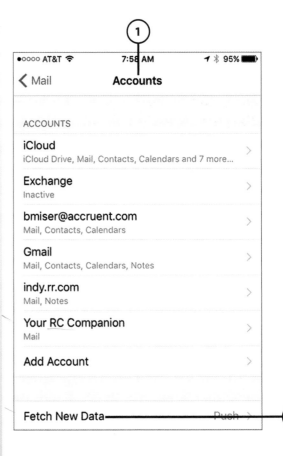

(**3**) To enable data to be pushed to your iPhone, slide the Push switch to on (green). To disable push to extend battery life, set it to off (white). This setting is global, meaning that if you disable Push here, it is disabled for all accounts even though you can still configure Push to be used for individual accounts. For example, if your iCloud account is set to use Push but Push is globally disabled, the iCloud account's setting is ignored and data is fetched instead.

(**4**) To change how an account's information is updated, tap it. The account's screen displays. The options on this screen depend on the kind of account it is. You always have Fetch and Manual; Push is displayed only for accounts that support it.

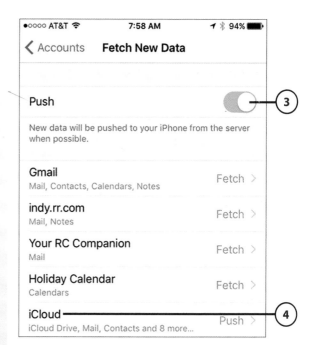

5 Tap the option you want to use for the account: Push, Fetch, or Manual.

If you choose Manual, information is retrieved only when you manually start the process by opening the related app (such as Mail to fetch your email) or by using the refresh gesture, regardless of the global setting.

If you choose Fetch, information is updated according to the schedule you set in step 9.

6 If you choose the Push option in step 5 and are working with an email account, choose the mailboxes whose information you want to be pushed by tapping them so they have a check mark; to prevent a mailbox's information from being pushed, tap it so that it doesn't have a check mark. (The Inbox is selected by default and can't be unselected.)

7 Tap Fetch New Data.

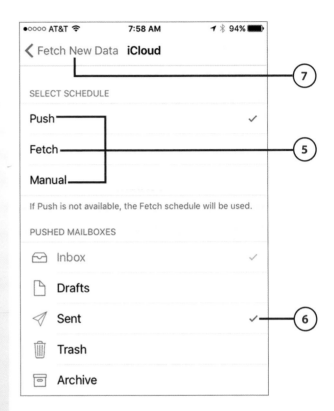

8 Repeat steps 5–7 until you have set the update option for each account. (The current option is shown to the right of the account's name.)

9 Tap the amount of time when you want the iPhone to fetch data when Push is turned off globally or for those accounts for which you have selected Fetch or that don't support Push; tap Manual if you want to manually check for information for Fetch accounts or when Push is off. Information for your accounts is updated according to your settings.

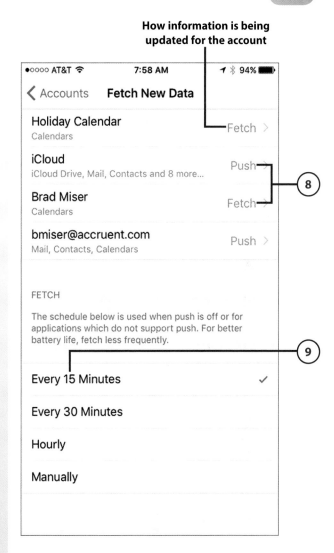

How information is being updated for the account

>>>Go Further

TIPS FOR MANAGING YOUR ACCOUNTS

As you add and use accounts on your iPhone, keep the following points in mind:

- You can temporarily disable any data for any account by moving to the Mail screen, tapping Accounts, and tapping that account. Set the switch for the data you don't want to use to off (white). You might be prompted to keep or delete that information; if you choose to keep it, the data remains on your iPhone but is disconnected from the account and is no longer updated. If you delete it, you can always recover it again by simply turning that data back on. For example, suppose you are going on vacation and don't want to deal with club email. Move to your club account and disable all its data. That data disappears from the related apps; for example, the account's mailboxes no longer appear in the Mail app. When you want to start using the account again, simply re-enable its data.

- If you want to completely remove an account from your iPhone, move to its configuration screen, swipe up the screen, and tap Delete Account. Tap Delete in the confirmation dialog box and the account is removed from your iPhone. (You can always sign in to the account to start using it again.)

- You can have different notifications for certain aspects of an account, such as email. See Chapter 2 for the details of configuring and using notifications. For example, you might want to hear a different sound when you receive club emails versus those sent to your personal account.

- You can change how information is updated at any time, too. If your iPhone is running low on battery, disable Push and set Fetch to Manual so you can control when the updates happen. When your battery is charged again, you can re-enable Push or set a Fetch schedule.

- You can access the Accounts tools to configure your online accounts and set the Fetch New Data option from the settings for any of the online account settings areas including Mail, Contacts, Calendar, Notes, and Reminders. The Accounts settings from any of these areas are global, meaning the change all of the account settings regardless of the settings area you used to access them.

Tap to personalize your iPhone to make it your own

Install apps so you can do all kinds of useful and fun things with your iPhone

In this chapter, you learn how to make an iPhone into your iPhone. Topics include the following:

→ Getting started
→ Working with the Settings app
→ Setting keyboard, language, and format options
→ Setting privacy and location services preferences
→ Setting a passcode and configuring Touch ID
→ Setting accessibility options
→ Setting restrictions for content and apps
→ Using the App Store app to find and install iPhone apps

Customizing How Your iPhone Works

You can configure the iPhone to make it work how you want it to. Taking the time to tailor your iPhone to your personal preferences and how you want to use it makes the iPhone easier, better, and more fun to use.

Getting Started

As you've seen in previous chapters, the Settings app enables you to configure various aspects of your iPhone, such as connecting your iPhone to a Wi-Fi network and configuring iCloud. The Settings app provides many other configuration tools that you can use to tailor how your iPhone works to suit your preferences. Perhaps the most important of these is the security of your iPhone that you can configure by setting a passcode and fingerprint recognition using Touch ID. You can also configure the keyboards available, language and region format options, accessibility options, and how content on your phone can be accessed. You use the Settings app to customize the iPhone in all of these areas as you see throughout this chapter.

Although the Settings app enables you to customize how your iPhone works in many ways, installing apps on your iPhone enables it to do so much more than it can "out of the box." You'll want to explore and download apps to completely customize how you use your iPhone; the possibilities of what your phone can do with apps are limitless!

Working with the Settings App

Aptly named, the Settings app is where you configure the many settings that change how your iPhone looks, sounds, and works. Most of the tasks in this chapter involve the Settings app. Rather than repeat the first couple of steps within each task, it is more efficient to show you how the app works so you can easily access the controls you need for each task.

Using the Settings App on Any iPhone

You can work with the Settings app on any iPhone as follows:

(1) On the Home screen, tap Settings. The Settings app opens. The app is organized in sections starting at the top with Airplane Mode, Wi-Fi, Bluetooth, and Cellular.

(2) Swipe up or down the screen to get to the settings area you want to use.

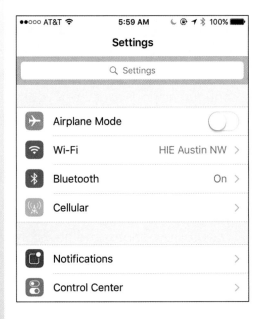

3 Tap the area you want to configure, such as Sounds & Haptics (iPhone 7 or 7 Plus) or Sounds (all other models).

4 Use the resulting controls to configure that area. The changes you make take effect immediately.

5 When you're done, you can leave the Settings app where it is or tap the back button, which is always located in the upper-left corner of the screen, until you get back to the main Settings screen to go into other Settings areas.

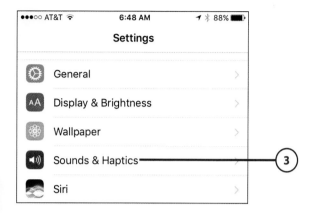

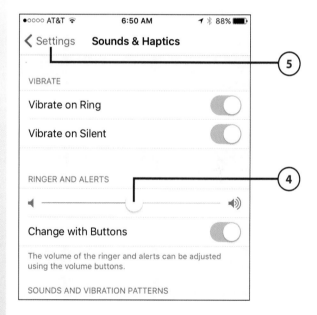

Searching for Settings

You can quickly find settings you need by searching for them:

(1) Move into the Settings app.

(2) Tap in the Search bar; if you don't see the Search bar, swipe down from the top of the Settings screen until it appears.

(3) Type the setting for which you want to search. As you type, potential matches are shown on the list of results. Matches can include a settings area, such as Sounds, and specific settings, such as the ringtone and vibrations used when you receive a call.

(4) Tap the setting you want to use.

(5) Configure the setting you selected in the previous step.

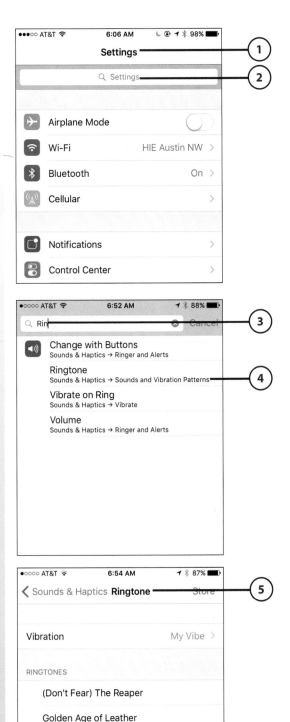

Using the Settings App on an iPhone Plus

When you hold an iPhone 6 Plus, 6s Plus, or 7 Plus in the horizontal orientation and use the Settings app, you can take advantage of the split-screen feature as follows:

(1) Hold the iPhone Plus so it is horizontal.

(2) Tap the Settings app to open it. In the left pane, you see the areas of the Settings app that you can configure. In the right pane, you see tools you can use to configure the selected setting. The two panes are independent, making navigation easier than with other iPhones.

(3) Swipe up or down on the left pane until you see the function, feature, or app you want to configure.

(4) Tap the function, feature, or app you want to configure, such as Sounds. Its controls appear in the right pane.

(5) Swipe up or down on the right pane until you see the specific setting you want to change.

(6) Tap the setting you want to configure, such as Ringtone. Its controls appear in the right pane.

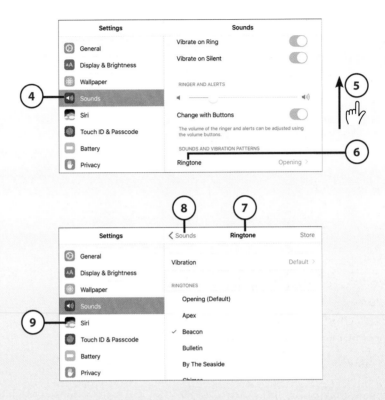

(7) Use the tools in the right pane to configure the setting you selected in step 6. These work just as described in the previous task and throughout this chapter except that you move within the right pane instead of changing the entire screen.

(8) To move back through the screens in the right pane, use the back button, which is labeled with the name of the screen you came from.

(9) Tap another area in the left pane to configure it. As you can see, the split screen makes it very easy to quickly switch between areas in the Settings app.

Setting Keyboard, Language, and Format Options

You'll be working with text in many apps on your iPhone. You can customize a number of keyboard- and format-related options so text appears and behaves the way you want it to.

Setting Keyboard Preferences

You use the iPhone's keyboard to input text in many apps, including Mail, Messages, and so on. A number of settings determine how the keyboard works.

(1) On the Settings screen, tap General.

(2) Swipe up the screen.

(3) Tap Keyboard.

(4) Tap Keyboards. This enables you to activate <u>more</u> keyboards so that you can choose a specific language's keyboard when you are entering text. At the top of the screen, you see the keyboards that are available to you.

(5) Tap Add New Keyboard.

Fun in Text

The Emoji keyboard allows you to include a huge variety of smiley faces, symbols, and other icons whenever you type. The Emoji keyboard is active by default; however, if you <u>don't see</u> it on the list of active keyboards, you can use these steps to activate it.

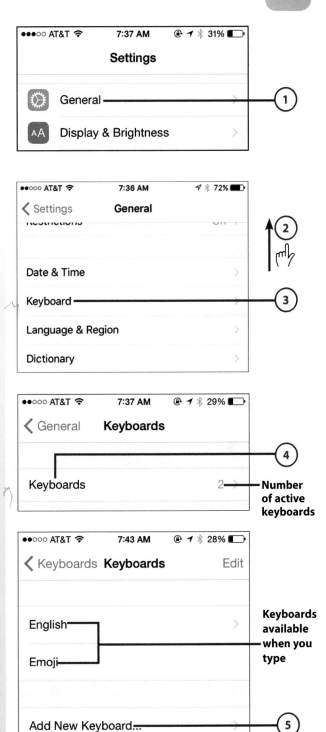

6 Swipe up and down the screen to browse the available keyboards.

7 Tap the keyboard you want to add.

8 Tap the keyboard you added in step 7.

9 Tap the keyboard layout you want to use.

10 Tap Keyboards.

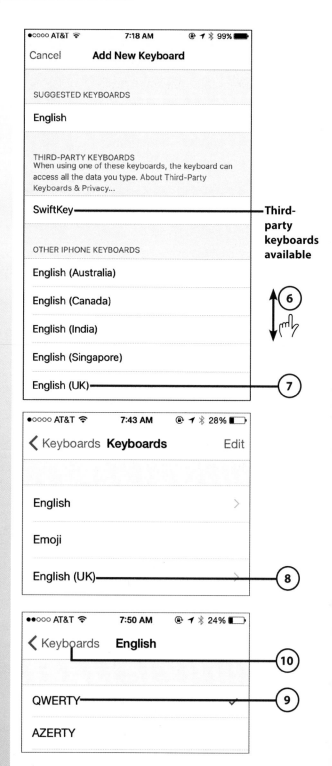

●○○○ AT&T 🔇   7:18 AM   @ ✓ ⚹ 99% ▬

Cancel   **Add New Keyboard**

SUGGESTED KEYBOARDS

English

THIRD-PARTY KEYBOARDS
When using one of these keyboards, the keyboard can access all the data you type. About Third-Party Keyboards & Privacy...

SwiftKey ———— Third-party keyboards available

OTHER IPHONE KEYBOARDS

English (Australia)

English (Canada)   **6**

English (India)

English (Singapore)

English (UK) ———— **7**

●○○○○ AT&T 🔇   7:43 AM   @ ✓ ⚹ 28% ▭

❮ Keyboards **Keyboards**   Edit

English   ❯

Emoji

English (UK) ———— **8**

●●○○○ AT&T 🔇   7:50 AM   @ ✓ ⚹ 24% ▭

❮ Keyboards **English**   **10**

QWERTY ———— **9**

AZERTY

(11) Repeat steps 5–10 to add and configure additional keyboards.

(12) Tap Keyboards.

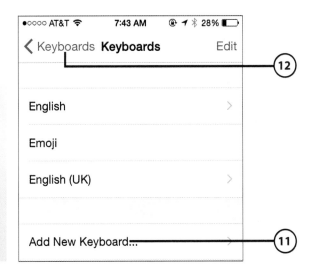

>>>Go Further

THIRD-PARTY KEYBOARDS

You can install and use keyboards from third parties (meaning not Apple) on your iPhone. To do this, open the App Store app and search for "keyboards for iPhone" or you can search for a specific keyboard by name if you know of one you want to try. (See "Using the App Store App to Find and Install iPhone Apps," later in this chapter for help using the App Store app.) After you have downloaded the keyboard you want to use, use steps 1–5 to move back to the Keyboards Settings screen. When you open the Add New Keyboard screen, you see a section called THIRD-PARTY KEYBOARDS in which you see the additional keyboards you have installed. Tap a keyboard in this section to activate it as you do with the default keyboards. When you move back to the Keyboards screen, you see the keyboard you just activated. Tap it to configure its additional options. Then you can use the new keyboard just like the others you have activated. Make sure you check out the documentation for any keyboards you download so you take advantage of all of their features.

(13) To prevent your iPhone from automatically capitalizing as you type, set Auto-Capitalization to off (white).

(14) To disable the automatic spell checking/correction, set Auto-Correction to off (white).

(15) To disable the iPhone's Spell Checker, set the Check Spelling switch to off (white).

(16) To disable the Caps Lock function, set the Enable Caps Lock to off (white).

(17) To disable the iPhone's Predictive Text feature (see Chapter 2, "Using Your iPhone's Core Features"), set the Predictive switch to off (white).

(18) To prevent the character you type from being shown in a magnified pop-up as you type it, set the Character Preview switch to off (white).

(19) To disable the shortcut that types a period followed by a space when you tap the spacebar twice, set the "." shortcut switch to off (white). You must tap a period and the spacebar to type these characters when you end a sentence.

(20) To disable the iPhone's dictation feature, set the Enable Dictation switch to off (white). The microphone key won't appear on the keyboard and you won't be able to dictate text.

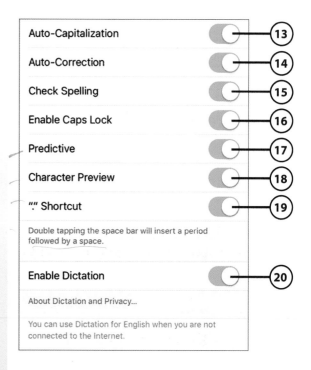

Auto-Capitalization	◉ —— (13)
Auto-Correction	◉ —— (14)
Check Spelling	◉ —— (15)
Enable Caps Lock	◉ —— (16)
Predictive	◉ —— (17)
Character Preview	◉ —— (18)
"." Shortcut	◉ —— (19)

Double tapping the space bar will insert a period followed by a space.

Enable Dictation	◉ —— (20)

About Dictation and Privacy...

You can use Dictation for English when you are not connected to the Internet.

Language Options

The keyboard options you see depend on the language being used. For example, if settings apply only to a specific language, you see them in that language's section.

Changing Keyboards

To delete a keyboard, move to the Keyboards Settings screen and swipe to the left on the keyboard you want to remove. Tap Delete. The keyboard is removed from the list of activated keyboards and is no longer available to you when you type. (You can always activate it again later.) To change the order in which keyboards appear, move to the Keyboards screen, tap Edit, and drag the keyboards up and down the screen. When you've finished, tap Done. (An explanation of how to switch between keyboards when you type is provided in Chapter 2.)

Creating and Working with Text Replacements

Text replacements are useful because you can use just a few letters to type a series of words. You type the replacement, and it is replaced by the phrase with which it is associated. To configure your text replacements, do the following:

1. Move to the Keyboards screen as described in steps 1–3 in the previous task.

2. Tap Text Replacement.

3. Review the current replacements.

4. To add a replacement, tap Add (+).

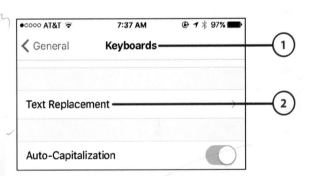

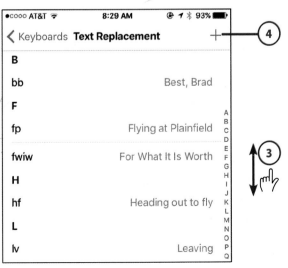

(5) Type the phrase for which you want to create a replacement.

(6) Type the shortcut you want to be replaced by the phrase you created in step 5.

(7) Tap Save. If the replacement doesn't contain any disallowed characters, it is created and you move back to the Text Replacement screen where you see your new text replacement. If there is an error, you see an explanation of the error; you must correct it before you can create the replacement.

(8) Repeat steps 4–7 to create other text replacements.

(9) When you've created all the replacements you want, tap Keyboards.

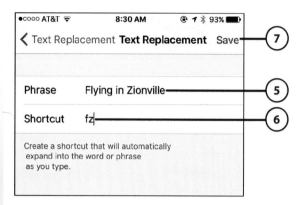

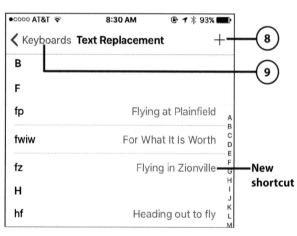

New shortcut

Shortcuts to Replacements

To change a replacement, tap it. Use the resulting screen to change the phrase or shortcut, and tap Save to update the replacement. To remove a replacement, swipe to the left on it and tap Delete. To search for a replacement, tap in the Search bar at the top of the screen and type the replacements you want to see; you can also use the index along the right side of the screen to find replacements. You can also tap Edit on the Shortcuts screen to change your replacements. And, yes, you can create a phrase without a replacement, but I don't really see much use for that!

Setting Language and Region Preferences

There are a number of formatting preferences you can set that determine how information is formatted in various apps. For example, you can choose how addresses are formatted by default by choosing the region whose format you want to follow.

(1) On the Settings screen, tap General.

(2) Swipe up the screen.

(3) Tap Language & Region.

(4) Tap iPhone Language.

(5) Swipe up and down the screen to view the languages with which your iPhone can work or tap in the Search bar and type a language you want to use. The current language is marked with a check mark.

(6) Tap the language you want to use.

(7) Tap Done.

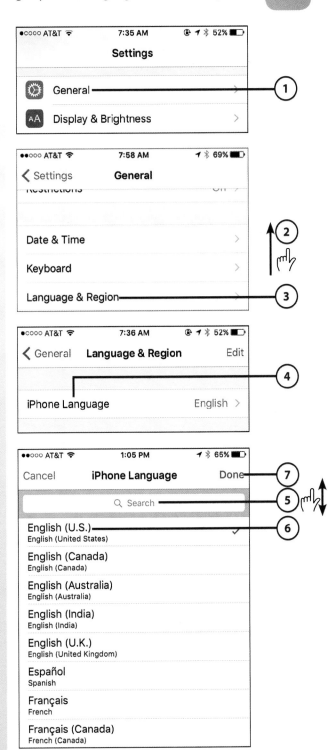

8 Tap to confirm the change in language you indicated. Your iPhone screen goes dark while the iPhone switches to the new language. When it comes back, you return to the Language & Region screen, and the language you selected starts being used.

9 Tap Add Language.

10 Using steps 5–7, find and tap a secondary language. This language is used when your primary language can't be, such as on websites that don't support your primary language.

11 Tap Done.

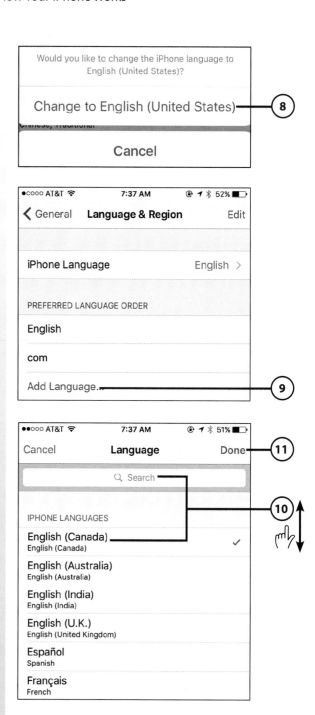

12 Tap the language you want to be primary to confirm it. The language you selected is configured and you move back to the Language & Region screen. The new language is shown on the list in the center of the screen.

13 To add more languages, tap Add Language and follow steps 10–12 to add more languages.

Order, Order!

To change the order of preference for the languages you have configured, tap Edit, drag the languages up or down the screen to set their order, and tap Done to save your changes.

14 Tap Region.

15 Swipe up and down the regions available to you. The current region is marked with a check mark.

16 Tap the region whose formatting you want to use; if there are options within a region, you move to an additional screen and can tap the specific option you want to use.

17 Tap Done. Your iPhone starts using the formatting associated with the region you selected.

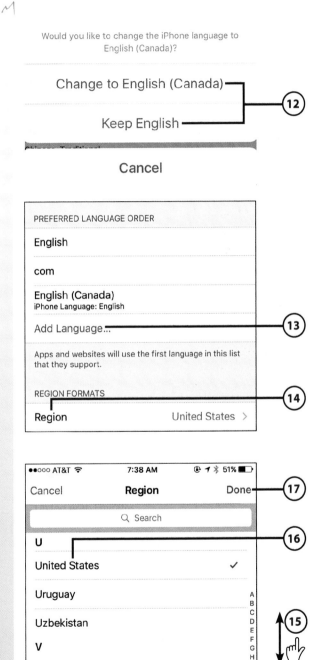

18. Tap Calendar.

19. Tap the calendar you want your iPhone to use.

20. Tap Language & Region.

21. Tap Temperature Unit.

22. Tap the unit in which you want temperatures to be displayed.

23. Tap Language & Region. Swipe up until you see the bottom of the screen where there are examples of the format options you have selected, such as the time and date format.

Setting Privacy and Location Services Preferences

Using its GPS or network connection, your iPhone's Location Services feature can determine where the phone is. This is useful in many situations, such as in the Maps app when you want to generate directions. Lots of other apps use this capability, too, such as apps that provide you location-specific information (the Uber app uses it to determine your location when you request a ride, for example). You can configure certain aspects of how these services work. And, if you don't want specific apps to be able to access your iPhone's current location, you can disable this feature for those apps. Of course, if you do, apps that rely on this capability won't work properly (they prompt you to allow access to this service as you try to use them).

You can also determine which apps can access certain kinds of information, such as the apps that are able to access your contact information in the Contacts app.

To configure privacy settings, do the following:

1. Move to the Settings screen and tap Privacy.

2. Tap Location Services.

3. To disable Location Services for all apps, set the Location Services switch to off (white); to leave it enabled, skip to step 5.

4. Tap Turn Off at the prompt. No apps are able to identify your location; skip the rest of these steps because they don't apply when Location Services is disabled.

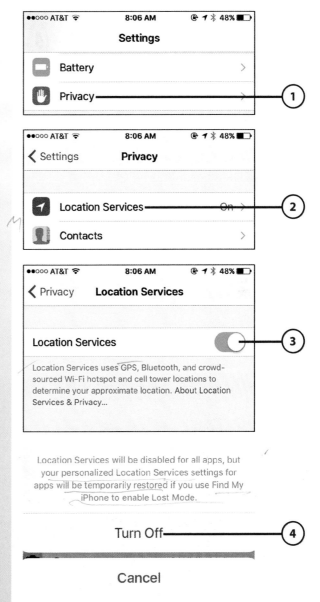

(5) Tap Share My Location. You can share your location with others in several areas, such as the Messages app.

(6) To prevent your location from being shared, set the Share My Location switch to off (white) and skip to step 10. If you leave this switch on (green), move to the next step.

(7) Tap From.

(8) Tap the device that should be used to identify your location (this only applies if you have multiple devices configured with your Apple ID).

(9) Tap Share My Location.

(10) Tap Location Services.

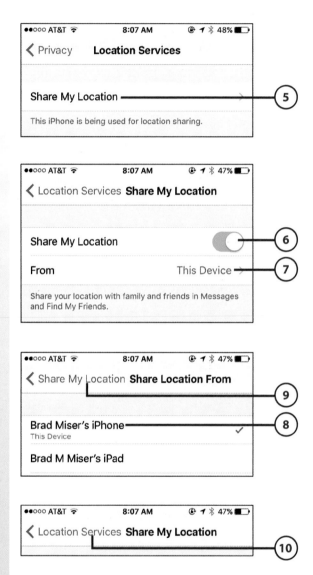

(11) Swipe up and down the list of apps on the Location Services screen. These are all the apps that have requested access to your iPhone's location. Along the right side of the screen, you see the current status of Location Sharing for the app. Always means that the app can always access your location. While Using means the app can only access your location information while you are using it. Never means that using location information for the app has been disabled (some apps won't be able to work properly when set to this status). Apps marked with a purple arrow have recently accessed your location; those that have done so within the past 24 hours are marked with a gray arrow. An outline purple arrow indicates that the app is using a geofence, which is a perimeter around a location that defines an area that is used to trigger some event, such as a reminder.

(12) Tap an app to configure its access to Location Services.

(13) Tap the status in which you want to place the app's access to your location. Some apps only have the Always or Never options, whereas others also have the While Using the App option.

(14) Tap Location Services.

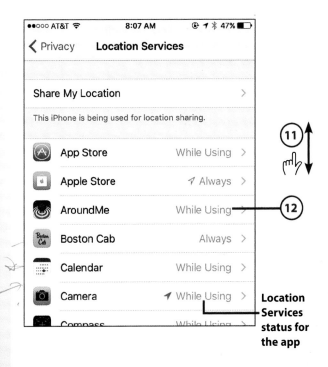

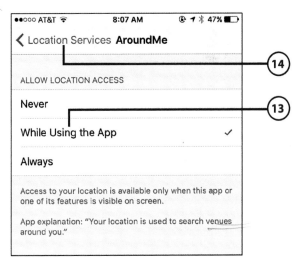

Location Services status for the app

15. Repeat steps 12–14 for each app whose access to your location you want to configure.

16. Tap System Services.

17. Enable or disable Location Services for the System Services you see. As with apps, if you disable Location Devices for a system function, it might not work properly.

18. Tap Location Services.

19. Tap Privacy. Next, allow or prevent apps from accessing data stored on your iPhone.

20. Tap the first app on the list; this example shows Contacts. A list of apps that have requested to use the app's data (in this example, contact information) is displayed. If the requesting app is able to use the app's data, its switch is on (green).

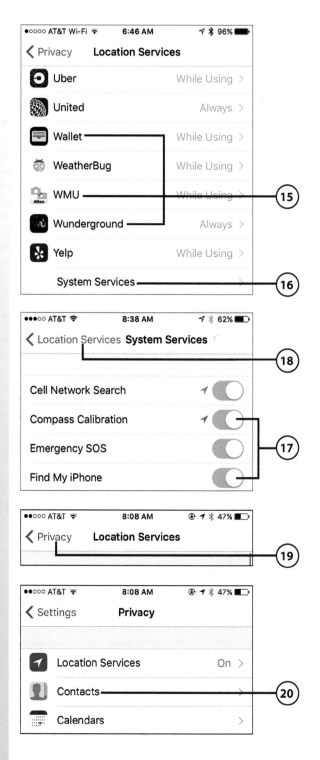

(21) Prevent a requesting app from accessing the app's data by setting its switch to off (white). That app is no longer able to use the data it requested (which can inhibit some of its functionality).

(22) Repeat step 21 for each app you see that you want to prevent from accessing the data.

(23) Tap Privacy.

(24) Repeat steps 20–23 for each app on the list. Most of time, you can just leave the permissions with the default setting (unless you want to block a specific app from using a certain kind of data).

>>>Go Further
MORE ON PRIVACY

Under the list of apps, you see the social accounts section that includes Facebook, Twitter, and other such social media apps. You can control which apps access your social media information similar to how you control which apps can use other types of information (such as your contact information).

Under the Diagnostics & Usage section, you can determine if information about performance of apps and your device is communicated back to Apple. You can also determine if information about the performance of apps is shared with app developers.

At the bottom of the Privacy screen, you see the Advertising option. If you tap this, you can limit the tracking of ads you view by setting the Limit Ad Tracking switch to on (green). Typically, this tracking is used by advertisers to present ads that are related to ads you have viewed (the point being to make the ads more effective). You can reset the identifier used to identify you by tapping Reset Advertising Identifier and then tapping Reset. You can tap View Ad Information to see your status with respect to advertising in Apple apps.

Setting a Passcode and Configuring Touch ID

Your iPhone contains data you probably don't want others to access. You can (and should) require a passcode so your iPhone can't be unlocked without the proper passcode being entered. This gives you a measure of protection should you lose control of your phone. If you have an iPhone 5s or later, you can record your fingerprints so that you can unlock your phone (by automatically entering the passcode) and enter your Apple ID password by pressing the Touch ID/Home button. The capability can also be used in other apps and services that require confirmation, such as Apple Pay and downloading apps from the App Store.

New! Third-party apps can also use Touch ID for various tasks, such as signing into your accounts. For example, if you use a banking app, the first time you log in after the app has been upgraded to support Touch ID, you're prompted to allow that app to use Touch ID. If you allow this, you won't need to type your password the next time you log in. Instead, you simply touch a recorded fingerprint to the Touch ID/Home button to sign in.

Configuring Your Passcode and Fingerprints

To configure the passcode you have to enter to unlock your iPhone, perform the following steps (note these steps show an iPhone that supports Touch ID; if your model doesn't have this, the steps are slightly different as you will only be configuring a passcode):

1 On the Settings screen, tap Touch ID & Passcode.

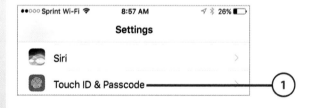

Already Have a Passcode?

When you first turned on your iPhone, you were prompted to enter a passcode and to record a fingerprint for Touch ID. If your iPhone already has a passcode set, when you perform step 1, you're prompted to enter your current passcode. When you enter it correctly, you move to the Touch ID & Passcode (iPhone 5s and later) or Passcode (other models) screen, and you can make changes to the current passcode, add new fingerprints, and so on. In that case, you can skip directly to step 5. If you want to change your current passcode, tap Change Passcode and follow steps 3 and 4 to change it. Then continue with step 5.

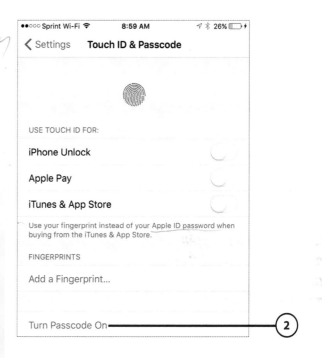

(**2**) Tap Turn Passcode On.

(**3**) Enter a six-digit passcode.

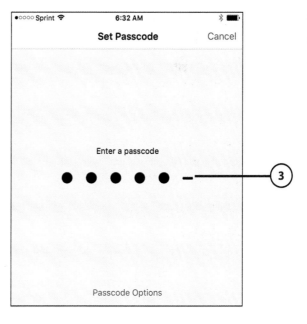

④ Re-enter the passcode. If the two passcodes match, the passcode is set.

⑤ Tap Require Passcode; when you use Touch ID to unlock your iPhone, you don't have an option for when the passcode is required, so if you are going to or already use Touch ID, skip to step 8.

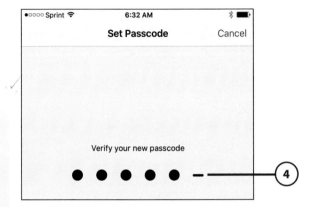

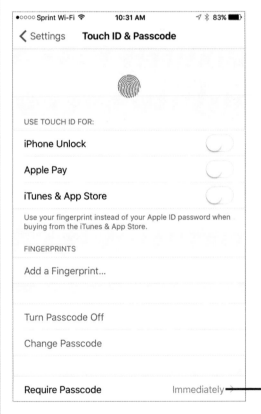

6 Tap the amount of time the iPhone is locked before the passcode takes effect. The shorter this time is, the more secure your iPhone is, but also the more frequently you'll have to enter the passcode if your iPhone locks frequently.

7 Tap Touch ID & Passcode.

8 If you have an iPhone 5s or later, tap Add a Fingerprint and continue to step 9; if you have a model that doesn't support Touch ID, skip to step 21.

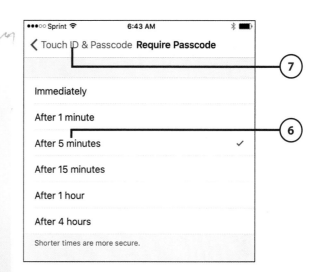

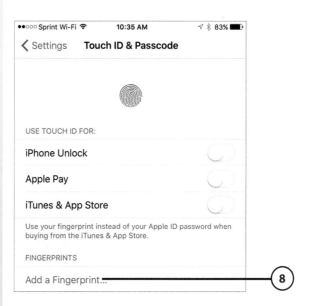

9 Touch the finger you want to record to the Touch ID/Home button, but don't press it. An image of a fingerprint appears.

10 Leave your finger on the Touch ID/Home button until you feel the phone vibrate, which indicates part of your fingerprint has been recorded and you see some segments turn red. The parts of your fingerprint that are recorded are indicated by the red segments; gray segments are not recorded yet. This step captures the center part of your finger.

11 Lift your finger off the Touch ID/Home button and touch the button again, adjusting your finger on the button to record other parts that currently show gray lines instead of red ones. Other segments of your fingerprint are recorded.

12 Repeat step 11 until all the segments are red. You are prompted to change your grip so you can record more of your fingerprint.

13 Tap Continue.

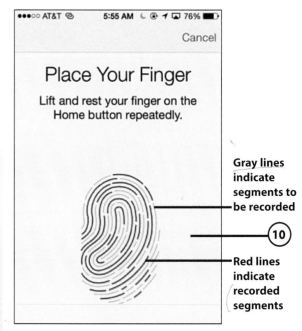

Gray lines indicate segments to be recorded

10

Red lines indicate recorded segments

13

14 Repeat step 11, again placing other areas of your finger to fill in more gray lines with red. This step captured the fingerprints more toward the edges of your fingers. When the entire fingerprint is covered in red lines, you see the Complete screen.

15 Tap Continue. The fingerprint is recorded and you move back to the Touch ID & Passcode screen. You see the fingerprint that has been recorded.

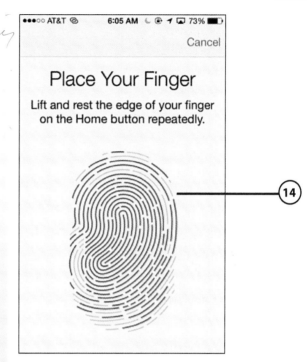

(16) Repeat steps 8–15 to record up to five fingerprints. These can be yours or someone else's if you want to allow another person to access your iPhone.

(17) To be able to use Touch ID to unlock your iPhone, ensure the iPhone Unlock switch is set to on (green).

(18) To use your fingerprint to make Apple Pay payments, set the Apple Pay switch to on (green). (Refer to Chapter 2 for more information about Apple Pay.)

(19) If it isn't enabled already and you want to also be able to enter your Apple ID password by touching your finger to the Touch ID/Home button, set the iTunes & App Store switch to on (green).

(20) Enter your Apple ID password and tap OK.

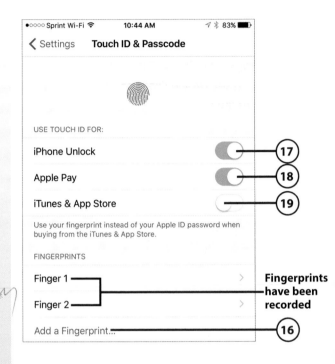

(21) Swipe up the screen until you see the Voice Dial switch.

(22) To prevent Voice Dial from working, set the Voice Dial switch to off (white). (Voice Dial enables you to make calls by speaking even if you don't use Siri.)

(23) Use the switches in the ALLOW ACCESS WHEN LOCKED section to enable or disable the related functions when your iPhone is locked. The options are Today View (the Today section of the Notifications Center), Notifications View (the Notifications view of the Notifications Center), Siri, Reply with Message, Home Control, and Wallet. If you set a switch to off (white), you won't be able to access the corresponding function when your iPhone is locked.

(24) If you don't want the iPhone to automatically erase all your data after an incorrect passcode has been entered 10 times, set the Erase Data switch to off (white).

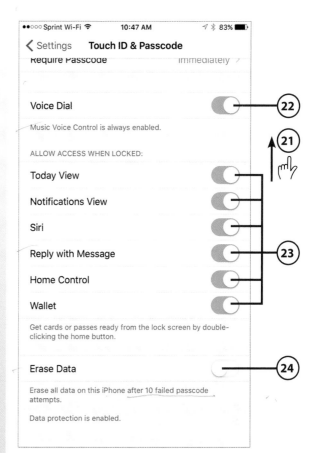

Automatic Erase

When you have enabled the Erase Data function and you enter an incorrect passcode when unlocking your iPhone, you see a counter showing the number of unsuccessful attempts. When this reaches 10, all the data on your iPhone is erased on the next unsuccessful attempt.

Making Changes

Any time you want to make changes to your passcode and fingerprint settings, move back to the Touch ID & Passcode (iPhone 5s or later) or Passcode (other models) screen. Before you can move back to this screen, you must enter your current passcode at the prompt. After you enter your current passcode, you move to the Touch ID & Passcode (iPhone 5s or later) or Passcode (other models) screen. To disable the passcode (not recommended), tap Turn Passcode Off, tap Turn Off, and enter the passcode. To change your passcode, tap Change Passcode. You then enter your current passcode and enter your new passcode twice. You return to the Passcode Lock screen, and the new passcode takes effect. You can change the other settings similar to how you set them initially as described in these steps. For example, you can add new fingerprints. To remove a fingerprint, move to the Fingerprints screen, swipe to the left on the fingerprint you want to remove, and tap Delete. You can rename a fingerprint by tapping it, editing its name on the resulting screen, and tapping Done (for example, you might want to name the fingerprints so you recognize them, such as My Right Thumb or Jim's Left Thumb).

Automatic Locking

For security purposes, you should configure your iPhone so that it locks automatically after a specific amount of idle time passes. To do this, you use the Auto-Lock setting on the Display & Brightness settings screen as explained in Chapter 6, "Customizing How Your iPhone Looks and Sounds."

Setting Accessibility Options

The iPhone has many features designed to help people who have hearing impairments, or visual impairments, or other physical challenges to be able to use it effectively.

You can enable and configure the Accessibility features on the Accessibility Settings screen.

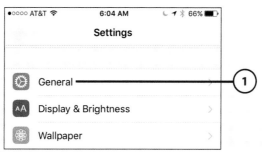

(1) On the Settings screen, tap General.

(2) Swipe up the screen until you see Accessibility.

(3) Tap Accessibility. The Accessibility screen is organized into different sections for different kinds of limitations. The first section is VISION, which includes options to assist people who are visually impaired.

(4) Use the controls in the VISION section to change how the iPhone's screens appear. Some of the options include

- **VoiceOver**—The iPhone guides you through screens by speaking their contents. To set this, tap VoiceOver and set the VoiceOver switch to on (green) to turn it on. The rest of the settings configure how VoiceOver works. For example, you can set the rate at which the voice speaks, what kind of feedback you get, and many more options.

- **Zoom**—This magnifies the entire screen. Tap Zoom and then turn Zoom on. Use the other settings to change how the zoom works, such as whether it follows where you are focused on the screen or remains fixed.

- **Magnifier**—This feature enables you to use your iPhone's camera like a magnifying glass. When you enable this, you can triple-press the Touch ID/Home button to activate it.

- **Display Accommodations**—These options change how your iPhone uses color. You can use the Invert Colors function to disable the Night Shift feature. The Color Filters tool enables you to customize how colors appear on the screen. The Reduce White Point switch, when enabled, reduces the intensity of bright colors.

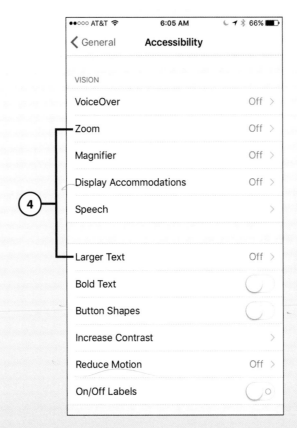

- **Speech**—Under the Speech option, Speak Selection causes a Speak button to appear when you select text, and Speak Screen provides the option to have the screen's content spoken. You can also determine if you hear feedback while you type, and you can configure the voices used, the rate of speech, and pronunciations.

- **Larger and Bold Text**—These increase the text size and add bold; these are in addition to the Text Size and Bold settings that you learn about in Chapter 6. You can make the text even larger than with those settings.

- **Other options**—You can also change button shapes, change contrast, reduce motion, and turn labels on or off.

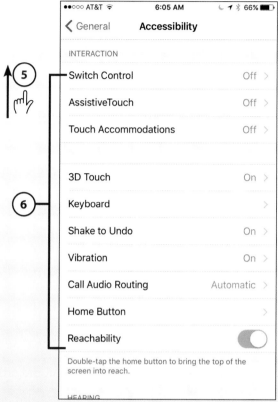

(5) Swipe up to see the INTERACTION section.

(6) Use the controls in this section to adjust how you can interact with the iPhone. The controls here include

- **Switch Control**—The controls on this screen enable you to configure an iPhone to work with an adaptive device so that you can control the iPhone with that device.

- **Assistive Touch**—These controls make an iPhone easier to manipulate; if you enable this, a white button appears on the screen at all times. You can tap this to access the Home screen, Notification Center, and other areas. You can also create new gestures to control other functions on the iPhone.

- **Touch Accommodations**—You can use the Touch Accommodation options to make it easier for you to use the touch screen. For example, you can change the amount of time you must touch the screen before it is recognized as a touch.

- **3D Touch**—This setting, which is only available on iPhone models that support 3D Touch, enables you to turn the 3D Touch feature off or on. If 3D Touch is on, you can determine how much pressure you need to apply to the screen to activate it.

Setting Restrictions for Content and Apps

You can restrict the access to specific content and apps on your phone. Suppose you let other people borrow your iPhone but don't want them to use certain apps or to see data you'd rather keep to yourself. You can enable a restriction to prevent someone from accessing these areas without entering the restriction code. You can also restrict the use of apps, movies, music, and other content based on the age rating that the app or other content has.

To restrict access to content or apps, perform the following steps:

1 On the Settings screen, tap General.

2 Swipe up the screen until you see Restrictions.

3 Tap Restrictions.

4 Tap Enable Restrictions.

5 Create a Restrictions Passcode. You have to enter this passcode to change the content restrictions or to be able to access restricted content.

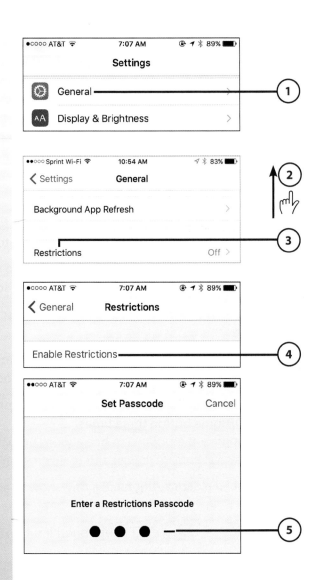

6 Re-enter your Restrictions Passcode. You return to the Restrictions screen, and the Allow switches are enabled.

7 In the ALLOW section, set the switch next to each function you want to disable to off (white). For example, to prevent web browsing, set the Safari switch to off (white); the Safari icon is removed from the Home screen and can't be used. With the other controls, you can prevent access to the Camera, FaceTime, iTunes Store, and so on.

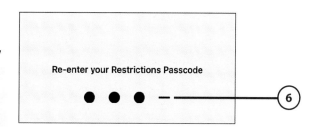

Dueling Passcodes

Your iPhone can have two passcodes: the Lock passcode and the Restrictions passcode. Each controls access to its respective functions. Limiting access to content and apps likely means you will be letting someone else use your phone. The person who will be using your iPhone might need to be able to unlock it unless you want to have to unlock it for them. If you want to allow her to unlock the phone, but want to restrict access to your Apple Pay information or Apple ID, create a fingerprint for that person, but disable Touch ID for Apple Pay and iTunes & App Stores (see the previous task for details). This enables the person to unlock and use your iPhone; you can control what she does by setting a Restrictions passcode and configuring permissions as described in these steps. (You don't want to give the person the passcode to the phone as that defeats the purpose of configuring restrictions.)

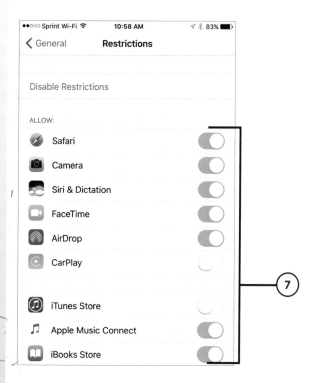

In-App Purchases

Some apps, especially games, allow you to make purchases while you are using the app. For example, you can buy additional levels for a game. To prevent in-app purchases, set the In-App Purchases switch to off (white). This is especially important if you let your phone be used by children or others who might inadvertently make purchases you don't want made.

8. Swipe up to see the ALLOWED CONTENT section.

9. Tap Ratings For.

10. Tap the country whose rating system you want to use for content on your iPhone.

Whose Ratings?

The country you select in step 10 determines the options you see in the remaining steps because the restrictions available depend on the location you select. These steps show the United States rating systems; if you select a different country, you see rating options for that country instead.

---

11. Tap Restrictions.

12. Tap Music, Podcasts & News.

13. To prevent content tagged as explicit from being played, set the EXPLICIT switch to off (white). Explicit content will not be available in the associated apps, such as Music or News.

14. Tap Restrictions.

15. Tap Movies.

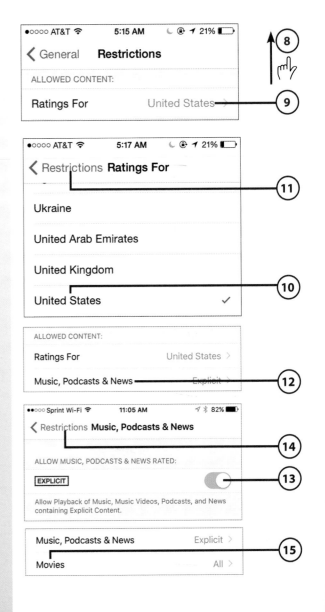

16 Tap the highest rating of movies that you want to be playable (for example, tap PG-13 to prevent R and NC-17 movies from playing); tap Allow All Movies to allow any movie to be played; or tap Don't Allow Movies to prevent any movie content from playing. Prevented movie ratings are highlighted in red.

17 Tap Restrictions.

18 Tap TV Shows and use the resulting screen to set the highest rating of TV shows that you want to be playable (for example, tap TV-14 to prevent TV-MA shows from playing); tap Allow All TV Shows to allow any show to be played; or tap Don't Allow TV Shows to prevent any TV content from playing. Prevented ratings are highlighted in red. Tap Restrictions to return to the Restrictions screen.

19 Use the Books option to enable or disable access to sexually explicit books.

20 Tap Apps and set the highest rating of app that you want to be available (for example, tap 12+ to prevent 17+ applications from working); tap Allow All Apps to allow any application to be used; or tap Don't Allow Apps to prevent all applications. Tap Restrictions to return to the Restrictions screen.

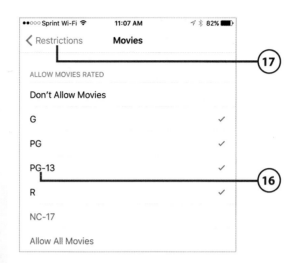

(21) Use the Siri option to restrict explicit language or content during web searches.

(22) Use the Websites option to control the websites that can be accessed. The options are to limit sites with adult content or to allow only specific websites to be visited. When you select the Specific Websites Only option, you can create a list of sites and only those sites can be visited.

(23) Swipe up the screen until you see the PRIVACY section.

(24) Use the settings in the PRIVACY section to determine whether apps can access information stored in each area and whether they should be locked in their current states. For example, you can prevent apps from accessing your calendars or photos. Configuring these is similar to the Privacy settings you read about earlier in this chapter.

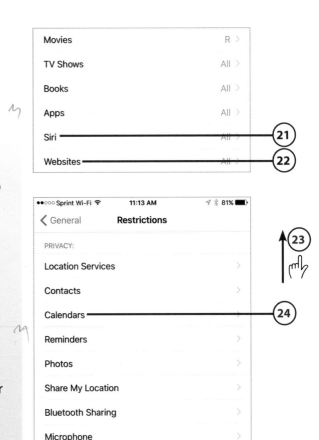

25 Swipe up the screen until you see the ALLOW CHANGES section.

26 Tap areas that you want to restrict, such as Cellular Data Use or Volume Limit and then tap Don't Allow Changes to prevent changes to that area.

27 To prevent multiplayer games in the Game Center, set the Multiplayer Games switch to off (white). Users will no longer be able to play games against other people.

28 To prevent new friends from being added in the Game Center, set the Adding Friends switch to off (white). Players will be restricted to the friends already allowed.

29 To prevent the screen from being recorded during game play associated with the Game Center, set the Screen Recording switch to off (white).

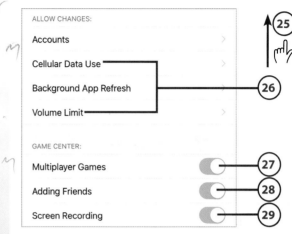

Removing Restrictions

To remove all restrictions, move to the Restrictions screen (your Restrictions passcode is required) and tap Disable Restrictions. Enter your Restrictions passcode, and the restrictions are removed.

Using the App Store App to Find and Install iPhone Apps

Installing apps on your iPhone enables you to add more functionality than you can probably imagine. As the old Apple ad use to proclaim "There's an app for that." And in all likelihood, there probably is an app for a lot of what you would like to use your iPhone for. The App Store app enables you to find, download, and install apps onto your iPhone.

Before you jump into the App Store, take a few moments to ensure your iPhone is configured for maximum ease and efficiency of dealing with new apps.

Configuring Your iPhone to Download and Maintain Apps

To download apps from the App Store, you need an Apple ID (if you need help getting or configuring an Apple ID, see Chapter 4, "Setting Up and Using iCloud and Other Online Accounts"). With your Apple ID configured on your phone in the iCloud area, make sure it is also ready to go for the App Store and ensure you can use Touch ID when you download apps (instead of typing your password).

(1) Open the Settings app.

(2) Tap iTunes & App Store.

3 Ensure the Apple ID you want to use to download apps is shown at the top of the screen; if it isn't, tap the Apple ID shown, tap Sign Out, and then sign into your Apple ID.

4 Ensure the Apps switch is on (green); this causes any apps you download to your iPhone to also automatically be downloaded to other devices (with which the apps are compatible, of course) that use the same Apple ID.

5 Ensure the Updates switch is on (green); this causes any updates to apps you have installed on your iPhone to be downloaded and installed automatically. I recommend you use this option so you can be sure you are always running the most current versions of your apps.

6 If you don't have an unlimited cellular data plan, you might want to set Use Cellular Data to off (white) so apps and other content are downloaded only when you are on a Wi-Fi network. If this is enabled (green), apps and content are downloaded to your iPhone when you are using a cellular network, which can consume significant amounts of your data plan. (Some apps or content are so large, they can only be downloaded when you are using a Wi-Fi connection).

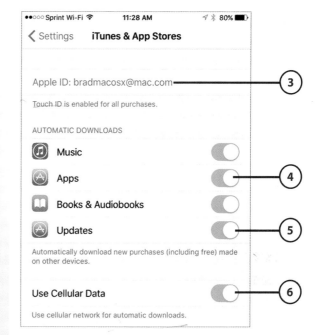

⑦ Use the information in the task "Setting a Passcode and Configuring Touch ID" earlier in this chapter to ensure the iTunes & App Store switch is enabled (green) so that you can use Touch ID to download apps instead of typing your password. (If it isn't enabled, tap the switch, enter your Apple ID password, and tap OK to enable it.)

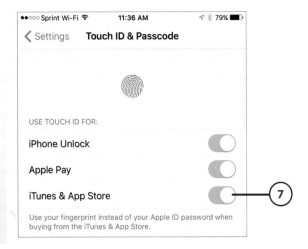

Using the App Store App to Find and Install iPhone Apps

The App Store app enables you to quickly and easily browse and search for apps, view information about them, and then download and install them on your iPhone with just a few taps.

When you use the App Store app, you can find apps to download using any of the following options:

- **Featured**—This tab takes you to apps featured in the Apps Store. This screen organizes apps in several categories. These categories change from time to time, but they typically include "best" types of apps (such as games), apps for specific purposes (for example, back-to-school shopping), and so on. Swipe up and down the screen to see all the categories available.

- **Categories** —This area shows you various categories of apps that you can browse.

- **Top Charts**—This takes you to lists of the top iPhone apps. This screen has three tabs at the top of the screen: Paid shows you the top apps for which you have to pay a license fee; Free shows you a similar list containing only free apps; and Top Grossing shows the apps that have been downloaded the most (rather than those that have made the most money).

- **Search**—This tool enables you to search for apps. You can search by name, developer, and other keywords.

- **Updates**—Through this option, you can get to the Purchased screen, which enables you to find and download apps you have previously downloaded to your iPhone or other device and shows you the update status of your apps on your iPhone. If you have automatic updates enabled, you see the list of updates made to the apps on your iPhone along with those that are pending; if you don't have automatic updates enabled, you can use this screen to download and install updates for your apps.

Finding and downloading any kind of app follows this same pattern:

1. **Find the app you are interested in.** You can use the options described in the previous list, find apps by browsing for them, or use the search option to find a specific app quickly and easily.

2. **Evaluate the app.** The information screen for apps provides lots of information that you can use to decide whether you want to download an app (or not). The information available includes a text description, screenshots, ratings and reviews from users, and so on.

3. **Download and install the app.**

The following tasks provide detailed examples for each of these steps.

Searching for Apps

If you know something about an app, such as its name, its developer, its purpose, or just about anything else, you can quickly search the App Store to find the app. Here's how to search for an app:

1. Move to the Home screen and tap App Store.

2. Tap Search.

③ Tap in the Search box.

④ Type a search term. This can be the type of app you are looking for based on its purpose (such as travel) or the name of someone associated with the app, its title, its developer, or even a topic. As you type, the app suggests searches that are related to what you are typing.

⑤ Tap the search you want to perform (to see the full list of search results, tap Search on the keyboard). The apps that meet your search term appear.

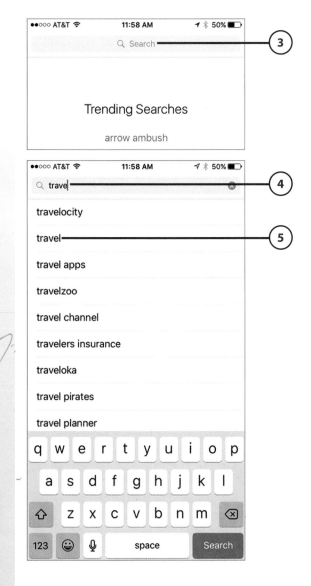

Related Apps

When the search results are on the screen, at the top (just under the Search bar), you see app searches that are related to the one you performed in some way in the Related bar. Tap a related search on this bar to use it to find other apps. As you use related searches, back (<) and forward (>) buttons appear in the Related bar so that you can move back and forth among the searches you have done. For example, tap the back button to get back to a previous search result.

6 Swipe up and down on the screen to review the apps in the search results.

7 If none of the apps are what you are looking for, tap the Clear button (x) in the Search box and repeat steps 4–6 (or use the Related Searches as described in the Related Apps note).

8 When you find an app of interest to you, tap it. You move to the app's information screen.

9 Use the app's information on the information screen to evaluate the app and decide whether you want to download it. You can read about the app, see screenshots, and read other peoples' reviews to help you decide. If you want to download the app, see "Downloading Apps" later in this chapter for the details.

Follow the Trends?

Before you enter a search term on the Search screen, you see the Trending Searches, which are the searches that are being performed most frequently. You can tap one of these to use it to search for apps.

Related searches

Browsing for Apps

If you don't know of a specific app you want, you can browse the App Store. To browse, you can tap any graphics or links you see in the App Store app. One of the most useful ways to browse for apps is by using categories:

(**1**) Open the App Store app.

(**2**) Tap Categories.

(**3**) Swipe up and down the screen to browse the list until you see a category of interest.

(**4**) Tap a category in which you are interested.

(**5**) If the category has subcategories, swipe up and down the screen to browse the subcategories; if you moved directly to apps, skip to step 7.

(**6**) Tap a subcategory in which you are interested.

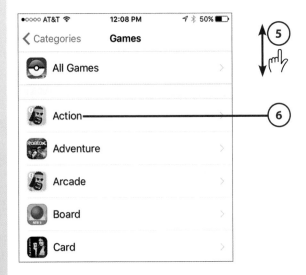

7 Swipe up and down to browse the groupings of apps, such as New Games We Love, All-Time Greats, and so on.

8 Swipe left and right on a grouping to browse the apps it contains.

See All, Know All

To browse all the apps in a category, tap the See All option at the top of the category's screen. You see all the apps in that category; swipe up and down the screen to browse the list. Tap an app to see its information.

9 Tap an app in which you are interested. You move to that app's information screen.

10 Use the information on the information screen to decide whether you want to download this app. You can read about the app, see screenshots, and read other peoples' reviews to help you decide. If you want to download the app, see "Downloading Apps" later in this chapter for the details. Or, you can continue browsing by tapping the name of the category in the top-left corner of the screen to return to the category list.

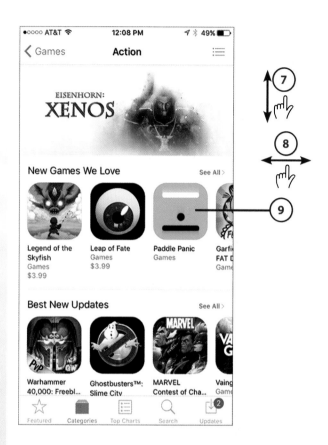

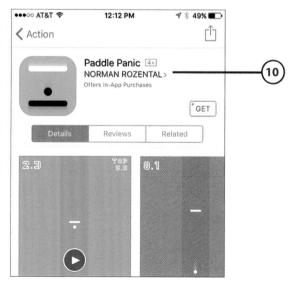

>>>Go Further
MORE ON FINDING APPS

Following are a few pointers to help you use the App Store:

- When you see a + inside an app's price or Get button, that means the app is a universal app, which means it runs equally as well on iPhones, iPads, and iPod touches.

- Some apps include video previews. When you see the Play button on an image, it is a video preview. Tap the Play button to watch it. Tap the Done button in the upper-left corner of the screen to move back to the screenshots.

- After you have used an app, you can add your own review by moving back to its Reviews tab and tapping Write a Review. You move to the Write a Review screen where you have to enter your iTunes Store account information before you can write and submit a review.

- You can read user reviews of the apps in the App Store. You should take these with a grain of salt. Some people have an issue with the developer, are reviewing an older version of the app, or are commenting on issues unrelated to the app itself, and that causes them to provide low ratings. The most useful individual user reviews are very specific, as in "I wanted the app to do x, but it only does y." It can be more helpful to look at the number of reviews and the average user rating than reading the individual reviews.

Downloading Apps

Downloading and installing apps is about as easy as things get, as you can see:

(1) In the App Store, view the app you want to download.

(2) Tap GET (for free apps) or the price (for apps that have a license fee). The button then becomes INSTALL, if it is a free app, or BUY if it has a license fee.

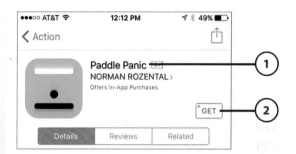

(3) Tap INSTALL or BUY. Depending on your iTunes & App Store settings, you might be prompted to sign in with your Apple ID and password to start the download. If you aren't prompted to confirm the download, you can skip the next step because the app starts downloading immediately.

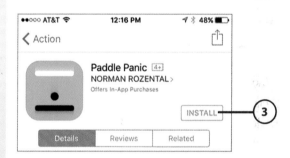

(4) If you are prompted to confirm the download, and you are using an iPhone 5s or later and have enabled Touch ID for store downloads, touch the Touch ID/Home button at the prompt; if you are using another model, or you don't use Touch ID for store downloads, type your Apple ID password, and then tap OK.

You see the progress of the process.

When the process is complete, the status information is replaced by the OPEN button.

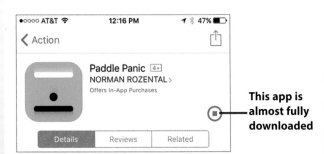

This app is almost fully downloaded

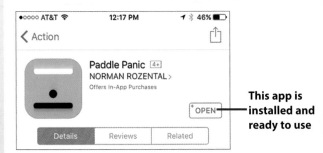

This app is installed and ready to use

>>>Go Further

MORE ON APPS

As you use the App Store app to install apps on your iPhone, keep the following hints handy:

- Like other software, apps are updated regularly to fix problems, add features, or make other changes. If you set the iTunes & App Store Updates setting to on (green) as described earlier in this chapter, updates to your apps happen automatically in the background. Your apps are always current so you don't have to update them manually. (More information on updating apps is in online Chapter 17, "Maintaining and Protecting Your iPhone and Solving Problems.")

- If you see the Download button (a cloud with a downward-pointing arrow) next to an app rather than Get or Buy, that means you have previously downloaded (and paid for if it isn't free) the app but it is not currently installed on your iPhone. Tap the button to download and install it.

- To let someone else know about an app, tap the Share button and then tap how you want to let him know; the options include AirDrop, Message, Mail, Twitter, and Facebook. To buy an app for someone, tap Gift.

- Apps can work in the background to keep their information current, such as Weather and Stocks. To configure this, open the Settings app, tap General, and tap Background App Refresh. Set Background App Refresh to on (green). To enable an app to work in the background, set its switch to on (green). To disable background activity for an app, set its switch to off (white).

- If you are having a problem with an app, move to the app's Details tab, swipe up the screen, and tap Developer Website. You move to the developer's website and can get information and help with the app.

- After you install an app, move to the Settings screen and look for the app's icon. If it is there, the app has additional settings you can use to configure the way it works. Tap the app's icon in the Settings app and use its Settings screen to configure it.

Customize the layout of the icons on your Home screens by placing icons where you want them

Place icons in folders to keep your Home screens organized

Tap to configure your iPhone's screen and sounds

Choose the image you want as wallpaper

In this chapter, you learn how to make an iPhone look, sound, and feel the way you want it to. Topics include the following:

→ Getting started
→ Customizing your Home screens
→ Setting the screen's brightness, lock/wake, text, view, and wallpaper options
→ Choosing the sounds and vibrations your iPhone makes

6

Customizing How Your iPhone Looks and Sounds

There are lots of ways that you can customize an iPhone to make it *your* iPhone so that it looks, sounds, and feels the way you want it to. You can design your Home screens; set the screen's brightness, text size, and wallpaper; and choose the sounds and vibrations your iPhone makes.

Getting Started

In Chapter 5, "Customizing How Your iPhone Works," you learned how to change many aspects of how your iPhone works. This chapter focuses on how you can change the way you interact with your iPhone and how it interacts with you. Following are key areas you can configure to personalize your iPhone's personality:

- **Home screens**—The iPhone's Home screens are the starting point for most everything you do because these screens contain the icons that you tap to access the apps and web page icons that you want to use. You see and use the Home screens constantly, so it's a good idea to customize them to your preferences. You can place icons on specific screens, and you can use folders to make your Home screens work better for you.

- **Screen brightness, Auto-Lock, Raise to Wake, text, view, and wallpaper options**—There are a number of ways you can change how your iPhone's screen looks and works. For example, you can set its brightness level and text size. You can also change the view you have; one option causes the screen to be zoomed in so icons and text are larger and easier to see.

- **Sounds**—Sound is one important way your iPhone uses to communicate with you. The most obvious of these sounds is the ringtone that plays when you receive a call. However, there are many other sounds you can choose to help you know when something is happening. You can also choose to disable sounds so that your iPhone isn't so noisy. You can also have your iPhone vibrate in conjunction with, or instead of, making sounds.

Notifications

Notifications are the primary way your iPhone communicates with you and there are many options you can configure to change your iPhone's visual, auditory, and vibratory notifications. These are explained in Chapter 2, "Using Your iPhone's Core Features."

Customizing Your Home Screens

The iPhone's Home screens are the starting point for anything you do. You access apps on your Home screens by tapping their icons.

The Home screens come configured with icons in default locations. You can change the location of these icons to be more convenient for you. As you install more apps, it's a good idea to organize your Home screens so that you can quickly get to the items you use most frequently. You can move icons around the same screen, move icons between the pages of the Home screen, and organize icons within folders. You can even change the icons that appear on the Home screens' Dock. You can also delete icons you no longer need.

Moving Icons Around Your Home Screens

You can move icons around on a Home screen, and you can move icons among screens to change where they are located.

1. Press the Touch ID/Home button to move to a Home screen if you aren't there already.

2. Swipe to the left or right across the Home screen until the page containing an icon you want to move appears.

3. Touch (don't tap because if you do, the app opens instead) and hold on any icon. After a moment, the icons begin jiggling, which indicates that you can move icons on the Home screens. You also see Delete buttons (x) in the upper-left corner of some icons, which indicate that you can delete both the icon and app or the web page link (more on this later in this section).

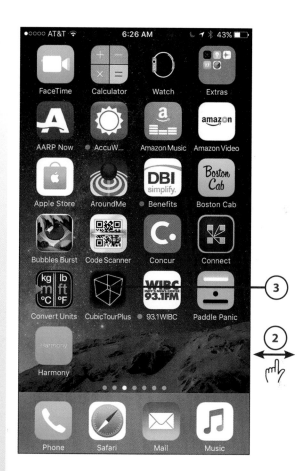

Touch But Don't Press (3D Touch Models)

If you are working with an iPhone 6s/6s Plus or later model that supports 3D Touch, don't press on icons when you want to move them; just touch your finger lightly to the screen. If you apply pressure, you might open the Quick Action menu instead. When you just touch an icon and leave your finger on the screen without any pressure, the icons become fuzzy briefly and then start jiggling to indicate you can move them.

(4) Touch and hold an icon you want to move; it becomes larger to show that you have selected it.

(5) Drag the icon to a new location on the current screen; as you move the icon around the page, other icons separate and are reorganized to enable you to place the icon in its new location.

(6) When the icon is in the location you want, lift your finger from the screen. The icon is set in that place.

(7) Tap and hold on an icon you want to move to a different page.

(8) Drag the icon to the left edge of the screen to move it to a previous page or to the right edge of the screen to move it to a later page. As you reach the edge of the screen, you move to the previous or next page.

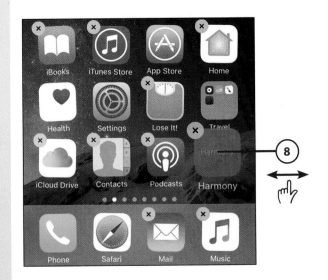

9 Drag the icon around on the new screen until it is in the location where you want to place it.

10 Lift your finger off the screen. The icon is set in its new place.

11 Continue moving icons until you've placed them in the locations you want; then press the Touch ID/Home button once. The icons are locked in their current positions, they stop jiggling, and the Delete buttons disappear.

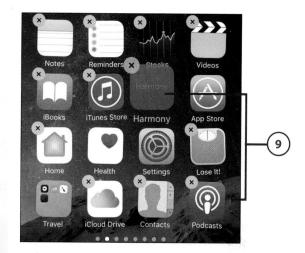

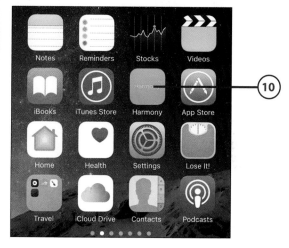

Creating Folders to Organize Apps on Your Home Screens

You can place icons into folders to keep them organized and to make more icons available on the same page. To create a folder, do the following:

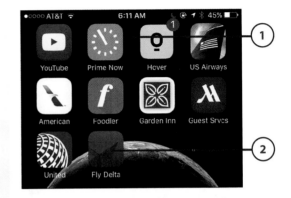

1. Move to the Home screen containing icons you want to place in a folder.

2. Touch and hold an icon until the icons start jiggling; the Delete buttons appear.

3. Drag one icon on top of another one that you want to be in the new folder together.

4. When the first icon is on top of the second and a border appears around the second icon, lift your finger. The two icons are placed into a new folder, which is named based on the type of icons you place within it. The folder opens and you see its default name.

5 Edit the name by tapping in the name field.

6 Change the default name for the folder or type a completely new name.

7 Tap Done.

8 Tap outside the folder to close it.

9 If you're done organizing the Home screen, press the Touch ID/Home button. The icons stop jiggling.

Locating Folders

You can move a folder to a new location in the same way you can move any icon. Touch and hold (don't tap or it opens instead) an icon until the icons start jiggling. Drag the folder icon to where you want it to be.

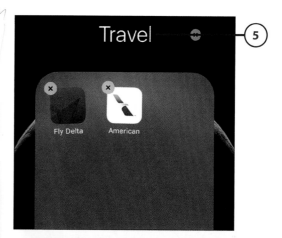

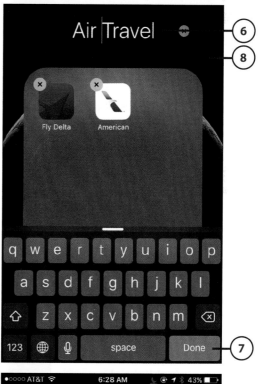

New folder containing two icons

Configuring the Home Screen Dock

The Dock on the bottom of the Home screen appears on every page. You can place any icons on the Dock that you want, including folder icons.

(1) Move to the Home screen containing an icon you want to place on the Dock.

(2) Touch and hold an icon until the icons start jiggling and the Delete buttons appear.

(3) Drag an icon that is currently on the Dock from the Dock onto the Home screen to create an empty space on the Dock.

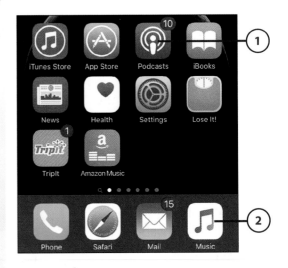

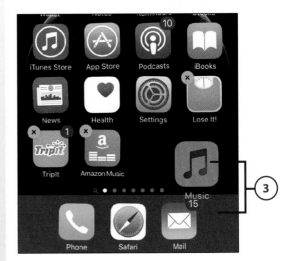

4 Drag an icon or folder from the Home screen onto the Dock.

5 Drag the icons on the Dock around so they are in the order you want them to be.

6 Press the Touch ID/Home button to set the icons in their current places.

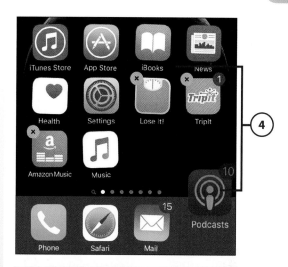

Deleting Icons

You can delete icons from a Home screen to remove them from your iPhone. When you delete an app's icon, its data is also deleted and you won't be able to use the app anymore (of course, you can download it again if you change your mind).

1 Move to the Home screen containing an icon you want to delete.

2 Touch and hold an icon until the icons start jiggling and the Delete buttons appear (you can delete icons that are inside folders, too).

3 Tap the icon's Delete button.

4 Tap Delete. If the icon was for an app, it and any associated data on your iPhone are deleted.

>>>Go Further
MORE ON ORGANIZING HOME SCREENS

Organizing your Home screens can make the use of your iPhone more efficient. Here are a few more things to keep in mind:

- You can place many icons in the same folder. When you add more than nine, any additional icons are placed on new pages within the folder. As you keep adding icons, pages keep being added to the folder to accommodate the icons you add to it. You can swipe to the left or right within a folder to move among its pages, just as you can to move among your Home screens.

- To change a folder's name, move to a screen showing the folder whose name you want to change. Touch and hold an icon until the icons jiggle. Tap the folder so that it opens, and then tap the current name. Edit the name, tap Done, and tap outside the folder to close it. Press the Touch ID/Home button to complete the process.

- To delete a folder, remove all the icons from it. The folder is deleted as soon as you remove the last icon from within it.

- You can delete icons for apps you've added to your iPhone or some of the default apps, such as the Stocks app. You can't delete some of the default apps, which is why their icons don't have Delete buttons like apps that you install do. If you don't use some of these default apps that you can't delete, move them to pages of your Home screen that you don't use very often so they don't get in your way, or create a folder for unused icons and store them there, out of your way.

- To return your Home screens to how they were when you first started using your iPhone, open the Settings app, tap General, Reset, Reset Home Screen Layout, and Reset Home Screen. The Home screens return to their default configurations. Icons you've added are moved onto the later pages.

Setting the Screen's Brightness, Lock/Wake, Text, View, and Wallpaper Options

There are a number of settings you can configure to suit your viewing preferences and how your iPhone locks/wakes:

- **Brightness**—Because you continually look at your iPhone's screen, it should be the right brightness level for your eyes. However, the screen is also a large user of battery power, so the dimmer an iPhone's screen is, the longer its battery lasts. You should find a good balance between viewing comfort and battery life. Fortunately, your iPhone has an Auto-Brightness feature that automatically adjusts for current lighting conditions.

- **Night Shift**—This feature changes the color profile of the screen after dark. It is supposed to make the light produced by the iPhone more suitable to darker conditions. You can set the color temperature to your preferences and can set a schedule if you want Night Shift to be activated automatically.

- **Auto-Lock**—The Auto-Lock setting causes your iPhone to lock and go to sleep after a specific amount of inactivity. This is good for security as it is less likely someone can pick up and use your phone if you let it sit for a while. It also extends battery life because it puts the iPhone to sleep.

- **Raise to Wake**—This setting, available on iPhone 6s/6s Plus and 7/7 Plus models, enables you to wake up the iPhone by lifting it up. This is useful because you don't even need to press a button, just lift the phone and you see the Lock screen, giving you quick access to notifications and widgets.

- **Text Size/Bold**—As you use your iPhone, you'll be constantly working with text so it's also important to configure the text size to meet your preferences. You can use the Bold setting to bold text to make it easier to read.

- **View**—The iPhone 6, 6s, 6 Plus, 6s Plus, 7, and 7 Plus offer two views. The Standard view maximizes screen space, and the Zoomed view makes things on the screen larger, making them easier to see, but less content fits on the screen. You can choose the view that works best for you.

- **Wallpaper**—Wallpaper is the image you see "behind" the icons on your Home screens. Because you see this image so often, you might as well have an image that you want to see or that you believe makes using the

Home screens easier and faster. You can use the iPhone's default wallpaper images, or you can use any photo available on your iPhone. You can also set the wallpaper you see on the iPhone's Lock screen (you can use the same image as on the Home screens or a different one). Although it doesn't affect productivity or usability of the iPhone very much, choosing your own wallpaper to see in the background of the Home and Lock screens makes your iPhone more personal to you and is just plain fun.

Setting the Screen Brightness and Night Shift

To set the screen brightness and Night Shift, perform the following steps:

1. In the Settings app, tap Display & Brightness.

2. Drag the slider to the right to raise the base brightness or to the left to lower it. A brighter screen uses more power but is easier to see.

3. If you don't want to use the Auto-Brightness feature, slide the switch to off (white) to disable this feature. The Auto-Brightness feature adjusts the screen brightness based on the lighting conditions in which you are using the iPhone. You get more battery life with Auto-Brightness on, but you might not be comfortable with the brightness of the screen when you use the iPhone where there isn't a lot of ambient light.

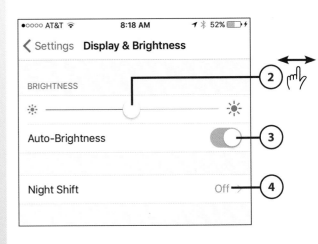

4. Tap Night Shift.

5 To have Night Shift activate automatically, set the Scheduled switch to on (green); if you don't want it to activate automatically, skip to step 11.

6 Tap the From/To setting.

7 To have Night Shift on between sunset and sunrise, tap Sunset to Sunrise and skip to step 10; to set a custom schedule for Night Shift, tap Custom Schedule.

8 Tap Turn On At and swipe up or down on the hour, minute, and AM/PM wheels to set the time when you want Night Shift to activate.

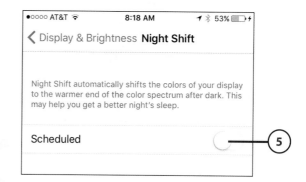

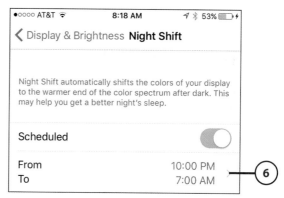

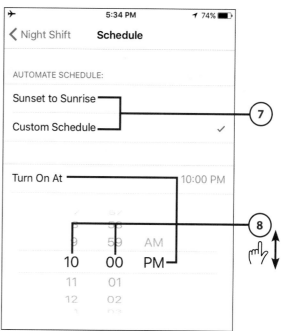

9 Tap Turn Off At and use the time wheels to set when you want Night Shift to turn off.

10 Tap Night Shift.

11 To manually turn on Night Shift at any time, set the Manually Enable Until Tomorrow switch to on (green). Night Shift activates and remains on until sunrise when it shuts off automatically. You can manually turn off Night Shift by setting the Manually Enable Until Tomorrow switch to off (white).

12 Drag the COLOR TEMPERATURE slider to the right to make the Night Shift effect more pronounced or to the left to make it less warm. If Night Shift isn't active when you drag the slider, it goes into effect as you move the slider so you can see the effect the temperature you select has.

13 Tap Display & Brightness.

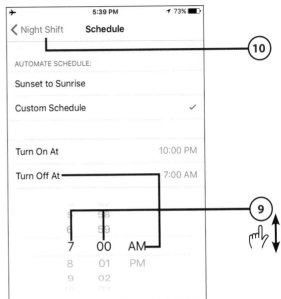

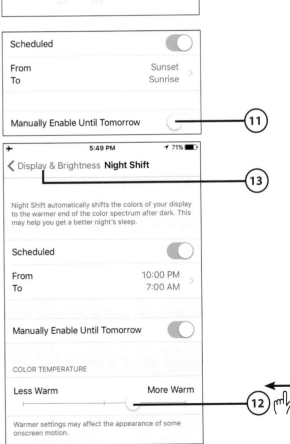

Setting Auto-Lock and Raise to Wake

To set the screen brightness, perform the following steps:

1. Open the Display & Brightness settings screen.

2. Tap Auto-Lock.

3. Tap the amount of idle time you want to pass before the iPhone automatically locks and goes to sleep. You can choose from 30 seconds or 1 to 5 minutes; choose Never if you want to manually lock your iPhone. I recommend that you keep Auto-Lock set to a relatively small value to conserve your iPhone's battery and to make it more secure. Of course, the shorter you set this time to be, the more frequently you have to unlock your iPhone. (If you configure your iPhone to unlock with Touch ID, unlocking your iPhone is as easy as touching the Home/Touch ID button.)

4. Tap Display & Brightness.

5. If you want to be able to wake your phone by lifting it, set the Raise to Wake switch to on (green); to disable this feature, leave the switch off (white).

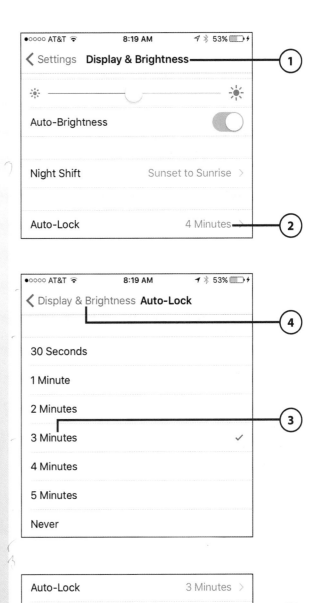

Setting Text Size and Bold

To change the text size or make all text bold, perform the following steps:

(1) Open the Display & Brightness settings screen.

(2) Tap Text Size. This control changes the size of text in all the apps that support the iPhone's Dynamic Type feature.

(3) Drag the slider to the right to increase the size of text or to the left to decrease it. As you move the slider, the text at the top of the screen resizes so you can see the effect of the change you are making.

(4) When you are happy with the size of the text, tap Display & Brightness.

(5) If you want to make all of the text on your iPhone bold, set the Bold Text switch to on (green) and move to step 6. If you don't want to bold the text, skip the next step.

(6) Tap Continue. Your iPhone restarts. All the text is in bold, making it easier to read.

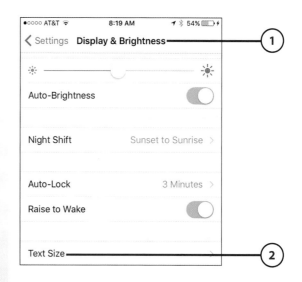

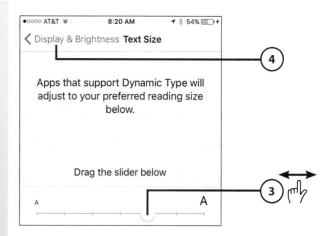

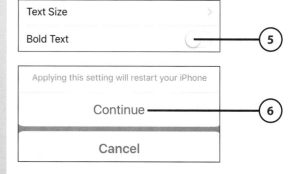

Choosing a View

To configure the view you use, perform the following steps:

1. Open the Display & Brightness settings screen.

2. Tap View; if you don't see this option, your iPhone doesn't support it and you can skip the rest of these steps.

3. Tap Standard.

4. Look at the sample screen.

5. Swipe to the left or right to see examples of what other screens look like in the Standard view.

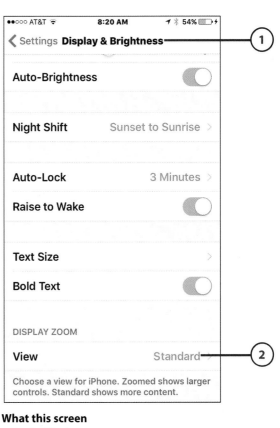

What this screen looks like in Standard view

(6) Look at the next sample screen.

(7) Swipe to the left or right to see examples of what other screens look like in the Standard view.

(8) Tap Zoomed. The sample screens change to reflect the Zoomed view.

(9) Swipe to the left and right to preview the other sample screens in the Zoomed view.

(10) If you want to keep the current view, tap Cancel and skip the rest of these steps.

(11) To change the view, tap the view you want.

(12) Tap Set (if Set is grayed out, the view you selected is already set and you can skip the rest of these steps).

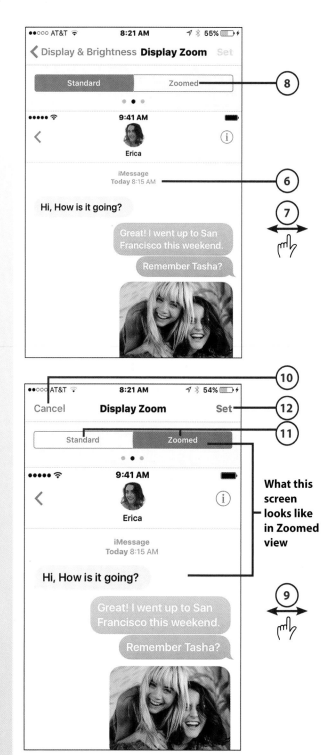

What this screen looks like in Zoomed view

(13) Tap Use Zoomed (this is Use Standard if you are switching to the Standard view). Your iPhone restarts and uses the new view.

Setting the Wallpaper on the Home and Lock Screens

To configure your wallpaper, perform the following steps:

(1) In the Settings app, tap Wallpaper. You see the current wallpaper set for the Lock and Home screens.

(2) Tap Choose a New Wallpaper. The Choose screen has two sections. The top section enables you to choose one of the default wallpaper images (Dynamic, Stills, or Live), whereas the lower section shows you the photos available on your iPhone. If you don't have any photos stored on your iPhone, you can only choose from the default images. To choose a default image, continue with step 3; to use one of your photos as wallpaper, skip to step 8.

Current wallpaper on your Lock screen

Current wallpaper on your Home screens

(3) Tap Dynamic if you want to use dynamic wallpaper, Stills if you want to use a static image, or Live if you want to use a Live Photo. These steps show selecting a Live Photo, but using a dynamic or still image is similar.

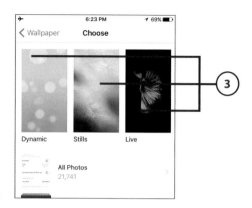

(4) Swipe up and down the screen to browse the images available to you.

(5) Tap the image you want to use as wallpaper.

(6) Tap Perspective to use the Perspective view of the wallpaper, tap Still if you want a static version of the image, or tap Live Photo to use a Live Photo. (See the sidebar "More on View Options" later in this chapter for an explanation of these terms.)

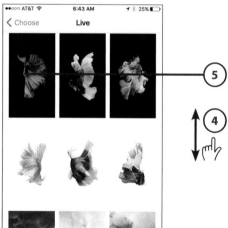

(7) Tap Set and move to step 15.

Wallpaper Options Explained

Dynamic wallpaper has motion (kind of like a screen saver on a computer). Stills are static images. Live Photos show motion when you tap and hold on them. Live Photos are available only on iPhone 6s/6s Plus or later models. On other models, you see only the Dynamic and Still options.

(**8**) To use a photo as wallpaper, swipe up the screen to browse the sources of photos available to you; these include All Photos, Favorites, Selfies, albums, and so on.

Working with Photos

To learn how to work with the photos on your iPhone, see Chapter 15, "Viewing and Editing Photos and Video with the Photos App."

(**9**) Tap the source containing the photo you want to use.

(**10**) Swipe up and down the selected source to browse its photos.

(**11**) Tap the photo you want to use. The photo appears on the Move and Scale screen, which you can use to resize and move the image around.

More on View Options

The Perspective view can be a bit difficult to describe because it is subtle. This view magnifies the wallpaper image when you tilt your iPhone. It is sometimes noticeable and sometimes not, depending on the image you are using for wallpaper. The best thing to do is to enable it to see if you notice any difference or disable it if you prefer not to use it for the specific images you use as wallpaper. You can enable or disable it at any time for your wallpaper on the Lock and Home screens. To change the view without changing the wallpaper, move to the Wallpaper screen

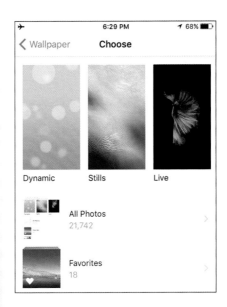

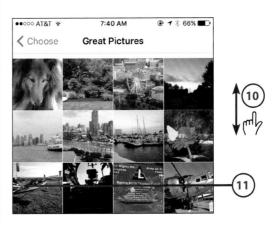

and tap the wallpaper (tap the Lock or Home screen) you want to change. Tap Perspective to use the Perspective view or Set if you don't want to use it. To save the view, tap Set or to leave it as it is, tap Cancel.

When you choose a Live Photo as wallpaper, you can touch and hold on the screen to see the image's motion. Note that when you apply a Live Photo to the Home screen wallpaper, it becomes a static image for which you can choose the Still or Perspective view.

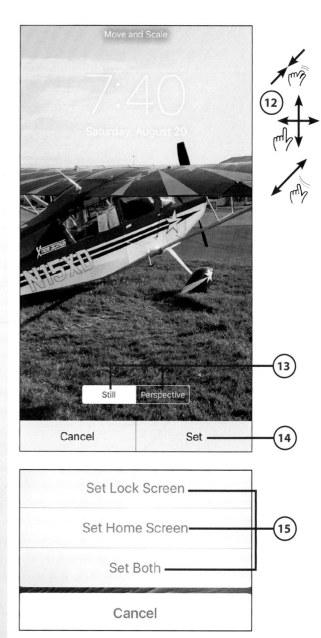

(12) Use your fingers to unpinch to zoom in or pinch to zoom out, and hold down and drag the photo around the screen until it appears as you want the wallpaper to look.

(13) Tap Perspective to use the Perspective view of the wallpaper (see the sidebar "More on View Options"), tap Still to use a static version of the image, or tap Live Photo to use a Live Photo (available only when you are working with a Live Photo on iPhone 6s, iPhone 6s Plus, or later models).

(14) Tap Set.

(15) Tap Set Lock Screen or Set Home Screen to apply the wallpaper to only one of those screens; tap Set Both to apply the same wallpaper in both locations. The next time you move to the screen you selected, you see the wallpaper you chose.

16 If you set the wallpaper in only one location, tap Choose (not shown on a figure) to move back to the Choose screen and repeat steps 3–15 to set the wallpaper for the other location.

New wallpaper on the Lock screen

New wallpaper on the Home screen

Choosing the Sounds and Vibrations Your iPhone Makes

Sound is one important way your iPhone uses to communicate with you. You can configure the sounds the phone uses in two ways. One is by choosing the general sounds your iPhone makes, which is covered in this section. You can also configure sounds specific apps use for notifications about certain events; this is covered in Chapter 2. You can also associate vibration patterns with various events, such as a receiving a phone call.

If you have an iPhone 7 or 7 Plus, it offers haptic feedback, which means the phone vibrates slightly when something happens, such as when you make a choice on a selection wheel. You can determine whether you want to feel this feedback or not. If you don't have one of these models, you won't see references to haptics on your Sounds screens.

To configure your iPhone's general sounds, vibrations, and haptics, do the following:

1. On the Settings screen, tap Sounds & Haptics (iPhone 7 and 7 Plus) or Sounds (all other models).

2. Set the Vibrate on Ring switch to on (green) if you want your iPhone to also vibrate when it rings.

3. Set the Vibrate on Silent switch to on (green) if you want your iPhone to vibrate when you have it muted.

4. Set the volume of the ringer and alert tones by dragging the slider to the left or right.

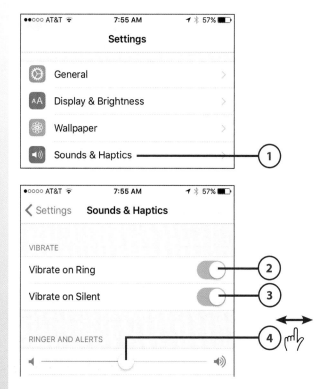

5 Set the Change with Buttons switch to on (green) if you want to also be able to change the volume using the volume buttons on the side of the phone.

6 Tap Ringtone. On the resulting screen, you can set the sound and vibration your iPhone uses when a call comes in.

7 Swipe up and down the screen to see all the ringtones available to you. There are two sections of sounds on this screen: RINGTONES and ALERT TONES. These work in the same way; alert tones tend to be shorter sounds. At the top of the RINGTONES section, you see any custom ringtones you have configured on your phone; a dark line separates those from the default ringtones that are below the custom ones.

8 Tap a sound, and it plays; tap it again to stop it.

9 Repeat steps 7 and 8 until you have selected the sound you want to have as your general ringtone.

10 If necessary, swipe down the screen so you see the Vibration section at the top.

11 Tap Vibration. A list of Standard and Custom vibrations is displayed.

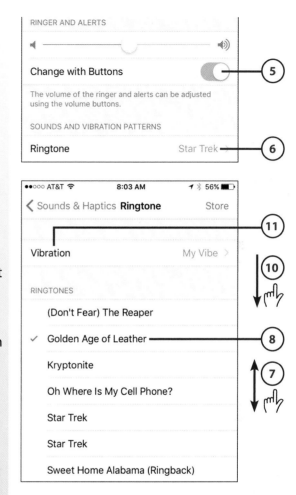

Individual Ringtones and Vibrations

The ringtone and vibration you set in steps 6–14 are the default or general settings. These are used for all callers except for people in your Contacts app for whom you've set specific ringtones or vibrations. In that case, the contact's specific ringtone and vibration are used instead of the defaults. See Chapter 7, "Managing Contacts," to learn how to configure specific ringtones and vibrations for your contacts.

12 Swipe up and down the screen to see all the vibrations available. The STANDARD section contains the default vibrations, and in the CUSTOM section you can tap Create New Vibration to create your own vibration patterns.

13 Tap a vibration. It "plays" so you can feel it. Tap it again to make it stop.

14 Repeat steps 12 and 13 until you've selected the general vibration you want to use; you can tap None at the bottom of the Vibration screen below the CUSTOM section if you don't want to have a general vibration.

15 Tap Ringtone.

16 Tap Sounds & Haptics. The ringtone you selected is shown on the Sounds screen next to the Ringtone label.

17 Tap Text Tone.

18 Use steps 7–14 with the Text Tone screen to set the sound and vibration used when you receive a new text. The process works the same as for ringtones, though the screens look a bit different. For example, the ALERT TONES section is at the top of the screen because you are more likely to want a short sound for new texts.

19 When you're done setting the text tone, tap Sounds & Haptics.

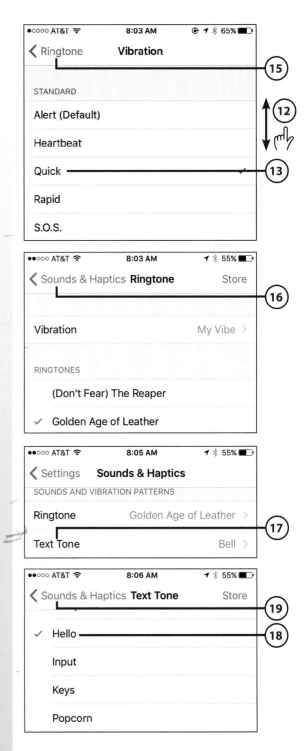

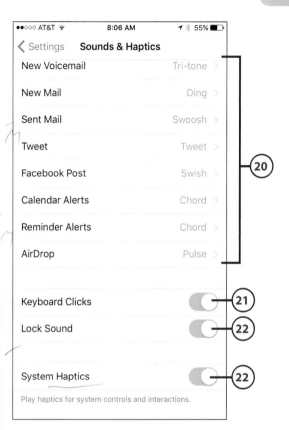

20. Using the same process as you did for ringtones and text tones, set the sound and vibrations for the rest of the events on the list.

21. If you don't like the audible feedback when you tap keys on the iPhone's virtual keyboard, slide the Keyboard Clicks switch to off (white) to disable that sound. The keyboard is silent as you type on it.

22. If you don't want your iPhone to make a sound when you lock it, slide the Lock Sound switch to off (white). Your iPhone no longer makes this sound when you press the Sleep/Wake button to put it to sleep and lock it.

23. Set the System Haptics switch to off (white) if you prefer not to experience vibratory feedback for events.

>>>Go Further

SOUNDING OFF

Following are some other sound- and vibration-related pointers:

- You can tap the Store button on the Ringtone, Text Tone, and other screens to move to the iTunes Store, where you can download ringtones and other sounds to your iPhone. See the online Chapter 16, "Working with Other Useful iPhone Apps and Features," for more information.

- You can create custom vibration patterns. On the Vibration screen, tap Create New Vibration. Tap the vibration pattern you want to create; when you're done tapping, tap Stop. Tap Record to start over. When you're done, tap Save. Name the pattern and tap Save. The patterns you create are available in the CUSTOM section on the Vibration screen. To remove a custom pattern, swipe to the left on it and tap Delete.

Use Settings to configure how contacts are displayed

Tap here to work with your contact information

Use your contact information in many apps

In this chapter, you learn how to ensure that your iPhone has the contact information you need when you need it. Topics include the following:

→ Getting started
→ Setting your Contacts preferences
→ Creating contacts on your iPhone
→ Working with contacts on your iPhone
→ Managing contacts on your iPhone

Managing Contacts

You'll be using your iPhone to make calls, get directions, send emails, and for many other tasks that require contact information, including names, phone numbers, email addresses, and physical addresses. It would be time consuming and a nuisance to have to remember and retype this information each time you use it. Fortunately, you don't have to do either because the Contacts app puts all your contact information at your fingertips (literally).

Getting Started

The Contacts app makes using your contact information extremely easy. This information is readily available on your phone in all the apps, such as Mail, Messages, and Phone, in which you need it. And, you don't need to remember or type the information because you can enter it by choosing someone's name, a business' name, or other information that you know about the contact. You can also access your contact information directly in the Contacts app and take action on it (such as placing a call).

To use contact information, it must be stored in the Contacts app. This can be accomplished in several ways. When you configure an online account on your iPhone, such as iCloud or Google, to include contact information, the contact information stored in that account is immediately available on your phone without you having to do anything else. (See Chapter 4, "Setting Up and Using iCloud and Other Online Accounts," for the steps to enable contact information in online accounts.) You can manually add new contact information to the Contacts app by capturing that information when you perform tasks (such as reading email). You can also enter new contact information directly in the Contacts app.

The Contacts app also makes it easy to keep your contact information current, such as adding more information, updating existing contacts, or removing contacts you no longer need.

Setting Your Contacts Preferences

Using the Settings app, you can determine how contacts are sorted and displayed, if or how names are shortened on various screens, your contact information, and which account should be the default for contact information. You can probably work with your contacts just fine without making any changes to your settings, but if you want to make adjustments, open the Settings app and tap Contacts. Use the information in the following table to change your contact settings.

Settings App Explained

To get detailed information on using the Settings app, see "Working with the Settings App" in Chapter 5, "Customizing How Your iPhone Works."

Contacts Settings

Setting	Description
Accounts	Use the Accounts setting to configure the online accounts you use to store contact information. See Chapter 4 for help setting up online accounts.
Sort Order	Tap First, Last to have contacts sorted by first name and then last name or tap Last, First to have contacts sorted by last name and then first name.

Setting	Description
Display Order	To show contacts in the format *first name, last name,* tap First, Last. To show contacts in the format *last name, first name,* tap Last, First.
Short Name	You can choose whether short names are used and, if they are, what form they take. Short names are useful because more contact information can be displayed in a smaller area , and they look "friendlier." To use short names, move the Short Name switch to the on position (green). Tap the format of the short name you want to use. You can choose from a combination of initial and name or just first or last name. If you want nicknames for contacts used for the short name when available, set the Prefer Nicknames switch to on (green).
My Info	Use this setting to find and tap your contact information in the Contacts app, which it can insert for you in various places and which Siri can use to call you by name; your current contact information is indicated by the label "me" next to the alphabetical index.
Default Account	Tap the account in which you want new contacts to be created by default (which is then marked with a check mark). If you have only one account configured for contacts, you don't have this option.
Contacts Found in Apps	If you don't want contact information in the various apps to be used, such as to automatically complete addresses when you create emails to, or try to identify callers when a number calling you is unknown, set the Contacts Found in Apps switch to off (white). You typically should leave this on (green) unless you find the automatic contact suggestions annoying or not helpful.

Where Contacts Are Stored Matters

You should store your contacts in an online account (for example, iCloud or Google), because the information is accessible on many devices and it is also backed up. If you don't have an online account, contact information is stored only on your iPhone. This is not good because, if something happens to your phone, you can lose all of your contacts.

Creating Contacts on Your iPhone

You can create new contacts on an iPhone in a number of ways. You can start with some information, such as the email address on a message you receive, and create a contact from it, or you can create a contact by manually filling in the contact information. In this section, you learn how to create a new contact starting with information in an email message and how to create a new contact manually.

Creating New Contacts from Email

When you receive an email, you can easily create a contact to capture the email address. (To learn how to work with the Mail app, see Chapter 9, "Sending, Receiving, and Managing Email.")

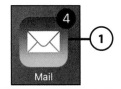

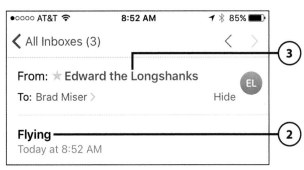

1. On the Home screen, tap Mail.

2. Use the Mail app to read an email message (see Chapter 9 for details).

3. Tap the email address from which you want to create a new contact. The contact's Info screen appears. You see as much information as could be gleaned from the email address, which is typically the sender's name and email address.

No Link?

If the name of someone you want to create a contact for isn't in blue, which means it is a link you can tap on, tap Details in the email's header. The header's full detail is shown and the names of people receiving the email become links that you can tap as described in step 3.

---

4 Tap Create New Contact. The New Contact screen appears. The name, email address, and any other information that can be identified are added to the new contact. The email address is labeled with the iPhone's best guess, such as other or home.

5 Use the New Contact screen to enter more contact information or update the information that was added (such as the label applied to the email address) and save the new contact by tapping Done. This works just like when you create a new contact manually, except that you already have some information—most likely, a name and an email address. For details on adding and changing more information for the contact, see the next task, "Creating Contacts Manually."

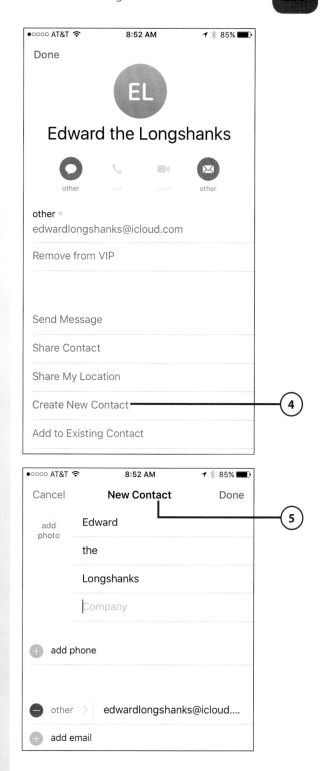

Contacts by Any Other Name...

At the top of the Contacts app's screen, you see All Contacts when you are display-ing all of your contacts. If you display only certain groups of contacts (groups are covered later in this chapter), the screen is named Contacts instead.

(**2**) Tap the Add (+) button. The New Contact screen appears with the default fields. (You can add more data fields as needed using the add field command.)

(**3**) To associate a photo with the contact, tap Add Photo. You can choose a photo already on your phone or take a new photo. These steps show using an existing photo. See the "Taking Photos" note for the steps to take a new photo.

(**4**) Tap Choose Photo.

Viewing Groups

In a contacts app on a computer, you can organize contacts into groups. If you see Contacts instead of All Contacts, you are viewing specific groups of con-tacts instead of all your contacts. The screens work in the same way; there is more on groups later in this chapter.

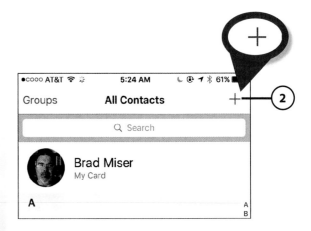

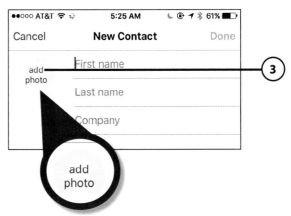

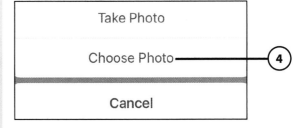

5 Use the Photos app to move to, select, and configure the photo you want to associate with the contact (see Chapter 15, "Viewing and Editing Photos and Video with the Photos App," for help with the Photos app).

6 Tap Choose. You return to the New Contact screen where the photo you selected is displayed.

7 Tap in the First field and enter the contact's first name; if you are creating a contact for an organization only, leave both name fields empty. (The Display Order preference determines whether the First or Last field appears at the top of the screen.)

8 Tap in the Last field and enter the contact's last name.

9 Enter the organization, such as a company, with which you want to associate the contact, if any.

10 Tap add phone to add a phone number. A new phone field appears along with the numeric keypad.

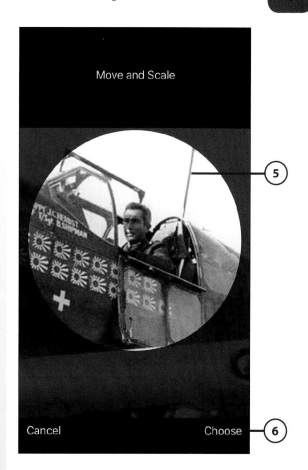

18 Type the contact's email address.

19 Tap the label for the email address to change it.

20 Tap the label you want to apply to the email address. You move back to the New Contact screen.

21 Repeat steps 17–20 to add more email addresses.

22 If necessary, swipe up the screen until you see Ringtone.

23 Tap Ringtone. The list of ringtones and alert tones available on your iPhone appears.

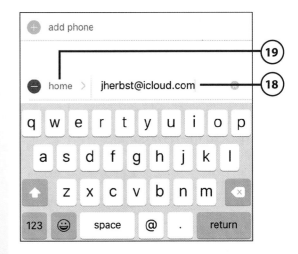

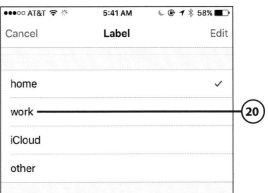

24 Set the Emergency Bypass switch to on (green) if you want sounds and vibrations for phone calls or new messages associated with the contact you are creating to play even when Do Not Disturb is on. (For more about Do Not Disturb and notifications, see Chapter 2, "Using Your iPhone's Core Features.")

25 Swipe up and down the list to see all of the tones available.

26 Tap the ringtone you want to play when the contact calls you. When you tap a ringtone, it plays so you can experiment to find the one that best relates to the contact. Setting a specific ringtone helps you identify a caller without looking at your phone.

27 Tap Vibration and use the resulting screen if you want to set a specific vibration for the contact. (For more on working with sounds and vibrations, see Chapter 6.)

28 Tap Done. You return to the New Contact screen, where the tone you selected appears.

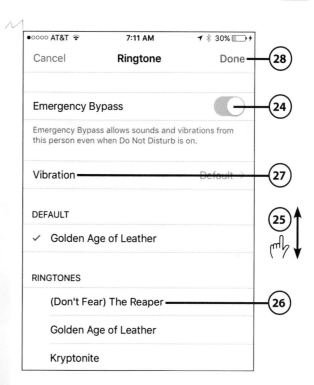

- When you have enabled the Emergency Bypass setting for a contact you see "Emergency Bypass On" in the Ringtone section of her contact information. If you've set a specific ringtone, you also see the name of that ringtone. If Emergency Bypass is turned off, you see only the name of the contact's ringtone.

- If you have an iPhone 6s/6s Plus or later model, you can touch and put pressure (called a Peek) on the Contacts icon. On the resulting Quick Action menu, you can show your contact info, create a new contact, or access your favorite contacts.

Working with Contacts on Your iPhone

There are many ways to use contact information. The first step is always finding the contact information you need, typically by using the Contacts app. Whether you access it directly or through another app (such as Mail), it works the same way. Then, you select the information you want to use or the action you want to perform.

Using the Contacts App

You can access your contact information directly in the Contacts app. For example, you can search or browse for a contact and then view the detailed information for the contact in which you are interested.

(1) On the Home screen, tap Contacts. The Contacts screen displays with the contacts listed in the view and sort format determined by the Contacts settings. (If the Groups screen appears, tap Done. You move back to the All Contacts or Contacts screen.)

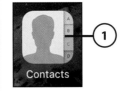

Contacts

You can find a contact to view by browsing (step 2), using the index (step 3), or searching (step 4). You can use combinations of these, too, such as first using the index to get to the right area and then browsing to find the contact in which you are interested.

(2) Swipe up or down to scroll the screen to browse for contact information; swipe up or down on the alphabetical index to browse rapidly.

(3) Tap the index to jump to contact information organized by the first letter of the format you selected in the Contact Preferences (last name or first name).

(4) Use the Search tool to search for a specific contact; tap in the tool, type the name (you can type last, first, company, and nickname), and then tap the contact you want to view on the results list.

(5) Tap a contact to view that contact's information.

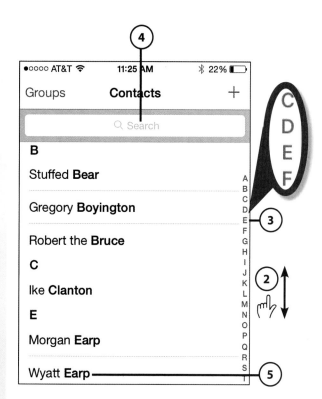

6 Swipe up and down the screen to view all the contact's information.

7 Tap the data or icons on the screen to perform actions, including the following:

- **Phone numbers**—Tap a phone number to call it. You can also tap one of the phone buttons just under the contact's image to call that number. For example, to call the number labeled as mobile, tap the mobile button.

- **Email addresses**—Tap an email address or the button with the address's label (such as other for the email address labeled as other) on it to create a new message to that address.

- **URLs**—Tap a URL to open Safari and move to the associated website.

- **Addresses**—Tap an address to show it in the Maps app.

- **FaceTime**—Tap video or FaceTime to start a FaceTime call with the contact.

- **Text**—Tap the message button or tap Send Message and choose the phone number or email address to which you want to send a text message.

- **Share Contact**—Tap Share Contact. The Share menu appears. To share the contact via email, tap Mail; to share it via a text, tap Message; or to share it using AirDrop, tap AirDrop.

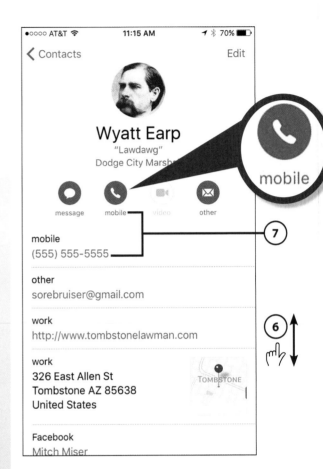

You can also share via Twitter or Facebook. Then, use the associated app to complete the task.

- **Favorites**—Tap Add to Favorites and choose the phone number or email address you want to designate as a favorite. You can use this in the associated app to do something faster. For example, if it's the Phone app, you can tap the Favorites tab to see your favorite contacts and quickly dial one by tapping it. You can also quickly access favorites from the FAVORITES widget by swiping to the right when you are on the Locked screen. You can add multiple items (such as cell and work phone numbers) as favorites for one contact.

8 To return to the Contacts list without performing an action, tap Contacts.

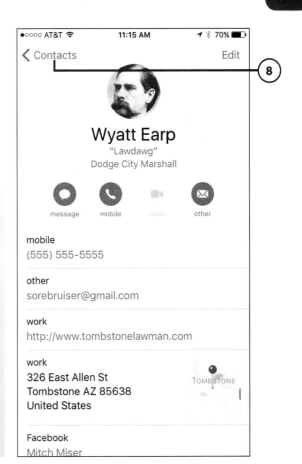

>>>Go Further

MAKE CONTACT

When working with your contacts, keep the following points in mind:

- **Last known contact**—The Contacts app remembers where you last were and takes you back there whenever you move into the Contacts app. For example, if you view a contact's details and then switch to a different app to send a message, and then go back to Contacts, you are returned to the screen you were last viewing. To move back to the main Contacts screen, tap Contacts in the upper-left corner of the screen.

- **Groups**—In a contact app on a computer, such as Contacts on a Mac, contacts can be organized into groups, which in turn can be stored in an online account, such as iCloud. When you sync, the groups of contacts move onto the iPhone. You can limit the contacts you browse or search; tap Groups on the Contacts screen.

The Groups screen displays the accounts (such as iCloud or Google) with which you are syncing contact information; under each account are the groups of contacts stored in that account. If a group has a check mark next to it, its contacts are displayed on the Contacts screen. To hide a group's contacts, tap it so that the check mark disappears. To hide or show all of a group's contacts, tap All *account*, where *account* is the name of the account in which those contacts are stored. To make browsing contacts easier, tap Hide All Contacts to hide all the groups and contacts; then, tap each group whose contacts you want to show on the Contacts screen.

Tap Done to move back to the Contacts screen. When you have selected a subset of your groups to view, the screen is labeled Contacts; when you have all groups displayed, the screen is called All Contacts.

- **Speaking of contacts**—You can use Siri to speak commands to work with contacts, too. You can get information about contacts by asking for it, such as "What is William Wallace's work phone number?" If you want to see all of a contact's information, you can say "Show me William Wallace." When Siri displays contact information, you can tap it to take action, such as tapping a phone number to call it. (See Chapter 12, "Working with Siri," for more on using Siri.)

It's Not All Good

Managing Contact Groups

When you create a new contact, it is associated with the account you designated as the default in the Contacts settings and is stored at the account level (not in any of your groups). You can't create groups in the Contacts app, nor can you change the group with which contacts are associated. You have to use a contacts app on a computer to manage groups and then sync your iPhone (which happens automatically when you use an online account, such as iCloud) to see the changes you make to your contact groups.

Accessing Contacts from Other Apps

You can also access contact information while you are using a different app. For example, you can use a contact's email address when you create an email message. When you perform such actions, you use the Contacts app to find and select the information you want to use. The following example shows using contact information to send an email message; using contact information in other apps (such as Phone or Messages) is similar.

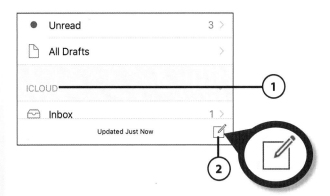

1. Open the app from which you want to access contact information (this example uses Mail).

2. Tap the Compose button.

3. Tap the Add (+) button in the To field.

4. Search, browse, or use the index to find the contact whose information you want to use.

5. Tap the contact whose information you want to use. (If a contact doesn't have relevant information, for example, if no email address is configured when you are using the Mail app, that contact is grayed out and can't be selected.)

   If the contact has only one type of the relevant information

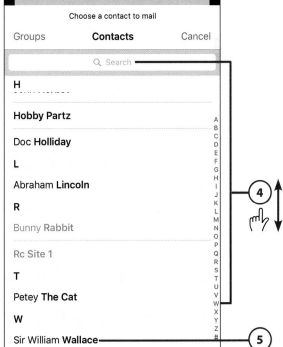

(such as a single email address, if you started in the Mail app), you immediately move back to the app and the appropriate information is entered, and you can skip to step 7.

(6) If the contact has multiple entries of the type you are trying to use, tap the information you want to use— in this case, the email address. The information is copied into the app and entered in the appropriate location.

(7) Complete the task you are doing, such as sending an email message.

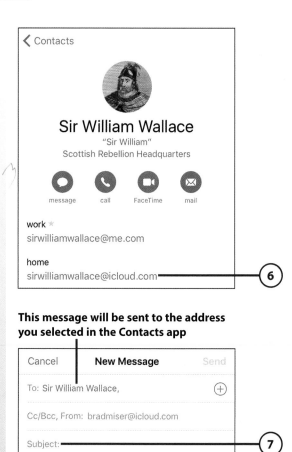

This message will be sent to the address you selected in the Contacts app

Managing Your Contacts on Your iPhone

When you sync contacts with an iCloud account, Google account, or other accounts, the changes go both ways. For example, when you change a contact on the iPhone, the synced contact manager application, such as Contacts, makes the changes for those contacts on your computer. Likewise, when you change contact information in a contact manager on your computer, those changes move to the iPhone. If you add a new contact in a contact manager, it moves to the iPhone, and vice versa. You can also change contacts manually in the Contacts app on your iPhone.

Updating Contact Information

You can change any information for an existing contact, such as adding new email addresses, deleting outdated information, and changing existing information.

1. View the contact's Info screen.

2. Tap Edit. The contact screen moves into Edit mode, and you see Unlock buttons.

3. Tap current information to change it; you can change a field's label by tapping it, or you can change the data for the field by tapping the information you want to change. Use the resulting tools, such as the phone number entry keypad, to make changes to the information. These tools work just like when you create a new contact (refer to "Creating Contacts Manually," earlier in this chapter).

4. To add more fields, tap Add (+) in the related section, such as add phone in the phone number section; then, select a label for the new field and complete its information. This also works just like adding a new field to a contact you created manually.

5. Tap a field's Unlock (–) button to remove that field from the contact.

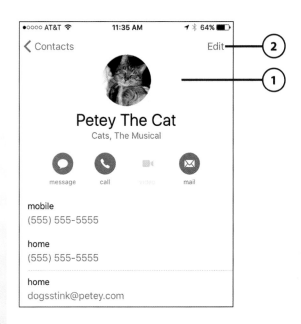

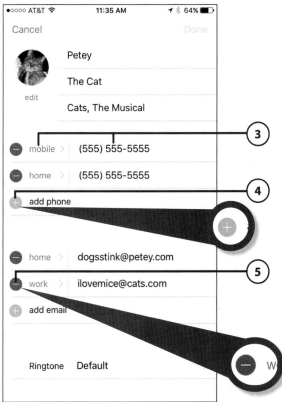

6 Tap Delete. The information is removed from the contact.

7 To change the contact's photo, tap the current photo, or the word *edit* under the current photo, and use the resulting menu and tools to select a new photo, take a new photo, delete the existing photo, or edit the existing one.

8 When you finish making changes, tap Done. Your changes are saved, and you move out of Edit mode.

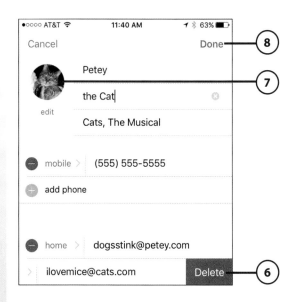

No Tones or Vibes?

If you leave the default tones or vibration patterns set for a contact, you won't see those fields when you view the contact. However, when you edit a contact, all the fields you need to add these to a contact become available.

Adding Information to an Existing Contact While Using Your iPhone

As you use your iPhone, you'll encounter information related to a contact that isn't currently part of that contact's information. For example, a contact might send you an email from a different email address than the one you have stored for her. When this happens, you can easily add the new information to the existing contact. Just tap the information to view it (such as an email address), and then tap Add to Existing Contact. Next, select the existing contact to which you want to add the new information. The new information is added to the contact. Depending on your iPhone model, tap Update or Done (or Cancel, if you decide not to keep the new information) to return to the app you are working in.

Deleting Contacts

To get rid of contacts, you can delete
them from the Contacts app.

(1) Find and view the contact you
want to delete.

(2) Tap Edit.

(3) Swipe up to get to the bottom
of the Info screen.

(4) Tap Delete Contact.

(5) Tap Delete Contact to confirm
the deletion. The app deletes
the contact, and you return to
the Contacts screen.

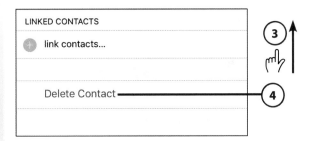

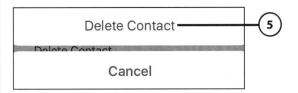

Tap to configure
Phone and FaceTime
settings

Tap to hear *and*
see the person
you want to talk
to

Tap to make calls,
listen to voicemail,
and more

In this chapter, you explore all the cell phone and FaceTime functionality that your iPhone has to offer. The topics include the following:

→ Getting started
→ Configuring phone settings
→ Making voice calls
→ Managing in-process voice calls
→ Receiving voice calls
→ Managing voice calls
→ Using visual voicemail
→ Communicating with FaceTime

Communicating with the Phone and FaceTime Apps

Although it's also a lot of other great things, such as a music player, web browser, email tool, and such, there's a reason the word *phone* is in *iPhone*. It's a feature-rich cell phone with amazing functionality, including visual voicemail, FaceTime, a speakerphone, conference calling, and easy-to-use onscreen controls. Plus your iPhone's phone functions are integrated with its other features. For example, when using the Maps application, you might find a location, such as a business, that you're interested in contacting. You can call that location just by tapping the number you want to call directly from the Maps screen.

Getting Started

Some of the key concepts you'll learn about in this chapter include:

- **Phone app**—The iPhone can run many different kinds of apps that do all sorts of useful things. The iPhone's cell phone functionality is provided by the Phone app. You use this app whenever you want to make calls, answer calls, or listen to voicemail.

- **Visual Voicemail**—The Phone app shows you information about your voicemails, such as the person who left each message, a time and date stamp, and the length of the message. The Phone app provides a lot more control over your messages, too; for example, you can easily fast forward to specific parts of a message that you want to hear. (This is particularly helpful for capturing information, such as phone numbers.) And if that wasn't enough, you can also read transcripts of voicemails so you don't have to listen to them at all.

- **FaceTime**—This app enables you to have videoconferences with other people (using iPhones or Mac computers) so that you can both see and hear them. Using FaceTime is intuitive so you won't find it any more difficult than making a phone call.

- **FaceTime Audio**—You can make FaceTime calls using only audio; this is similar to making a phone call. One difference is that when you are using a Wi-Fi network to place a FaceTime audio call, there are no extra costs for the call, no matter if you are calling someone next-door or halfway around the world.

Configuring Phone Settings

Of course, we all know that your ringtone is the most important phone setting, and you'll want to make sure your iPhone's ringtones are just right. Use the iPhone's Sounds settings to configure custom or standard ringtones and other phone-related sounds, including the new voicemail sound. These are explained in Chapter 6, "Customizing How Your iPhone Looks and Sounds."

You can also have different ringtones for specific people so you can know who is calling just by the ringtone (configuring contacts is explained in Chapter 7, "Managing Contacts").

And you'll want to configure notifications for the Phone app. These include alerts, the app's badge, and sounds. Configuring notifications is explained in Chapter 2, "Using Your iPhone's Core Features."

It is likely that you can use the Phone app with its default settings just fine. However, you might want to take advantage of some of its features by configuring the settings described in the following table. To access these settings, open the Settings app and tap Phone.

Provider Differences

The settings for the Phone app depend on the cell phone provider you use. The table lists most, but certainly not all, of the options you might have available. Depending on the provider you use, you may see more, fewer, or different settings than shown in the table. It's a good idea to open your Phone settings to see the options available to you.

Phone Settings

Section	Setting	Description
N/A	My Number	Shows your phone number for reference purposes.
CALLS	Announce Calls	When you enable this setting, the name of the caller (when available) is announced when the phone rings. Tap Always to always have the name announced, Headphones & Car to have the caller announced only when you are using headphones or your car's audio system, Headphones Only to have announcements only when you are using headphones, or Never if you don't want these announcements.
CALLS	Call Blocking & Identification	Tap this to see a list of people who you are currently blocking. You can tap someone on the list to see more information or swipe to the left and tap Unblock to unblock someone. Tap Block Contact to block someone in your Contacts app.

Section	Setting	Description
CALLS	Wi-Fi Calling	When enabled, you can place and receive calls via a Wi-Fi network. This is particularly useful when you are in a location with poor cellular reception, but you have access to a Wi-Fi network. When you set the Wi-Fi Calling on This iPhone switch to on (green), you're prompted to confirm your information. When you do, the service starts and you see the Update Emergency Address option; this is used to record your address so if you can place emergency calls via Wi-Fi, your location can be determined. Note that even when you see this option, it might not be supported in your area. You need to try configuring it to know for sure.
CALLS	Calls on Other Devices	When enabled, and your iPhone is on the same network as other iOS devices (such as iPads) or Macs, you can take incoming calls and place calls from those devices. This can be useful when you aren't near your phone or simply want to use a different device to have a phone conversation. It can also be annoying because when a call comes in, all the devices using this feature start "ringing." When the Allow Calls on Other Devices switch is on (green), you can choose the specific devices calls are allowed on by setting their switches to on (green).
CALLS	Respond with Text	When calls come in, you have the option to respond with text. For example, you might want to say "Can't talk now, will call later." There are three default text responses or you can use this setting to create your own custom text responses.
CALLS	Call Forwarding	Enables you to forward incoming calls to a different phone number.
CALLS	Call Waiting	Enables or disables the call waiting feature.

Section	Setting	Description
CALLS	Show My Caller ID	Shows or hides your caller ID information when you place a call.
CALLS	Blocked	Enables you to block incoming calls and text messages. Step-by-step instructions to block calls are in online Chapter 17, "Maintaining and Protecting Your iPhone and Solving Problems."
N/A	Change Voicemail Password	Use this option to change your voicemail password.
N/A	Dial Assist	Enable the Dial Assist feature if you want the correct country code to be added to numbers in your country when dialing those numbers from outside your country or if you want the correct area codes to be added when you dial a local number. For example, if you live in the United States and don't want the correct prefixes added to U.S. phone numbers when you dial them from outside the United States, turn off Dial Assist (white). You then have to add any prefixes manually when dialing a U.S. number from outside the United States.
N/A	SIM PIN	Your iPhone uses a Subscriber Identity Module (SIM) card to store certain data about your phone; the SIM PIN setting enables you to associate a personal ID number (PIN) with the SIM card in an iPhone. To use your account with a different phone, you can remove the SIM card from your iPhone and install it in other phones that support these cards. If you set a PIN, that PIN is required to use the card in a different phone.
N/A	*Provider* Services, where *Provider* is the name of your provider	This area provides information about your account, such as the numbers you can dial for checking balances, paying bills, and other account management. You can also access your account by tapping the link at the bottom of the screen.

Making Voice Calls

There are a number of ways to make calls with your iPhone; after a call is in progress, you can manage it in the same way no matter how you started it.

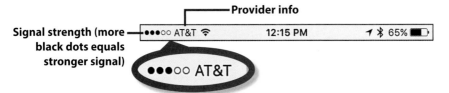

Provider info

Signal strength (more black dots equals stronger signal)

You can tell you are able to make a call or receive calls using your cellular network when you see your provider's information at the top of the screen along with the strength of the signal your phone is receiving. As long as you see at least one dark dot, you should be able to place and receive calls via the cellular network. More dots are better because they mean you have a stronger signal, meaning the call quality will be better.

Wi-Fi calling is available

If the Wi-Fi calling feature is enabled and your phone is connected to a Wi-Fi network, you see the Wi-Fi calling icon for your provider at the top of the screen.

With a reasonably strong cellular signal or connection to a Wi-Fi network with Wi-Fi calling enabled, you are ready to make calls.

Which Network?

When you leave the coverage area for your provider and move into an area that is covered by another provider that supports roaming, your iPhone automatically connects to the other provider's network. When you are roaming, you see a different provider near the signal strength indicator at the top of the screen. For example, if AT&T is your provider and you travel to Toronto, Canada, the provider might become Rogers instead of AT&T, which indicates you are roaming. (In some cases, your provider might send you a text message explaining the change in networks, including information about roaming charges.) Although the connection is automatic, you need to be aware of roaming charges, which can be significant depending on where you use your iPhone and what your default network is. Before you travel outside of your default network's coverage, check with your provider to determine the roaming rates that apply to where you are going. Also, see if there is a discounted roaming plan for that location. If you don't do this before you leave, you might get a nasty surprise when the bill arrives because roaming charges can be substantial.

Dialing with the Keypad

The most obvious way to make a call is to dial the number.

1. On the Home screen, tap Phone. The Phone app opens.

2. If you don't see the keypad, tap Keypad.

3. Tap numbers on the keypad to dial the number you want to call. If you dial a number associated with one or more contacts, you see the contact's name and the type of number you've dialed just under the number. (If you make a mistake in the number you are dialing, tap the Delete button located to the right of the number you are dialing at the top of the screen to delete the most recent digit you entered.)

4. Tap the receiver button. The app dials the number, and the Call screen appears.

5. Use the Call (not shown) screen to manage the call; see "Managing In-Process Voice Calls" for the details.

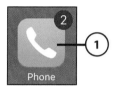

Phone

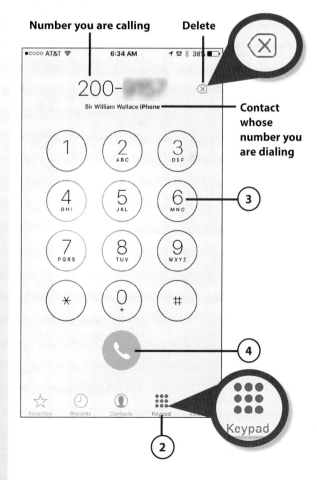

Number you are calling   **Delete**

Contact whose number you are dialing

Keypad

Nobody's Perfect

If your iPhone can't complete the call for some reason, such as not having a strong enough signal, the Call Failed screen appears. Tap Call Back to try again and maybe try moving to another location that might have a stronger signal or tap Done to give up. When you tap Done, you return to the screen from which you came.

Dialing with Recents

As you make, receive, or miss calls, your iPhone keeps tracks of all the numbers on the Recents list. You can use the Recents list to make calls.

1. On the Home screen, tap Phone.

2. Tap Recents.

3. Tap All to see all calls.

4. Tap Missed to see only calls you missed.

5. If necessary, browse the list of calls.

6. To call the number associated with a recent call, tap the title of the call, such as a person's name, or the number if no contact is associated with it. The app dials the number, and the Call screen appears. Skip to step 10.

7. To get more information about a recent call, for example, to see exactly what time yesterday the call was made, tap its Info button (i). The Info screen appears.

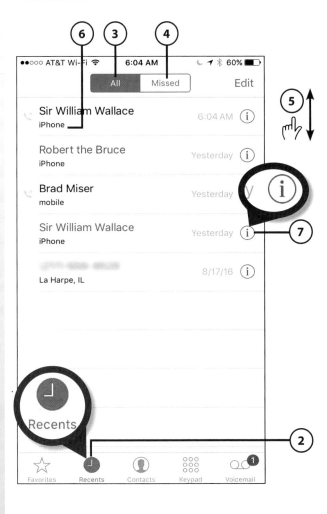

Info on the Recents Screen

If you have a contact on your iPhone associated with a phone number, you see the person's name and the label for the number (such as mobile). If you don't have a contact for a number, you see the number itself. If a contact or number has more than one call associated with it, you see the number of recent calls in parentheses next to the name or number. If you initiated a call, you see the phone icon next to the contact's name and label.

8 Read the information about the call or calls. For example, if the call is related to someone in your Contacts list, you see detailed information for that contact. If there are multiple recent calls, you see information for each call, such as its status (Missed Call, Canceled Call, or Outgoing Call, for example) and time.

9 Tap a number on the Info screen. The app dials the number, and the Call screen appears.

Going Back

To return to the Recents screen without making a call, tap Recents located in the top-left corner of the screen.

10 Use the Call screen to manage the call (not shown); see "Managing In-Process Voice Calls" later in this chapter for the details.

Dialing from the FAVORITES Widget

New! Using the FAVORITES widget, you can quickly call a favorite. Use the following steps.

Managing Widgets

If you don't see the FAVORITES widget, you need to add it. See Chapter 2 for the steps to manage your widgets.

(1) From the Home or Lock screen, swipe to the right to open your widgets.

(2) Swipe up or down until you see the FAVORITES widget.

(3) Tap Show More to see the full list of favorites. The list expands.

(4) Tap the person you want to call.

(5) Use the Call screen to manage the call (not shown); see the next section for the details.

You've Got the Touch

If your iPhone supports 3D Touch (iPhone 6s/6s Plus and later), you can also place calls to favorites by pressing on the Phone app. The FAVORITES pane appears; tap a favorite to place a call. You can also access the most recent voicemail or see the most recent call.

Managing In-Process Voice Calls

When you place a call, there are several ways to manage it. The most obvious is to place your iPhone next to your ear and use your iPhone like any other phone you've ever used. As you place your iPhone next to your ear, the controls on its screen become disabled so you don't accidentally tap onscreen buttons with the side of your face or your ear. When you take your iPhone away from your ear, the Call screen appears again and the iPhone app's controls become active again.

When you are on a call, press the Volume buttons on the left side of the iPhone to increase or decrease its volume. Some of the other things you can do while on a call might not be so obvious, as you learn in the next few tasks.

Following are some of the buttons on the Call screen that you can use to manage an active call:

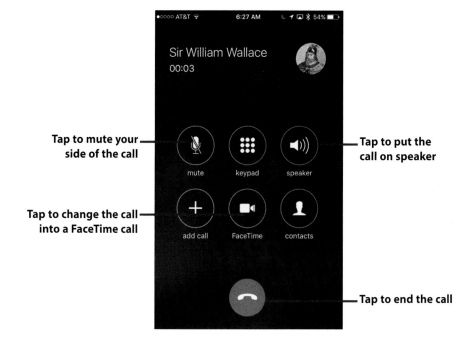

- Mute your side of the call by tapping Mute. You can hear the person on the other side of the call, but he can't hear anything on your side.

- Tap Speaker to use the iPhone's speakers to hear the call. You can speak with the phone held away from your face, too.

- Tap FaceTime to convert the voice call into a FaceTime call (read more on FaceTime later in this chapter).

- When you're done with the call, tap the receiver button to hang up.

Contact Photos on the Call Screen

If someone in your contacts calls you, or you call her, the photo associated with the contact appears on the screen. Depending on how the image was captured, it either appears as a small icon at the top of the screen next to the contact's name or fills the entire screen as the background wallpaper.

Entering Numbers During a Call

You often need to enter numbers during a call, such as to log in to a voicemail system, access an account, or enter a meeting code for an online meeting.

1. Place a call using any of the methods you've learned so far.

2. Tap Keypad.

3 Tap the numbers you want to enter.

4 When you're done, tap Hide. You return to the Call screen.

Making Conference Calls

Your iPhone makes it easy to talk to multiple people at the same time. You can have two separate calls going on at any point in time. You can even create conference calls by merging them together. Not all cell providers support two on-going calls or conference calling, though. If yours doesn't, you won't be able to perform the steps in this section.

1 Place a call using any of the methods you've learned so far.

2 Tap add call.

3 Tap the button you want to use to place the next call. Tap Favorites to call a favorite, tap Recents to use the Recents list, tap Contacts to place the call using the Contacts app, or tap Keypad to dial the number. These work just as they do when you start a new call.

4 Place the call using the option you selected in step 3. Doing so places the first call on hold and moves you back to the Call screen while the Phone app makes the second call. The first call's information appears at the top of the screen, including the word hold so you know the first call is on hold. The app displays the second call just below that, and it is currently the active call.

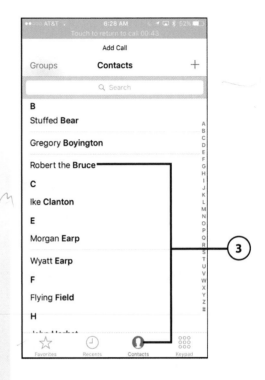

Similar but Different

If you tap contacts instead of add call, you move directly into the Contacts screen. This might save you one screen tap if the person you want to add to the call is in your Contacts app.

(5) Talk to the second person you called; the first remains on hold.

(6) To switch to the first call, tap it on the list or tap swap. This places the second call on hold and moves it to the top of the call list, while the first call becomes active again.

(7) Tap merge calls to join the calls so all parties can hear you and each other. The iPhone combines the two calls, and you see a single entry at the top of the screen to reflect this.

Merging Calls

As you merge calls, your iPhone attempts to display the names of the callers at the top of the Call screen. As the text increases, your iPhone scrolls it so you can read it. Eventually, the iPhone replaces the names with the word Conference.

Number of Callers

Your provider and the specific technology of the network you use can limit the number of callers you place in a conference call. When you reach the limit, the add call button is disabled.

(5)
The first call is placed on hold

(6)

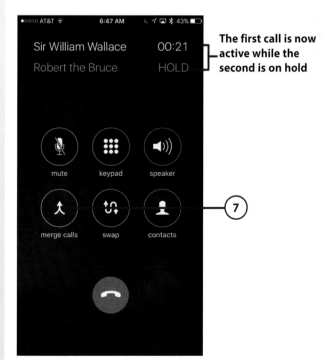

The first call is now active while the second is on hold

(7)

8 To add another call, repeat steps 2–7. Each time you merge calls, the second line becomes free so you can add more calls.

9 To manage a conference call, tap the Info button (i) at the top of the screen.

10 To speak with one of the callers privately, tap Private (if the Private buttons are disabled, you can't do this with the current calls). Doing so places the conference call on hold and returns you to the Call screen showing information about the active call. You can merge the calls again by tapping merge calls.

11 Tap End to remove a caller from the call. The app disconnects that caller from the conference call. When you have only one person left on the call, you return to the Call screen and see information about the active call.

12 Tap Back to move back to the Call screen. You move to the Call screen and can continue working with the call, such as adding more people to it.

13 To end the call for all callers, tap the receiver button.

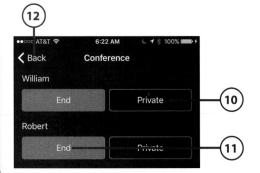

It's Not All Good

Watch Your Minutes

When you have multiple calls combined into one, depending on your provider, the minutes for each call can continue to count individually. So if you've joined three people into one call, each minute of the call might count as three minutes against your calling plan. Before you use this feature, check with your provider to determine what policies govern conference calling for your account.

Using Another App During a Voice Call

Tap to return to the call ——————————

A call is active, and you can use other apps while still talking

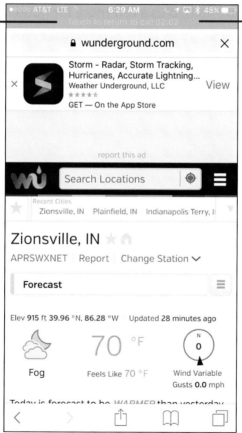

If your provider's technology supports it, you can use your iPhone for other tasks while you are on a call. When you are on a call, press the Touch ID/Home button once to move to the Home screen and then tap a different app (placing the call in speaker mode before you switch to a different app or using the headphones

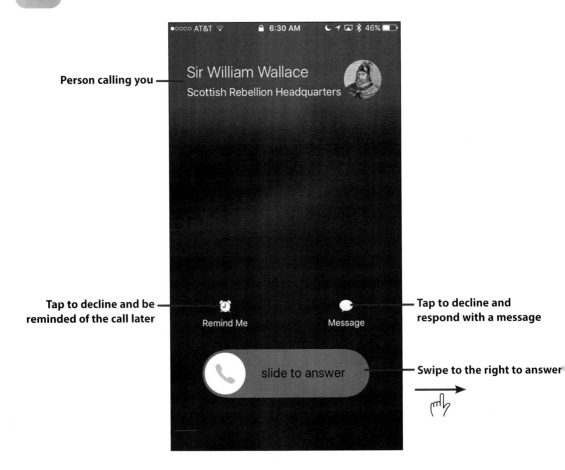

Person calling you —

Sir William Wallace
Scottish Rebellion Headquarters

Tap to decline and be —
reminded of the call later

Remind Me

Message

— Tap to decline and
respond with a message

slide to answer

— Swipe to the right to answer

- **Silence the ringer**—To silence the ringer without sending the call directly to voicemail, press the Sleep/Wake button once or press either volume button. The call continues to come in, and you can answer it even though you shut off the ringer.

- **Respond with a message**—Tap Message to send the call to voicemail and send a message back in response. You can tap one of the default messages, or you can tap Custom to create a unique message (earlier in the chapter, you learned where you can configure these messages). Of course, the device the caller is using to make the call must be capable of receiving messages for this to be useful.

- **Decline the call but be reminded later**—Tap Remind Me and the call is sent to voicemail. Tap In 1 hour or When I leave to set the timeframe in which you want to be reminded. A reminder is created in the Reminders app to call back the person who called you, and it is set to alert you at the time you select.

Silencio!

To mute your iPhone's ringer, slide the Mute switch located above the Volume switch toward the back so the orange line appears. The Mute icon (a bell with a slash through it) appears on the screen to let you know you turned off the ringer. To turn it on again, slide the switch forward. The bell icon appears on the screen to show you the ringer is active again. To set the ringer's volume, use the Volume controls (assuming that setting is enabled) when you aren't on a call and aren't listening to an app, such as the Music app.

Answering Calls During a Call

As mentioned earlier, your iPhone can manage multiple calls at the same time. If you are on a call and another call comes in, you have a number of ways to respond.

- **Decline incoming call**—Tap Send to Voicemail to send the incoming call directly to voicemail. (Note that the caller can't tell that you declined a call, it simply goes to voicemail.)
- **Place the first call on hold and answer the incoming call**—Tap Hold & Accept to place the current call on hold and answer the incoming one. After you do this, you can manage the two calls just as when you call two numbers from your iPhone. For example, you can place the second call on hold and move back to the first one, merge the calls, and add more calls.
- **End the first call and answer the incoming call**—Tap End & Accept to terminate the active call and answer the incoming call.
- **Respond with message or get reminded later**—These options work just as they do when you are dealing with any incoming phone call.

Auto-Mute

If you are listening to music or video when a call comes in, the app providing the audio, such as the Music app, automatically pauses. When the call ends, that app picks up right where it left off.

Managing Voice Calls

You've already learned most of what you need to know to use your iPhone's cell phone functions. In the following sections, you learn the rest.

Clearing Recent Calls

Previously in this chapter, you learned about the Recents tool that tracks call activity on your iPhone. As you read, this list shows both completed and missed calls; you can view all calls by tapping the All tab or only missed calls by tapping Missed. On either tab, missed calls are always in red, and you see the number of missed calls in the badge on the Recents tab since you last looked at the list. You also see how you can get more detail about a call, whether it was missed or made.

Over time, you'll build a large Recents list, which you can easily clear.

1 Tap Phone.

2 Tap Recents.

3 Tap Edit.

4 Tap Clear to clear the entire list; to delete a specific recent call, skip to step 6.

5 Tap Clear All Recents. The Recents list is reset.

Delete Faster

On the Recents screen, you can delete an individual recent item by swiping to the left on it (starting to the left of the i button) and tapping Delete.

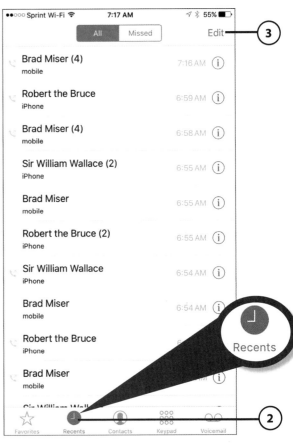

6 Tap a recent item's unlock button.

7 Tap Delete. The recent item is deleted.

8 When you are done managing your recent calls, tap Done.

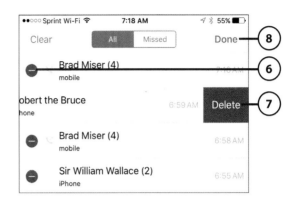

Adding Calling Information to Favorites

Earlier you learned how simple it is to place calls to someone on your Favorites list. There are a number of ways to add people to this list, including adding someone on your Recents list.

1 Move to the Recents list.

2 Tap the Info button (i) for the person you want to add to your favorites list. The Info screen appears. If the number is associated with a contact, you see that contact's information.

3 Swipe up to move to the bottom of the screen.

4 Tap Add to Favorites. If the person has multiple types of contact information, such as phone numbers, email addresses, and so on, you see each type of information available.

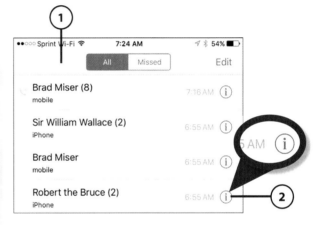

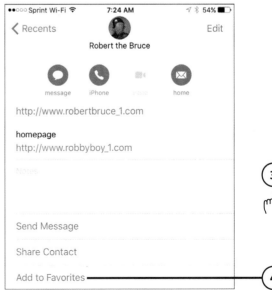

Finding and Listening to Voicemails

Working with voicemails is simple and quick.

1. Move into the Phone app and tap Voicemail (if you pressed or swiped on a new message notification, you jump directly to the Voicemail screen).

2. Swipe up and down the screen to browse the list of voicemails. Voicemails you haven't listened to are marked with a blue circle.

3. To listen to or read a voicemail, tap it. You see the timeline bar and controls and the message plays.

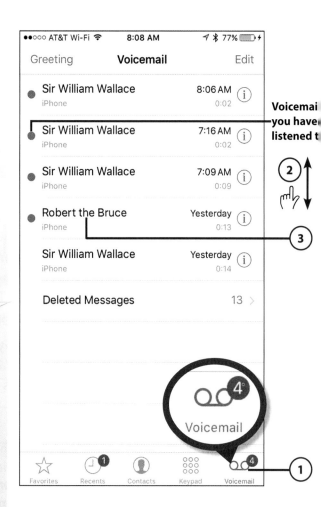

Voicemai
you have
listened t

④ Read the message if you don't want to listen to it.

⑤ Tap the Pause button to pause a message.

⑥ Tap Speaker to hear the message on your iPhone's speaker.

⑦ To move to a specific point in a message, drag the Playhead to the point at which you want to listen.

Moving Ahead or Behind

You can also drag the Playhead while a message is playing to rewind or fast-forward it. This is also helpful when you want to listen to specific information without hearing the whole message again.

⑧ Tap Call Back to call back the person who left the message.

⑨ Tap Delete to delete the message.

⑩ Tap the Share button to share the message, and then tap how you want to share it, such as Message or Mail. For example, when you tap Mail, you send the voicemail to someone else using the Mail app, so he can listen to the message.

⑪ Tap the Info button (i) to get more information about a message. The Info screen appears. If the person who left the message is on your contacts list, you see her contact information. The number associated with the message is highlighted in blue.

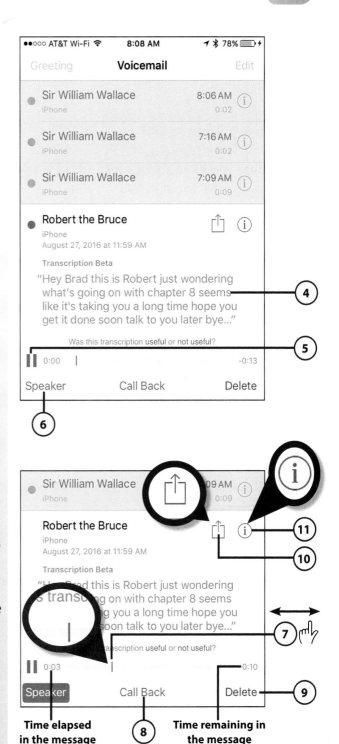

Time elapsed in the message

⑧

Time remaining in the message

(12) Swipe up or down the screen to review the caller's information.

(13) Tap Voicemail.

(14) To listen to a message you have listened to before (one that doesn't have a blue dot), tap the message and then tap the Play button. It begins to play. You can also read its transcript.

Deleting Messages

To delete a voicemail message that isn't the active message, tap it so it becomes the active message and then tap Delete. Or swipe to the left on the message you want to delete, and then tap Delete. Or swipe quickly all the way to the left on the message to delete it.

Listening to and Managing Deleted Voicemails

When you delete messages, they are moved to the Deleted Message folder. You can work with deleted messages as follows:

(1) Move to the Voicemail screen.

(2) If necessary, swipe up the screen until you see the Deleted Messages option.

(3) Tap Deleted Messages.

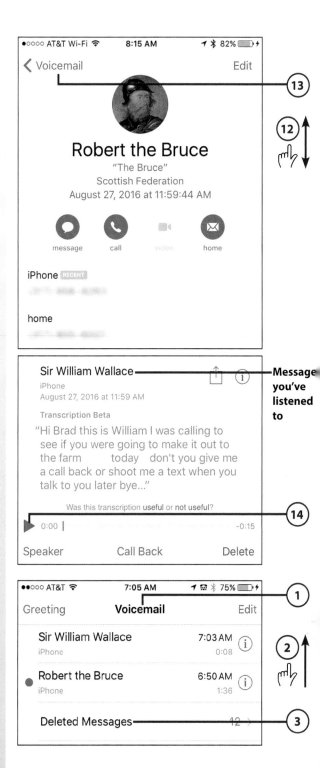

●○○○○ AT&T Wi-Fi 📶　　8:15 AM　　　🛬 ✳ 82% 🔋⚡

❮ Voicemail　　　　　　　　　Edit

Robert the Bruce
"The Bruce"
Scottish Federation
August 27, 2016 at 11:59:44 AM

　message　　call　　video　　home

iPhone RECENT

home

Sir William Wallace
iPhone
August 27, 2016 at 11:59 AM

Transcription Beta

"Hi Brad this is William I was calling to see if you were going to make it out to the farm　　today　don't you give me a call back or shoot me a text when you talk to you later bye..."

Was this transcription useful or not useful?

▶ 0:00 |　　　　　　　　　　-0:15

Speaker　　　Call Back　　　Delete

●●○○○ AT&T 📶　　7:05 AM　　🛬 📼 ✳ 75% 🔋⚡

Greeting　　**Voicemail**　　Edit

Sir William Wallace　　7:03 AM ⓘ
iPhone　　　　　　　　　0:08

● Robert the Bruce　　6:50 AM ⓘ
iPhone　　　　　　　　　1:36

Deleted Messages　　　　12 ❯

Message you've listened to

What's Missed?

In case you're wondering, your iPhone considers any call you didn't answer to be a missed call, if you just didn't answer the call or declined it. So if someone calls and leaves a message, that call is included in the counts of both missed calls and new voicemails. If the caller leaves a message, you see a notification informing you that you have a new voicemail and showing who it is from (if available). If you don't answer and the caller doesn't leave a message, it's counted only as a missed call and you see a notification showing a missed call along with the caller's identification (if available).

4 Swipe up or down the screen to browse all the deleted messages.

5 Tap a message to listen to it or to read its transcript.

6 Tap the Play button to hear the message. You can use the other playback tools just like you can with undeleted messages.

7 Tap Undelete to restore the deleted message. The iPhone restores the message to the Voicemail screen.

8 Tap Clear All to remove all deleted messages permanently. (If this is disabled, close the open message by tapping it.)

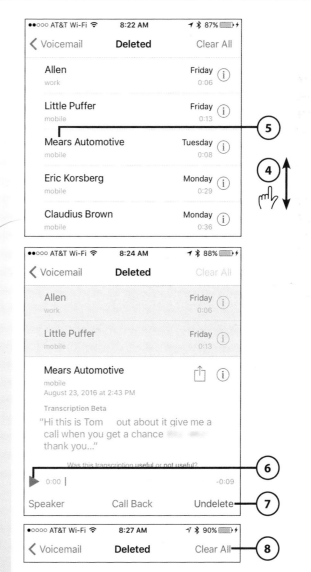

9. Tap Clear All at the prompt. The deleted messages are erased and you return to the Deleted screen.

10. Tap Voicemail to return to the Voicemail screen.

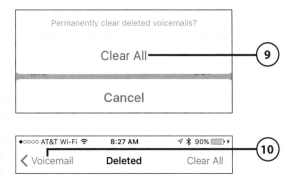

Lost/Forgot Your Password?

If you have to restore your iPhone or it loses your voicemail password for some other reason and you can't remember it, you need to have the password reset to access your voicemail on the iPhone. For most cell phone providers, this involves calling the customer support number and accessing an automated system that sends a new password to you via a text message. For AT&T, which is one of the iPhone providers in the United States, call 611 on your iPhone and follow the prompts to reset your password (which you receive via a text). No matter which provider you use, it's a good idea to know how to reset your voicemail password because it is likely you will need to do so at some point.

Communicating with FaceTime

FaceTime enables you to see, as well as hear, people with whom you want to communicate. This feature exemplifies what's great about the iPhone; it takes complex technology and makes it simple. FaceTime works great, but there are two conditions that have to be true for you and the people you want some FaceTime with. To be able to see each other, both sides have to use a device that has the required cameras (this includes iPhone 4s and newer, iPod touches third generation and newer, iPad 2s and newer, and Macs running Snow Leopard and newer), and have FaceTime enabled (via the settings on an iOS device as you saw earlier or via the FaceTime application on a Mac). And each device has to be able to communicate over a network; an iPhone or cellular iPad can use a cellular data network (if that setting is enabled) or a Wi-Fi network while Macs have to be connected to the Internet through a Wi-Fi or other type of network. When these conditions are true, making and receiving FaceTime calls are simple tasks.

In addition to making video FaceTime calls, you can also make audio-only FaceTime calls. These work similarly to making a voice call except the minutes don't count against your voice plan when you use a Wi-Fi network (if you are making the call over the cellular network, the data does count against your data plan, so be careful about this).

Assuming you are in a place where you don't have to pay for the data you use, such as when you use a Wi-Fi network, you don't have to pay for a FaceTime call (video or audio-only) either.

Configuring FaceTime Settings

FaceTime is a great way to use your iPhone to hear and see someone else. There are a few FaceTime settings you need to configure for FaceTime to work. You can connect with other FaceTime users via your phone number, an email address, or your Apple ID.

1. Move to the Settings screen.

2. Tap FaceTime.

3. If the FaceTime switch is off (white), tap the FaceTime switch to turn it on (green). If the FaceTime switch is on and you see an Apple ID, you are already signed into an account; in this case, you see the current FaceTime settings and can follow along starting with step 7 to change these settings. You can sign out of the current account by tapping it, and then tapping Sign Out; proceed to step 4 to sign in with a different account.

4 To use your Apple ID for FaceTime calls, tap Use your Apple ID for FaceTime. If you don't sign in to an Apple ID, you can still use FaceTime, but it is always via your cellular connection, which isn't ideal because then FaceTime counts under your voice minutes on your calling plan or as data on your data plan.

5 Enter your Apple ID and password. (An Apple ID might be entered already; if so, you can use it or replace it with a different one.)

6 Tap Sign In.

7 Configure the email addresses you want people to use to contact you for FaceTime sessions by tapping them to enable each address (enabled addresses are marked with a check mark) or to disable addresses (these don't have a check mark). (If you don't have any email addresses configured on your iPhone, you are prompted to enter email addresses.)

8 Tap the phone number or email address by which you will be identified to the other caller during a FaceTime call.

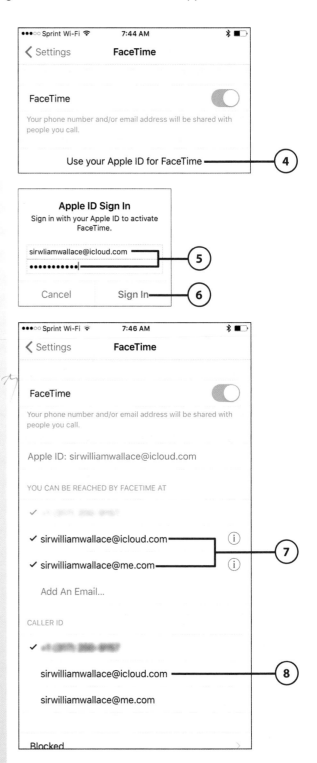

Managing Addresses

You can add more email addresses at any time by tapping Add An Email and following the onscreen prompts to add and confirm the new addresses. To remove an address from FaceTime, tap its Info button (i) and then tap Remove This Email.

Blocking FaceTime

If you tap Blocked at the bottom of the FaceTime Settings screen, you can block people from making calls, sending messages, or making FaceTime requests to your iPhone. Tap Add New and then tap the contact you want to block.

Making FaceTime Calls

FaceTime is a great way to communicate with someone because you can hear and see him (or just hear him if you choose an audio-only FaceTime call). Because iPhones have cameras facing each way, it's also easy to show something to the person you are talking with. You make FaceTime calls starting from the FaceTime, Contacts, or Phone apps and from the FAVORITES widget. No matter which way you start a FaceTime session, you manage it in the same way.

Careful

If your iPhone is connected to a Wi-Fi network, you can make all the FaceTime calls you want because you have unlimited data. However, if you are using the cellular data network, be aware that FaceTime calls may use data under your data plan. If you have a limited plan, it's a good idea to use FaceTime primarily when you are connected to a Wi-Fi network. (Refer to Chapter 3, "Connecting Your iPhone to the Internet, Bluetooth Devices, and iPhones/iPods/iPads," for information on connecting to Wi-Fi networks.)

To start a FaceTime call from the Contacts app, do the following:

(1) Use the Contacts app to open the contact with whom you want to chat (refer to Chapter 7 for information about using the Contacts app).

Playing Favorites

If you've set a FaceTime contact as a favorite, you can open the Phone app, tap Favorites, and tap the FaceTime favorite to start the FaceTime session.

(2) To place an audio-only FaceTime call, tap the FaceTime audio button. (The rest of these steps show a FaceTime video call, but a FaceTime audio-only is very similar to voice calls described earlier in this chapter.)

(3) Tap the contact's FaceTime video button. The iPhone attempts to make a FaceTime connection. You hear the FaceTime "chirping" and see status information on the screen while the call is attempted. When the connection is complete, you hear a different tone and see the other person in the large window and a preview of what he is seeing (whatever your iPhone's front-side camera is pointing at—

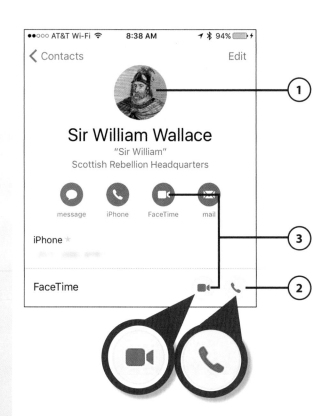

mostly likely your face—in the small window. If the person you are trying to FaceTime with isn't available for FaceTime for some reason (perhaps he doesn't have a FaceTime-capable device or is not connected to the Internet), you see a message saying that the person you are calling is unavailable for FaceTime and the call terminates.

4 After the call is accepted, manage the call as described in the "Managing FaceTime Calls" task later in this chapter.

Preview window

4

>>>Go Further

MORE INFORMATION ABOUT FACETIME CALLS

As you make FaceTime calls, following are some other bits of information for your consideration:

- **Failing FaceTime**—If a FaceTime request fails, you can't really tell the reason why. It can be a technical issue, such as none of the contact information you have is FaceTime-enabled, the person is not signed into a device, or the person might have declined the request. If you repeatedly have trouble connecting with someone, contact him to make sure he has a FaceTime-capable device and that you are using the correct FaceTime contact information.

- **Leave a Message**—On the FaceTime Unavailable screen, you can tap Leave a Message to send a text or iMessage message to the person with whom you are trying to FaceTime.

- **Transform a call**—You can transform a voice call into a FaceTime session by tapping the FaceTime button on the Call screen. When you transform a call into a FaceTime session, the minutes no longer count against the minutes in your calling plan because all communication happens over the Wi-Fi network or your cellular data plan if you enabled that option and aren't connected to a Wi-Fi network. (The voice call you started from automatically terminates when the switch is made.)

- **FaceTime app**—To use the FaceTime app to start a call, tap the FaceTime icon on the Home screen. Tap the Video tab to make a video call or the Audio tab to make an audio-only call. Tap the Add (+) button to use your contacts to start the call. You can also enter a name, email address, or phone number in the bar at the top of the screen (if you haven't made or received any FaceTime calls before, you won't see the tabs until you make your first call). Tap a person on the Recents list to place a FaceTime call to that person. Once you've connected, you manage the FaceTime session as described in the rest of this chapter.

- **FaceTime with Siri**—You can also place a FaceTime call using Siri by activating Siri and saying "FaceTime *name*" where *name* is the name of the person with whom you want to FaceTime. If there are multiple options for that contact, you must tell Siri which you want to use. After you've made a selection, Siri starts the FaceTime call.

- **FaceTime with the FAVORITES widget**—And for yet another option, you can open the FAVORITES widget and tap the FaceTime icon for the person with whom you want to have a FaceTime conversation.

Receiving FaceTime Calls

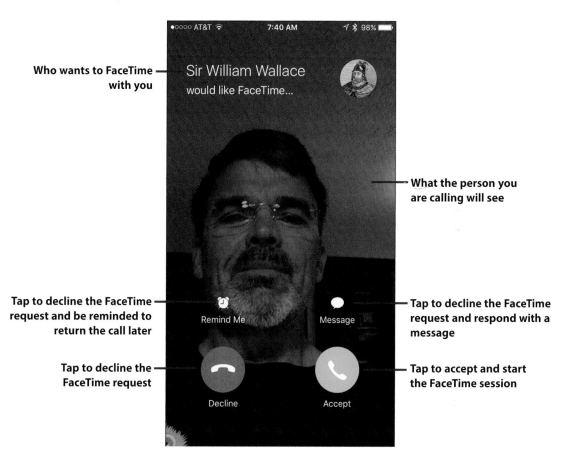

Who wants to FaceTime with you

What the person you are calling will see

Tap to decline the FaceTime request and be reminded to return the call later

Tap to decline the FaceTime request and respond with a message

Tap to decline the FaceTime request

Tap to accept and start the FaceTime session

When someone tries to FaceTime with you, you see the incoming FaceTime request screen message showing who is trying to connect with you and the image you are currently broadcasting. Tap Accept to accept the request and start the FaceTime session. Manage the FaceTime call as described in the upcoming "Managing FaceTime Calls" task.

Tap Remind Me to decline the FaceTime request and create a reminder or Message to decline the request and send a message. These options work just as they do for a voice call (you have the same custom message options). You can also press the Sleep/Wake button to decline the request.

When a FaceTime request comes in while your iPhone is locked, you swipe to the right on the slider to accept the call or use the Remind Me or Message options if you don't want to take the call (this is the same as when you receive a voice call via the Phone app).

If you decline the FaceTime request, the person trying to call you receives a message that you're not available (and a message if you choose that option). She can't tell whether there is a technical issue or if you simply declined to take the call.

Tracking FaceTime Calls

FaceTime calls are tracked just as voice calls are. Open the FaceTime app and tap Video to see recent video FaceTime calls or Audio to see recent audio FaceTime calls. On the recents list, FaceTime calls are marked with the video camera icon. FaceTime audio-only calls are marked with a telephone receiver icon. FaceTime calls that didn't go through are in red and are treated as missed calls. You can do the same tasks with recent FaceTime calls that you can with recent voice calls.

Managing FaceTime Calls

During a FaceTime call (regardless of who placed the call initially), you can do the following:

- Drag the preview window, which shows the image that the other person is seeing, around the screen to change its location. It "snaps" into place in the closest corner when you lift up your finger.

- Move your iPhone around, change the angle at which you are holding it, and move it closer to or further away from you to change the images you are broadcasting to the other person. Use the preview window to see what the other person is seeing.

- Tap Mute to mute your side of the conversation. Your audio is muted and you see the Mute icon in the preview window. Video continues to be broadcast so the other person can still see you.

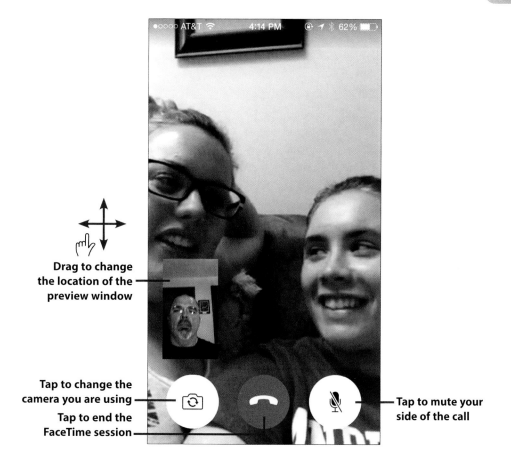

Drag to change the location of the preview window

Tap to change the camera you are using

Tap to end the FaceTime session

Tap to mute your side of the call

- To use the camera on the backside of the iPhone, tap the Change Camera button. The other person now sees whatever you have the camera on the back of the iPhone pointed at. If the other person changes her camera, you see what her backside camera is pointing at.

8 Replace the current text with the signature you want to use.

9 If you selected the Per Account option in step 6, repeat steps 7 and 8 to create a signature for each account.

10 Tap Mail. When you create a new email message (how to do this is covered later in "Sending Email"), the signatures you created are automatically added to the end of new messages. You can change the other Mail settings using a similar pattern and the description of the options in the following table.

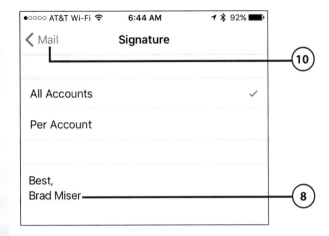

No Signatures, Please

If you don't want any text automatically appended to your messages, choose the All Accounts option and then delete all the text in the signature box.

To access the settings in the following table, first tap the Settings icon on the Home screen, tap the option listed in the Settings Area column, and then move to the location to make changes to the setting (for example, to change the amount of text shown in email previews, open the Settings app; tap Mail; move to the MESSAGE LIST section; and then tap Preview). For each setting, you see a description of what it does along with options (if applicable).

Mail and Related Settings

Settings Area	Location	Setting	Description
Mail	Accounts	Email accounts	You can configure the accounts used in the Mail app to determine which accounts can receive or send email on your iPhone (see Chapter 4 for details).
Mail	Accounts	Fetch New Data	Determines when new email is downloaded to your iPhone (see Chapter 4 for a complete explanation of the options).
Mail	MESSAGE LIST	Preview	Determines the number of lines you want to display for each email when you view the Inbox and in other locations, such as alerts. This preview enables you to get the gist of an email without opening it. More lines give you more of the message but take up more space on the screen.
Mail	MESSAGE LIST	Show To/ Cc Label	Slide the switch to on (green) to always see a To or Cc label next to the subject line on messages in your inboxes. This helps you know when you are included in the To line or as a Cc, which usually indicates whether you need to do something with the message or if it is just for your information.

Settings Area	Location	Setting	Description
Mail	COMPOSING	Increase Quote Level	When this option is enabled (green), the text of an email you are replying to or forwarding (quoted content) is automatically indented. Generally, you should leave this enabled so it is easier for the recipients to tell when you have added text to an email, versus what is from the previous email messages' quoted content.
Mail	COMPOSING	Signature	Signatures are text that is automatically added to the bottom of new email messages that you create. For example, you might want your name and email address added to every email you create. The previous steps explain how to set your signatures. (Note that the default signature is "Sent from my iPhone.")
Mail	COMPOSING	Default Account	Determines which email account is the default one used when you send an email (this setting isn't shown if you have only one email account). You can override the default email account for an email you are sending by choosing one of your other email addresses in the From field.
Display & Brightness	N/A	Text Size	Changes the size of text in all apps that support Dynamic Type (Mail does). Drag the slider to the right to make text larger or to the left to make it smaller.
Display & Brightness	N/A	Bold Text	Changes text to be bold when the Bold Text switch is set to on (green).

More on Marking Addresses

When you configure at least one address on the Mark Addresses screen, all addresses from domains except those listed on the Mark Addresses screen are in red text on the New Message screen. This is useful to prevent accidental email going to places where you don't want it to go. For example, you might want to leave domains associated with a club of which you are a member off this list so that whenever you send email to addresses associated with your club, the addresses appear in red to remind you to pay closer attention to the messages you are sending.

Email Notifications and Sounds

If you want to be alerted whenever new email is received and when email you create is sent, be sure to configure notifications for the Mail app. These include whether unread messages are shown in the Notification Center, the type of alerts, whether the badge appears on the Mail icon, whether the preview is shown, the alert sounds and vibrations, and whether new messages are shown on the Lock screen. For a detailed explanation of configuring notifications, refer to Chapter 2, "Using Your iPhone's Core Features."

Working with Email

The iPhone's Mail app offers lots of great features and is ideally suited for working with email on your iPhone. The Mail app offers a consolidated Inbox, so you can view email from all your accounts at the same time. Also, the Mail app organizes your email into threads (assuming you didn't disable this feature), which makes following a conversation convenient.

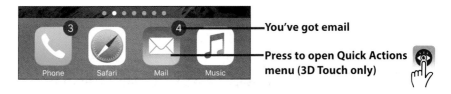

You've got email

Press to open Quick Actions menu (3D Touch only)

When you move to a Home screen, you see the number of new email messages you have in the badge on the Mail app's icon (assuming you haven't disabled this); tap the icon to move to the app. Even if you don't have any new email, the Mail icon still leads you to the Mail app. Other ways Mail notifies you of new messages include by displaying visual notifications and playing vibrations and new mail sounds. (You determine which of these options is used for each email account by configuring its notifications as explained in the "Email Notifications and Sounds" note.)

If you are using an iPhone that supports 3D Touch (6s/6s Plus or later models), you can press on the Mail icon to open the Quick Actions menu and choose an action you want to perform. For example, you can start a new email message by tapping New Message or move directly to your VIP email by tapping VIP. You can move to the most recent messages from one of your VIPs by tapping him in the MAIL widget.

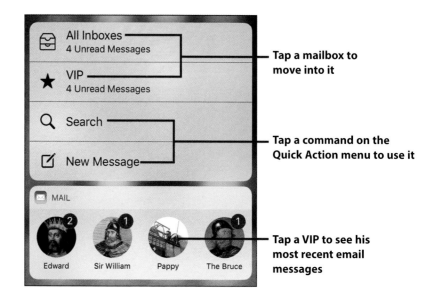

Tap a mailbox to move into it

Tap a command on the Quick Action menu to use it

Tap a VIP to see his most recent email messages

VIP

You can designate people with whom you correspond as a Very Important Person (VIP). Mail has options specifically for your VIPs, such as a dedicated inbox, the MAIL widget, and so on. You learn more about working with VIPs later in this chapter.

About Assumptions

The steps and figures in this section assume you have more than one email account configured and are actively receiving email from those accounts on your iPhone. If you have only one email account active, your Mailboxes screen contains that account's folders instead of mailboxes from multiple accounts and the Accounts sections that appear in these figures and steps. Similarly, if you disable the Organize by Thread setting, you won't see messages in threads as these figures show. Instead, you work with each message individually.

The Mail app enables you to receive and read email for all the email accounts configured on your iPhone. The Mailboxes screen is the top-level screen in the app and is organized into two sections.

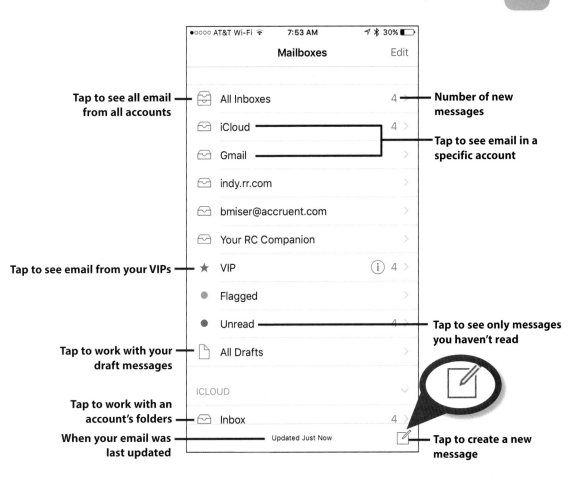

Tap to see all email from all accounts — All Inboxes — Number of new messages

Tap to see email in a specific account

Tap to see email from your VIPs — VIP

Tap to see only messages you haven't read — Unread

Tap to work with your draft messages — All Drafts

Tap to work with an account's folders — Inbox

When your email was last updated — Updated Just Now

Tap to create a new message

The Inboxes section shows the Inbox for each account along with folders for email from people designated as VIPs, your unread messages, and your draft messages (those you've started but haven't sent yet). Next to each Inbox or folder the number of new emails in that Inbox or folder is shown. (A new message is simply one you haven't viewed yet.) At the top of the section is All Inboxes, which shows the total number of new messages to all accounts; when you tap this, the integrated Inbox containing email from all your accounts is displayed.

The Accounts section shows each email account with another counter for new messages. The difference between these sections is that the Inbox options take you to just the Inbox for one or all of your accounts, whereas the Account options take you to all the folders under each account.

Receiving and Reading Email

To read email you have received, perform the following steps:

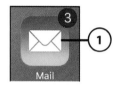

(1) On the Home screen, tap Mail. Mail opens. When you open Mail, you move back to the screen you were last on, for example, if you were reading an email you return to it. If the Mailboxes screen isn't showing, tap the back button in the upper-left corner of the screen until you reach the Mailboxes screen.

(2) To read messages, tap the Inbox that contains messages you want to read, or tap All Inboxes to see the messages from all your email accounts. Various icons indicate the status of each message, if it has attachments, if it is from a VIP, or if it is part of a thread. A message is part of a thread when it has double right-facing arrows along the right side of the screen—individual messages have only one arrow.

Pulling on Threads

A thread is a group of emails that are related to the same subject. For example, if someone sends an email to you saying how wonderful the *My iPhone* book is, and you reply with a message saying how much you agree, those two messages would be grouped into one thread. Other messages with the same subject are also placed in the thread.

3 Swipe up or down the screen to browse the messages. You can read the preview of each message to get an idea of its contents.

4 If a message you are interested in is in a thread, tap its arrows. (If it isn't part of a thread, skip to step 6.) The thread expands (the double arrows point down instead of to the right) and you can see the messages it contains. The first message in the thread appears in a gray bar. The responses to the message appear under it in a lighter shade of gray; the responses don't have a subject because they are all related to the subject of the thread.

Collapsing Threads
To collapse an expanded thread, tap the downward-facing arrows. You see only the most recent message in the thread again.

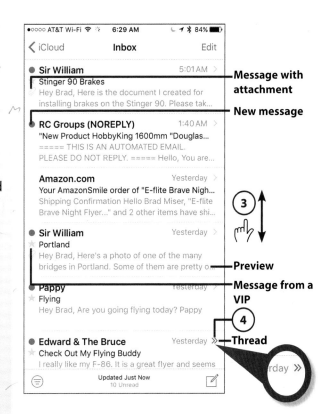

Message with attachment

New message

3

Preview

Message from a VIP

4

Thread

5 Swipe up or down the screen to browse the messages in the thread.

6 To read a message (whether in a thread or not), tap it. As soon as you open a message, it's marked as read and the new mail counter reduces by one. You see the message screen with the address information at the top, including whom the message is from and whom it was sent to. Under that the message's subject along with time and date it was sent are displayed. Below that is the body of the message. If the message has an attachment or is a reply to another message, the attachment or quoted text appears toward the bottom of the screen.

7 Swipe up and down the screen to read the entire message.

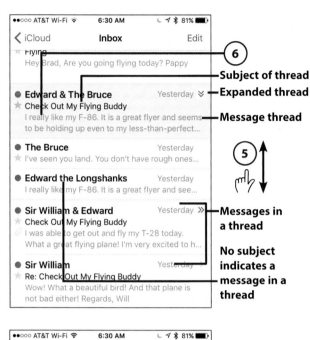

Subject of thread
Expanded thread
Message thread

Messages in a thread

No subject indicates a message in a thread

Quoted message

8 If the message contains an attachment, swipe up the screen to get to the end of the message. Some types of attachments, most notably photos, appear directly in the message and you don't have to download them to the device. If an attachment hasn't been downloaded yet, it starts to download automatically (unless it is a large file). If the attachment hasn't been downloaded automatically, which is indicated by a downward-facing arrow in the attachment icon, tap it to download it into the message. When an attachment finishes downloading, its icon changes to represent the type of file it is. If the icon remains generic, it might be of a type the iPhone can't display, and you would need to open it on a computer or other device.

Standard Motions Apply

You can use the standard finger motions on email messages, such as unpinching or tapping to zoom, swiping directions to scroll, and so on. You can also rotate the phone to change the orientation of messages from vertical to horizontal; this makes it easier to type.

9 Tap the attachment icon to view it.

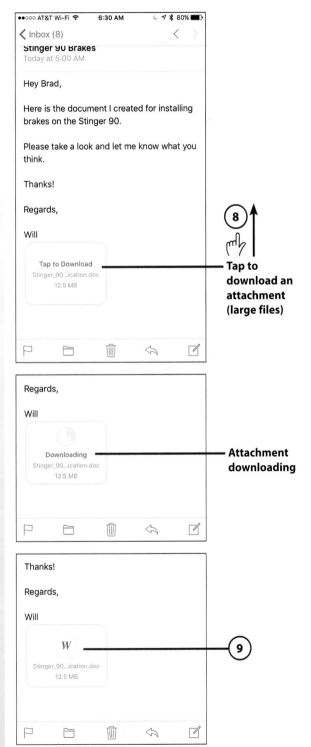

Tap to download an attachment (large files)

Attachment downloading

(10) Scroll the document by swiping up, down, left, or right on the screen.

(11) Unpinch or double-tap to zoom in.

(12) Pinch or double-tap to zoom out.

(13) Tap the Share button to see the available actions for the attachment.

(14) Swipe to the left or right to see all the available options.

(15) Tap the action you want to take, such as opening the attachment in a different app, printing it, sharing it via email, and so on. Tap Cancel to return to the attachment if you don't want to do any of these. If you open the attachment in an app, work with the attachment in that app. To return to the email, tap Mail in the top-left corner of the screen to return to the Mail app.

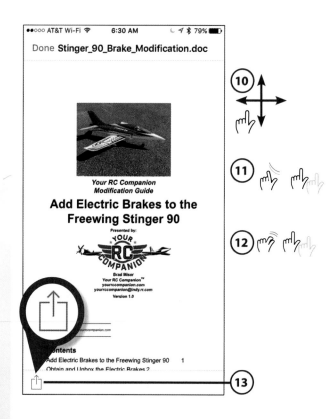

Details, Details

When you view the sender or other people involved in a message as described in step 17, if the names aren't in blue, tap Details. This causes the names to become links.

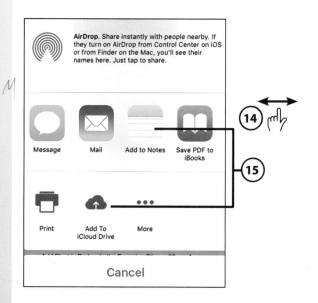

16 Tap Done (depending on the type of attachment you were viewing, you might tap the back button instead).

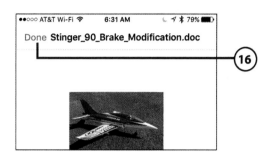

17 To view information for an email address, such as who sent the message, tap it. The Info screen appears. On this screen, you see as much information for the person as is available. If it is someone in the Contacts app, you see all of the information stored there, and you can place a call, send a message, and so on. If it is not someone in the Contacts app, you see the person's email address along with actions you might want to perform, such as creating a contact for him or adding new information to an existing contact. (See Chapter 7, "Managing Contacts," for information about working with contacts.)

18 Tap Done to return to the message.

19 To read the next message in the current Inbox, tap the right arrow. (If the arrow is disabled, you are viewing the most recent email in the inbox.)

20 To move to a previous message in the current Inbox, tap the left arrow. (If the arrow is disabled, you are viewing the oldest message in the inbox.)

21 To move back to see the entire Inbox, tap the back button, which is labeled with the name of the inbox from which you came.

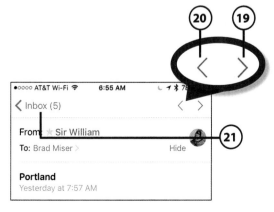

Reading Threads

If you want to read all the messages in a thread instead of individual messages it contains, tap the thread (instead of tapping its arrows to expand it). The thread opens, and you see the title of the thread at the top of the screen in a gray bar. You can browse up and down the thread's screen to read all of the messages it contains. When you are done with the thread, tap the back button (which may be called Inbox or Back depending on what you are viewing) to return to the current inbox.

Two Other Ways to Open New Email

You can view a preview of email messages in notifications you receive and press or swipe on the notification to get to the full message. You can also use Siri to get and read new email. If that isn't enough ways, you can also use the Mail widget to quickly get to email from your VIPs.

Receiving and Reading Email on an iPhone Plus

The iPhone 6 Plus', 6s Plus', and 7 Plus' larger screen provides some additional functionality that is unique to those models. You can access this by holding the Plus horizontally when you use the Mail app.

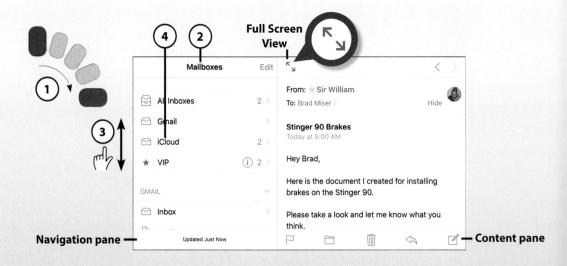

(**1**) Open the Mail app and hold the iPhone so it is oriented horizontally. The mail window splits into two panes. On the left is the Navigation pane, where you can move to and select items you want to view. When you select something in the left pane, it appears in the Content pane on the right, which shows the email message you were most recently reading.

(**2**) In the left pane, navigate to the Mailboxes screen by tapping the back button until it disappears.

(**3**) Swipe up or down the Navigation pane to browse the mailboxes and accounts available to you. Notice that the two panes are independent. When you browse the left pane, the right pane doesn't change.

(**4**) Tap the mailbox or account whose contents you want to view.

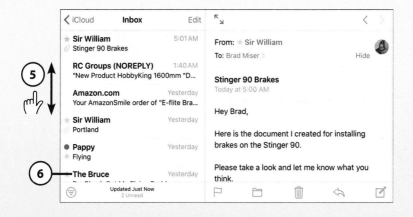

(**5**) Swipe up and down the messages to browse all of them in the mailbox you selected.

(**6**) Tap the message or thread that you want to read. If you tap a thread, the messages it contains appear in the left pane; browse the messages in the thread by swiping up and down the screen and then tap the message in the thread that you want to read. The message currently selected is highlighted in gray.

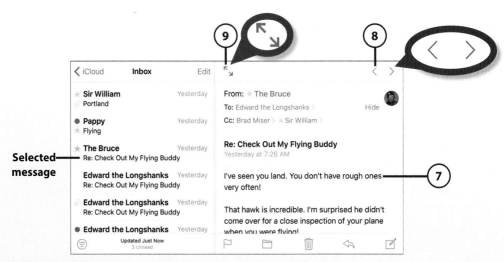

Selected message

7 Read the message.

8 Use the other tools to work with it; these work just like they do on other models and when you hold the iPhone vertically. For example, tap the left arrow to move to the previous message in the current Inbox.

9 To read the message in full screen, tap the Full Screen View button. The Content pane uses the entire screen.

10 Work with the message.

11 When you're done, tap the back button, which is labeled with the name of the mailbox or folder containing the message you are reading. The screen splits into two panes again.

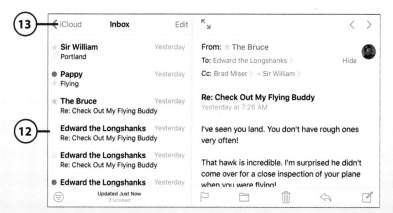

(12) Select and read other messages.

(13) When you're done, tap the back button, which is labeled with the name of the mailbox or folder whose contents you are browsing.

Using 3D Touch for Email

You can use the 3D Touch feature (iPhone 6s/6s Plus or later models) for email as follows:

(1) Browse a list of email messages.

(2) Press and hold on an email in which you are interested. A Peek of that email appears.

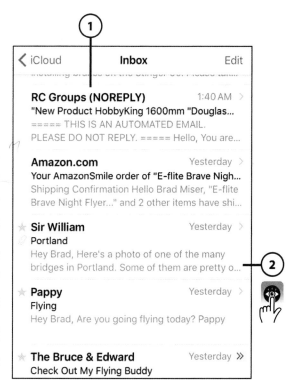

3 Review the preview of the email that appears in the Peek.

4 To open the email so you can read all of it, press down slightly harder until it pops open and use the steps in the earlier task to read it (skip the rest of these steps).

5 To see actions you can perform on the email, swipe up on the Peek.

6 Tap the action you want to perform, such as Reply, to reply to the email.

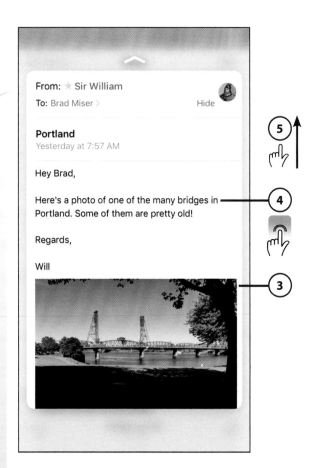

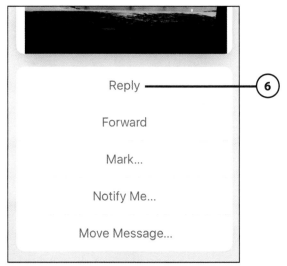

MORE ON RECEIVING AND READING EMAIL

Check out these additional pointers for working with email you receive:

- If more messages are available than are downloaded, tap the Load More Messages link. The additional messages download to the inbox you are viewing.

- You can change the amount of detail you see at the top of the message screen by tapping Details to show all of the detail, such as the entire list of recipients, or Hide to collapse that information.

- A thread is started based on its subject and sender. As replies are made, the messages continue to be categorized by subject because Re: is appended to it. It even remains in the thread if the initial subject continues to be in the message but other words are added.

- If a message includes a photo, Mail displays the photo in the body of the email message if it can. You can zoom in or out and scroll to view it just as you can for photos in other apps.

- If you tap a PDF attachment in a message and the iBooks app is installed on your iPhone, you're prompted to select Quick Look or Open in iBooks. If you select Open in iBooks, the document opens in the iBooks app where you can read it using the powerful features it offers for reading ebooks and other documents.

- Some emails, especially HTML messages, are large and don't immediately download in their entirety. When you open a message that hasn't been fully downloaded, you see a message stating that this is the case. Tap the link to download the rest of the message.

- If you have other apps with which an attachment is compatible, you can open the attachment in that app. For example, if you have Pages installed on your iPhone and are viewing a Word document attachment, you can tap the Share button and tap Open in Pages to open the document in the Pages app. You can get the same options by touching and holding on the attachment's icon in the body of a message until the Action menu appears.

8 Follow the same procedures from steps 2–4 to add recipients to the Bcc field.

9 If the account from which you want to send the email message is shown on the From line, skip to step 11; to change the account from which the email is sent, tap the From field. The account wheel appears at the bottom of the screen.

10 Swipe up or down the wheel until the From address you want to use is shown between the lines.

11 Tap in the Subject line. The account selection wheel closes.

12 Type the subject of the message.

13 If you want to be notified when someone replies to the message you are creating, tap the bell; if not, skip to step 16.

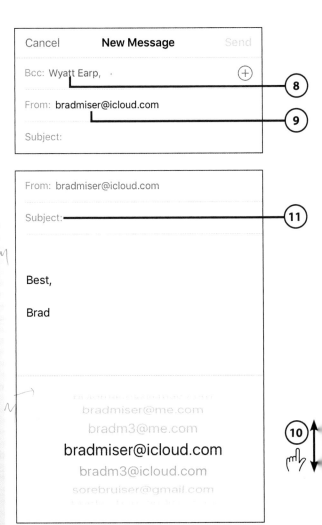

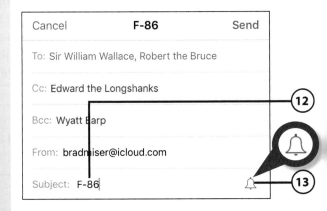

14 Tap Notify Me. When anyone replies to the message, you are notified.

15 If you don't see the body of the message, swipe up the screen and it appears.

16 Tap in the body of the message, and type the message above your signature. Mail uses the iOS's text tools, attempts to correct spelling, provides Predictive Text, and makes suggestions to complete words. To accept a proposed change, tap the spacebar when the suggestion appears on the screen; to ignore a correction, tap the x in the suggestion box. If the Predictive Text feature is enabled, you can tap the words shown above the keyboard that you want to enter. You can also use the copy-and-paste feature to move text around, and you can edit text using the spell checker and other text tools. (Refer to Chapter 2 for the details of working with text.)

17 To make the keyboard larger, rotate the iPhone so that it is horizontal.

18 When you finish the message, tap Send. The progress of the send process is shown at the bottom of the screen; when the message has been sent, you hear the send mail sound you configured, which confirms that the message has been sent. If you enabled the reply notification for the message, you are notified when anyone replies to it.

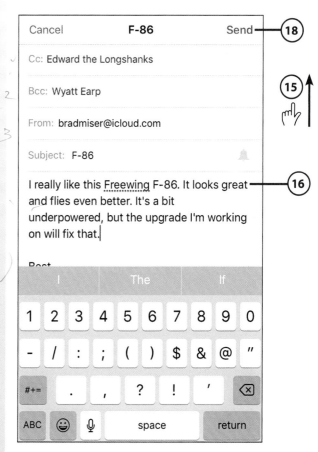

Start Writing Now, Finish Writing and Send Later

If you want to save a message you are creating without sending it, tap Cancel. A prompt appears; select Save Draft to save the message; if you don't want the message, tap Delete Draft instead. When you want to work on a draft message again, touch and hold down the Compose button. After a moment, you see your most recent draft messages; tap the draft message you want to work on. You can make changes to the message and then send it or save it as a draft again. (You can also move into the Drafts folder to select and work with draft messages; moving to this folder is covered later in this chapter.)

Using Mail's Suggested Recipients

As you create messages, Mail suggests recipients based on the new message's current recipients. For example, if you regularly send emails to a group of people, when you add two or more people from that group, Mail suggests others you might want to include. As you add others to the message, Mail continues suggesting recipients based on the current recipient list. You can use these suggestions to quickly add more recipients to a new message.

1. Create a new message.

2. Add at least two recipients. Just below the To line, Mail suggests additional recipients for the new message based on other messages you have created.

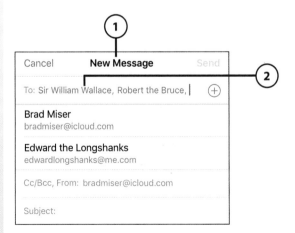

3 Tap the additional recipients you want to add to the new message. As you select these recipients, Mail keeps making suggestions and new people appear in the gray bars.

4 When you're done adding To recipients, tap in the next field you want to complete and continue creating the new message.

Replying to Email

Email is all about communication, and Mail makes it simple to reply to messages.

1 Open the message you want to reply to.

2 Tap the arrow button.

3 Tap Reply to reply to only the sender or, if there was more than one recipient, tap Reply All to reply to everyone who received the original message. The Re: screen appears showing a new message. Mail pastes the contents of the original message at the bottom of the body of the new message below your signature. The original content is in blue and is marked with a vertical line along the left side of the screen.

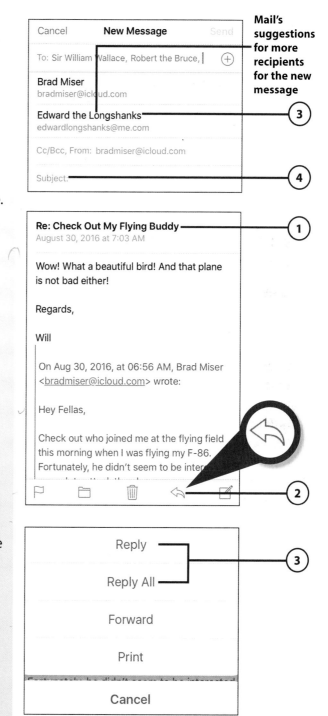

Including a Photo or Video in a Message

To add a photo or video to a message you create (new, reply, or forward), tap twice in the body. Swipe to the left on the resulting toolbar (if you don't see it immediately) until you see the Insert Photo or Video command, and then tap it. Use the Photos app (see Chapter 15, "Viewing and Editing Photos and Video with the Photos App," for information about this app) to move to and select the photo or video you want to attach. Tap Choose. The photo or video you selected is added to the message.

(**4**) Use the message tools to add or change the To, Cc, or Bcc recipients.

(**5**) Write your response.

(**6**) Tap Send. Mail sends your reply.

Sending Email from All the Right Places

You can send email from a number of places on your iPhone. For example, you can share a photo with someone by viewing the photo, tapping the Share button, and then tapping Mail. Or you can tap a contact's email address to send an email from your contacts list. In all cases, the iPhone uses Mail to create a new message that includes the appropriate content, such as a photo or link; you use Mail's tools to complete and send the email.

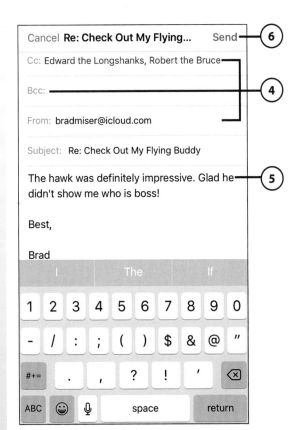

Print Email from Your iPhone

If you need to print a message, tap the arrow button at the bottom of the screen and tap Print. To learn about printing from your iPhone, refer to Chapter 2.

Forwarding Emails

When you receive an email you think others should see, you can forward it to them.

(**1**) Read the message you want to forward.

(**2**) If you want to include only part of the current content in the message you forward, tap where you want the forwarded content to start. This is useful (and considerate!) when only a part of the message applies to the people to whom you are forwarding it. If you want to forward the entire content, skip to step 4.

(**3**) Use the text selection tools to select the content you want to include in your forwarded message.

(**4**) Tap the arrow button.

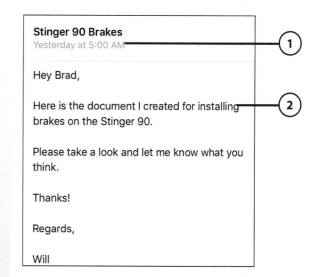

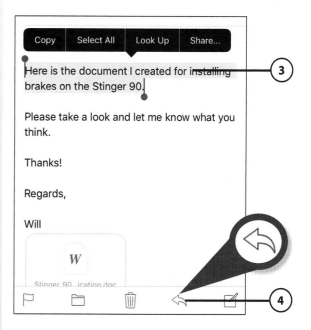

Understanding the Status of Email

When the message is replied to, you receive a notification

Message you've forwarded

Message you've flagged

Message with attachments

Unread message

Message from a VIP

Message to which you've replied

When you view an Inbox or a message thread, you see icons next to each message to indicate its status (except for messages that you've read but not done anything else with, which aren't marked with any icon unless they are from a VIP).

Managing Email from the Message Screen

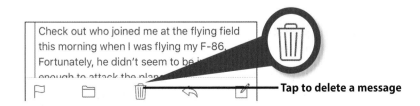

Tap to delete a message

To delete a message while reading it, tap the Trash button. If you enabled the warning preference, confirm the deletion and the message is deleted. If you disabled the confirmation prompt, the message is deleted immediately.

Dumpster Diving

As long as an account's trash hasn't been emptied (this happens automatically after a specified time), you can work with a message you've deleted by moving to the account's screen and opening its Trash folder.

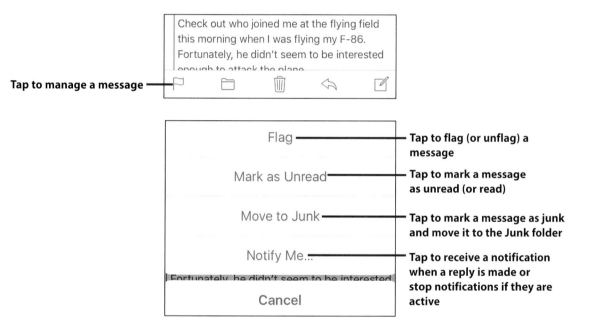

Tap to manage a message

Flag — **Tap to flag (or unflag) a message**

Mark as Unread — **Tap to mark a message as unread (or read)**

Move to Junk — **Tap to mark a message as junk and move it to the Junk folder**

Notify Me... — **Tap to receive a notification when a reply is made or stop notifications if they are active**

Cancel

To take other action on a message you are reading, tap the Flag icon. On the menu that opens, you can choose a number of commands. The action you select is performed on the message you are viewing.

Where Has My Email Gone?

When you send an email to the Archive folder, it isn't deleted. To access messages you've archived, tap the back button in the upper-left corner of the screen until you get to the Mailboxes screen. Tap the account to which email you've archived was sent. Then tap the Archive folder.

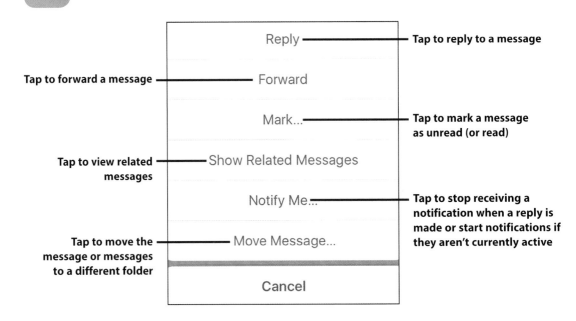

Tap to reply to a message

Tap to forward a message — Forward

Reply — Tap to reply to a message

Mark... — Tap to mark a message as unread (or read)

Tap to view related messages — Show Related Messages

Notify Me... — Tap to stop receiving a notification when a reply is made or start notifications if they aren't currently active

Tap to move the message or messages to a different folder — Move Message...

Cancel

Managing Multiple Emails at the Same Time

You can also manage email by selecting multiple messages on an Inbox screen, which is more efficient because you can take action on multiple messages at the same time.

1. Move to an Inbox screen showing messages you want to manage.

2. Tap Edit. A selection circle appears next to each message, and actions appear at the bottom of the screen.

3 Select the message(s) you want to manage by tapping their selection circles. As you select each message, its selection circle turns blue and is marked with a check mark. At the top of the screen, you see how many messages you have selected.

When you use an iPhone Plus in the horizontal orientation, you see the selection screen on the left and a preview of what you have selected in the right pane. Even though it looks a bit different, it works in the same way.

4 To delete the selected messages, tap Trash. Mail deletes the selected messages and exits Edit mode. (If you enabled the warning prompt, you have to confirm the deletion.)

5 To change the status of the selected messages, tap Mark.

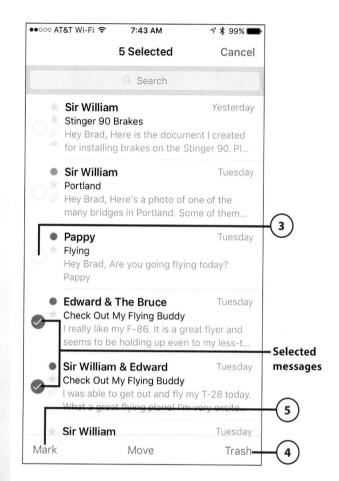

Selected messages

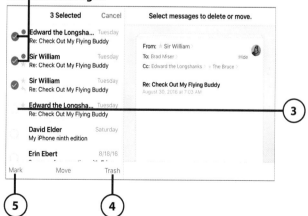

Makin' Mailboxes

You can create a new mailbox to organize your email. Move to the Mailboxes screen and tap Edit. Then, tap New Mailbox located at the bottom of the screen. Type the name of the new mailbox. Tap the Mailbox Location and then choose where you want the new mailbox located (for example, you can place the new mailbox inside an existing one). Tap Save. You can then store messages in the new mailbox.

Organizing Email from the Inbox

Like deleting messages, organizing email from the Inbox can be made more efficient because you can move multiple messages at the same time.

1. Move to an Inbox screen showing messages you want to move to a folder.

2. Tap Edit. A selection circle appears next to each message. Actions appear at the bottom of the screen.

3. Select the messages you want to move by tapping their selection circles. As you select each message, its selection circle turns blue and is marked with a check mark.

4. Tap Move. You're prompted to move the messages into the folder you most recently moved messages into or to choose a different folder.

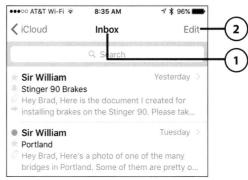

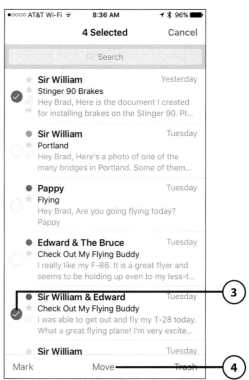

5 To move the messages into a folder you have previously used, tap Move to *"foldername"* where *foldername* is the name of that folder and skip the rest of these steps.

6 To move the message into a folder that wasn't the one you used most recently, tap Other Mailbox. The Mailboxes screen appears. At the top of this screen is the message you are moving. Under that are the mailboxes available under the current account.

7 Swipe up and down the screen to browse the mailboxes available in the current account.

On an iPhone Plus held horizontally, you see the list of folders in the left pane and a preview of the selected messages in the right pane.

8 Tap the mailbox to which you want to move the selected messages. They are moved into that folder, and you return to the previous screen, which is no longer in Edit mode.

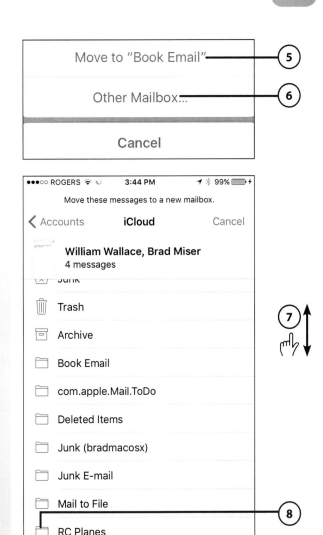

Picking at Threads

When you select a thread, you select all the messages in that thread. Whatever action you select is taken on all the thread's messages at the same time.

3 Touch and hold on an image (if you are using an iPhone that supports 3D Touch, don't press down when you touch or you peek at the image instead).

4 Swipe to the left until you see the Save Image buttons.

5 Tap Save Image to save just the image you touched or tap Save *X* Images, where *X* is the number of images attached to the message. (If there is only one image, the command is just Save Image.) The images are saved in the Photos app on your iPhone. (See Chapter 15 for help working with the Photos app.)

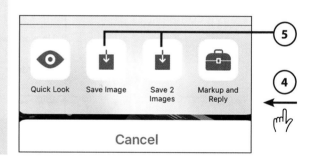

Changing Mailboxes

You can change the mailboxes that appear on the Mailboxes screen. Move to the Mailboxes screen and tap Edit. To cause a mailbox to appear, tap it so that it has a check mark in its circle. To hide a mailbox, tap its check mark so that it shows an empty circle. For example, you can show the Attachments mailbox to make messages with attachments or the All Drafts mailbox that contains your draft messages easier to get to. Drag the Order button for mailboxes up or down the screen to change the order in which mailboxes appear. Tap Add Mailbox to add a mailbox not shown on the list. Tap Done to save your changes.

Filtering Email

New! You can quickly filter the email messages in an inbox as follows:

1. Open the inbox you want to filter.

2. Tap the Filter button. The contents of the inbox are filtered by the current criteria, which is indicated by the terms under "Filtered by." The filter button is highlighted in blue to show the inbox is filtered.

3. Tap the current filter criteria.

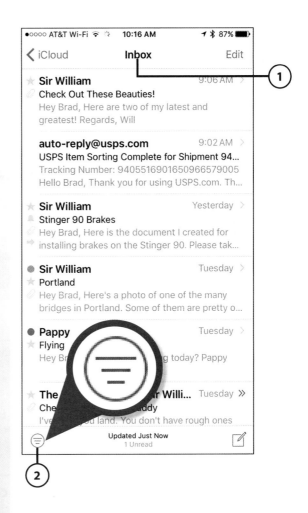

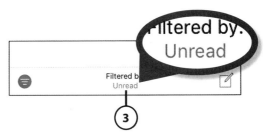

(6) To search in all your mailboxes, tap All Mailboxes, or to search in only the current mailbox, tap Current Mailbox.

(7) To search for the term in the subject field, tap Subject, or to search in the body, tap Message.

(8) Work with the messages you found, such as tapping a message to read it. When you are done reading a message, tap the back button in the upper-left corner of the screen to return to the search results.

(9) To clear a search and exit Search mode, tap Cancel.

(10) To clear a search but remain in Search mode, tap the Clear (x) button.

When you use an iPhone Plus horizontally, searching is even better, because you can select a found message in the search results in the left pane and read it in the right pane.

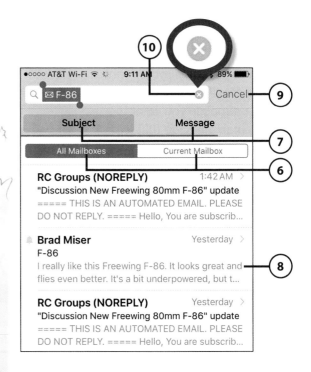

Working with VIPs

The VIP feature enables you to indicate specific people as your VIPs. When a VIP sends you email, it is marked with a star icon and goes into the special VIP mailbox so you can access these important messages easily. You can also create specific notifications for your VIPs, such as a unique sound when you receive email from a VIP (see Chapter 2).

Selected message

Designating VIPs

To designate someone as a VIP, per-form the following steps:

1. View information about the person you want to be a VIP by tapping his name in the From or Cc fields as described earlier in the chapter.

2. On the Info screen, tap Add to VIP. The person is designated as a VIP and any email from that person receives the VIP treatment.

Accessing VIP Email

To work with VIP email, do the following:

1. Move to the Mailboxes screen.

2. Tap VIP.

Marking Junk Email

You can perform basic junk email management on your iPhone by doing the following:

(1) When you view a message that is junk, tap the Flag button.

(2) Tap Move to Junk. The message is moved from the inbox to the Junk folder for the account to which it was sent. Future messages from the same sender go into the Junk folder automatically.

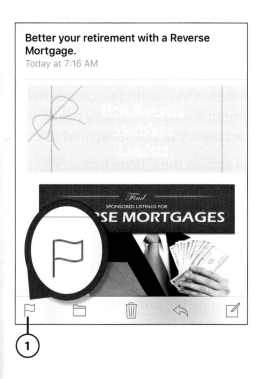

Better your retirement with a Reverse Mortgage.
Today at 7:16 AM

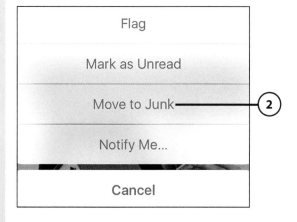

Flag

Mark as Unread

Move to Junk

Notify Me...

Cancel

Junk It

You can also move a message to the Junk folder by swiping slowly to the left on it, tapping More, and then tapping Move to Junk. If you swipe quickly all the way to the left side of the screen, you'll delete the message instead.

Junk It or Trash It?

The primary difference between moving a message to the Junk folder or deleting it is that when you mark a message as junk, future messages from the same sender are moved to the Junk folder automatically. When you delete a message, it doesn't change how future messages from the same sender are handled.

or send an email. Texting/messaging is designed for relatively short messages. It is also a great way to share photos and videos quickly and easily. And if you communicate with younger people, you might find they tend to respond quite well since texting is a primary form of communication for them.

There are two types of messages that you can send with and receive on your iPhone using the Messages app.

The Messages app can send and receive text messages via your cell network based on telephone numbers. Using this option, you can send text messages to and receive messages from anyone who has a cell phone capable of text messaging.

You can also use the iMessage function within the Messages app to send and receive messages via an email account, to and from other iOS devices (using iOS 5 or newer), or Macs (running OS X Lion or newer). This is especially useful when your cell phone account has a limit on the number of texts you can send via your cell account; when you use iMessage for texting, there is no limit on the amount of data you can send when you are connected to the Internet using a Wi-Fi network and so you incur no additional costs for your messages. This is also really useful because you can send messages to, and receive messages from, iPod touch, iPad, Apple Watch, and Mac users. The limitations to iMessage are that it only works on those supported devices, and the people with whom you are messaging have to set up iMessage on their device (which isn't difficult).

You don't need to be overly concerned about which type is which because the Messages app makes it clear which type a message is by color and text. It uses iMessage when available and automatically uses cellular texting when it isn't possible to use iMessage.

You can configure iMessage on multiple devices, such as an iPhone and an iPad. This means you have the same iMessages on each device. So, you can start a conversation on your iPhone, and then continue it on an iPad at a later time.

Preparing the Messages App for Messaging

Like most of the apps described in this book, there are settings for the Messages app you can configure to choose how the app works for you. For example, you can configure iMessage so you can communicate via email addresses and configure how standard text messages are managed. You can also choose to block messages from specific people.

Setting Your Text and iMessage Preferences

Perform the following steps to set up Messages on your iPhone:

(1) Move to the Settings app and tap Messages.

(2) Set the iMessage switch to on (green).

(3) Tap Use your Apple ID for iMessage.

Already Signed In to an Apple ID?

If you have already signed in to an Apple ID for Messages, you can start with step 5 to configure the settings being used for your messages. If you want to change the Apple ID currently being used for iMessage, tap Send & Receive, tap the Apple ID shown at the top of the iMessage screen, and then tap Sign Out. You can then use these steps to sign in to a different Apple ID for Messages.

---

(4) Type your Apple ID and associated password, and then tap Sign In.

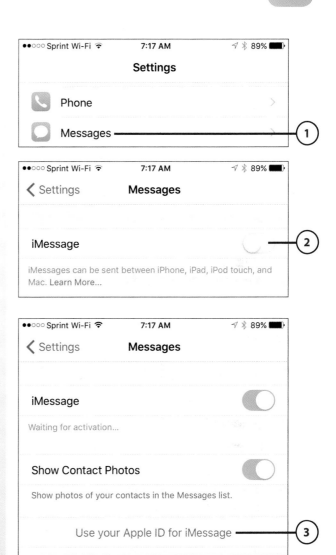

(5) Set the Show Contact Photos switch to on (green) if you want images associated with your contacts to appear in messages.

(6) Tap Text Messaging Forwarding; if you don't see this option, your cell phone carrier doesn't support it and you can skip to step 12.

(7) Set the switch to on (green) for a device on which you want to be able to receive and send text messages using your iPhone's cell phone function (this doesn't affect messages sent via iMessages). A code appears on the device for which you turned on the switch (in this case, Brad's Mac Mini).

(8) Type the code into the Text Message Forwarding box on the iPhone.

(9) Tap Allow.

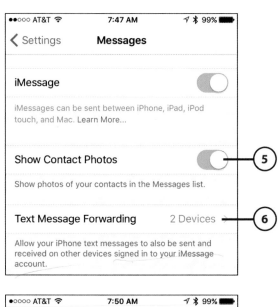

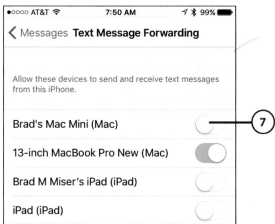

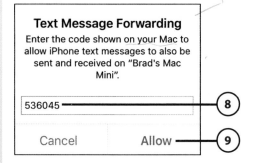

10 Repeat steps 7 through 9 to enable other devices to receive text messages via your iPhone's cell phone function.

11 Tap Messages.

12 Slide the Send Read Receipts switch to on (green) to notify others when you read their messages. Be aware that receipts apply only to iMessages (not texts sent over a cellular network).

13 Slide the Send as SMS switch to on (green) to send texts via your cellular network when iMessage is unavailable. If your cellular account has a limit on the number of texts you can send, you might want to leave this set to off (white) so you use only iMessage when you are texting. If your account has unlimited texting, you should set this to on (green).

14 Tap Send & Receive. At the top of the iMessage screen, you see the Apple ID via which you'll send and receive iMessages. On the rest of the screen are the phone number and email addresses that can be used with the Messages app.

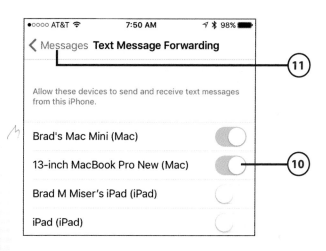

(15) To prevent an email address from being available for messages, tap it so it doesn't have a check mark; to enable an address so it can be used for messages, tap it so it does have a check mark.

(16) Tap the phone number or email address you want to use by default when you start a new text conversation. Each number or email address becomes a separate conversation in the Messages app, so choose the number or address you want to use most frequently to start new conversations.

(17) Tap Messages.

(18) Set the MMS Messaging switch to off (white) if you don't want to allow photos and videos to be included in messages sent via your phone's cellular network. You might want to disable this option if your provider charges more for these types of messages—or if you simply don't want to deal with anything but text in your messages.

(19) Set the Group Messaging switch to on (green) to keep messages you send to a group of people organized by the group. When enabled, replies you receive to messages you send to groups (meaning more than one person on a single message) are shown on a group message screen where each reply from anyone in the group is included on

the same screen. If this is off (white), when someone replies to a message sent to a group, the message is separated out as if the original message was just to that person. (The steps in this chapter assume Group Messaging is on.)

(20) Set the Show Subject Field switch to on (green) to add a subject field to your messages. This divides text messages into two sections; the upper section is for a subject, and you type your message in the lower section. This is not commonly used, and the steps in this chapter assume this setting is off.

(21) Set the Character Count switch to on (green) to display the number of characters you've written compared to the number allowed (such as 59/160). When it is off, you don't see a character count for messages you send. Technically, text messages you send via the cellular network are limited to 160 characters, so showing the character count helps you see where you are relative to this limit (iMessages don't have a limit). I don't use this setting so you won't see it in the figures in this chapter, but if character count is important to you, you should enable this.

(22) Use the Blocked option to block people from texting you (see the next task).

(23) Tap Keep Messages.

(24) Tap the length of time for which you want to keep messages.

(25) If you tapped something other than Forever, tap Delete. The messages on your iPhone older than the length of time you selected in step 24 are deleted.

(26) Tap Messages.

(27) If you want messages from people or organizations not in the Contacts app to be put on a separate list, set the Filter Unknown Senders switch to on (green). When this switch is on, you see a separate tab for messages from people you might not know; notifications for those messages are also disabled. This can be useful if you receive a lot of messages from people you don't know and don't want to be annoyed by notifications about those messages. (This feature is explained in the section "Working with Messages from People You Might Not Know" later in this chapter.)

(28) Tap Expire.

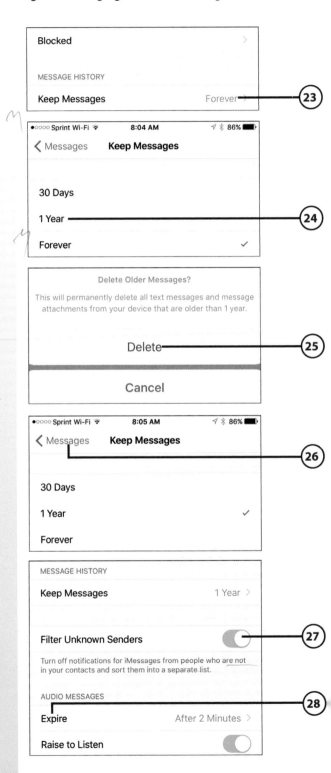

29 Choose the time after which you want audio messages to expire and be deleted from your iPhone. The options you see depend on your cell phone provider. For example, if you tap After 2 Minutes, audio messages are automatically deleted two minutes after you listen to them. This is good because audio messages require a lot of storage space, and deleting them keeps that space available for other things. Other choices may be After 1 Year or Never (if you don't want audio messages to ever be deleted).

30 Tap Messages.

31 To be able to listen to audio messages by lifting the phone to your ear, set the Raise to Listen switch to on (green). If you set this to off (white), you need to manually start audio messages.

32 To have the images in your messages sent at a lower quality level, set the Low Quality Image Mode switch to on (green). This can be a useful setting if you or the recipients of your messages have limited data plans because lower quality images require less data to transmit and receive. If you tend to use all or most of your data allowance each month and send a lot of images, you might want to enable this setting and see if that reduces your data use.

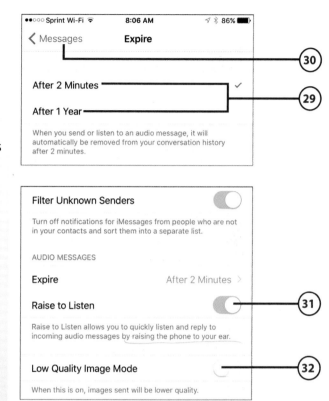

Removing and Adding Addresses

To remove an address from iMessage, tap Send & Receive, tap the email's Info button (i) and then tap Remove This Email. Tap Remove Email Address at the prompt, and you are no longer able to use that address for iMessage. You can add more email addresses for iMessage messages by tapping Add Another Email. Enter the email address you want to add. If you use an email that is not associated with your Apple ID, a verification email is sent to that address. You need to click the link in that email to be able to use the address with the Messages app. When the address is verified, you see it on the list of options for messaging. You also receive notifications on other devices on which the same Apple ID is configured informing you that the addresses have been enabled for iMessage on your iPhone.

Avoiding Scam Email

When you enable email addresses for iMessage, the resulting confirmation message should contain only a link you click to verify the address you provided. If you receive an email asking for your Apple ID or other identifying information, this is not from Apple and you should delete it without responding to it.

Audio Messages

There are two types of audio messages you can send via the Messages app. Instant audio messages are included as part of the message itself. Audio, such as voice memos, can also be attached to messages. The Expire settings only affect instant audio messages. Audio that is attached to messages is not deleted automatically.

Blocking People from Messaging or Texting You

To block a phone number or email address from sending you a message, you might want to have a contact configured with that information so you can identify blocked people later. Refer to Chapter 7, "Managing Contacts," for the steps to create contacts. Creating a contact from a message you receive is especially useful for this purpose. When you start receiving messages from someone you want to block, use a message to create a contact. Then use the following steps to block that contact from sending messages to you:

(1) Move to the Messages screen in the Settings app.

(2) Swipe up the Messages screen.

(3) Tap Blocked.

(4) Tap Add New.

(5) Use the Contacts app to find and tap the contact you want to block. (Note that contacts without email addresses or phone numbers that don't have the potential to send messages to you are grayed out and cannot be selected.) You return to the Blocked screen and see the contact on your Blocked list. Any messages from the contact, as long as they come from an email address or phone number included in his contact information, won't be sent to your iPhone.

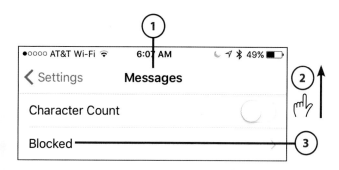

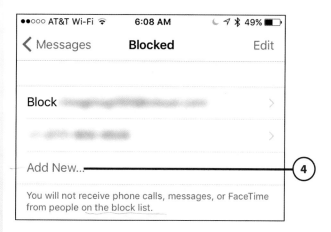

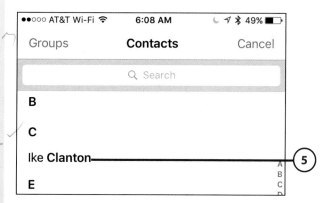

(6) Repeat steps 4 and 5 to block other addresses or phone numbers for the person you are blocking or to block other people.

> >>>Go Further

MORE ON MESSAGES CONFIGURATION

Following are a few more Messages configuration tidbits for your consideration:

- You can use only one Apple ID for iMessages at a time. To change the account you are using, move to the iMessage screen by tapping Send & Receive on the Messages Settings screen. Then tap the Apple ID shown. Tap Sign Out. You can then sign in to a different Apple ID.

- SMS stands for Short Message Service, which is what text messages use. MMS stands for Multimedia Messaging Service, which adds the ability to include multimedia elements (photos, video, sound, and so on) in text messages. All text devices and accounts support SMS, but they don't all support MMS.

- You should also configure the notifications the Messages app uses to communicate with you. You can configure the alert styles (none, banners, or alerts), badges on the icon to show you the number of new messages, sounds and vibrations when you receive messages, and so on. Messages also supports repeated alerts, which by default is to send you two notifications for each message you receive but don't read. Configuring notifications is explained in detail in Chapter 2, "Using Your iPhone's Core Features."

- To unblock someone so you can receive messages from them again, move to the Messages screen in the Settings app, tap Blocked, swipe to the left across the contact you want to unblock, and tap Unblock.

- You can also block someone without creating a contact first. To do this, move to the details screen for the conversation containing the person you want to block (you learn how to work with conversations later in this chapter). Tap the person, email address, or number you want to block. On the resulting screen, tap Block this Caller. Tap Block Contact at the prompt. That person is blocked from sending you messages.

Sending Messages

You can use the Messages app to send messages to people using a cell phone number (as long as the device receiving it can receive text messages) or an email address that has been registered for iMessage. If the recipient has both a cell number and iMessage-enabled email address, the Messages app assumes you want to use iMessage for the message.

When you send a message to more than one person and at least one of those people can use only the cellular network, all the messages are sent via the cellular network and not as an iMessage.

More on Mixed Recipients

If one of a message's recipients has an email address that isn't iMessage-enabled (and doesn't have a phone number), the Messages app attempts to send the message to that recipient as an email message. The recipient receives the email message in an email app on his phone or computer instead of through the Messages app.

Whether messages are sent via a cellular network or iMessage isn't terribly important, but there are some differences. If your cellular account has a limit on the number of texts you can send, you should use iMessage when you can because those messages won't count against your limit. Also, when you use iMessage, you don't have to worry about a limit on the number of characters in a message. When you send a message via a cellular network, your messages might be limited to 160 characters.

When you send messages to or receive messages from a person or a group of people, you see those messages in a conversation. Every message sent among the same people is added to that conversation. When you send a message to a person or group you haven't messaged before, a new conversation is created. If you send a message to a person or group you have messaged before, the message is added to the existing conversation.

Messages on an iPhone running iOS 10 can include lots of different elements, including effects, Digital Touches, content from apps, and more. When you include these items in your messages sent to other people using devices running iOS 10 or Macs running MacOS Sierra or later, they'll be received as you intended.

If they are using devices that aren't running iOS 10 or Macs running MacOS Sierra, messages with these enhancements might or might not be what you intend. For example, if the recipient is using an older version of the iOS, a Digital Touch message comes in as a static image. If the recipient is using a device not running the iOS at all, such as an Android device, it can be hard to predict what will happen to messages if you enhance them. So, keep the recipients of your messages in mind and adjust their content accordingly.

Creating a New Message and Conversation

You can send messages by entering a number or email address manually or by selecting a contact from your contacts list.

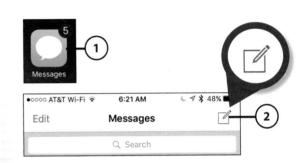

(1) On the Home screen, tap Messages.

(2) Tap New Message (if you don't see this button, tap the back button in the upper-left corner of the screen until you do). If you haven't used the Messages app before, you skip this step and move directly to the New Message screen in the next step.

3 Type the recipient's name, email address, or phone number. As you type, the app attempts to match what you type with a saved contact or to someone you have previously messaged and shows you a list of suggested recipients. You see phone numbers or email addresses for each recipient on the list. Phone numbers or addresses in blue indicate the recipient is registered for iMessages and your message is sent via that means. Messages to phone numbers in green are sent as text messages over the cellular network. If a number or email address is gray, you haven't sent any messages to it yet; you can tap it to attempt to send a message. You also see groups you have previously messaged.

4 Tap the phone number, email address, or group to which you want to send the message. The recipients' names are inserted into the To field. Or, if the information you want to use doesn't appear, just type the complete phone number (as you would dial it to make a call to that number) or email address.

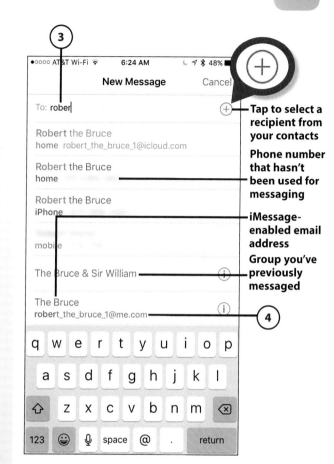

Tap to select a recipient from your contacts

Phone number that hasn't been used for messaging

iMessage-enabled email address

Group you've previously messaged

Straight to the Source

You can tap the Add button (+) in the To field to use the Contacts app to select a contact to whom you want to address the message. (See Chapter 7 for information about using the Contacts app.)

Go to the Group

You can tap the Info button (i) next to a group on the suggested recipients list to see the people that are part of that group.

5 If you want to send the message to more than one recipient, tap in the space between the current recipient and the Add button (+) and use steps 3 and 4 to enter the other recipients' information, either by selecting contacts using the Add button (+), or by entering phone numbers or email addresses. As you add recipients, they appear in the To field. (If you addressed the message to a number or email address that matches a number in your contacts, the contact's name replaces the number in the To field. If not, the number or email address remains as you entered it.)

6 Tap in the Message bar, which is labeled iMessage if you entered iMessage addresses or Text Message if you entered a phone number. The cursor moves into the Message bar and you are ready to type your message.

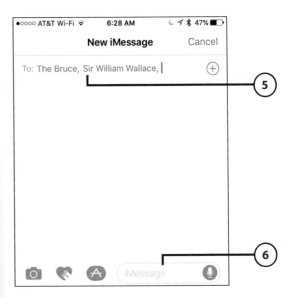

Change Your Mind?

To remove a contact or phone number from the To box, tap it once so it becomes highlighted in blue and then tap the Delete key on the keyboard.

⑦ Type the message you want to send in the Message bar.

⑧ Tap the Send button (circle with an upward-facing arrow), which is blue if you are sending the message via iMessage or green if you are sending it via the cellular network. The Send status bar appears as the message is sent; when the process is complete, you hear the message sent sound and the status bar disappears.

If the message is addressed to iMessage recipients, your message appears in a blue bubble in a section labeled iMessage. If the person to whom you sent the message enabled his read receipt setting, you see when he reads your message.

If you sent the message via the cellular network instead of iMessage, you see your message in a green bubble in a section labeled Text Message.

When you send a message, you see a new conversation screen if the message was not sent to someone or a group of people with whom you were previously messaging. If you

When the message was sent   **Recipients of the message**   **Message sent to more than one person**   **This message has been sent via iMessage**

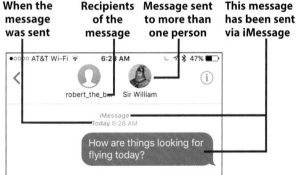

When the message was sent   **Recipient of the message**   **This message has been sent via a cellular network**

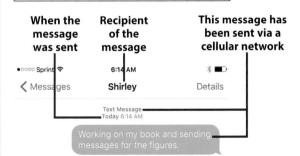

have previously sent messages to the same recipient or recipients, you move back to the existing conversation screen and your new message is added to that conversation instead.

You see icons and the names of each person who received the message; if there are more than two or three people, the icons "stack" on top of each other. (If you sent a message via a cellular text, you only see the person's name or number.)

>>>Go Further

TEXT ON

Following are some additional points to help you take your texting to the next level (where is the next level, anyway?):

- **iMessage or cell**—If the recipient has an iOS device or Mac that has been enabled for iMessage, text messages are sent via iMessage when possible even if you choose the recipient's phone number.

- **Group messaging**—If you've enabled the Group Messaging setting, when you include more than one recipient, any messages sent in reply are grouped in one conversation. If this setting isn't enabled, each reply to your message appears in a separate conversation.

- **Larger keyboard**—Like other areas where you type, you can rotate the iPhone to be horizontal where the keyboard is larger as is each key. This can make texting easier, faster, and more accurate.

- **Recents**—When you enter To information for a new message, included on the list of potential recipients are people being suggested to you by your iPhone. When a suggested recipient has an Info button (i), tap that button, tap Ignore Contact, and then tap Ignore at the prompt to prevent that person from being suggested in the future.

Sending Messages in an Existing Conversation

As you learned earlier, when you send a message to or receive a message from one or more people, a conversation is created. You can add new messages to a conversation as follows:

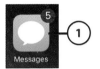

(1) On the Home screen, tap Messages. You see a list of conversations on the Messages screen. If you were previously in a conversation, you see the messages in that conversation and the people involved at the top of the screen instead. Tap the back button, which is the left-facing arrow in the top-left corner of the screen to return to the conversation list on the Messages screen.

On the list, the conversation containing the most recent message you've sent or received is at the top; coversations get "older" as you move down the screen.

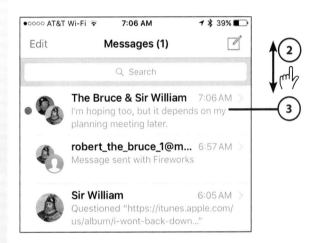

(2) Swipe up or down the screen or tap in the Search bar and type names, numbers, or email addresses to find the conversation to which you want to add a message.

(3) Tap the conversation to which you want to add a message. At the top of the screen, you see the people involved in the conversation. Under that, you see the current messages in the conversation.

(5) Tap other effects to see what they do.

Ah, Forget It

If you decide you don't want to add an effect, tap the Delete button (x) located under the effects along the right side of the screen and you return to your unadorned message, which you can then send without any bells or whistles.

(6) To send the message with the current Bubble effect, tap the Send button and skip the rest of these steps. Your message is sent and the recipient sees the effect on the message's bubble when he opens the message.

(7) Tap Screen to apply a Screen effect.

(8) Swipe to the left or right. Each time you swipe, a new Screen effect is applied and you see it on the screen.

(9) When you find the effect you want to use, tap the Send button. Your message is sent and each recipient sees the effect in the background of the Messages screen when she opens the message.

Message with the Loud Bubble effect applied

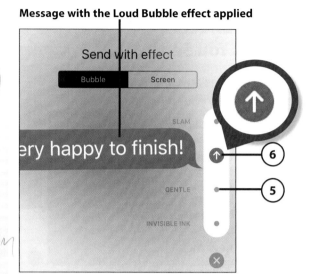

Message with the Confetti Screen effect applied

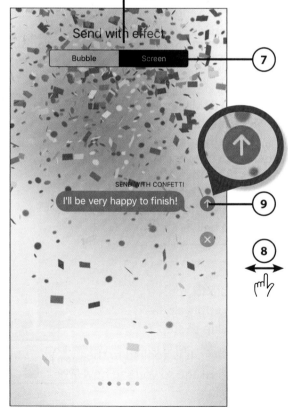

Including Photos or Video in Messages You Send

New! You can add any image, photo, or video stored on your iPhone in a conversation, or you can take a photo or video to include in a message.

(**1**) Move into the conversation with the person or people to whom you want to send a photo, or start a new conversation.

(**2**) If you see the Camera button, skip to step 3; if not, tap the right-facing arrow next to the Message bar.

(**3**) Tap the Camera button. A panel appears that allows you to add photos or videos in three ways. Perform steps 4 through 11 to send photos you've recently taken. Perform steps 12 through 20 to send any photo or video stored on your iPhone. Start with step 21 to take a new photo or video and send it.

Send a Video? No Problemo.
The steps in this task show sending photos in messages. You can send videos in exactly the same way.

(**4**) Send a photo or video you've taken recently by swiping to the left on the photo panel. You see your recent photos and videos.

(**5**) Tap the first photo or video you want to send. The photo or video is marked with a check mark and is added to the message you are sending.

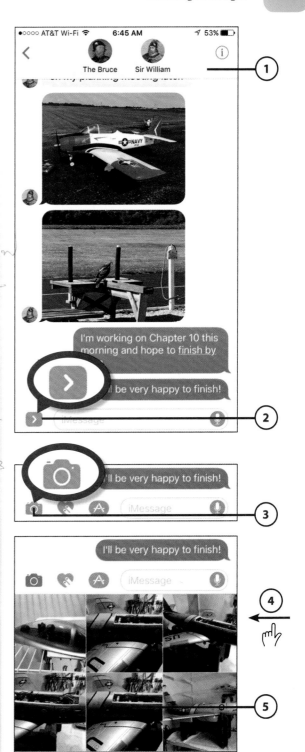

14 Swipe up or down the screen to find the source containing the photos or videos you want to send. (For more information about using the Photos app to find and select photos, see Chapter 15, "Viewing and Editing Photos and Video with the Photos App.")

15 Tap the source containing the photos or videos you want to send.

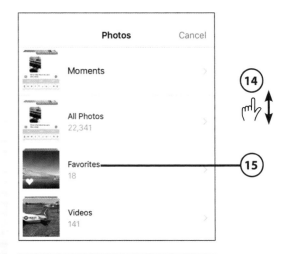

16 Swipe up or down the screen until you see the photo or video you want to send.

17 Tap the photo or video you want to send.

18 Tap Choose. You move back to the conversation and see the image in the Message bar.

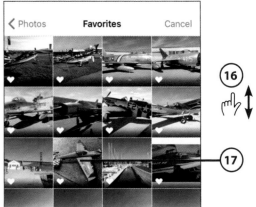

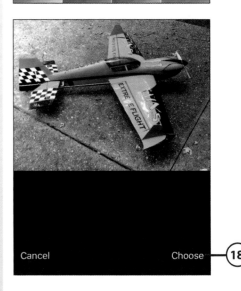

19 Type the message you want to send with the photo or video.

20 Tap the Send button.

21 If you don't see the camera window or the Camera button, swipe to the right until you do.

22 To use the full Camera app to take the photo or video, go on to step 23; to take a photo using the small camera window you see on the screen, position the image that you want to take and tap the Shutter button. The photo is taken and added to the message; skip to step 29.

23 Tap the Camera button.

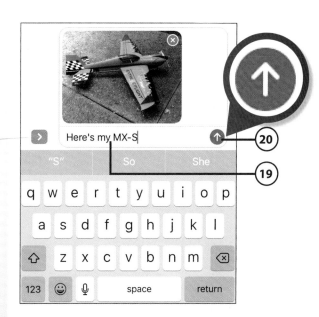

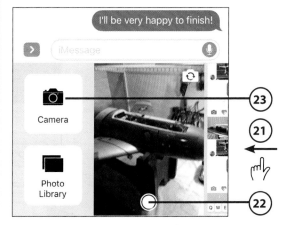

Using Digital Touches in Messages You Send

New! You can enhance your messages with Digital Touches, which are dynamic images you draw with your fingers, or you can use the default images.

(1) Move into the conversation with the person or people to whom you want to send a Digital Touch.

(2) If you see the Digital Touch button, skip to step 3; if not, tap the right-facing arrow next to the Message bar.

(3) Tap the Digital Touch button. The Digital Touch panel opens.

iOS 10 Required

Like effects, the recipient must be using a device running iOS 10 or Macs running MacOS Sierra to receive Digital Touches as you see them when you send them. If you send a Digital Touch message to devices not running iOS 10 or Macs running MacOS Sierra, it appears as a static image in the message.

(4) To send one of the default Digital Touches, move to step 8; to create your own Digital Touch, tap the upward-facing arrow to open the Digital Touch screen in full screen mode.

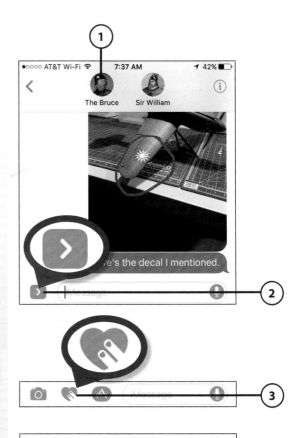

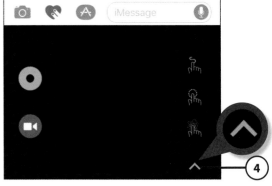

Use the Small Screen

You can create Digital Touches directly in the window in the center of the Digital Touch panel. Putting it in full screen mode gives you more room to work but takes slightly longer. To create a Digital Touch directly in the panel, use the Digital Touch drawing tools directly in the small window and then tap the Send button to send it.

Tap to delete the drawing

(5) Tap the color you want to use. The current color's icon has a dot in the center to show it's selected.

(6) Use your finger to draw or write on the screen. You can change the color at any time; for example, you can use different colors in a drawing or for each letter in a word. Drawing on the Digital Touch screen is much like using colored pencils on paper.

Start Over

To get rid of the contents of the Digital Touch screen, tap the Delete button (x).

(7) Tap the Send button to send it. The full screen mode Digital Touch pane collapses and you see a preview of your Digital Touch as it sends.

6 Set the Automatically Add Apps switch to on (green) if you want apps that can work within Messages and that are installed on your phone to be automatically added to the App Drawer. If you leave this switch off (white), you have to manually add apps to the drawer. I recommend you leave this switch off because automatically adding the apps can clutter the App Drawer with apps you might not use often.

7 To add a new and updated app to your App Drawer, set its switch to on (green).

8 Swipe up and down the screen to browse all of the apps available to be shown in the App Drawer.

9 Display an app in the App Drawer by setting its switch to on (green).

10 Remove an app from the App Drawer by setting its switch to off (white).

11 When you're done managing the apps, tap Done. You return to the App Drawer and see the apps available there.

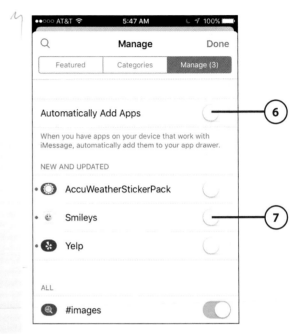

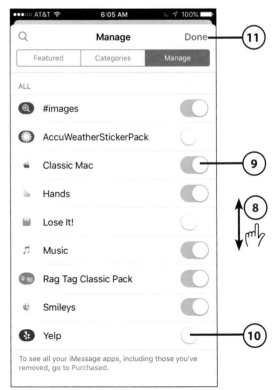

12 Tap outside the App Drawer to close it.

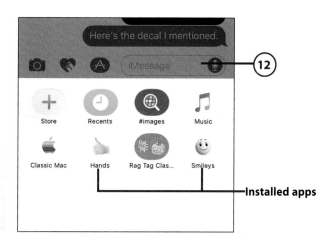

>>>Go Further

ADDING OTHER IMESSAGE APPS

When you open the Store within Messages, you can also find and download apps that work within Messages but that aren't associated with apps already installed on your iPhone. Tap the Featured tab to browse apps that are being highlighted in the store, use the Categories tab to browse for apps by their category, or tap the magnifying glass icon to search for apps. You can evaluate, download, and install these apps from the App Store just like apps you use outside of Messages. See Chapter 5, "Customizing How Your iPhone Works," for information about using the App Store app to download and install apps on your iPhone.

Adding Content from Apps to Messages You Send

New! You can use the apps on the Messages' App Drawer to add content to the messages you send. As you saw in the previous task, there are many different types of apps available and each works according to the type of content you can use. Some are quite simple, such as providing icons or images you can easily add to messages, whereas others are a bit more complicated, for example, you can use the #images app to search for and add images to your messages. Using any of these apps to add content to your messages follows a similar pattern, so once you see how to use one of them, you can use any of them fairly easily.

You can use the #images app to add static images and animated gif images to your messages as follows:

1. Move into a conversation or start a new one.

2. Tap the Apps button. The app drawer opens.

3. Swipe all the way to the right to see the app content you've most recently added to messages.

4. Tap recent content to add it to the current message. The content, such as an icon, is added to the Message bar and you can skip to step 11.

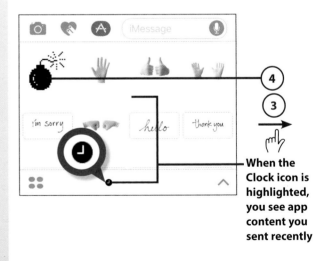

When the Clock icon is highlighted, you see app content you sent recently

5. Swipe to the left to browse the installed apps until you see the app you want to use.

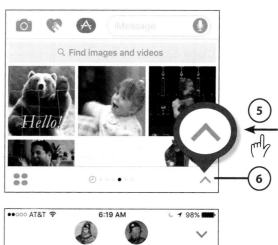

Straight to the App

To move directly to an app, open the App Drawer and tap the app you want to use.

6. Tap the up-facing arrow to expand the app to full screen; this step is optional because you can use the app in the collapsed view in the same way.

7. Type a search term. Search terms that match what you type are listed.

8. Tap the search you want to perform.

9. Swipe up and down the screen to browse all the images that match your search.

10. Tap the image you want to add to the conversation.

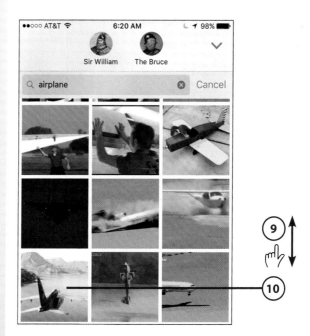

Current Locations

When a current location is added to a conversation, it is static, meaning it is only the location at that point in time. It appears as a map thumbnail in the conversation. Recipients can tap it to zoom in on the location, and then tap Directions to Here to generate directions from their location to the one sent as the current location.

Which Device?

If you have multiple devices that can provide your location, you are prompted to use the current device when you share location. Tap the Use button to have your location be determined by the device you are using.

5 Tap how long you want your location information to be shared.

6 To stop sharing your location, tap Stop Sharing My Location. If you selected to share it for one hour or until the end of the day, location sharing stops automatically at the time you selected.

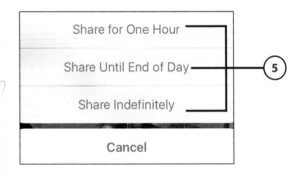

Share for One Hour

Share Until End of Day — **5**

Share Indefinitely

Cancel

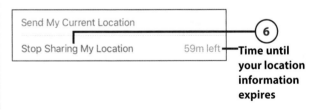

Send My Current Location

Stop Sharing My Location   59m left

6

Time until your location information expires

Using Quick Actions to Send Messages

You can use the Quick Actions feature on iPhones that support 3D Touch with the Messages app as follows:

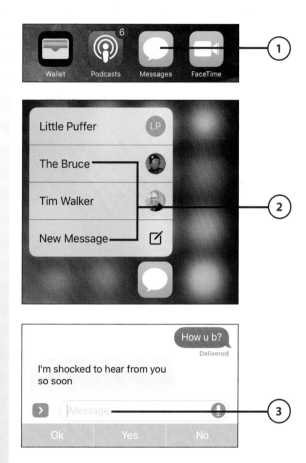

(1) Press on the Messages icon. The Quick Actions menu appears. You see the three most recent people with whom you've been messaging and the New Message command.

(2) Tap the person to whom you want to send a message or tap New Message to send a message to someone not shown on the list. If you choose a person, you move into an existing conversation with that person or a new conversation is started. If you choose New Message, you move to the New Message screen. These tasks are done just like when you start from the Messages app.

(3) Complete and send the message.

Receiving, Reading, and Replying to Messages

Text messaging is about communication, so when you send messages you expect to receive responses. People can also send new messages to you. As you learned earlier, the Messages app keeps messages grouped as a conversation consisting of messages you send and replies you receive to the same person or group of people.

Receiving Messages

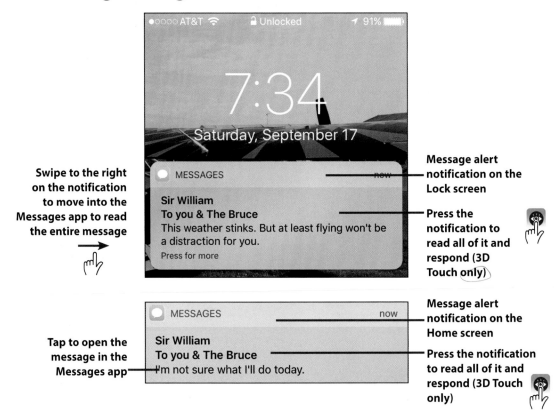

Swipe to the right on the notification to move into the Messages app to read the entire message

Message alert notification on the Lock screen

Press the notification to read all of it and respond (3D Touch only)

Tap to open the message in the Messages app

Message alert notification on the Home screen

Press the notification to read all of it and respond (3D Touch only)

When you aren't currently using the Messages screen in the Messages app and receive a new message (as a new conversation or as a new message in an ongoing conversation), you see, hear, and feel the notifications you have configured for the Messages app. (Refer to Chapter 2 to configure your message notifications.)

If you are on the Messages screen in the Messages app when a new message comes in, you hear and feel the new message notification sound and/or vibration, but a notification does not appear. On the conversation list, any conversations containing a new message are marked with a blue circle showing the number of new messages in that conversation.

If a new message is from someone with whom you have previously sent or received a message, and you haven't deleted all the messages to or from those recipients (no matter how long it has been since a message was added to that conversation), the new message is appended to an ongoing conversation. That conversation then moves to the top of the list of conversations in the Messages app. If there isn't an existing message to or from the people involved in a new message, a new conversation is started and the message appears at the top of that list.

Speaking of Texting

Using Siri to hear and speak text messages can be useful. Check out Chapter 12, "Working with Siri," for examples showing how you can take advantage of this great feature. One of the most useful Messages commands is to activate Siri and say "Get new messages." Siri reads any new messages you have received.

Reading Messages

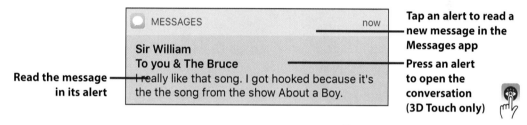

Read the message in its alert

Tap an alert to read a new message in the Messages app

Press an alert to open the conversation (3D Touch only)

You can get to new messages you receive by doing any of the following:

- Read a message in its alert. Tap a banner alert notification from Messages. You move into the message's conversation in the Messages app.

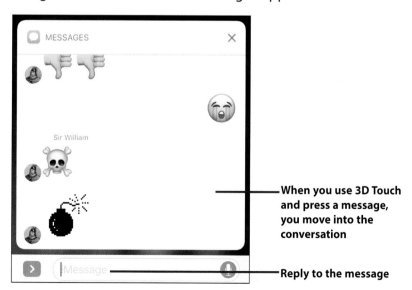

When you use 3D Touch and press a message, you move into the conversation

Reply to the message

• If you are using an iPhone that supports 3D Touch, you can press on an alert to open the conversation to which the message was added. You can read all the messages it contains and reply to those messages.

Conversations with new messages are marked with a blue dot

Tap a conversation with a new message to read the new message

• Open the Messages app and tap a conversation containing a new message; these conversations appear at the top of the Messages list and are marked with a blue circle. The conversation opens and you see the new message.

• Swipe to the right on a message notification when it appears on the Lock screen. You move into the conversation to which the message was sent (you might need to unlock your phone first).

• If you receive a new message in a conversation that you are currently viewing, you immediately see the new message.

However you get to a message, you see the new message in either an existing conversation or a new conversation. The newest messages appear at the bottom of the screen. You can swipe up and down the screen to see all of the messages in the conversation. As you move up the screen, you move back in time.

Messages sent to you are on the left side of the screen and appear in a gray bubble. Just above the bubble is the name of the person sending the message; if you have an image for the contact, that image appears next to the bubble. The color of your bubbles indicates how the message is sent: Blue indicates an iMessage and green indicates a cellular message.

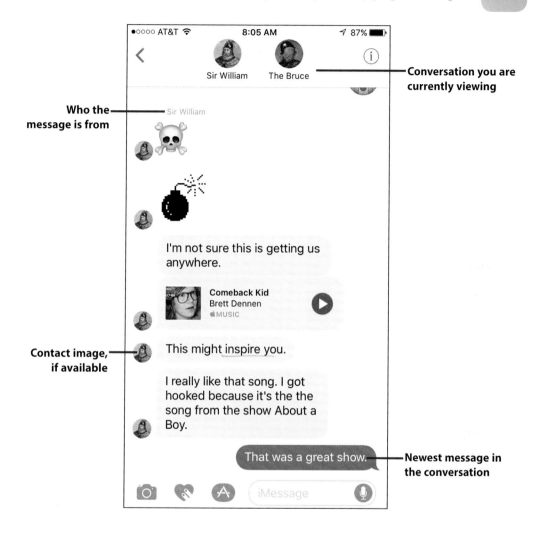

Conversation you are currently viewing

Who the message is from

Contact image, if available

Newest message in the conversation

Viewing Images or Video You Receive in Messages

When you receive a photo or video as an attachment, it appears in a thumbnail along with the accompanying message.

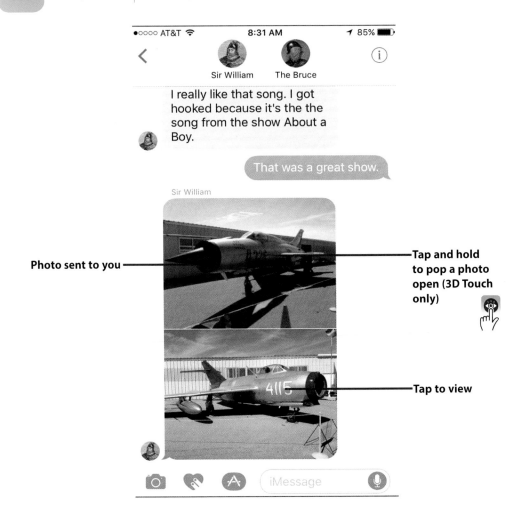

Photo sent to you

Tap and hold to pop a photo open (3D Touch only)

Tap to view

Tap to return to the conversation

Number of photos in the conversation

Swipe to see other photos or videos in the conversation

Tap to bring a list of recent photos in the conversation

Tap to share

To view a photo or video attachment, tap it. You see the photo or video at a larger size. You can rotate the phone, zoom, and swipe around the photo just like viewing photos in the Photos app (see Chapter 15 for details). You can watch a video in the same way, too.

Tap the Share button to share the photo with others via a message, email, tweet, Facebook, and so on. (When you hold an iPhone Plus horizontally, all the buttons are at the top of the screen.)

If there is more than one photo or video in the conversation, you see the number of them at the top of the screen. Swipe to the left or right to move through the available photos.

Tap the List button to see a list of the recent photos in the conversation (this only appears if there is more than one photo in the conversation).

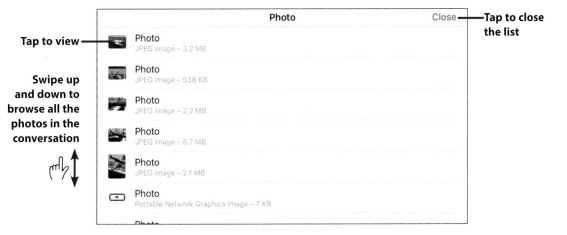

Tap a photo on the list to view it. Tap Close to return to the photo you were viewing.

To move back to the conversation, tap Close.

When you use an iPhone that supports 3D Touch and you press on a photo, it opens in a Peek. If you continue pressing on the photo, it opens in the view window just like when you tap on it in the conversation.

When you are peeking at a photo, swipe up on it to reveal options. You can copy the photo so you can paste it elsewhere, save the photo in the Photos app, or forward it to others.

**Swipe up
for options**

Press to view

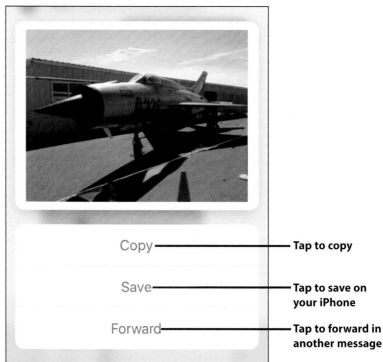

Copy ———————————— **Tap to copy**

Save ———————————— **Tap to save on
your iPhone**

Forward ———————————— **Tap to forward in
another message**

No 3D Touch?

If your iPhone doesn't support 3D Touch, you can save a photo by touching the photo (don't apply pressure) and using the Save command on the resulting menu. You can also copy or forward it from this menu.

Listening to Audio in Messages You Receive in Messages

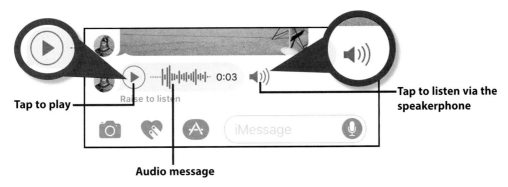

Tap to play — Audio message — Tap to listen via the speakerphone

When you receive an audio message, you can tap the Play button to play it, or, if you enabled the Raise to Listen option, lift the phone to your ear and the message plays automatically. Tap the Speaker icon to hear the message via the iPhone's speakerphone.

Tap to pause

While the message is playing, you see its status along with the Pause button, which you can tap to pause the message. After the message finishes, you see a message saying that it expires in 2 minutes or 1 year, depending on your settings. That message is quickly replaced by Keep.

Speakerphone is on

Tap to show the Trash Can button so you can delete the audio

Raise to talk

Keep

Tap to save the audio message

Keep

Tap Keep to save the message on your phone. (Keep disappears indicating the audio is saved.)

Kept Audio Messages

When one or more of the recipients of an audio message that you sent keeps it, a status message is added to the conversation on your phone, so you know who keeps audio messages you have sent. And, others know when you keep their messages, too.

Replying to Messages from the Messages App

To reply to a message, read the message and do the following:

1 Read, watch, or listen to the most recent message.

2 Use the photos, Digital Touch, or App tools to reply with content of that type as you learned about earlier in this chapter.

3 Tap in the Message bar if you want to reply with text.

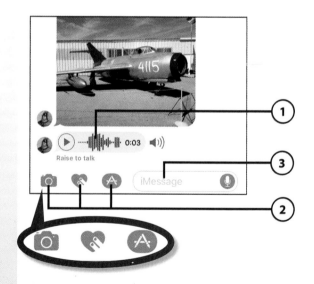

4. Type your reply or use the Dictation feature to speak your reply (this is translated to text; it's not recording and embedding an audio message).

5. Tap the Send button.

Mix and Match

The Messages app can switch between types of messages. For example, if you have an iMessage conversation going but can't access the iMessage service for some reason, the app can send messages as a cellular text. It can switch the other way, too. The app tries to send iMessages first if it can but chooses whichever method it needs to get the messages through. (If you disabled the Send as SMS option, messages are only sent via iMessage.)

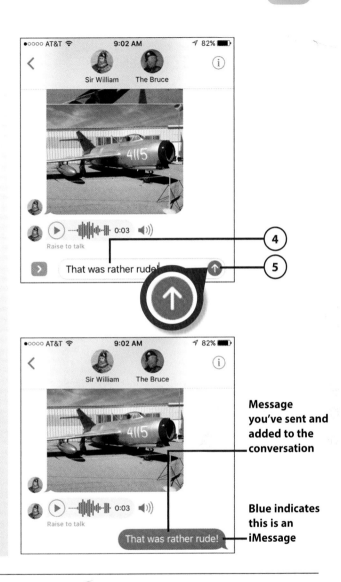

Message you've sent and added to the conversation

Blue indicates this is an iMessage

More Tricks of the Messaging Trade

My Acquisitions Editor Extraordinaire pointed out that when people have cellular data turned off, they can't receive messages. You don't see a warning in this case; you can only tell the message wasn't delivered because the Delivered status doesn't appear under the message. The message is delivered as soon as the other person's phone is connected to the Internet again, and its status is updated accordingly on your phone. Also, when an iMessage can't be delivered, you can tap and hold on it; then tap Send as Text Message. The app tries to send the message via SMS instead of iMessage.

Replying to Messages from a Banner Alert

If you have banner alerts configured for your messages, you can reply directly from the alert from either the Home or Lock screens:

① Press on the notification (3D Touch) or swipe to the right (non-3D Touch). The conversation opens.

② Type your reply or tap the right-facing arrow to add other types of content to your response.

③ Tap the Send button. Your message is added to the conversation.

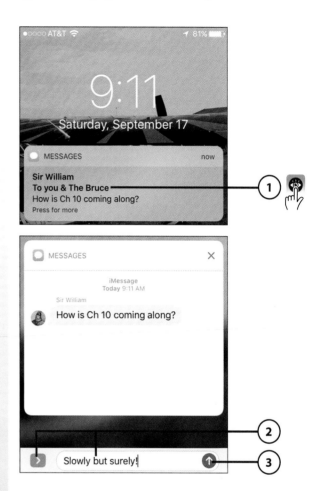

Having a Messages Conversation

Messaging is all about the back-and-forth communication with one or more people. You've already learned the skills you need, so put them all together. You can start a new conversation by sending a message to one or more people with whom you don't have an ongoing conversation; or you can add to a conversation already underway.

Seen But Not Read

Don't take the Read status too literally. All it means is that the conversation to which your message was added has been viewed. Of course, the Messages app can't know whether the recipient actually read the message.

1. Send a new message to a person or add a new message to an existing conversation. You see when your message has been delivered. If you sent the message to an individual person via iMessages and he has enabled his Read Receipt setting, you see when he has read your message and you see a bubble as he is composing a response. (If you are conversing with more than one person, the person doesn't have her Read Receipt setting enabled, or the conversation is happening via the cellular network, you don't see either of these.)

As the recipient composes a response, you see a bubble on the screen where the new message will appear when it is received (again, only if it is an iMessage with a single individual). Of course, you don't have to remain on the conversation's screen waiting for a response. You can move to a different conversation or a different app. When the response comes in, you are notified per your notification settings.

2. Read the response.

3. Send your next message.

4. Repeat these steps as long as you want. Conversations remain in the Messages app until you remove them. Messages within conversations remain forever (unless you delete them, for one year, or for 30 days depending on your Keep Messages setting as shown earlier in this chapter).

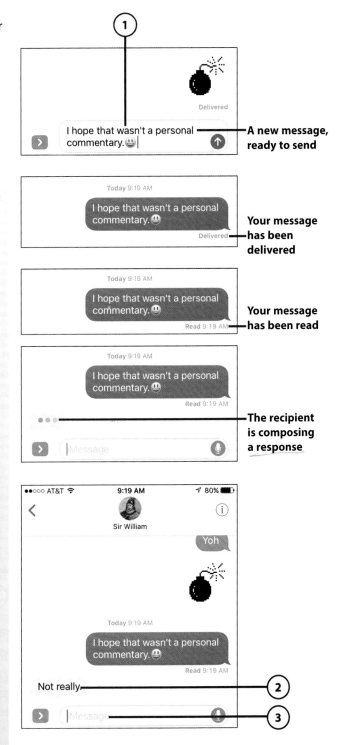

A new message, ready to send

Your message has been delivered

Your message has been read

The recipient is composing a response

(4) Read the new messages or view other new content in the conversation. Your messages are on the right side of the screen in green (cell network) or blue (iMessage), whereas the other people's messages are on the left in gray. Messages are organized so the newest message is at the bottom of the screen.

(5) Swipe up and down the conversation screen to see all the messages it contains.

(6) To add a new message to the conversation, tap in the Message bar, type your message, and tap the Send button.

(7) Swipe down to scroll up the screen and move back in time in the conversation.

(8) To see details about the conversation, tap the Info button (i). The Details screen appears. At the top of the screen, you see location information for the people with whom you are texting if it is available.

(9) If you are working with a group message and want to give it a name, tap Enter a Group Name. If you are working with a conversation involving one other person or don't want to name the group, skip to step 11.

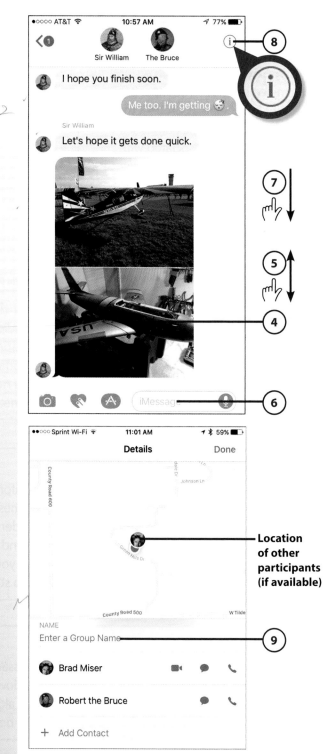

Location of other participants (if available)

10 Enter the name of the group, and tap Done.

11 To place a voice call or audio-only FaceTime call to one of the participants in the conversation, tap the phone icon. If the person has a phone number configured, you're prompted to choose Voice Call or FaceTime Audio. When you make a choice, that call is placed. If the person only has an email address, an audio-only FaceTime call is placed over the Internet. You move into the Phone or FaceTime app and use that app to complete the call. (See Chapter 8, "Communicating with the Phone and FaceTime Apps," for the details about those apps.) Move to the Home screen and tap Messages or use the App Switcher to return to the Messages app.

12 Send a private message to one of the participants by tapping the Messages button.

13 Place a FaceTime video call by tapping the Video Camera icon. You move into the FaceTime app to complete the call. When you're done, move to the Home screen and tap Messages or use the App Switcher to return to the Messages app.

14 To view a participant's contact information or send an email, tap the person whose information you want to view.

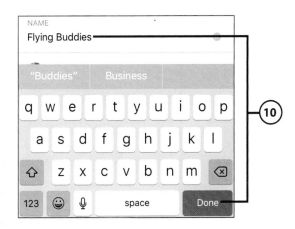

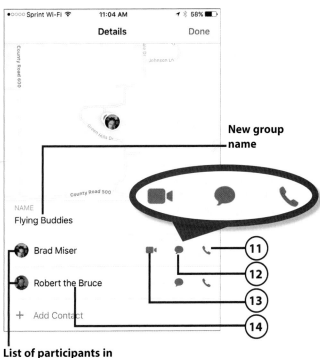

New group name

List of participants in the conversation

(15) Work with the contact information as described in Chapter 7.

(16) Tap the back button to return to the Details screen.

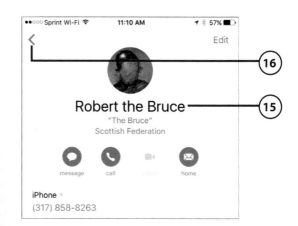

Receiving and Reading Messages on an iPhone Plus

The larger screen on the iPhone Plus provides some additional functionality that is unique to it. You can access this by holding the iPhone Plus horizontally when you use the Messages app.

(1) Open the Messages app and hold the iPhone so it is oriented horizontally. The window splits into two panes. On the left is the Navigation pane, where you can move to and select conversations you want to view. When you select a conversation in the left pane, its messages appear in the Content pane on the right.

(2) Swipe up or down the Navigation pane to browse the conversations available to you. Notice that the two panes are independent. When you browse the left pane, the right pane doesn't change.

(3) Tap the conversation containing messages you want to read. The messages in that conversation appear in the Content pane on the right.

List of conversations

Messages in selected conversation

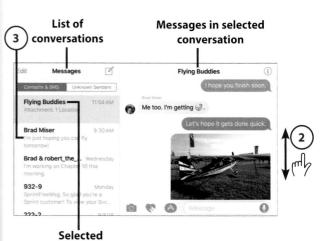

Selected conversation

4 Swipe up and down the Content pane to read the messages in the conversation.

5 Listen to embedded audio, use app content (such as to play music), or work with attachments just like when you hold the iPhone vertically.

6 To add a message to the conversation, tap in the Send bar, type your message, and tap Send. Of course, you can embed audio, attach photos or video, add content from apps, or send your location just as you can when using Messages when you hold the iPhone vertically.

7 Work with the conversation's details by tapping the Info button (i).

8 Change conversations by tapping the conversation you want to view.

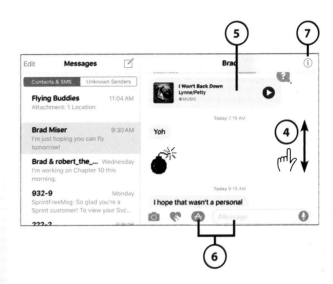

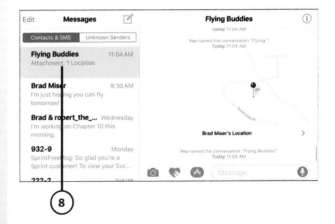

Using 3D Touch for Messages

You can use the 3D Touch feature with the Messages app as follows:

1. Browse your messages.

2. Tap and hold on a message in which you are interested. A Peek of that message appears.

3. Review the preview of the messages that appear in the Peek.

4. Open the message so you can read the conversation of which it is a part by pressing down slightly harder until it pops open. Use the steps in the earlier task to read it (skip the rest of these steps).

5. See actions you can perform on the message by swiping up on the Peek.

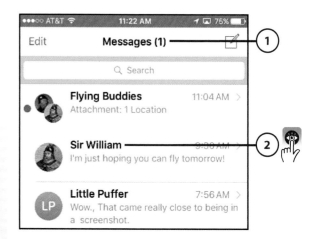

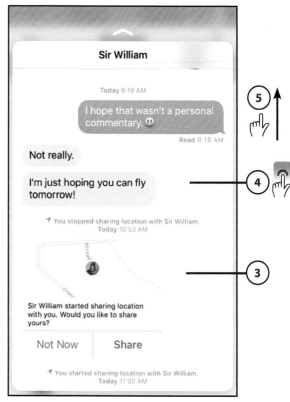

6 Tap the action you want to perform, such as Thank you, to reply to the message with that message. If you tap Custom, you can create a custom reply to the message as you can when you view the conversation.

Browsing Attachments to Conversations

As photos and videos are added to a conversation, they are collected so you can browse and view them at any time:

1 Move to the conversation in which you want to browse attachments.

2 Tap the Info button (i).

3 Swipe up until you see the Images and Attachments tabs.

4 Tap Images to see images attached to the conversation or Attachments to work with other types of attachments (such as documents).

5 Swipe up and down on the attachments until you see one you want to view.

6 Tap the attachment you want to view.

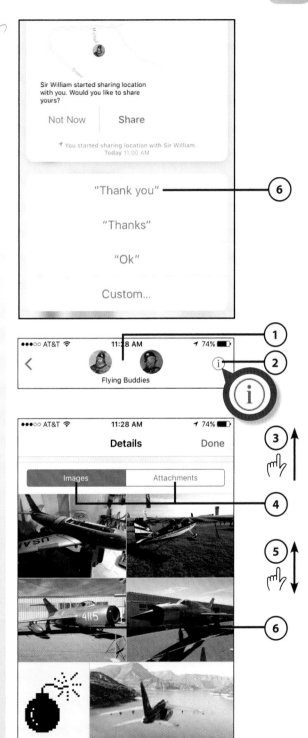

(7) View the attachment, such as looking at a photo.

(8) Tap Done to return to the Details screen.

Keep Quiet!

You can disable notifications for a specific conversation by tapping its Info button (i) to move to the Details screen. Set the Do Not Disturb switch to on (green). You no longer are notified when new messages arrive in that conversation. Set the switch to off (white) to have notifications resume.

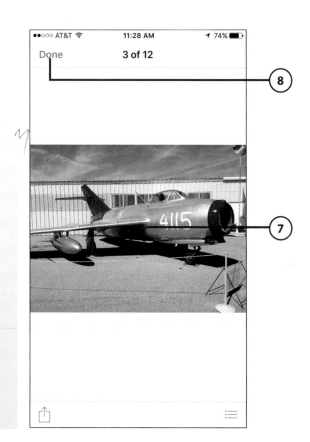

Working with Messages from People You Might Not Know

As you use Messages, it is likely you'll receive messages from people who aren't in your contacts or who you haven't sent messages to before. The Messages app can filter these messages for you and put them on the Unknown Senders tab so you can easily identify messages that are from people who you might not know.

To use this functionality, the Filter Unknown Senders switch on the Messages Settings screen must be turned on (green). (The details of configuring Messages settings are provided in "Setting Your Text and iMessage Preferences" earlier in this chapter.) When this switch is on, you see two tabs in the Messages app. The Contacts & SMS tab lists conversations with people who are contacts or with whom you have communicated previously. The Unknown Senders tab lists conversations from people who aren't contacts or with whom you haven't communicated previously. (If the Filter Unknown Senders switch is off, you don't see these tabs, which is the case for most of the figures in this chapter.)

The messages that get put on the Unknown Senders tab are usually either from someone who you do know, but who you don't have a contact created for and whom you've never messaged with; someone who mistakenly sent a message to the wrong address; or someone who is trying to contact you for nefarious purposes.

If you enable the Filter Unknown Senders feature, you can work with "suspicious" messages as follows:

(1) Open the Messages app.

(2) Tap the Unknown Senders tab.

(3) Tap a message to read it to determine if it is a legitimate message for you.

(4) Review the identification of the sender as best Messages can determine it, such as an email address.

(5) Read the message.

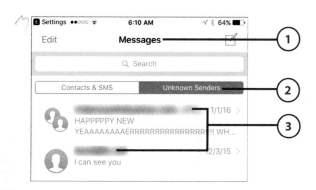

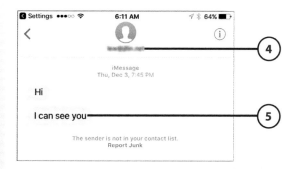

(6) If the message is from someone you don't recognize and don't want to receive future messages from, tap Report Junk. The sender's message is deleted from the Messages app and the associated email address or phone number is blocked so you won't receive any more messages from the sender.

(7) If you do recognize the person and want to receive future messages normally, tap the Info button (i). On the resulting Details screen, tap the sender's contact information and then tap Create New Contact to create a new contact for the person or Add to Existing Contact to update a current contact with new information. (For information about creating or updating contacts, see Chapter 7.)

Responding to a Message with Icons

New! You can quickly respond to messages with an icon as follows:

(1) View a conversation.

(2) If you are using an iPhone with 3D Touch, press and hold on a message you want to respond to; if you are using a non-3D Touch phone, just touch and hold on a message. You can respond to any message, even if it's one you sent.

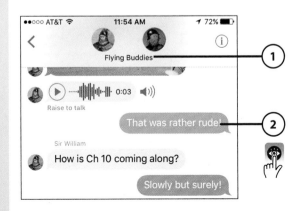

3 Tap the icon you want to add to the message; for example, tap the thumbs-down icon to indicate you don't like a message. The icon you select is added to the message.

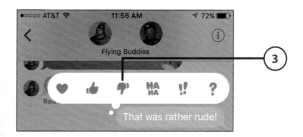

Deleting Messages and Conversations

Old text conversations never die, nor do they fade away (if you have your Keep Messages setting set to Forever, that is). All the messages you receive from a person or that involve the same group of people stay in the conversation. Over time, you can build up a lot of messages in one conversation, and you can end up with lots of conversations. (If you set the Keep Messages setting to be 30 Days or 1 Year, messages older than the time you set are deleted automatically.)

Long Conversation?

When a conversation gets very long, the Messages app won't display all its messages. It keeps the more current messages visible on the conversation screen. To see earlier messages, swipe down on the screen to move to the top and tap Load Earlier Messages.

When a conversation gets too long, if you just want to remove specific messages from a conversation, or, if you want to get rid of messages to free up storage space, take these steps:

1 Move to a conversation containing an abundance of messages.

2 If you are using an iPhone with 3D Touch, press and hold on a message you want to delete; if you are using a non-3D Touch phone, just touch and hold on a message to be deleted.

3 Tap More. The message on which you tapped is marked with a check mark to show it is selected.

Be a Copycat
Tap Copy to copy a message so you can paste it in other messages or in other apps.

Delete Them All!
To delete the whole conversation, instead of performing step 4, tap Delete All, which appears in the upper-left corner of the screen. Tap Delete Conversation in the confirmation box. The conversation and all its messages are deleted.

4 Tap other messages you want to delete. They are marked with a check mark to show you have selected them.

5 Tap the Trash Can button.

6 Tap Delete *X* Messages, where *X* is the number of messages you have selected. The messages are deleted and you return to the conversation.

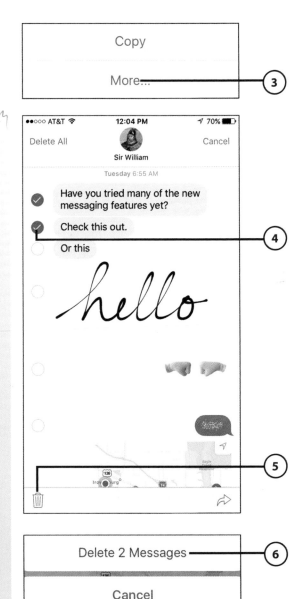

Pass It On
If you want to send one or more messages to someone else, perform steps 1–4. Tap the Forward button that appears in the lower-right corner of the screen. A new message is created, and the messages you selected are pasted into it. Select or enter the recipients to whom you want to send the messages, and tap Send.

Deleting Conversations

If a conversation's time has come, you can delete it.

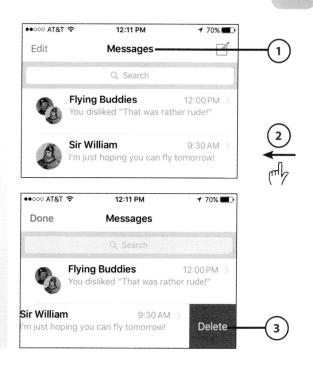

(1) Move to the Messages screen.

(2) Swipe to the left on the conversation you want to delete.

(3) Tap Delete. The conversation and all the messages it contains are deleted.

>>>Go Further
TEXTING LINGO

People frequently use shorthand when they text. Here is some of the more common shorthand you might see. This list is extremely short, but there are many websites dedicated to providing this type of information if you are interested. One that boasts of being the largest list of text message acronyms is www.netlingo.com/acronyms.php.

- **FWIW**—For What It's Worth
- **LOL**—Laughing Out Loud
- **ROTFL**—Rolling On the Floor Laughing
- **CU**—See You (later)
- **PO**—Peace Out
- **IMHO**—In My Humble Opinion

- **TY**—Thank You
- **RU**—Are You
- **BRB**—Be Right Back
- **CM**—Call Me
- **DND**—Do Not Disturb
- **EOM**—End of Message
- **FSR**—For Some Reason
- **G2G**—Got to Go

- **IDK**—I Don't Know
- **IKR**—I Know, Right?
- **ILU**—I Love You
- **NM or NVM**—Never Mind
- **OMG**—Oh My God
- **OTP**—On the Phone
- **P911**—Parent Alert
- **PLZ**—Please

Go here to figure out where and when you're supposed to be

Tap here to configure your calendar, date, and time preferences

In this chapter, you explore all the calendar functionality your iPhone has to offer. Topics include the following:

→ Getting started
→ Setting calendar, date, and and time preferences
→ Working with calendars

Managing Calendars

When it comes to time management, your iPhone is definitely your friend. Using the iPhone's Calendar app, you can view calendars that are available on all your devices. You can also make changes to your calendars on your iPhone, and they appear on the calendars on your other devices so you have consistent information no matter which device you happen to be using at any time. You can also include other people in your events and manage events others invite you to attend.

Getting Started

The Calendar app does what it sounds like: It allows you to manage one or more calendars. This app has lots of features designed to help you work with multiple calendars and accounts, manage events that other people are invited to, and more. You don't have to use all these features, and you might just want to use its basic functionality, such as to record doctor appointments, dinner reservations, and similar events for which it is important to know the time and date (and be reminded when those times and dates are approaching).

Setting Calendar, Date, and Time Preferences

There are a number of calendar, date, and time options you can configure using the Settings app. Following is an example showing how to determine how many months of events are available in the Calendar app on your iPhone. You can configure other calendar, date, and time settings using similar steps and the descriptions of the settings in the lists that follow these steps.

To configure how far back in time calendars on your iPhone go, perform the following steps:

1 Tap Settings on the Home screen.

2 Swipe up the screen.

3 Tap Calendar.

4 Tap Sync.

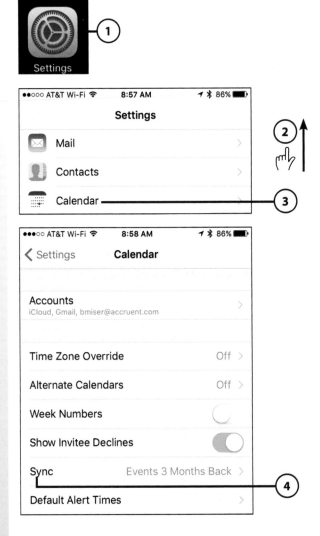

5 Tap the amount of time you would like to see on your calendars. For example, to show events as far back as three months, tap Events 3 Months Back.

6 Tap Calendar. The Calendar app shows events as far back in time as you selected in step 5. You can change the other calendar, time, and date settings using a similar pattern and the description of the options in the following lists.

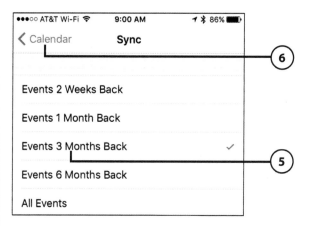

To change the calendar settings, open the Settings app and tap Calendar. Use the settings described in the following list to make changes to how the app works:

- **Accounts**—Use this area to determine which online accounts store your calendar information. See Chapter 4, "Setting Up and Using iCloud and Other Online Accounts," for information about configuring online accounts.

- **Time Zone Override**—When disabled, the time for events is based on your current time zone. When enabled, the time zone for events on the calendars is overridden with the time zone for a city you select. This is useful if you always want event times to be based on a specific time zone. (See the Go Further sidebar at the end of this list for a more in-depth explanation of this setting.)

- **Alternate Calendars**—You can choose among different types of calendars, such as Chinese or Hebrew.

- **Week Numbers**—When this switch is on (green), week numbers appear on your calendars in the Month view.

- **Show Invitee Declines**—When enabled (the switch is green) and someone declines a meeting, they are shown on the Invitee list as having declined. When disabled (the switch is white), invitees who decline an event are removed from the list.

- **Sync**—Determines how far back events are synced onto your calendars. You can choose 2 weeks, 1 month, 3 months, 6 months, or all events.

- **Default Alert Times**—Determines the default alert times for birthdays, events, and all-day events. When you set the Time to Leave switch to on (green), the Calendar app can use your travel time to configure an event's alert. You can change the alert time for any event on your calendar; this setting just determines the initial time.

- **Start Week On**—Determines the first day of the week.

- **Default Calendar**—Determines which calendar is used for new events by default (you can override this setting for any events you create).

- **Location Suggestions**—When this switch is on (green), the Calendar app makes suggestions about the location of events when you create them.

- **Events Found in Apps**—When on (green) and the iPhone's software detects event information in an email, message, or other location, it presents a prompt that enables you to easily add that event to a calendar.

>>>*Go Further*

MORE ON TIME ZONE OVERRIDE

The Time Zone Override feature can be a bit confusing. If Time Zone Override is on, the iPhone displays event times according to the time zone you select on the Time Zone Override screen. When Time Zone Override is off, the time zone used for calendars is the iPhone's current time zone, which is set automatically based on your location or your manual setting. This means that when you change time zones (automatically or manually), the times for calendar events shift accordingly. For example, if an event starts at 3:00 p.m. when you are in the Eastern time zone, its start time becomes 12:00 p.m. if you move into the Pacific time zone.

When Time Zone Override is on, the dates and times for events become fixed based on the time zone you select for Time Zone Override. If you change the time zone the iPhone is in, no change to the dates and times for events is shown on the calendar because they remain set according to the time zone you selected for the Time Zone Override. Therefore, an event's actual start time might not be accurately reflected for the iPhone's current time zone because it is based on the fixed Time Zone Override city instead of the time zone where you are currently located.

To configure how your iPhone displays and manages the date and time, open the Settings app, tap General, tap Date & Time, and change the settings described in the following list:

- **24-Hour Time**—Turning this switch on (green) causes the iPhone to display 24-hour instead of 12-hour time.

- **Set Automatically**—When this switch is on (green), your iPhone sets the current time and date automatically based on the cellular network it is using. When it is off (white), controls appear that you use to manually set the time zone, time, and date.

Notifications

The Calendar app can communicate with you in various ways, such as displaying alerts or banners when something happens that you might want to know about; for example, you can be alerted with a banner when you receive an invitation to an event. Configuring notifications for this app makes it even more useful. The information you need to configure notifications is explained in Chapter 2, "Using Your iPhone's Core Features."

Working with Calendars

The Calendar app helps you manage your calendars; notice I wrote *calendars* rather than *calendar*. That's because you can have multiple calendars in the app at the same time. For example, you might have a calendar for work and one for a club. Or, you might want a calendar dedicated to your travel plans, and then share that calendar with people who care about your location.

In most cases, you start by adding existing calendar information from an iCloud, Google, or similar account. From there, you can use the Calendar app to view your calendars, add or change events, and much more. Any changes you make in the Calendar app are automatically made in all the locations that use calendars from the same account.

The best option for storing your calendar information is an online account (such as iCloud or Google) because you can easily access your calendar information from many devices, and your calendars are kept in sync automatically. To learn how to configure an online account for calendar information, refer to Chapter 4.

(5) Change the name of the calendar by tapping it and then making changes on the keyboard; when you're done making changes, swipe down the screen to close the keyboard.

(6) To share the calendar with someone, tap Add Person, enter the email address of the person with whom you are sharing it, and tap Add. (Sharing calendars is explained in more detail later in this chapter.)

(7) If the calendar is shared and you don't want to be notified when shared events are changed, added, or deleted, set the Show Changes switch to off (white). When this switch is enabled (green) and a change is made to a shared calendar, you receive notifications about the changes that were made. If the calendar is not shared, you won't see this switch.

(8) Swipe up the screen.

(9) Tap the color you want events on the calendar to appear in.

(10) If you want alerts to be enabled (active) for the calendar, set the Event Alerts switch to on (green).

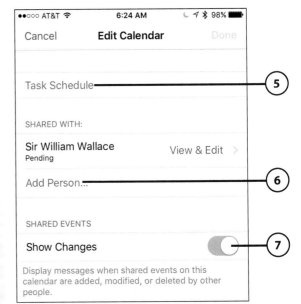

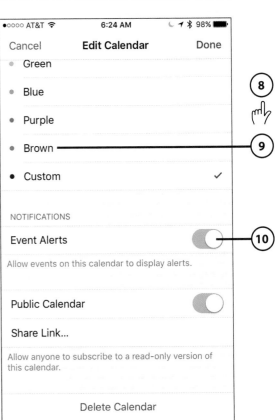

11 To make the calendar public so that others can subscribe to a read-only version of it, set the Public Calendar switch to on (green), tap Share Link, and then use the resulting Share tools to invite others to subscribe to the calendar (more on this later in this chapter).

12 To remove the calendar entirely (instead of hiding it from view), tap Delete Calendar and then tap Delete Calendar at the prompt. The calendar and all its events are deleted. (It's usually better just to hide a calendar as described in step 2 so you don't lose its information.)

13 Assuming that you didn't delete the calendar, tap Done.

14 Edit other calendars as needed.

15 Tap Done. The app moves into viewing mode, and the calendars you enabled are displayed.

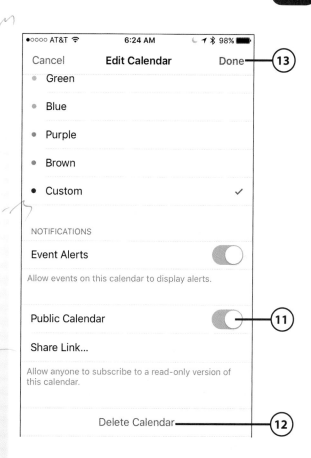

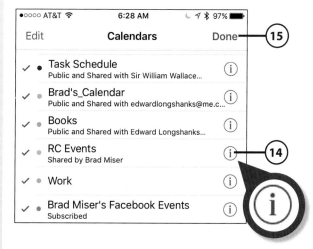

Another Way to Edit

You can also change a calendar by tapping Edit at the upper-left of the Calendars screen and then tapping the calendar you want to edit. When you are done editing calendars, tap Done.

>>>Go Further

ALL OR NOTHING

You can make all your calendars visible by tapping the Show All Calendars button at the top of the screen; tap Hide All Calendars to do the opposite. After all the calendars are shown or hidden, you can tap individual calendars to show or hide them. You can show all the calendars from the same account by tapping the All command at the top of each account's calendar list, such as All iCloud to show all your iCloud calendars. Tap this again to hide all the account's calendars.

Navigating Calendars

The Calendar app uses a hierarchy of detail to display your calendars. The highest level is the year view that shows the months in each year. The next level is the month view, which shows the days of the month (days with events are marked with a dot). This is followed by the week/day view that shows the days of the week and summary information for the events on each day. The most detailed view is the event view, which shows all the information for a single event.

Viewing Calendars

You can view your calendars from the year level all the way down to the day/week view. It's easy to move among the levels to get to the time period you want to see. Here's how:

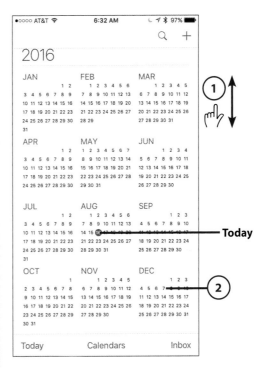

Today

1. Starting at the year view, swipe up and down until you see the year in which you are interested. (If you aren't in the year view, keep tapping the back button located in the upper-left corner of the screen until that button disappears.)

2. Tap the month in which you are interested. The days in that month display, and days with events are marked with a dot.

3. Swipe up and down the screen to view different months.

4. To see the detail for a date, tap it. There are two ways to view the daily details: the Calendar view or the List view. Steps 5 through 8 show the Calendar view, whereas steps 9 through 11 show the List view. Each of these views has benefits, and, as you can see, it is easy to switch between them.

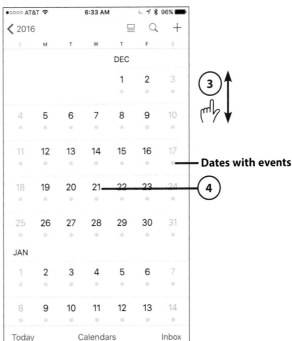

Dates with events

Today Is the Day

To quickly move to the current day, tap Today, located at the bottom of the screen.

(5) To see the Calendar view, ensure the List button is not selected (isn't highlighted). At the top of the screen are the days of the week you are viewing. The date in focus is highlighted with a red circle when that day is today and a black circle for any other day. Below this area is the detail for the selected day showing the events on that day.

(6) Swipe to the left or right on the dates or date being displayed to change the date for which detailed information is being shown.

(7) Swipe up or down on the date detail to browse all its events.

(8) Tap an event to view its detail and skip to step 12.

(9) See the events in List view by tapping the List button so it is highlighted.

(10) Swipe up and down to see the events for each day.

(11) Tap an event to view its detail.

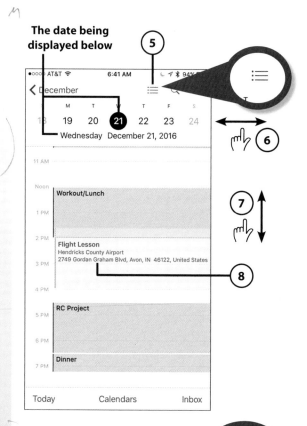

The date being displayed below

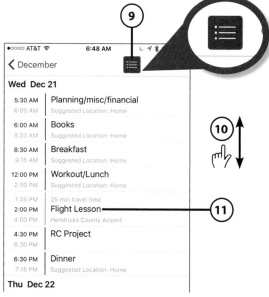

12 Swipe up and down the screen to see all of the event's information.

13 Read information about the event.

14 Tap the Calendar or Alert fields to change these settings; tap the Invitees area to get information about people you've invited to the event.

15 Tap attachments to view them.

16 Tap any links to move to information related to the event.

17 Read notes associated with the event.

18 Tap a location to get directions to it.

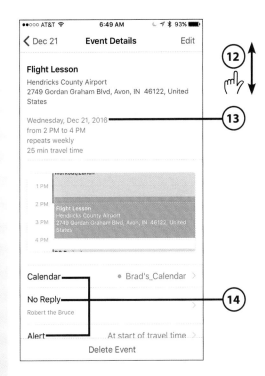

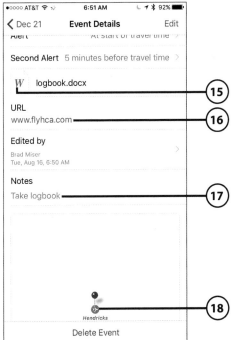

19 Use the Maps app to get directions (see online Chapter 16, "Working with Other Useful iPhone Apps and Features," for more information).

20 Tap Calendar to return to the Calendar app.

21 Tap the date to move back to the week/day view.

22 Tap the back button (labeled with the month you are viewing) to move back to the month view.

(23) To view your calendars in the multiday view, rotate your iPhone so it is horizontal. You can do this while in the week/day view or the month view.

(24) Swipe left or right to change the dates being displayed.

(25) Swipe up or down to change the time of day being displayed.

(26) Tap an event to see its detail.

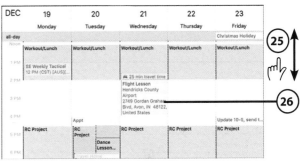

Current Time or Event

When you are viewing today in the Calendar view, the red line stretching horizontally across the screen indicates the current time, which is shown at the left end of that line. When you are viewing today in the List view, the current event is indicated by the text "Now" in red along the right edge of the screen.

Using 3D Touch for Events (iPhone 6s/6s Plus and Later)

You can use the 3D Touch feature on an iPhone 6s/6s Plus or later models with the Calendar app as follows:

(1) Browse events, such as when you use the List view.

(2) Tap and hold on an event in which you are interested. A Peek of that event appears.

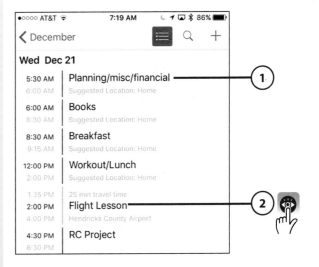

3. Review the preview of the event that appears in the Peek.

4. To open the event so you can see all of its detail, press down slightly harder until it pops open and use the steps in the earlier task to work with it (skip the rest of these steps).

5. To see actions you can perform on the event, swipe up on the Peek.

6. Tap the action you want to perform, such as Delete Event, to delete the event from your calendar.

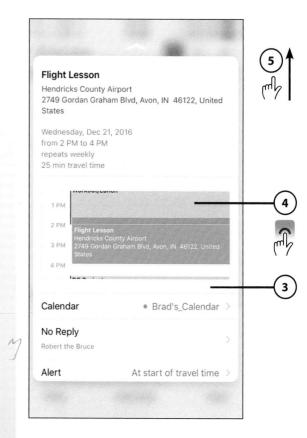

What's Next?

To quickly see the next event on your calendar, move to a Home screen or the Lock screen and swipe to the right to open the Widget Center. Find the UP NEXT widget, which shows you the next event on your calendar; you might want to move this to the top of the Widget Center if you use it regularly. (For more on working with widgets, see Chapter 2.)

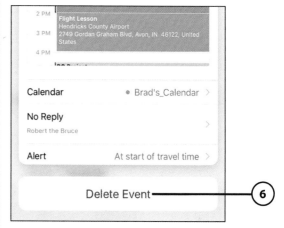

Adding Events to a Calendar

There are a number of ways you can add events to your calendar. You can create an event in an app on a computer, website, or other device and sync that event onto the iPhone through an online account. You can also manually create events in the Calendar app on the iPhone. Your events can include a lot of information, or they can be fairly basic. You can choose to create the basic information on your iPhone while you are on the move and complete it later from a computer or other device, or you can fill in all the details directly in the Calendar app.

(1) Tap the Add button (+), which appears in the upper-right corner of any of the views when your phone is vertical (except when you are viewing an event's details). The initial date information is taken from the date currently being displayed, so you can save a little time if you view the date of the event before tapping the Add button.

(2) Tap in the Title field and type the title of the event.

(3) Tap the Location bar and type the location of the event; if you allow the app to use Location Services, you're prompted to find and select a location; if not, just type the location and skip to step 6.

Location Prompt

The first time you create an event, you might be prompted to allow the Calendar app to access your location information. When you allow the app to use Location Services, you can search for and select event locations. The app can use this information to include an estimate of travel time for the event and to display events on a map when you view their detail.

(4) Type the location in the Search bar. Sites that meet your search are shown below. The results screen has several sections including Recents, which shows locations you've used recently, and Locations, which are sites that the app finds that match your search criteria.

(5) Tap the location for the event. You return to the new event screen and see the location you entered.

(6) To set the event to last all day, set the All-day switch to the on position (green); when you select the All-day option, you provide only the start and end dates (you don't enter times as described in the next several steps). To set a specific start and end time, leave this setting in the off position (white); you set both the dates and times as described in the following steps.

(7) To set a timeframe for the event, tap Starts. The date and time tool appears.

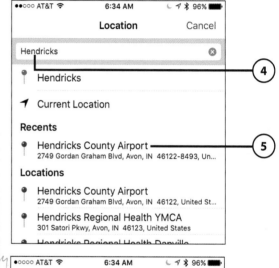

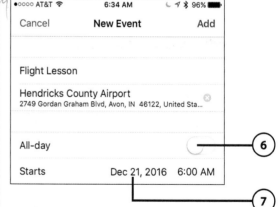

8 Swipe up or down on the date wheel until the date on which the event starts appears in the center.

9 Swipe up or down on the hour wheel until the event's starting hour is shown.

10 Scroll and select the starting minute in the same way.

11 Swipe up or down on the hour wheel to select AM or PM.

12 If you want to associate the event with a specific time zone, tap Time Zone; if not, skip to step 14.

13 Search for and select the time zone with which the event should be associated.

14 Tap Ends.

15 Use the date and time tool to set the ending date and time (if applicable) for the event; these work the same way as for the start date and time.

16 Tap Ends. The date and time tool closes.

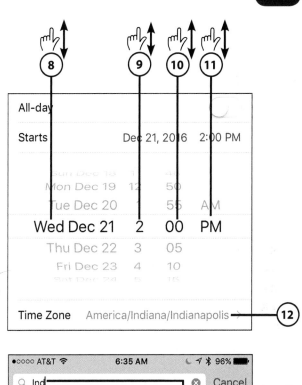

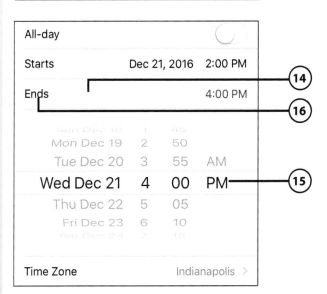

Your Results Might Vary

The fields and options available when you create a new event are based on the calendar with which the event is associated. For example, an iCloud calendar might have different options than a Google calendar does. If you aren't creating an event on your default calendar, it's a good idea to associate the event with a calendar before you fill in its details (to do that, perform step 31 before you do step 2).

Different Ending Time Zone?

The Calendar app assumes the time zone associated with the ending date and time is the same as for the starting date and time. If you want to set a different ending time zone, tap Time Zone below the Ends section and choose a different time zone as described in steps 12 and 13.

No Changes?

When you change a selection on most of the screens you see, you automatically return to the previous screen; for example, when you select a time zone, you immediately return to the New Event screen. If you don't make a change, you can return to the previous screen by tapping New Event in the upper-left corner of the screen. If you start to perform a search for something, such as time zone, but decide not to finish it, tap Cancel and then tap New Event.

(17) To make the event repeat, tap Repeat and follow steps 18–23. (For a nonrepeating event, keep the default, which is Never, and skip to step 24.)

(18) Tap the frequency at which you want the event repeated, such as Every Day, Every Week, etc.; if you want to use a repeat cycle not shown, tap Custom and create the frequency with which you want the event to repeat.

Custom Repeat

To configure a custom repeat cycle for an event in step 18, such as the first Monday of every month, tap Custom on the Repeat screen. Then use the Frequency (Monthly for the example) and Every (for example, On the first Monday) settings to configure the repeat cycle. Tap Repeat to return to the Repeat screen and then tap New Event to get back to the event you are creating.

(19) Tap End Repeat to set a time at which the event stops repeating.

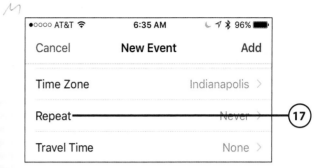

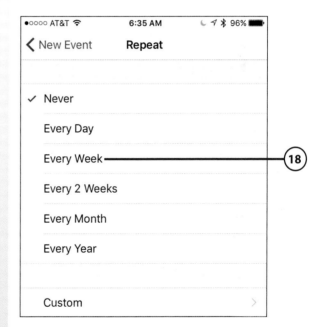

20 Tap Never to have the event repeat ad infinitum, and then skip to step 23.

21 Tap On Date to set an end to the repetition.

22 Use the date tool to set the date for the last repeated event.

23 Tap New Event.

24 To configure travel time for the event, tap Travel Time; if you don't want to configure this, skip to step 31.

25 Set the Travel Time switch to on (green).

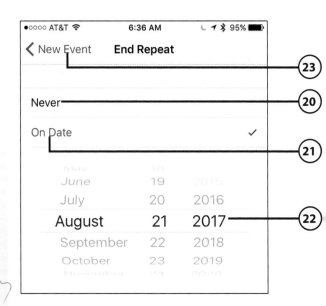

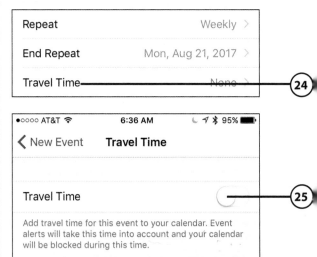

Add travel time for this event to your calendar. Event alerts will take this time into account and your calendar will be blocked during this time.

26 To manually set a travel time for the event, tap it and skip to step 30.

27 Tap Starting Location to build a travel time based on a starting location.

No Change Needed

If you don't make a change to one of the settings, such as on the Repeat screen, tap the back (labeled New Event) button in the upper-left corner of the screen to get back to the New Event screen.

28 To use your current location as the starting point, tap Current Location. Alternatively, use the search tool to find a starting location, and then tap it to select that location. This works just like setting a location for the event.

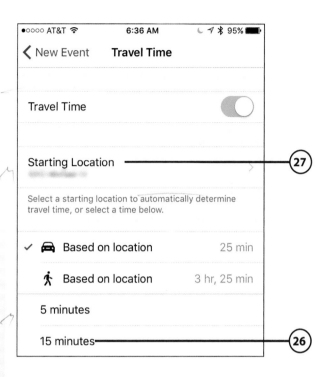

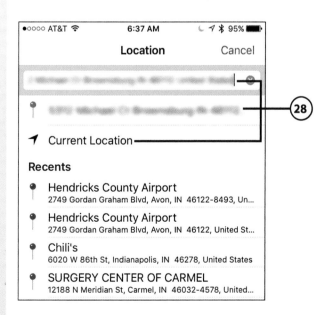

29 Tap the method you will use to travel to the location.

30 Tap New Event.

31 To change the calendar with which the event is associated, tap Calendar (to leave the current calendar selected, skip to step 33).

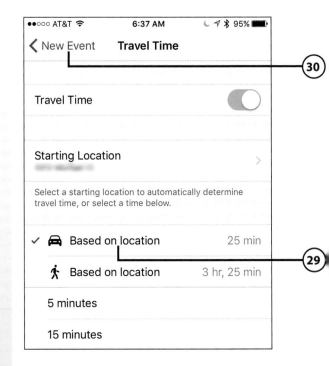

32 Tap the calendar with which the event should be associated.

33 To invite others to the event, tap Invitees; if you don't want to invite someone else, skip to step 38.

34 Enter the email addresses for each person you want to invite; as you type, the app tries to identify people who match what you are typing. You can tap a person to add him to the event or keep entering the email address until it is complete. You can also use the Add button (+) to choose people in your Contacts app (see Chapter 7, "Managing Contacts," for help using that app).

35 Repeat step 34 until you've added everyone you want to invite.

36 Tap Done. You move to the Invitees screen and see those whom you invited.

Automatic Sharing

When you add an event to a calendar that is shared with others, the people with whom the calendar is shared are invited to the event automatically.

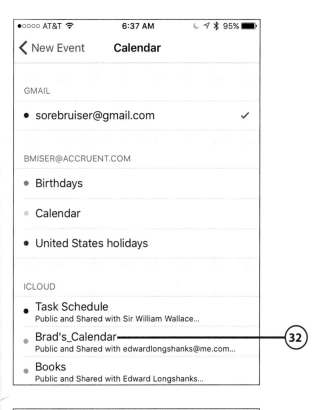

Tap to use the Contacts app to select a contact's email address

(37) Tap New Event.

(38) To set an alert for the event that is different than the default, tap Alert; if you want to use the default alert, skip to step 40.

(39) Tap when you want to see an alert for the event. You can choose a time relative to the time you need to start traveling or relative to the event's start time.

(40) To set a second alert that is different than the default, tap Second Alert; to use the default, skip to step 42.

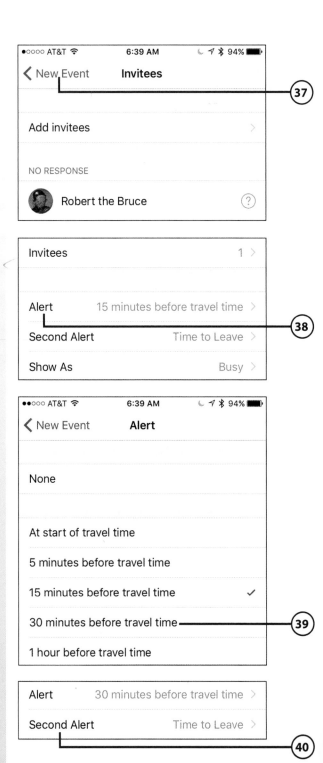

41 Tap when you want to see a second alert for the event. If you have included travel time in the event, the At or before start of travel time options are useful because they alert you relative to when your journey should begin.

42 To indicate your availability during this event, tap Show As.

43 Tap the availability status you want to indicate during the event. If someone can access your availability through their calendar application, this is the status they see if they try to book an event at the same time.

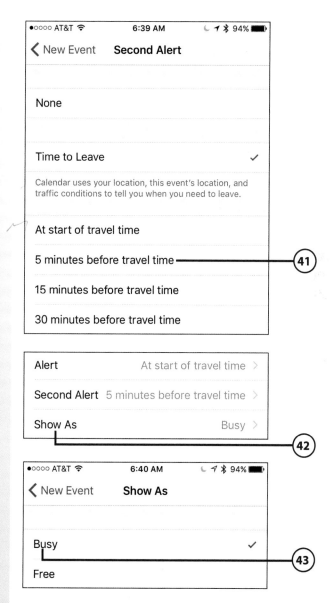

44 Tap in the URL field to enter a URL associated with the event.

45 Type the URL.

46 Tap Done.

47 Tap in the Notes field and type information you want to associate with the event.

48 Tap Add. The event is added to the calendar you selected, and invitations are sent to its invitees. Alerts trigger according to the event's settings.

A Better Way to Create Events

Adding a lot of detail to an event in the Calendar app can be challenging. One effective and easy way to create events is to start with Siri. You can activate Siri and say something like "Create meeting with William Wallace in my office on November 15 at 10 a.m." Siri creates the event with as much detail as you provided (and might prompt you to provide additional information, such as which email address to use to send invitations). When you get to a computer or iPad, edit the event to add more information, such as website links. When your calendar is updated on the iPhone, via syncing, the additional detail for the event appears in the Calendar app, too. (See Chapter 12, "Working with Siri," for detailed information about using Siri.)

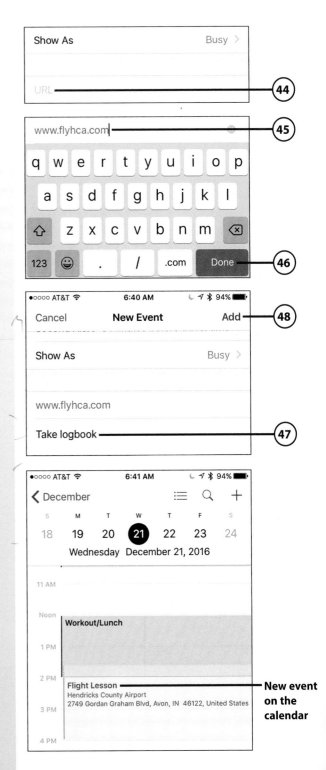

New event on the calendar

Using Quick Actions with the Calendar App (iPhone 6s/6s Plus and Later)

You can use the Quick Actions feature on an iPhone 6s/6s Plus or later models with the Calendar app as follows:

(1) Press on the Calendar icon. The Quick Actions menu appears. At the top, you see the next event on your calendar.

(2) To add a new event, choose Add Event and use the steps in the previous task to create the event.

(3) Tap an event to view its event's details. You move to the event and can see all of its information.

Searching Calendars

You can search for events to locate specific ones quickly and easily. Here's how:

(1) Tap the Search tool.

(6) Slide the Allow Editing switch to off (white); the person will be able to view but not change the calendar.

(7) Tap Edit Calendar.

(8) When you're done sharing the calendar, tap Done.

(9) When you are finished configuring calendar sharing, tap Done.

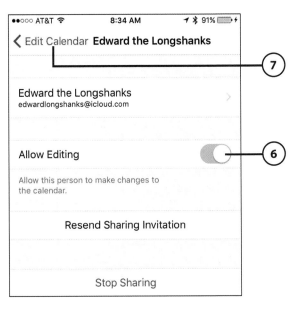

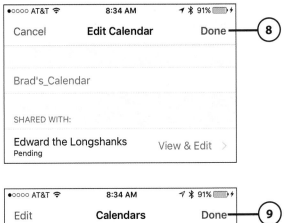

Managing Calendars, Events, and Invitations

Following are some more points about the Calendar app you might find helpful:

- You can also use the List view when you are viewing the calendar in month view. Tap the List button (just to the left of the Search button). The list opens at the bottom of the screen and shows the events on the day currently selected (indicated in the black circle unless the day selected is today, in which case the circle is red).

- You can see today's events at any time by swiping down from the top of the screen to open the Notification Center and then swiping to the right to open the Widgets screen. In the UP NEXT box, you see information about the next event on your calendar. You can view the current day's calendar in the CALENDAR widget; tap an event in the widget to see its detail. (See Chapter 2 for more information about working with the Notification Center and widgets.)

- When an event's alarm goes off, an onscreen notification appears (according to the notification settings for the Calendar app) and the calendar event sound you've selected plays. When an alert notification appears, the event's title, location (if one is set), and time appear. You have to take some action, the minimum of which is viewing the event by pressing it (3D Touch) or tapping it (other models). When a banner notification appears, you see the event's name and location. You can press (3D Touch iPhones) or tap (non-3D Touch iPhones) the event to view its details or ignore it and it moves off the screen after a few moments. You can also swipe up from the bottom of the notification to manually close it.

- If an event gets canceled after you accept it or indicated maybe, you receive a notification in your Inbox that displays a strikethrough through the event's title. Tap Delete to remove the event from your calendar.

- When you receive an invitation, the event is tentatively added to your calendar until you make a decision about it. The status changes as you accept, tentatively accept (Maybe), or decline invitations.

- Siri is useful for working with calendars, especially for creating events. See Chapter 12 for detailed information about using Siri.

>>>Go Further

OTHER USEFUL APPS FOR MANAGING YOUR TIME

Your iPhone includes a couple more apps that can help you manage your time. The Clock app enables you to easily see the current time in multiple locations, set alarms, set a consistent time for sleep every day, use a stopwatch, and count down time with a timer. The Reminders app enables you to create reminders for events, tasks you need to perform, or just about anything else. You can learn a bit more about these apps in online Chapter 16.

Go here to set
up Siri

Speak to Siri to send
and listen to
messages, create and
manage events, make
calls, and much more

Dictate text
instead of
typing

Working with Siri

Siri is Apple's name for the iPhone's and iPad's voice recognition feature. This technology enables your iPhone to "listen" to words you speak so that you can issue commands just by saying them, such as "Send text message to Sam," and the iPhone accomplishes the tasks you speak. This technology also enables the iPhone to take dictation; for example, you can speak words that you want to send in a text or email instead of typing them on the keyboard.

Getting Started

Siri gives you the ability to talk to your iPhone to control it, to get information, and to dictate text. Siri also works with lots of iPhone apps—this feature enables you to accomplish many tasks by speaking instead of using your fingers on the iPhone's screen. For example, you can hear, create, and send text messages; reply to emails; make phone and FaceTime calls; create and manage events and reminders; and much more. Using dictation, you can speak text into any supported app instead of typing.

In fact, Siri does so many things, it's impossible to list them all in a short chapter like this one; you should give Siri a try for the tasks you perform and to get the information you need, and, in many cases, Siri can handle what you want to do.

Think of Siri as your own personal, digital assistant to help you do what you want to do more quickly and easily (especially when you are working in handsfree mode).

You don't have to train Siri very much to work with your voice either; you can speak to it normally and Siri generally does a good job understanding what you say. Also, you don't have to use any specific kind of phrases when you have Siri do your bidding. Simply talk to Siri like you talk to people (well, you probably won't be ordering other people around like you do Siri, but you get the idea).

Your iPhone has to be connected to the Internet for Siri and dictation to work. That's because the words you speak are sent over the Internet, transcribed into text, and then sent back to your iPhone. If your iPhone isn't connected to the Internet, this can't happen, and if you try to use it, Siri reports that it can't complete its tasks.

Because your iPhone is likely to be connected to the Internet most of the time (via Wi-Fi or a cellular network when you have cellular data enabled), this really isn't much of a limitation—but it is one you need to be aware of.

You'll find many examples in this chapter to get you going with specific tasks; from there, you can explore to learn what else Siri can do for you.

Setting Up Siri

Several settings affect how Siri works. In most cases, you can leave these settings in their default positions (including those you selected the first time you turned your iPhone on) and start using Siri right away (beginning with "Understanding Siri's Personality" later in this chapter).

If you decide you want to make changes to Siri's settings, you can use the information in the table that follows to understand the options available to you.

To access Siri's settings, tap Settings on the Home screen and then tap Siri. For each of these settings, you see a description of what it does along with options (if applicable). (Siri must be enabled by setting the Siri switch to on [green] and then tapping Enable Siri before the rest of the settings become visible.)

The Settings App Explained

To get detailed information on using the Settings app, see "Working with the Settings App" in Chapter 5, "Customizing How Your iPhone Works."

Siri Settings

Setting	Description
Siri	To enable Siri, set this switch to on (green) and then tap Enable Siri. Siri is then ready to do your bidding. To disable Siri, set the switch to off (white) and tap Turn Off Siri.
Access on Lock Screen	When this switch is on (green), you can activate and use Siri without unlocking your iPhone. This can be convenient, but it also makes your phone vulnerable to misuse because someone else may be able to activate Siri (for example, to send a text message) without using a passcode or providing a recognized thumbprint. The phone must be unlocked to complete some tasks, but some can be done while the phone is still locked.
Allow "Hey Siri"	When this switch is on (green), you can activate Siri by saying, "Hey Siri" (in addition to pressing and holding the Touch ID/Home button). The first time you turned your iPhone on, you were prompted to speak the phrases Siri uses to recognize when you want its attention. When this switch is off (white), you can only activate Siri with the other options. When you enable it again, you might have to go through the recognition process again.
Language	Set the language you want Siri to use to speak to you.
Siri Voice	Choose the accent and gender of the voice that Siri uses to speak to you (the options you see depend on the language you have selected).
Voice Feedback	Choose when Siri provides verbal feedback as it works for you. When Always On is selected, Siri provides verbal feedback at all times. If you want to control Siri's voice feedback with the ring (Mute) switch, choose Control with Ring Switch. If you want voice feedback only when you are operating in handsfree mode, such as when you are using the iPhone's EarPods or a Bluetooth headset, tap Hands-free Only. Regardless of this setting, you always see Siri's feedback on the screen.
My Info	Choose your contact information in the Contacts app, which Siri uses to address you by name, take you to your home address, etc.
App Support	Some third-party apps also can use Siri. When you access this area, you see information about those apps and switches that determine if those apps can use Siri or not.

Speak your command or ask a question. As you speak, the line at the bottom of the screen oscillates to show you that Siri is hearing your input, and Siri displays what it is hearing you say at the top of the screen. When you stop speaking, Siri goes into processing mode.

After Siri interprets what you've said, it provides two kinds of feedback to confirm what it heard: It displays what it heard on the screen and provides audible feedback to you (unless it's disabled through the settings you learned about earlier). Siri then tries to do what it thinks you've asked and shows you the outcome.

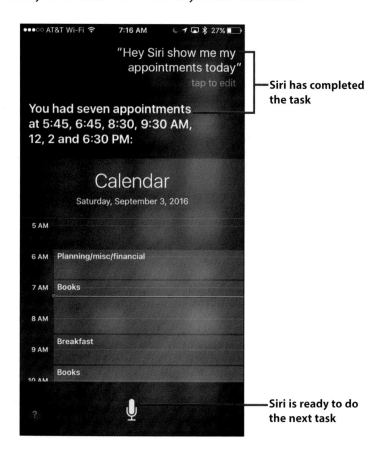

Siri has completed the task

Siri is ready to do the next task

If it needs more input from you, you're prompted to provide it and Siri moves into "listening" mode automatically. If Siri asks you to confirm what it is doing or to make a selection, do so. Siri completes the action and displays what it has done; it also audibly confirms the result (again unless audible feedback is disabled as described earlier). If you want Siri to do more for you, tap the Microphone icon at the bottom of the screen and speak your command. If you want to work with the object Siri created for you in its associated app, tap the object Siri presents.

Also, how Siri interacts with you can depend on how it was activated. For example, if you started the interaction using the verbal "Hey Siri" option, Siri assumes you want to interact verbally and might respond with other options than you would see or hear when you activate Siri manually. When you ask Siri to show you your appointments for the day in this mode, you see the summary, but then Siri asks if you want to hear the details; if you say yes, Siri reads each event to you. When you activate Siri by using the Touch ID/Home button with the same request, Siri stops after showing you the summary.

When you're done with Siri, you can lock the iPhone or press the Touch ID/Home button to move back to the Home screen or to the app you were using.

Siri uses this pattern for all the tasks it does, but often Siri needs to get more information from you, such as when there are multiple contacts that match the command you've given. Siri prompts you for what it needs to complete the work. Generally, the more specific you make your initial command, the fewer steps you have to work through to complete it. For example, if you say "Meet Will at the park," Siri might require several prompts to get you to tell it who Will is and what time you want to meet him at the park. If you say "Meet William Wallace at the park on 10/17 at 10 a.m.," Siri can likely complete the task in one step.

The best way to learn how and when Siri can help you is to try it—a lot. You find a number of examples in the rest of this chapter to get started.

Following are some other Siri tidbits:

- If Siri doesn't automatically quit "listening" mode after you've finished speaking, tap the oscillating line. This stops "listening" mode and Siri starts processing your request. You need to do this more often when you are in a noisy environment because Siri might not be able to accurately discern the sound of you speaking versus the ambient background noise.

- If you are having trouble with Siri understanding commands, speak a bit more slowly and make sure you clearly enunciate and end your words. If you tend to have a very short pause between words, Siri might run them all together, making them into something that doesn't make sense or that you didn't intend.

- Don't pause too long between words or sentences because Siri interprets pauses of a certain length to mean that you are done speaking, and it goes into processing mode. Practicing with Siri helps you develop a good balance between speed and clarity.

- If Siri doesn't understand what you want, or if you ask it a general question, it often performs a web search for you. Siri takes what it thinks you are looking for and does a search. You then see the results page for the search Siri performed, and you might have to manually open and read the results by tapping the listing you want to see. It opens in the Safari app. In some cases, Siri reads the results to you.

- When Siri presents information to you on the screen, you can often tap that information to move into the app with which it is associated. For example, when you tap an event that Siri has created, you move into the Calendar app, where you can add more detail using that app's tools, such as inviting people to an event, changing the calendar it's associated with, and so on.

- When Siri needs direction from you, it presents your options on the screen, including Yes, Cancel, Confirm, or lists of names. You can speak these items or tap them to select them.

- Siri is very useful for some tasks, such as creating reminders, responding to text messages, getting directions, and so on, but not so useful for others, such as inputting search criteria, because it can take longer to use Siri than to type your input.

- Siri is not so good at editing text you dictate. In many cases, your only option is to replace the text you've dictated. For short text blocks, such as text messages or tweets, this can be fine, but for longer blocks of text, you have to use the virtual keyboard to make changes to portions of text. You can use Siri to quickly dictate blocks of text and then edit that text using the iPhone's text-editing tools.

- To use Siri effectively, you should experiment with it by trying to say different commands or similar commands in different ways. For example, when sending emails, you can include more information in your initial command to reduce the number of steps because Siri doesn't have to ask you for more information. Saying "Send an email to Wyatt Earp home about flying" requires fewer steps than saying "Send email" because you've given Siri more of the information it needs to complete the task, and so it won't have to prompt you for who you want to send it to, which address you want to use, or what the subject of the email is.

- When Siri can't complete a task that it thinks it should be able to do, it usually responds with the "I can't connect to the network right now," or "Sorry, I don't know what you mean." This indicates that your iPhone isn't connected to the Internet, the Siri server is not responding, or Siri just isn't able to complete the command for some other reason. If your iPhone is connected to the Internet, try the command again or try rephrasing the command.

- When Siri can't complete a task that it knows it can't do, it responds by telling you so. Occasionally, you can get Siri to complete the task by rephrasing it, but typically you have to use an app directly to get it done.

- If you have a passcode set to protect your iPhone's data (which you should), Siri might not be able to complete some tasks because the phone is locked. If that happens, Siri prompts you to unlock your phone, which you can do by touching the Home/Touch ID button or entering your passcode, and continue with what you were doing.

- Siri can retrieve all sorts of information for you. This can include schedules, weather, directions, unit conversions, and so on. When you need something, try Siri first, as trying it is really the best way to learn how Siri can work for you.

- Siri sees all and knows all (well, not really, but it sometimes seems that way). If you want to be enlightened, try asking Siri questions. Some examples are:

> *What is the best phone?*
>
> *Will you marry me?*
>
> *What is the meaning of life?*
>
> *Tell me a joke.*
>
> And so on.

Some of the answers are pretty funny, and you don't always get the same ones so Siri can keep amusing you. I've heard it even has responses if you curse at it, though I haven't tried that particular option.

Learning How to Use Siri by Example

As mentioned earlier in this chapter, the best way to learn about Siri is to use it. Following are a number of tasks for which Siri is really helpful. Try these to get some experience with Siri and then explore on your own to make Siri work at its best for you.

Using Siri to Make Voice Calls

You can use Siri to make calls by speaking. This is especially useful when you are using your iPhone in handsfree mode.

(1) Activate Siri (such as by pressing and holding the Touch ID/Home button).

Speeding Up Siri

You can combine these steps by saying "Hey Siri, call Robert Bruce iPhone." This is an example where providing Siri with more information when you speak gets the task done more quickly.

(2) Say "Call *name*" or "Call *name numberlabel*," where *name* is the person you want to call and *numberlabel* is the label of the specific number you want to call, such as home, work, iPhone, and so on. Siri identifies the contact you named. If the contact has only one number or you were specific about which number you want to call, Siri places the call and you move into the Phone app. If you weren't specific about the number

you want to call (you simply said "Call *name*") and the person has multiple numbers, Siri lists the numbers available and asks you which number to use.

(3) Speak the label for the number you want to call, or tap it. Siri dials the number for you and you move to the Phone app as if you had dialed the number yourself.

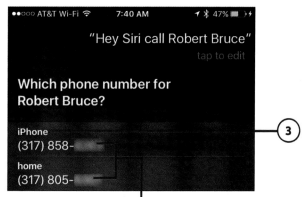

Siri has found multiple numbers for Robert

Placing FaceTime Calls

You can also use Siri to make FaceTime calls by saying "FaceTime *name*."

Composing New Email with Siri

To create email with Siri, do the following:

(1) Say "Hey Siri, send email to *name*," where *name* is the person you want to email. Siri creates a new email addressed to the name you spoke. (If the recipient has more than one email address, Siri prompts you to choose the address you want to use.) Next, Siri asks you for the subject of the email.

More Than One Recipient?

To send an email to more than one recipient, say "and" between each name as in, "Send email to William Wallace and Edward Longshanks." Siri adds each address before and after the "and."

② Speak the subject of the email.
Siri inserts the subject, and then
prompts you for the body of the
message.

③ Speak the body of the email.
As you speak, you can include
punctuation; for example, to end
a sentence, say the word "period"
or to end a question, say the
words "question mark." When Siri
completes the email, it displays
the message on the screen and
prompts you to send it.

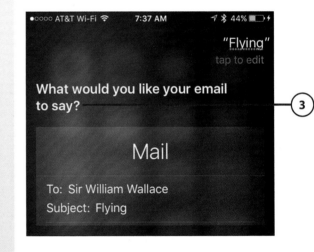

4. Say "send" to send the email or "cancel" to delete it. If you say "send," Siri sends the message, confirms it will be sent, and plays the sent mail sound when it is.

Replying to Emails with Siri

You can also use Siri to speak replies to emails you've read. Here's how:

1. Open the message to which you want to reply.

2. Say "Hey Siri, reply to this email." Siri prompts you for what you want your reply to say.

3. Complete and send the reply; this works just like when you create a new message.

>>>Go Further

DOING MORE IN EMAIL WITH SIRI

Following are some other ways to use Siri for email:

- If you tell Siri to "Read email," Siri tells you how many emails are in your Inboxes and starts reading the time and date of the most recent email message followed by the subject and sender of the message. Siri then does the same for the next email until it has read a number of them. When it gets to the last message it reads, it prompts you to ask if you want to hear the entire list. On the screen, Siri lists the emails; you can tap an email message to read it yourself.

- Siri can read the content of email messages to you when you speak commands that tell it which email you want it to read, such as "Read most recent email," or "Read last email from William Wallace." Siri reads the entire message to you.

- To edit an email Siri created, say "Change." Siri prompts you to change the subject, change the message, cancel it, or send it. If you choose one of the change options, you can replace the subject or the body of the message. To change just some of the subject or body or to change the recipients, tap the message and edit it in the Mail app.

- You can start a new and completely blank email by saying "New email." Siri prompts you for the recipients, subject, and body.

- You can retrieve your email at any time by activating Siri and saying "Check email." Siri checks for new email and then announces how many emails you have received since the oldest message in your Inboxes was received. If you don't have any new email messages, Siri announces how many emails you have previously received and that remain in your Inbox.

- If you just want to know about new email messages, say "Check new email" instead. Siri reports back on new email you have received, but doesn't provide any information on email messages you've previously read.

- You can determine if you have emails from a specific person by asking something like, "Any email from William Wallace?" Siri's reply includes the number of emails in your Inboxes from William and displays them on the screen. Tap an email to read it.

- You can forward an email you are reading by saying "Forward this email" and then following Siri's lead to complete the process.

Having Messages Read to You

You can use Siri to read new text messages to you from the Messages app. When you receive new text messages, do the following to have Siri read them to you:

(1) When you receive a text notification, activate Siri.

(2) Speak the command "Read text messages." (You can combine steps 1 and 2 by saying, "Hey Siri, read text messages.") Siri reads all the new text messages you've received, announcing the sender before reading each message. You have the option to reply (covered in the next task) or have Siri read the message again.

Siri reads each new message in turn until it has read all of them and then announces, "That's it" to let you know it has read all of them.

Siri only reads new text messages to you when you aren't on the Messages screen. If you've already read all your messages and you aren't in the Messages app, when you speak the command "Read text messages," Siri tells you that you have no new messages.

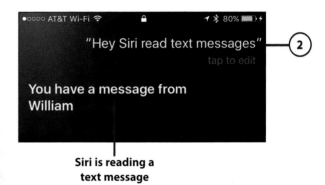

Siri is reading a text message

Reading Old Messages

To read an old message, move back to the conversation containing the message you want to hear. Activate Siri and say the command "Read text message." Siri reads the most recent text message to you.

Replying to Messages with Siri

You can also use Siri to speak replies to messages you've received. Here's how:

1. Listen to a message.

2. At the prompt asking if you want to reply, say "Yes." Siri prepares a reply to the message.

3. Speak your reply. Siri displays your reply.

4. At the prompt, say "Send" to send it, "Cancel" to delete it, or "Change" to replace it. If you tell Siri that you want to send the message, Siri sends it and then confirms that it was sent.

Sending New Messages with Siri

To send a new message to someone, do the following:

(1) Say "Hey Siri, send text to *name*," where *name* is the person you want to text. Siri confirms your command and prepares to hear your text message.

(2) Speak your message. Siri listens and then prepares your message.

(3) If you want to send the message, say "Send." Siri sends the message.

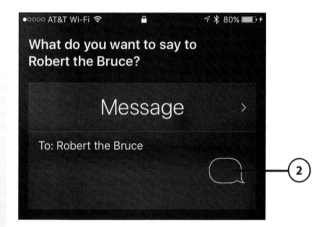

>>>Go Further

DOING MORE MESSAGING WITH SIRI

Following are some other ways to use Siri with messaging:

- If you say "Change" after you have created a new message, Siri prompts you to replace the message with a different one. If you say "Review" after creating a new message, Siri reads your message back to you. If you say "Cancel," Siri stops the process and deletes the message.

- To send a text message to more than one recipient, say "and" between each name, as in, "Send text to William Wallace and Edward Longshanks."

- You can speak punctuation, such as "period" or "question mark" to add it to your message.

- You can tap buttons that Siri presents on the screen, such as Send or Cancel, to take those actions on the message you are working on.

- Messages you receive or send via Siri appear in the Messages app just like messages you receive or send by tapping and typing.

- You can dictate into a text message you start in the Messages app (you learn about dictating later in this chapter).

Using Siri to Create Events

Siri is useful for capturing meetings and other events you want to add to your calendars. To create an event by speaking, use the following steps:

(1) Activate Siri.

(2) Speak the event you want to create. There are a number of variations in what you can say. Examples include "Set up a meeting with William Wallace on Friday at 10 a.m." or "Doctor appt on Thursday at 1 p.m." and so on. If you have any conflicts with the event you are setting up, Siri lets you know about them. (Again, you can combine these two steps by speaking "Hey Siri" and then immediately speaking a command to create the event.)

(3) Say "Confirm" if you don't have any conflicts or "Yes" if you do and you still want to have the appointment confirmed; you can also tap Confirm. Siri adds the event to your calendar. Say "Cancel" to cancel the event.

(4) To add more information to an event Siri has created for you, tap it on the confirmation screen after you have confirmed it (not shown on the figure). You move into the Calendar app and can edit the event just like events you create within that app.

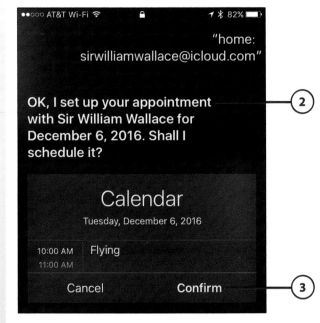

Invitees

If you include the name of someone for whom you have an email address, Siri automatically sends invitations. If you include a name that matches more than one contact, Siri prompts you to choose the contact you want to invite. If the name doesn't match a contact, Siri enters the name but doesn't send an invitation.

Using Siri to Create Reminders

Using Siri to create reminders can be another useful thing you do with Siri, assuming you find reminders useful, of course. Here's how:

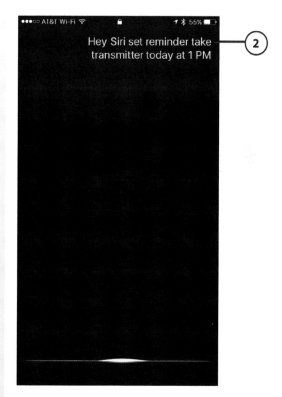

Hey Siri set reminder take transmitter today at 1 PM

1. Activate Siri.

2. Speak the reminder you want to create. Here are some examples:

   Remind me to buy the A-10 at Motion RC.

   Remind me to finish Chapter 10 at 10 a.m. on Saturday.

   Remind me to buy milk when I leave work.

   Siri provides a confirmation of what you asked. If you didn't mention a time or date when you want to be reminded, Siri prompts you to provide the details of when you want to be reminded.

3. Speak the date and time when you want to be reminded. If you included a date and time in your original reminder request, you skip this step. Unlike some of the other tasks, Siri creates the reminder without confirming it with you.

④ If you don't want to keep the reminder, activate Siri and say "Remove" or tap Remove.

⑤ To add detail to the reminder, tap it. You move into the Reminders app and can add more information to the reminder as you can when you create one manually.

>>>*Go Further*

GOING FURTHER WITH SIRI TO MANAGE TIME

Following are some other ways to use Siri with the Calendar, Reminders, and Clock apps:

- You can change events with Siri, too. For example, if you have a meeting at 3 p.m., you can move it by saying something like "Move my Friday 3 p.m. meeting to Friday at 6 p.m."

- You can get information about your events with Siri by saying things such as:

    Show me today's appointments.
    Do I have meetings on November 3?
    What time is my first appointment tomorrow?
    What are my appointments tomorrow?

    Siri tells you about the events and shows you what they are on the screen. You can tap any event to view it in the Calendar app.

- You can speak to your iPhone to set alarms. Tell Siri what you want and when you want the alarm to be set. For example, you can say something like "New alarm *alarmname* 6 a.m. tomorrow," where *alarmname* is the label of the alarm. Siri sets an alarm to go off at that time and gives it the label you speak. It displays the alarm on the screen along with a status button so you can turn it off if you change your mind. You don't have to label alarms, and you can just say something like "Set alarm 6 a.m. tomorrow." However, a label can be useful to issue other commands. For example, if an alarm has a name, you can turn off an alarm by saying "Turn off *alarmname*." Any alarms you create with Siri can be managed just like alarms you create directly in the Clock app.

- To set a countdown timer, tell Siri to "Set timer for *x* minutes," where *x* is a number of minutes (you can do the same to set a timer for seconds or hours, too). Siri starts a countdown for you and presents it on the screen. You can continue to use the iPhone however you want. When the timer ends, you see and hear an alert. You can also reset the time, pause it, and so on by speaking.

- You can get information about time by asking questions, such as "What time is it?" or "What is the date?" You can add location information to the time information, too, as in "What time is it in London, England?"

- Tapping any confirmation Siri displays takes you back into the related app. For example, if you tap a clock that results when you ask what time it is, you can tap that clock to move into the Clock app. If you ask about your schedule today, you can tap any of the events Siri presents to move into the Calendar app to work with them.

- When you use Siri to create events and reminders, they are created on your default calendar (events) or reminder list (reminders).

Using Siri to Get Information

Siri is a great way to get information about lots of different topics in many different areas. You can ask Siri for information about a subject, places in your area, unit conversion (such as inches to centimeters), and so on. Just try speaking what you want to learn to best get the information you need. Here's an example looking for Chinese restaurants in my area:

(1) Activate Siri.

(2) Say something like, "Show me Chinese restaurants close to me." (Or a faster way is to combine steps 1 and 2 by saying "Hey Siri, show me Chinese restaurants in my area.") Siri presents a list of results that match your query and even provides a summary of reviews at the top of the screen. (You must have Location Services enabled for this to work. Refer to Chapter 5, "Customizing How Your iPhone Works," for information about configuring Location Services.)

Siri is also useful for getting information about topics. Siri responds by conducting a web search and showing you the result. For example, suppose you want to learn about William Wallace. Activate Siri and say, "Tell me about William Wallace." Siri responds with information about your topic.

If you like Chinese food (or just about anything else), Siri can help you find it

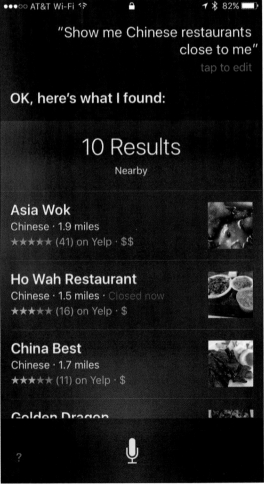

You can have Siri read the information by activating Siri and saying "Read." Siri reads the results (this doesn't always work; it works best when the results are presented via Wikipedia or something similar).

Using Siri to Play Music

You can also play music by telling Siri the music you want to hear.

1. Activate Siri.

2. Tell Siri the music you want to hear. There are a number of variations in what you can say. Examples include

   Play album Time of My Life.
   Play song "Gone" by Switchfoot.
   Play playlist Jon McLaughlin.

   Siri provides a confirmation of what you asked and begins playing the music.

3. Tap Open Music to move into the Music app to control the music with your fingers.

Want to learn about something—just ask Siri

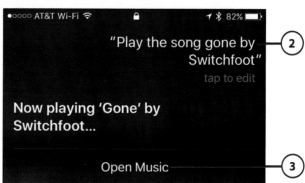

>>>Go Further

MORE SPOKEN COMMANDS FOR MUSIC

There are a number of commands you can speak to find, play, and control music (and other audio). "Play *artist*" plays music by the artist you speak. "Play *album*" plays the album you name. In both cases, if the name includes the word "the," you need to include "the" when you speak the command. "Shuffle" plays a random song. "Play more like this" uses the Genius to find songs similar to the one playing and plays them. "Previous track" or "next track" does exactly what they sound like they do. To hear the name of the artist for the song currently playing, say "Who sings this song?" You can shuffle music in an album or playlist by saying "Shuffle playlist *playlistname*." You can stop the music, pause it, or play it by speaking those commands.

Using Siri to Get Directions

With Siri, it's easy to get directions— you don't even have to stop at a gas station to ask.

1. Activate Siri.

2. Speak something like "Give me directions to the airport." If you want directions starting from someplace other than your current location, include that in the request, such as "Get directions from the Eagle Creek Airpark to the Indianapolis International Airport."

3. If Siri needs you to confirm one or more of the locations, tap the correct one. Siri uses the Maps app to generate directions.

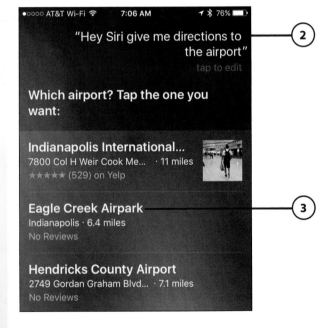

4 Tap Go to start turn-by-turn instructions.

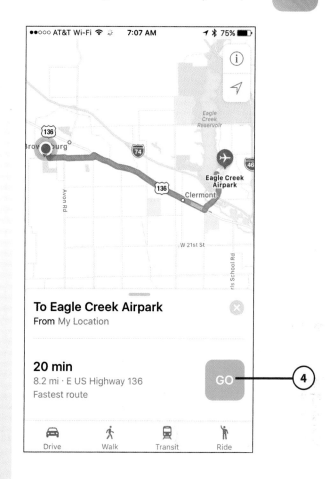

Using Siri to Open Apps

As you accumulate apps on your iPhone, it can take several taps and swipes to get to a specific app, such as one that is stored in a folder that isn't on the page of the Home screen you are viewing. With Siri, you can open any app on your phone with a simple command.

(1) Say "Hey Siri, open *appname*," where *appname* is the name of the app you want to open.

(2) If your phone needs to be unlocked to open the app, unlock it (such as by touching the Touch ID button). Siri opens the app for you, and you move to the last screen in that app you were using.

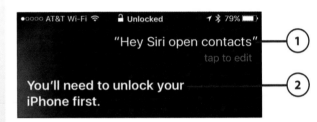

It's Not All Good

When Siri Misunderstands

Voice commands to Siri aren't perfect. Make sure you confirm your commands by listening to the feedback Siri provides when it repeats them or reviewing the feedback Siri provides on the screen. Sometimes, a spoken command can have unexpected results, which can include making a phone call to someone in the Contacts app. If you don't catch such a mistake before the call is started, you might be surprised to hear someone answering your call instead of hearing music you intended to play. You can put Siri in listening mode by tapping the Microphone button, and then saying "no" or "stop" to stop Siri should a verbal command go awry.

④ Using Dictation to Speak Text Instead of Typing

You can use the iPhone's dictation capability to speak text into any app, such as Mail, Messages, and so on.

In fact, any time you see the Microphone button on the keyboard, dictation is available to you. Here's how this works:

① In the app you are using, put the cursor where you want the text you dictate to start. For example, if you are creating an email, tap in the body.

② Tap the Microphone key on the virtual keyboard.

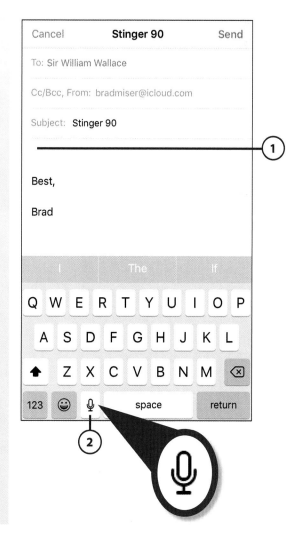

6 Tap In New Tab to have the web pages you are opening appear in a new tab. (You learn about Safari tabs in "Opening New Pages in a New Tab").

7 Tap In Background to have web pages you are opening open in the background. (You learn about this option in "Opening New Pages in the Background").

8 Tap Safari. When you tap and hold on a link, the resulting web page opens according to the option you selected in step 6 or 7. You can change other Safari settings using a similar pattern and the description of the options in the following table.

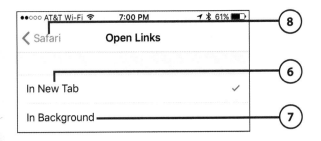

Safari Settings

Settings Area	Location	Setting	Description
SEARCH	Search Engine	Search Engine	Enables you to choose your default search tool; the options are Bing, DuckDuckGo, Google (default), and Yahoo!.
SEARCH	N/A	Search Engine Suggestions	When this switch is on (green), Safari asks your default search engine for suggestions related to what you type in the Address/Search bar. This makes search easier because you can type your search term in the bar instead of first moving to the search web page.
SEARCH	N/A	Safari Suggestions	When this switch is on (green), Safari makes suggestions related to what you type in the Address/Search bar. This makes search easier because you can type your search term in the bar instead of first moving to the search web page.

Settings Area	Location	Setting	Description
SEARCH	Quick Website Search	Quick Website Search	When this switch is on (green), you can perform a search at a specific website by typing its name before your search term. For example, you can type "wiki william wallace" in the Address/Search box and the first section of the results will be entries in the Wikipedia related to William Wallace; this saves you the steps of moving to the search engine results, and then tapping the articles you want to read because you can do this directly from the Search screen instead.
SEARCH	N/A	Preload Top Hit	When this switch is on (green), the sites you move to or find more frequently are loaded while you search, making accessing them faster.
GENERAL	Passwords	Passwords	When you tap this setting and confirm your security (with Touch ID or a passcode), you see the list of passwords stored on your iPhone. Tap a password to see its details or edit it. Swipe to the left on a password, and then tap Delete to remove it.
GENERAL	Autofill	Autofill	These settings enable you to automatically log in to websites and to quickly complete forms on the Web by automatically filling in key information for you. Set the Use Contact Info switch to on (green), and then tap your contact information in the Contacts app. You can determine what data is saved on your iPhone by setting the following switches on (green) or off (white): Names and Passwords or Credit Cards. Tap Saved Credit Cards to view or change existing credit card information or to add new credit cards to Safari.
GENERAL	N/A	Frequently Visited Sites	When this switch is on (green) and you move into the Address/Search bar, Safari shows a section of sites that you visit frequently, making them easier to return to.

Settings Area	Location	Setting	Description
GENERAL	Favorites	Favorites	Use this option to choose the folder of bookmarks for sites that you use most frequently. The bookmarks in the folder you select appear at the top of the screen when you move into the Address/Search bar, making them fast and easy to use.
GENERAL	Open Links	Open Links	This tells Safari the option you want to see when you tap and hold a link on a current web page to open a new web page. The In New Tab option causes Safari to open and immediately take you to a new tab displaying the web page with which a link is associated. The In Background option causes Safari to open pages in the background for links you tap so you can view them later.
GENERAL	N/A	Block Pop-ups	Some websites won't work properly with pop-ups blocked, so you can use this setting to temporarily enable pop-ups by sliding the switch to off (white). When the Block Pop-ups switch is on (green), pop-ups are blocked.
PRIVACY & SECURITY	N/A	Do Not Track	To enable private browsing, which means Safari doesn't track and keep a list of the sites you visit, set the Do Not Track switch to on (green). With this setting on, you won't be able to use the History list to return to sites you visited.
PRIVACY & SECURITY	Block Cookies	Block Cookies	This enables you to choose the kind of cookies you want to allow to be stored on your iPhone. The Always Block option blocks all cookies. The Allow from Current Website Only setting allows cookies only from the website you are currently viewing to be stored on your phone. Allow from Websites I Visit blocks cookies from sites you didn't visit directly. This is the setting I recommend you choose because it enables websites you visit to store information on your iPhone while blocking cookies from sites you didn't visit. The Always Allow option accepts all cookies (not recommended).

Settings Area	Location	Setting	Description
PRIVACY & SECURITY	N/A	Fraudulent Website Warning	If you don't want Safari to warn you when you visit websites that appear to be fraudulent, set the Fraudulent Website Warning switch to off (white).
PRIVACY & SECURITY	N/A	Check for Apple Pay	When you visit websites that support Apple Pay with this switch enabled (green), you can use your Apple Pay account to make payments for goods or services. (Refer to Chapter 2, "Using Your iPhone's Core Features," for information about Apple Pay.)
PRIVACY & SECURITY	N/A	Clear History and Website Data	When you tap this command and confirm it by tapping Clear History and Data at the prompt, Safari removes the websites you have visited from your history list. The list starts over, so the next site you visit is added to your history list again—unless you have enabled private browsing. It also removes all cookies and other website data that have been stored on your iPhone.
READING LIST	N/A	Use Cellular Data	The Reading List enables you to store web pages on your iPhone for offline reading. If you want to allow pages to be saved to your iPhone when you are using its cellular data connection, slide the Use Cellular Data switch to the on (green) position. When it is off (white), you can use this feature only when connected to Wi-Fi.
Advanced	Website Data	Website Data	Website Data displays the amount of data associated with websites you have visited; swipe up on the screen and tap Remove All Website Data to clear this data.
Advanced	N/A	JavaScript	Set this switch to off (white) to disable JavaScript functionality (however, some sites won't work properly without JavaScript).
Advanced	N/A	Web Inspector	This switch controls a feature that is used by website developers to see how their sites work on an iPhone.

9) Repeat steps 5–8 until you see a bookmark you want to visit.

10) Tap the bookmark you want to visit. Safari moves to that website.

11) Use the information in the section "Viewing Websites" later in this chapter to get information on viewing the web page.

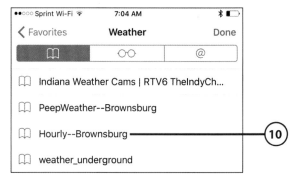

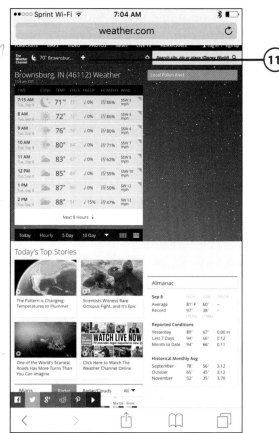

Playing Favorites

You might see two Favorites folders on the Bookmarks screen. The folder marked with a star is the folder you designated, using the Safari settings described previously in this chapter, as the place to store Favorites on your iPhone. If you use Safari on a computer, you can also configure bookmarks and folders of bookmarks on its Bookmarks bar. When these bookmarks are synced from your computer to the iPhone, they might be stored in a folder of bookmarks also called Favorites and shown with the standard folder icon. If you set this synced folder in your iPhone's Safari settings to also be its Favorites folder, you won't have to deal with this potentially confusing situation of having two Favorites folders.

iPhone Web Pages

Some websites have been specially formatted for mobile devices. These typically have less complex information on each page, so they load faster. When you move to a site like this, you might be redirected to the mobile version automatically, or you might be prompted to choose which version of the site you want to visit. On the mobile version, there is typically a link that takes you to the "regular" version, too. (It's sometimes called the Desktop, Full, or Classic version.) Sometimes the version formatted for handheld devices offers less information or fewer tools than the regular version. Because Safari is a full-featured browser, you can use either version.

Using Your Favorites to Move to Websites

Using the Safari settings described earlier, you can designate a folder of bookmarks as your Favorites. You can get to the folders and bookmarks in your Favorites folder more quickly and easily than navigating to it as described in the previous section. Here's how to use your Favorites:

(1) On the Home screen, tap Safari. (If you are in Safari and have the Bookmarks screen open, tap Done to close it.)

(2) Tap in the Address/Search bar (if you don't see the Address/ Search bar, tap at the top of the screen to show it). Just below the Address/Search bar are your Favorites (bookmarks and folders of bookmarks). The keyboard opens at the bottom of the screen.

8 Use the information in the section "Viewing Websites" later in this chapter to view the web page.

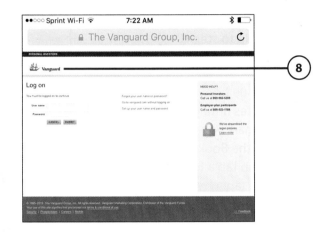

Typing URLs to Move to Websites

A Uniform Resource Locator (URL) is the Internet address of a web page. URLs can be relatively simple, such as www.apple.com, or they can be quite long and convoluted. The good news is that by using bookmarks, you can save a URL in Safari so you can get back to it using its bookmark (as you learned in the previous two tasks) and thus avoid typing URLs more than once. To use a URL to move to a website, do the following:

1 On the Home screen, tap Safari. (If you are in Safari and have the Bookmarks screen open, tap Done to close it.)

2 Tap in the Address/Search bar (if you don't see the Address/Search bar, tap at the top of the screen). The URL of the current page becomes highlighted, or if you haven't visited a page, the Address/Search bar is empty. Just below the Address/Search bar, your Favorites are displayed. The keyboard appears at the bottom of the screen.

3 If an address appears in the Address/Search bar, tap the Clear button (x) to remove it.

4 Type the URL you want to visit. If it starts with www (which almost all URLs do), you don't have to type "www". As you type, Safari attempts to match what you are typing to a site you have visited previously and completes the URL for you if it can. Just below the Address/Search bar, Safari presents a list of sites that might be what you are looking for, organized into groups, such as Suggested Websites.

5 If one of the sites shown is the one you want to visit, tap it. You move to that web page; skip to step 8.

6 If Safari doesn't find a match, continue typing until you enter the entire URL.

7 Tap Go. You move to the web page.

8 Use the information in the section "Viewing Websites" to view the web page.

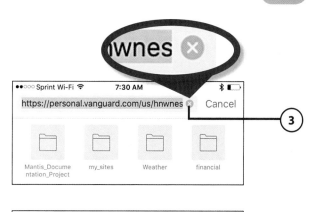

Shortcut for Typing URLs

URLs include a top-level domain code that represents the type of site (theoretically anyway) that URL leads to. Common examples are .com (commercial sites) and .edu (educational sites). To quickly enter a URL's code, tap and hold the period key to see a menu from which you can select other options, such as .net or .edu. Select the code you want on the keyboard, and it is entered in the Address/Search bar.

Using Your Browsing History to Move to Websites

As you move about the Web, Safari tracks the sites you visit and builds a history list (unless you enabled the Do Not Track option, in which case this doesn't happen and you can't use History to return to previous sites). You can use your browsing history list to return to sites you've visited.

1. Tap the Bookmarks button.

2. If you aren't on the Bookmarks screen, tap the back button until you move to the Bookmarks screen. (Safari remembers your last location, so if you were last on the Bookmarks screen, you don't need to tap any buttons to get back there.)

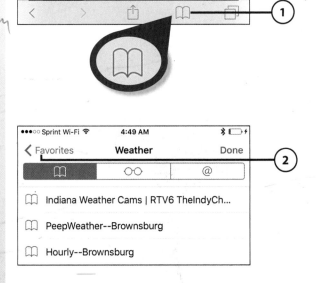

(3) If necessary, swipe down the Bookmarks page until you see the History folder.

(4) Tap History.

(5) Swipe up and down the page to browse all the sites you've visited. The more recent sites appear at the top of the screen; the further you move down the screen, the further back in time you go. Earlier sites are collected in folders for various times, such as This Morning, or Monday Afternoon.

(6) Tap the site you want to visit. The site opens and you can use the information in the section "Viewing Websites" to view the web page.

Erasing the Past

To clear your browsing history, tap the Clear button at the bottom of the History screen. At the prompt, tap the timeframe that you want to clear; the options are The last hour, Today, Today and yesterday, or All time. Your browsing history for the period of time you selected is erased. (Don't you wish it was this easy to erase the past in real life?)

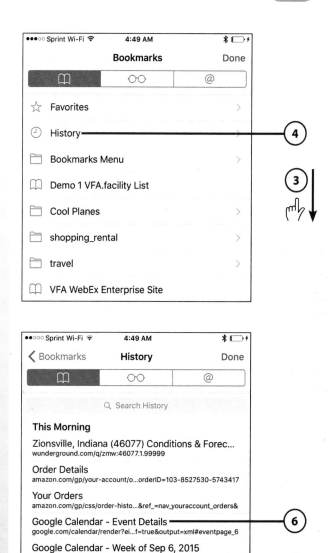

Viewing Websites

Even though your iPhone is a small device, you'll be amazed at how well it displays web pages designed for larger screens.

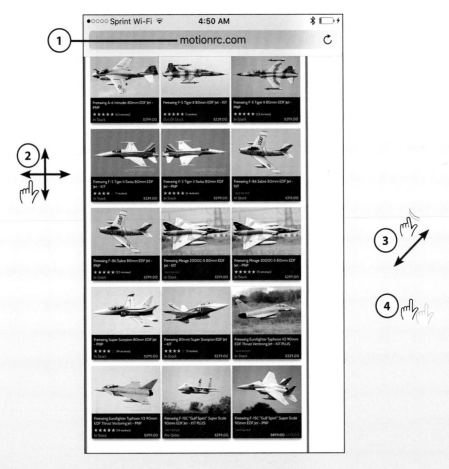

① Use Safari to move to a web page as described in the previous tasks.

② To browse around a web page, swipe your finger right or left, or up or down.

③ Zoom in manually by unpinching your fingers.

④ Zoom in automatically by tapping twice on the screen.

Where Did the URL Go?

When you first move to a URL, you see that URL in the Address/Search bar. After you work with a site, the Address/Search bar is hidden and the URL is replaced with the high-level domain name for the site (such as *sitename*.com, *sitename*.edu, and so on). To see the Address/Search bar again, tap the top of the screen. To see the full URL again, tap in the Address/Search bar.

(5) Zoom out manually by pinching your fingers.

(6) Zoom out a column or a figure by tapping it twice.

(7) Tap a link to move to the location at which it points. Links can come in many forms, including text (most text that is a link is in color and underlined) or graphics. The web page to which the link points opens and replaces the page currently being displayed.

Do More with Links

To see options for a link, tap and hold your finger down for a second or so. (If you are using an iPhone that supports Touch 3D, this can be a bit tricky. If you apply pressure, a Peek appears instead of the menu. To see the menu, place your finger on the screen and hold it there, but don't put any pressure on it.) When you lift your finger, a menu appears. Tap Open to open the page to replace the current page at which the link points (this is the same as tapping a link once). Tap Open in Background to open the page in a new Safari window that opens in the background, or tap Open in New Tab to open the new page in the new tab. The command that appears depends on the Open Links Safari setting that you learned about earlier in this chapter. Tap Add to Reading List to add the page to your Reading List. If the link is an image, tap Save Image to save the image on your phone. Tap Copy to copy the link's URL so that you can paste it elsewhere, such as in an email message. Tap Cancel to return to the current page and take no action.

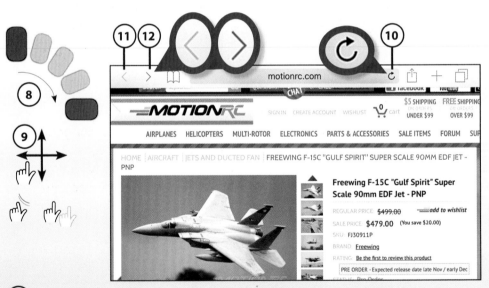

⑧ To view the web page in landscape orientation, rotate the iPhone so that it is horizontal.

⑨ Scroll, zoom in, and zoom out on the page to read it, as described in steps 2–7.

⑩ Tap Refresh to refresh a page to update its contents. (Note: While a page is loading, this is the stop button [x]; tap it to stop the rest of the page from loading.)

⑪ To move to a previous page you've visited, tap the Back button (left-facing arrow). (If the arrow is grayed out, it means you are at the beginning of the set of pages you have visited.)

⑫ To move to a subsequent page, tap the Forward button (right-facing arrow). (If the arrow is grayed out, it means you are at the end of the set of pages you have visited.)

13 As you move around, the Address/Search bar at the top of the page and the toolbar at the bottom of the page are hidden automatically; to show them again, tap the top or bottom of the screen (on the iPhone 6/6s Plus or later models, tap the top of the screen when the phone is horizontal).

Different Phones, Different Look

The type of iPhone you are using to browse the Web affects how pages look and where controls are located. For example, when you use an iPhone 5s, you see black at the top and bottom of the screen whereas you see white there on an iPhone 7. Also, when you rotate an iPhone 5s, the tools are at the top and bottom of the screen, but on an iPhone 7, the controls are all at the top of the screen.

Working with Multiple Websites at the Same Time

When you move to a web page by using a bookmark, typing a URL, or tapping a link on the current web page, the new web page replaces the current one. However, you can also open and work with multiple web pages at the same time so that a new web page doesn't replace the current one.

When you work with multiple web pages, each open page appears in its own tab. You can use the tab view to easily move to and manage your open web pages.

You can also close open tabs, and you can even open web pages that are open on other devices on which your iCloud account has been configured and Safari syncing enabled.

There are two ways to open a new web page in a new tab. One is to tap and hold on a link on the current web page; you can use the resulting Open command to open the new page. There are two options for this approach; the one you use is determined by the Open Links preference set as described earlier in this chapter. The In Background option causes the new page to open and move to the background. This is most useful when you want to read the new page at a later time, such as when you are done with the current one. The In New Tab option causes the new page to open and move to the front so you see it instantly while moving the current page and its tab to the background.

The second way to open a new web page in a new tab is by using the Tab Manager.

These options are described in the following tasks.

Tapping Without Holding

When you tap, but don't hold down, a link on a web page, the web page to which the link points opens and replaces the current web page—no new tab is created. When you tap and hold a link, the behavior is determined by the setting you chose in the preferences as covered in a task earlier in this chapter ("Setting Safari Preferences"). To make things a bit more complicated, if your phone supports 3D Touch (iPhone 6s/6s Plus and later), don't apply pressure to the screen when you tap; if you do, a Peek appears instead (you learn about this in "Using 3D Touch with Safari").

Opening New Pages in the Background

If you enabled the In Background option for the Open Links preference, you can open new web pages by doing the following:

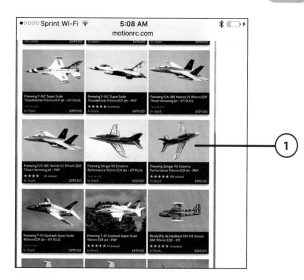

① Tap and hold (but don't press) on the link you want to open in the background.

② Tap Open in Background. The page to which the link points opens. The only result you see is the current page "jumping" down to the Tab Manager button in the lower-right corner of the screen.

③ Continue opening pages in the background; see "Using Tab View to Manage Open Web Pages" later in this chapter to learn how to use the tab view to move to pages that are open in the background.

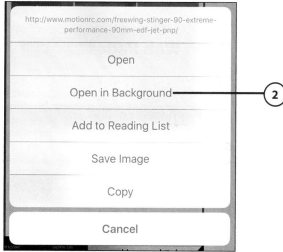

Opening New Pages in a New Tab

If you enabled the In New Tab option for the Open Links preference, you can open new pages by doing the following:

① Tap and hold on the link you want to open in the background.

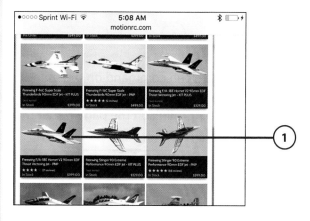

6 Tap a Close button (x) to close a tab; alternatively swipe to the left on the tab you want to close.

7 To open a new tab, tap the Add button (+) to create a new tab that shows your Favorites screen; navigate to a new page in that tab using the methods described in other tasks (tapping bookmarks or typing a URL).

8 Tap Done to close the tab view. The tab view closes, and the page you were most recently viewing is shown.

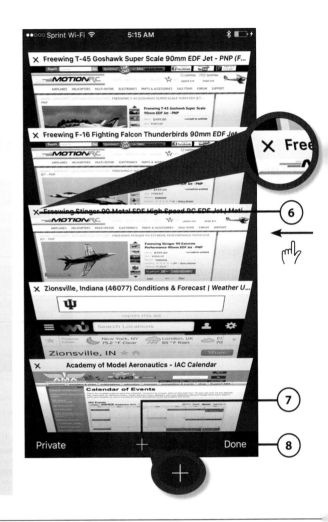

Tabs Are Independent

Each tab is independent. So, when you are working with a tab and use the back/forward buttons to move among its pages, you are just moving among the pages open under that tab. Pages open in other tabs are not affected.

Opening Web Pages That Are Open on Other Devices

When you enable iCloud Safari syncing, iCloud tracks the websites you have open on all the devices on which you have Safari syncing enabled, including your iPhone, iPads, and Macs. This is really handy when you have pages open on another device and want to view them on your iPhone. (Pages open on your iPhone are available on your other devices, too.) To view a page you have open on another device, do the following:

(1) Open the tab view.

(2) Swipe up the screen until you see the pages open on other devices. There is a section for each device; sections are labeled with the device's name. In each device's section, you see the pages open in Safari on those devices.

(3) Tap the page you want to view. The page opens on the iPhone and becomes a new tab.

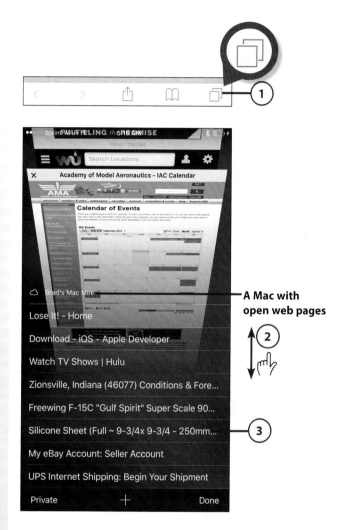

A Mac with open web pages

Keep Private Things Private

If you aren't browsing in Private mode and tap the Private button at the bottom of the tab view, Safari moves into Private mode and stops tracking the sites you visit. Tap the Private button again to return to the previous state. If you are browsing in Private mode, tapping the Private button shows or hides the tabs in the tab view.

Saving and Organizing Bookmarks

In addition to moving bookmarks from a computer or iCloud onto your iPhone, you can save new bookmarks directly in your iPhone (they are synced onto other devices, too). You can also organize bookmarks on your iPhone to make them easier and faster to access.

Creating Bookmarks

When you want to make it easy to return to a website, create a book-mark with the following steps:

1. Move to a web page for which you want to save a bookmark.

2. Tap the Share button.

3. Tap Add Bookmark. The Add Bookmark screen appears, showing the title of the web page you are viewing, which will also be the name of the bookmark initially; its URL; and the Location field, which shows where the bookmark will be stored when you create it.

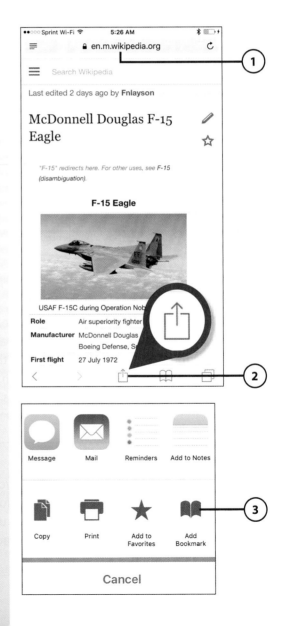

4 Edit the bookmark's name as needed, or tap the Clear button (x) to erase the current name, and then type the new name of the bookmark. The titles of some web pages are quite long, so it's a good idea to shorten them so the bookmark's name is easier to read on the iPhone's screen.

5 Tap the current folder shown under Location. The Location section expands and you see all of the folders of bookmarks on your phone. The folder that is currently selected is marked with a check mark.

6 Swipe up and down the screen to find the folder in which you want to place the new bookmark. You can choose any folder on the screen; folders are indented when they are contained within other folders.

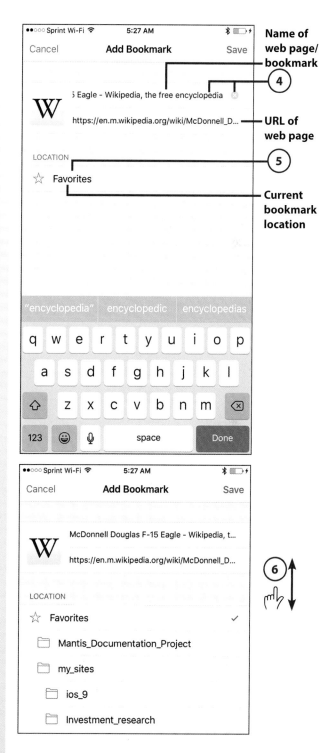

Name of web page/bookmark

4

URL of web page

5

Current bookmark location

6

(7) Tap the folder in which to store the new bookmark. You return to the Add Bookmark screen, which shows the location you selected.

(8) Tap Save. The bookmark is created and saved in the location you specified. You can use the bookmark to return to the website at any time.

Organizing Bookmarks

You've seen how bookmarks can be contained in folders, which is a good thing because you're likely to have a lot of them. You can change the names and locations of your existing bookmarks and folders as follows:

(1) Move to the Bookmarks screen showing the bookmarks and folders you want to change. (You can't move among the Bookmarks screens while you are in Edit mode so you need to start at the location where the items you want to change are located.)

(2) Tap Edit. Unlock buttons appear next to the folders and bookmarks you can change (some folders, such as the History folder, can't be changed and you won't see controls for those folders). The order icons also appear on the right side of the screen, again only for folders or bookmarks you can change.

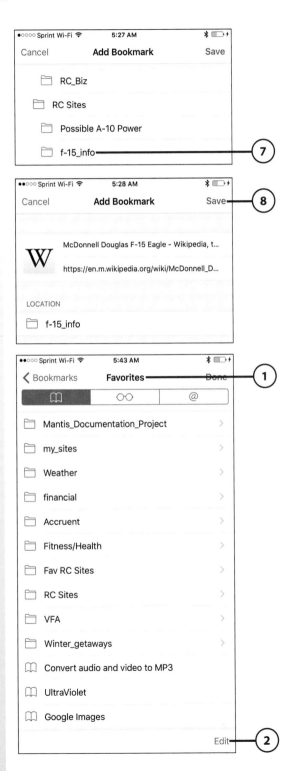

3) Touch the order icon next to the bookmark or folder you want to move and drag it up or down the screen to change the order in which it appears on the screen. When you drag a folder or bookmark between other items, they slide apart to make room for the folder or bookmark you are dragging. The order of the items in the list is the order in which they appear on the Bookmarks screen.

4) Tap a folder to change its name or location.

5) Change the name in the name bar.

6) To change the location of the folder, tap the Location bar, which shows the folder's current location.

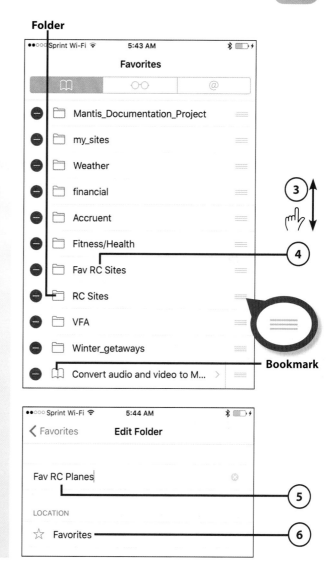

Folder

••○○○ Sprint Wi-Fi 🛜	5:43 AM		🔋 ⚡

Favorites

| 📖 | ◯◯ | @ |

- 🗂 Mantis_Documentation_Project
- 🗂 my_sites
- 🗂 Weather
- 🗂 financial
- 🗂 Accruent
- 🗂 Fitness/Health
- 🗂 Fav RC Sites
- 🗂 RC Sites
- 🗂 VFA
- 🗂 Winter_getaways
- 📖 Convert audio and video to M... ›

Bookmark

| ••○○○ Sprint Wi-Fi 🛜 | 5:44 AM | 🔋 ⚡ |

‹ Favorites **Edit Folder**

Fav RC Planes

LOCATION

☆ Favorites

Can't Move?

If you have only one bookmark you've added, you can't move them around as described here because Safari won't let you "disturb" the default bookmarks and folders (such as Favorites and History). You can only delete default bookmarks.

7. Swipe up and down the list of folders until you see the folder in which you want to place the folder you are working with.

8. Tap the folder into which you want to move the folder you are editing.

9. Tap the back button, which is labeled with the location from which you came. You move back to the prior Bookmarks screen, which reflects any changes you made.

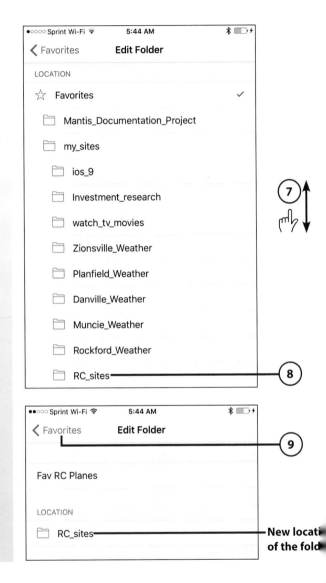

Editing a Bookmark

If the bookmark you want to change isn't on the Bookmarks screen you are currently viewing, tap Done to exit Edit mode. Then open the folder containing the bookmark you want to change and tap Edit. You are able to change the bookmark.

10 Tap a bookmark you want to change.

11 Change the bookmark's name in the name bar.

12 If you want to change a bookmark's URL, tap the URL bar and make changes to the current URL. For example, you might want to change it to have the bookmark point to a site's home page rather than the page you are viewing.

13 To change the location of the folder or bookmark, tap the Location bar and follow steps 7 and 8.

14 Tap Done. You move back to the previous screen, and any changes you made—such as changing the name or location of a bookmark—are reflected.

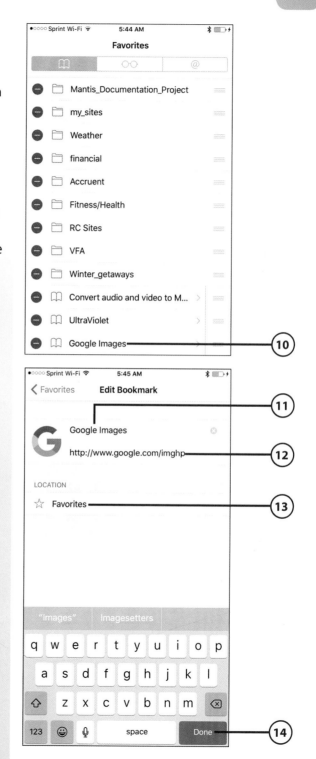

⑮ Tap New Folder to create a new folder.

⑯ Enter the name of the folder.

⑰ Follow steps 6–8 to choose the location in which you want to save the new folder.

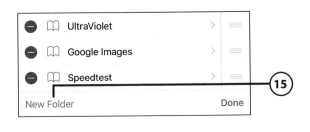

⑱ Tap Done. The new folder is created in the location you selected. You can place folders and bookmarks into it by using the Location bar to navigate to it.

⑲ Tap Done. Your changes are saved, and you exit Edit mode.

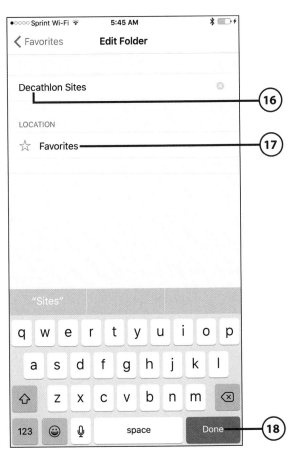

Browsing Both Ways

As you browse, make sure you try both the horizontal and vertical orientations. Safari sometimes offers different features in the two orientations on different models. For example, when you open the Bookmarks screen and rotate an iPhone 6 Plus, 6s Plus, or 7 Plus, the screen is divided into two panes. On the left is the Bookmarks pane you are viewing and the right pane shows the web page you were browsing. If you tap a bookmark, the web page in the right pane becomes the page at which the bookmark points.

Deleting Bookmarks or Folders of Bookmarks

You can get rid of bookmarks or folders of bookmarks you don't want any more by deleting them:

(1) Move to the screen containing the folder or bookmark you want to delete.

(2) Swipe to the left on the folder or bookmark you want to delete.

(3) Tap Delete. The folder or bookmark is deleted. Note that when you delete a folder, all the bookmarks it contains are deleted, too.

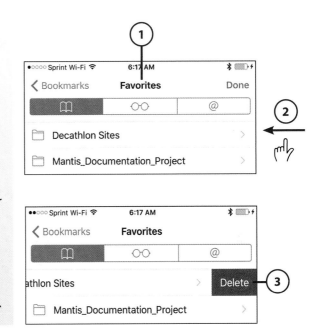

Using 3D Touch with Safari

Like other default iPhone apps, Safari supports 3D Touch, which you can use in a couple of ways.

Perform a Peek to see the Quick Actions menu

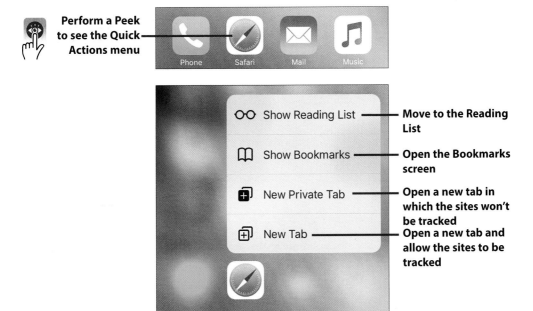

Show Reading List — **Move to the Reading List**

Show Bookmarks — **Open the Bookmarks screen**

New Private Tab — **Open a new tab in which the sites won't be tracked**

New Tab — **Open a new tab and allow the sites to be tracked**

When you press and hold on the Safari app's icon, you see the Quick Actions menu. You can select from among its options to quickly perform actions in Safari. For example, choose New Tab to open a new tab in which you can navigate to a web page, or choose Show Bookmarks to jump to the Bookmarks page.

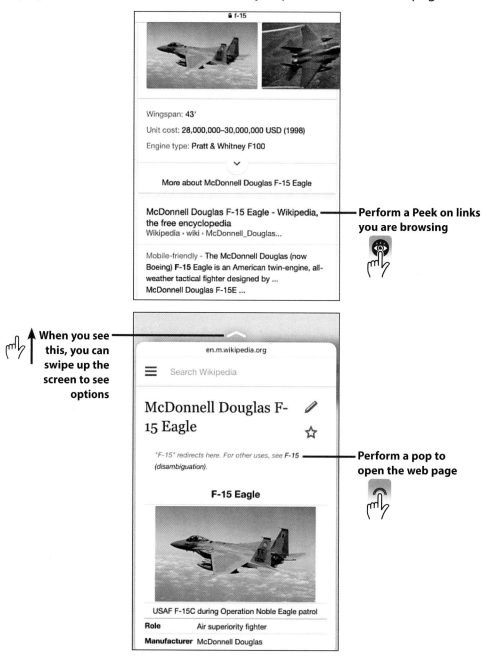

Perform a Peek on links you are browsing

When you see this, you can swipe up the screen to see options

Perform a pop to open the web page

When you are browsing links, such as when you have performed a search, or your bookmarks, press on a link or a bookmark in which you are interested to perform a Peek on it. In the Peek window, you see the web page for the link or web page on which you peeked. If you continue to press on the Peek, it pops open so you can view the web page in Safari. When you perform a Peek on some screens, such as the links resulting from a search, you see an upward-facing arrow at the top of the screen; this indicates you can swipe up the screen to reveal a menu of commands. Tap a command to perform it. For example, tap Open in New Tab to open the web page in a new tab in Safari.

Sharing Web Pages

Safari makes it easy to share web pages that you think will be valuable to others. There are many ways to share, including AirDrop, Message, Mail, Twitter, and Facebook. A couple of examples will prepare you to use any of them.

Emailing a Link to a Web Page

You can quickly email links to web pages you visit.

1. Use Safari to navigate to a web page whose link you want to email to someone.

2. Tap the Share button.

3. Tap Mail. A new email message is created, and the link to the web page is inserted into the body. The subject of the message is the title of the web page.

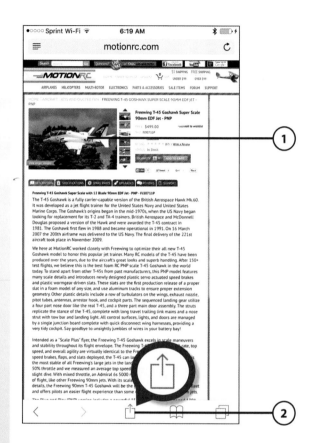

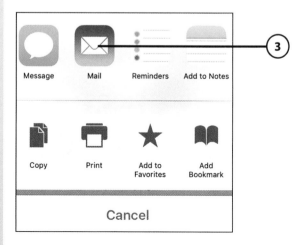

4 Complete and send the email message. (Refer to Chapter 9, "Sending, Receiving, and Managing Email," for information about the Mail app.) When the recipient receives your message, he can visit the website by tapping the link included in the email message.

Messaging a Web Page

If you come across a page that you want to share with someone via Messages, Safari makes it easy.

1 Use Safari to navigate to a web page whose link you want to message to someone.

2 Tap the Share button.

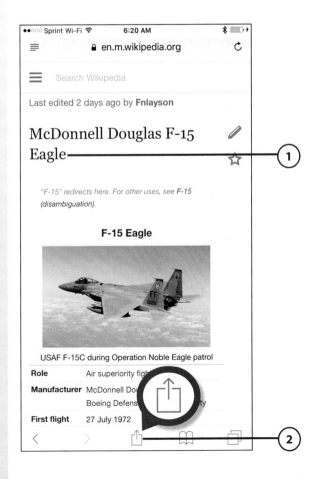

(3) Tap Message. A new message is created, and the link to the web page is inserted.

(4) Address the message.

(5) Enter text you want to send along with the link to the web page.

(6) Tap the Send button. Your message is sent. The recipients can visit the web page by tapping the link included in the message.

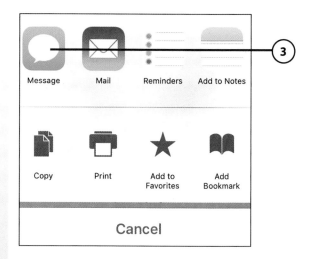

>>>Go Further
MORE WAYS TO SHARE THE WEB

If you want to share a web page in the old-fashioned way, you can print it by opening the Share menu and tapping Print (assuming you have your iPhone set up to print, as explained in Chapter 2). If you tap Copy, the web page's address is copied to the clipboard, so you can paste into documents, emails, notes, or messages. You can also share via Twitter and Facebook.

Signing In to Websites Automatically

If you enable Safari to remember usernames and passwords, it can enter this information for you automatically. When Safari encounters a site for which it recognizes and can save login information, you are prompted to allow Safari to save that information. This doesn't work with all sites; if you aren't prompted to allow Safari to save login information, you can't use this feature with that site. When saved, this information can be entered for you automatically.

(1) Move to a web page that requires you to log in to an account.

(2) Enter your account's username and password.

(3) Tap the button to log in to your account, such as Continue, Sign In, Submit, Login, and such. You are prompted to save the login information.

(4) Tap Save Password to save the information. The next time you move to the login page, your username and password are entered for you automatically. Tap Never for This Website if you don't want the information to be saved and you don't want to be prompted again. Tap Not Now if you don't want the information saved but do want to be prompted again later to save it.

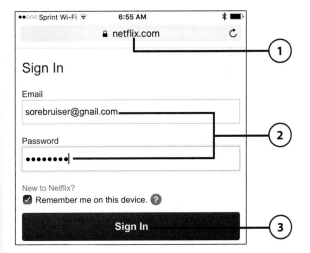

>>>Go Further

LETTING SAFARI CREATE PASSWORDS FOR YOU

If you have enabled the Names and Passwords setting, Safari can create passwords for you. Go to a website that requires you to create a password, such as when you register for a new account. When you tap in a field that Safari recognizes as requiring a password, tap Suggest Password. Safari presents a password for you; most of these are not easy to remember, but that doesn't matter because it is saved for you automatically so you won't have to enter it manually. If you want to use the recommended password, tap Use Suggested Password; Safari enters the password in the password and verify password fields. When syncing is enabled, the password is stored on the synced devices, too, so you are able to sign in from those devices just as easily.

Take photos and videos

Configure photo and camera settings

Take photos and videos and quickly send them to others

In this chapter, you explore all the photo and video functionality that your iPhone has to offer. Topics include the following:

→ Getting started
→ Setting your Photos & Camera preferences
→ Using the Camera app to take photos and videos with your iPhone

14

Taking Photos and Video with Your iPhone

The iPhone's cameras and Camera app capture high-quality photos and video. Because you'll likely have your iPhone with you at all times, it's handy to capture photos with it whenever and wherever you are. And, you can capture video just as easily.

Whether you've taken photos and video on your iPhone or added them from another source, the Photos app enables you to edit, view, organize, and share your photos. (To learn how to use the Photos app with the great photos and video you take, see Chapter 15, "Viewing and Editing Photos and Video with the Photos App.") You'll likely find that taking and working with photos and videos are among the most useful things your iPhone can do.

Getting Started

Each generation of iPhone has had different and more sophisticated photo and video capabilities and features than the previous versions. All current versions sport high-quality cameras; in fact, there is a camera on each side of the iPhone. One takes photos of what you are looking at (the back-facing camera, located on the backside of the phone), whereas the other takes photos of what the screen is facing (the front-facing camera, which is usually for taking selfies, located on the face of the phone).

Current generations also have a flash; can zoom; take burst, panoramic, and time-lapse photos; and have other features you expect from a high-quality digital camera. The iPhone 6s/6s Plus and 7/7 Plus models can also take Live Photos, which capture a small amount of video along with the photo.

The iPhone 7 and 7 Plus have image stabilization, more resolution, and other enhancements to enable them to take even higher quality photos and video with both the back-facing and front-facing cameras.

The iPhone 7 Plus has two back-facing cameras: one is the wide-angle camera that all models have (in different versions depending on the model), and the other camera has a telephoto lens. These two cameras give the iPhone 7 Plus unique photo capabilities, which are a Telephoto mode that enables you to capture much better quality photos using both optical zoom and software zoom. It also enables you to take Portrait photos in which the subject is in very sharp focus and the background in a soft blur.

The iPhone's photo and video capabilities and features are probably the largest area of differences between the various models. Because of the fairly large variation in capabilities of iPhone models that can run iOS 10, it's impossible to cover all the differences in this chapter; the iPhone 7 and iPhone 7 Plus are the most advanced models, so they are the focus of this chapter. If you have a different model, some of the tasks described might not be applicable to you, or some of the details in this chapter might be different than what you see on your iPhone if it is an older model. However, all models can do most of the tasks in this chapter so even if you don't have an iPhone 7 or 7 Plus, you can still take lots of different kinds of photos and videos.

Additionally, the iPhone's photo and video capabilities have been increasingly tied into iCloud. For example, you can store your entire photo library under your iCloud account; this offers many benefits, including backing up all your photos, making it easy to access your photos from any device, and being able to quickly share your photos with others. Therefore, I've assumed you are using iCloud and have configured it to work with photos as described in Chapter 4, "Setting Up and Using iCloud and Other Online Accounts." Like differences in iPhone camera capabilities, if you don't use iCloud with your photos, some of the information in this chapter doesn't apply to you and what you see on your phone might look different than what you see in this chapter.

Setting Your Photos & Camera Preferences

The following table describes options in the Settings app that you can access by tapping Settings, and then tapping Photos & Camera. The default settings allow you to take photos and video without making any changes to these settings, but it's good to know where they are and what they do if you decide to change how your apps work.

Settings App Explained

To get detailed information on using the Settings app, see "Working with the Settings App" in Chapter 5, "Customizing How Your iPhone Works."

Photos & Camera Settings

Section	Setting	Description
N/A	iCloud Photo Library	When enabled, all your photos are stored in the cloud so that you can access them from multiple devices. Additionally, this ensures that your photos are backed up in the event something happens to your iPhone. I recommend you enable this option to protect your photos, even if you only use your iPhone for photos and video. The only downside is that photos can require large amounts of storage. You might need to upgrade your iCloud storage space at some point to store all of your photos and video there.

Section	Setting	Description
N/A	Optimize iPhone Storage	If you select this option, only versions of your photos that are optimized for the iPhone are stored on your phone; this saves space so that you can keep more photos and videos on your iPhone, while providing images with perfect quality for displaying on the iPhone's screen. Full resolution photos are uploaded to the cloud so you can still use them with devices that are capable of displaying them in all their glory.
N/A	Download and Keep Originals	This option downloads full resolution versions of your photos and videos on your iPhone. They consume more space than optimized versions, and you aren't likely to be able to tell the difference when viewing them on your iPhone, so Optimize iPhone Storage is the better option.
N/A	Upload to My Photo Stream	When enabled, all your photos are automatically uploaded to your iCloud Photo Stream when you are connected to the Internet with Wi-Fi. New photos are also downloaded from the cloud to your iPhone and other devices with this setting enabled.
N/A	Upload Burst Photos	Later in this chapter, you learn about Burst photos, which are a series of photos taken rapidly. This setting determines if all of the photos in a burst are uploaded to the cloud or only photos you tag as favorites are uploaded. Because burst photos can take up a lot of space, it's usually better to leave this disabled. If you leave this disabled, when you select favorite photos in a burst series, only those photos are uploaded.
N/A	iCloud Photo Sharing	When enabled, you can share your photos with others and subscribe to other people's Photo Streams to share their photos.
PHOTOS TAB	Summarize Photos	When this switch is on (green), you see thumbnails for only some of the photos in a collection, and the timeframe of each group is larger. If you set this to off (white), you see a thumbnail of every photo in your collections, which takes up much more screen space and you have to scroll more to move among your collections. This setting affects how you see Collections view and Years view only.

Section	Setting	Description
MEMORIES	Show Holiday Events	With this switch enabled (green), the Photos app attempts to collect photos taken on the holidays in your country into memories (which you learn about in Chapter 15). When disabled (white), the Photos app ignores holidays when it creates memories for you.
CAMERA	Grid	When this switch is on (green), you see a grid on the screen when you are taking photos with the Camera app. This grid can help you align the subject of your photos in the image you are capturing.
CAMERA	Record Video	Use the options under this menu to determine how video is recorded. The options available depend on the model of iPhone you have. You can choose from among different combinations of resolution and frame rate. Higher resolution and frame rates mean better-quality video, but also larger files.
CAMERA	Record Slo-mo	The selections under this menu determine the resolution and frame rate for slow-motion video. Like regular video, the higher the resolution and frame rate, the better quality the resulting video is and the file sizes are larger.
HDR (High Dynamic Range)	Keep Normal Photo	When this switch is on (green), the HDR (read more about this in a later sidebar) and the normal version of photos are stored. When this switch is off (white), only the HDR version of the photo is stored.

Using the Camera App to Take Photos and Videos with Your iPhone

You use the Camera app to take photos and video with your iPhone. This app has a number of controls and features. Some features are easy to spot whereas others aren't so obvious. By the end of this section, you'll know how to use these features to take great photos and video with your iPhone.

The general process for capturing photos or video follows:

1. Choose the type of photo or video you want to capture.

2. Set the options for the type of photo or video you selected.

3. Take the photos or video.

4. View and edit the photos or video you captured using the Photos app.

The information you need to accomplish steps 1 through 3 of this process is provided in tables and tasks throughout this chapter. The details for step 4 are provided in Chapter 15.

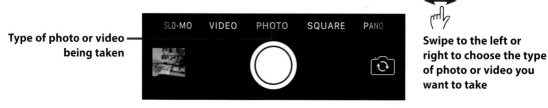

Type of photo or video being taken

Swipe to the left or right to choose the type of photo or video you want to take

The first step in taking photos or video is to choose the type of photo or video that you want to capture. You do this by swiping to the left or right on the selection bar just above the large shutter button at the bottom of the Camera app's screen, as shown in the previous figure. The option shown in yellow at the center of the screen just above the shutter button is the current type of photo or video you are capturing. The options available in the Camera app are explained in the following table.

Types of Photo and Video iPhones Can Capture

Type of Photo or Video	Description
TIME-LAPSE	Captures a video with compressed time so that the time displayed in the video occurs much more rapidly than "real time." This is what is often used to show a process that takes a long time, such as a plant growing, in just a few seconds.
SLO-MO	Takes slow motion video so that you can slow down something that happens quickly.
VIDEO	Captures video at a real-time speed. The steps to take video are provided in the task "Taking Video," later in this chapter.
PHOTO	Captures still photos (or Live Photos on iPhone 6s/6s Plus or later models). Step-by-step instructions showing how to use this option are provided in the task "Taking Photos," later in this chapter.
SQUARE	Takes "square" photos in which the height and width are the same.
PANO	Takes panoramic photos that enable you to capture very wide images. An example of capturing a panoramic photo is provided in the task "Taking Panoramic Photos," later in this chapter.

Type of Photo or Video	Description
Telephoto (iPhone 7 Plus only)	Zooms in using optical and digital zooming when taking photos in the PHOTO and other modes. This provides zoom from 1x to 10x, which is a higher level of zoom than all other models. The steps to use this feature are provided in "Taking Telephoto Photos (iPhone 7 Plus Only)," later in this chapter.
PORTRAIT (iPhone 7 Plus only)	Captures a photo with the subject in very sharp focus while blurring the background. This provides an almost 3D effect and causes the subject of the photo to be shown in what appears to be much more detail than with other options. See "Taking Portrait Photos (iPhone 7 Plus Only)" later in this chapter for details.

When you choose the type of photo or video you want to take, there are quite a few options you can select (the options available to you depend on the specific model of iPhone you are using). When you select options, the icons you see on the screen change to reflect your selection. For example, when you choose a self-timed photo, the Self-timer icon changes to show the time delay you have selected. And not all options are available at the same time. For example, you can't set the flash and HDR to go on at the same time because you can't take HDR images with the flash.

The following table describes the icons and tools available on the Camera app's screen. (Remember that the specific icons and tools you see depend on the type of photo or video you are capturing and the model of iPhone you are using.)

Photo and Video Options and Icons

Icon	Description
⚡	**Flash**. When you tap this icon, you see a menu with the flash options, which are Auto (the app uses the flash when required), On (flash is always used), or Off (flash is never used). Tap the option you want to use and the menu closes. When the flash is set to on, the icon is yellow.
⚡	**Flash Being Used**. When this icon appears on the screen, it indicates the flash will be used when taking a photo or video.

Icon	Description
HDR	**High Dynamic Range (HDR).** Tap this to set the HDR options. (You learn more about HDR in the "More on Taking Photos and Video" Go Further sidebar later in this chapter.) The options are Auto, On, or Off. When the flash is set to on, this is disabled and you see a line through the HDR icon because you can't use the flash with HDR images.
◎	**Live Photo on.** When this feature is enabled, you take Live Photos (see the "And Now a Few Words on Live Photos (iPhone 6s/6s Plus and Later Models)" note following this table) and the Live Photos icon is yellow. To turn Live Photos off, tap this icon. This feature is only available on 6s/6s Plus and later models.
◎	**Live Photo off.** When disabled, you take static photos and the Live icon is white. To turn Live Photos on, tap this icon. This feature is only available on 6s/6s Plus and later models.
⏲	**Self-timer.** When you tap this icon, a menu appears on which you can choose a 3- or 10-second delay for photos. When you choose a delay, the icon is replaced with one showing the delay you set. When you tap the shutter button, the timer starts and counts down the interval you selected before capturing the image.
◐	**Filter.** When you tap this button, a palette of filters appears. You can tap a filter to apply it to the photo or video you are capturing. For example, you can apply the Instant filter to make a photo look like it was taken on an old instant camera. When you apply a filter, you see the image with the filter applied. Generally, it's better to apply filters after you take a photo so that you have an original, unfiltered version of the photo (this is covered in the task "Applying Filters to Photos" in Chapter 15).
◐	**Filter applied.** When the Filter icon is in color, you know a filter is currently applied. Tap the icon, and then tap the None option in the center of the screen to remove the filter.
📷	**Change Camera.** When you tap this icon, you toggle between the back-facing and front-facing camera (the front-facing camera is typically used for selfies).
◯	**Shutter.** This button changes based on the type of photo or video you are taking. For example, when you are taking a photo, this button is white as shown. When you take a video, it becomes red. It looks a bit different for other types as well, such as TIME-LAPSE. Regardless of what the button looks like, its function is the same. Tap it to start the process, such as to take a photo or start capturing video. If applicable, tap it again to stop the process, such as stopping video capture. To take burst photos, you touch and hold it to capture the burst.
00:00:08	**Timer.** When you capture video, the timer shows the elapsed time of the video you are capturing.

Icon	Description
	Focus/exposure box. When you frame an image, the camera uses a specific part of the image to set the focus, exposure, and other attributes. The yellow box that appears on the screen indicates the focus/exposure area. You can manually set the location of this box by tapping on the part of the image that you want the app to use to set the image's attributes. The box moves to the area on which you tapped and sets the attributes of the image based on that area.
	Exposure slider. When you tap in an image you are framing, the sun icon appears next to the focus/exposure box. If you tap this icon, you see the exposure slider. Drag the sun up to increase the exposure or down to decrease it. The image changes as you move the slider so you can see its effect immediately.
AE/AF LOCK	**AE/AF lock**. When you tap an image to set the location of the focus/exposure box and keep your finger on the screen for a second or so, the focus and exposure becomes locked based on the area you selected. This icon indicates that the exposure and focus are locked so you can move the camera without changing the focus or exposure used when you capture the image. Tap the screen to release the lock and refocus on another area.
	Faces found. When your iPhone detects faces, it puts this box around them and identifies the area as a face. You can use faces to organize photos by applying names to the faces in your photos.

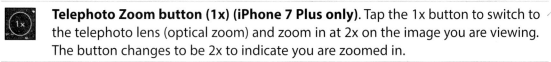

Icon	Description
	Zoom slider. You can unpinch on an image to zoom in or pinch on an image to zoom out. When you do, the Zoom slider appears on the screen. This indicates the relative level of zoom you are applying. You can also drag the slider toward the – to zoom out or drag it toward the + to zoom in to change the level of zoom you are using.
	Telephoto Zoom button (1x) (iPhone 7 Plus only). Tap the 1x button to switch to the telephoto lens (optical zoom) and zoom in at 2x on the image you are viewing. The button changes to be 2x to indicate you are zoomed in.
	Telephoto Zoom button (2x) (iPhone 7 Plus only). This indicates you are currently using the telephoto lens and are zoomed in at 2x. When this button appears, you can further zoom in as described in the Telephoto Zoom slider description. Tap the 2x button to return to using the wide-angle lens, at which point the button becomes the 1x button again.
	Telephoto Zoom button (10x) (iPhone 7 Plus only). This indicates you are currently using the telephoto lens and are zoomed in at 10x.

Icon	Description

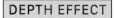

Telephoto Zoom slider (iPhone 7 Plus only). When you touch and hold on the Telephoto Zoom button, you see this slider. Swipe to the right to increase the level of zoom or to the left to decrease it. You can choose a zoom level from 2x to 10x. When you lift your finger, the slider disappears.

DEPTH EFFECT (iPhone 7 Plus only). This appears when you are in Portrait mode. The yellow box on the screen indicates the part of the image that will be in sharp focus. Everything outside of this box will have a soft blur applied.

And Now a Few Words on Live Photos (iPhone 6s/6s Plus and Later Models)

The iPhone 6s/6s Plus and later models can capture Live Photos. A Live Photo is a static image, but it also has a few of what Apple calls "moments" of video around the static image that you take. To capture a Live Photo, you set the Live function to on (the icon is yellow) and take the photo as you normally would. When you are viewing a Live Photo you have taken, tap and hold on the photo to see the motion associated with that photo. When you aren't tapping and holding on a Live Photo, it looks like any other photo you've taken.

Taking Photos

You can use the Camera app to capture photos, like so:

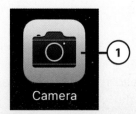

Camera

① On the Home screen, tap Camera.

② To capture a horizontal photo, rotate your iPhone so that it's horizontal; of course, you can use either orientation to take photos just as you can with any other camera.

(3) Swipe up or down (right or left if the phone is vertical) on the selection bar until PHOTO is in the center and in yellow.

(4) If you want to change the camera you are using, tap the Change Camera button. When you change the camera, the image briefly freezes, and then the view changes to the other camera. The front-facing camera (the one facing you when you look at the screen) has fewer features than the back-facing camera does. These steps show taking a photo with the back-facing camera.

(5) Set the Flash, HDR, Live, and Self-timer options you want to use for the photo; see the previous table for an explanation of these options you can use and how they work.

Part of the image being used to set brightness, focus, and exposure

(6) Frame the image by moving and adjusting the iPhone's distance and angle to the object you are photographing; if you have the Grid turned on, you can use its lines to help you frame the image the way you want it. When you stop moving the phone, the Camera app

indicates the part of the image that is used to set focus, brightness, and exposure with the yellow box. If this is the most important part of the image, you are good to go. If not, you can set this point manually by tapping where you want the focus to be (see step 9).

7 Zoom in by unpinching on the image. The camera zooms in on the subject and the Zoom slider appears.

8 Unpinch on the image or drag the slider toward the + to zoom in or pinch on the image or drag the slider toward the – to zoom out to change the level of zoom until it's what you want to use.

9 Tap the screen to manually set the area of the image to be used for setting the focus and exposure. The yellow focus box appears where you tapped.

10 To change the exposure, swipe up on the sun icon to increase the brightness or down to decrease it.

(11) Continue making adjustments in the framing of the image, the zoom, focus point, and brightness until it is the image you want to take.

(12) Tap the Shutter button on the screen, either Volume button on the side of the iPhone, or the switch on the EarPods. The Photo app captures the photo, and the shutter closes briefly while the photo is recorded. When the shutter opens again, you're ready to take the next photo.

(13) Tap the Thumbnail button to see the photo you most recently captured.

(14) Use the photo-viewing tools to view the photo (see Chapter 15 for the details).

(15) Tap the Trash Can button to delete a photo, and then tap Delete Photo.

(16) Edit the photo by tapping the Adjust button and using the resulting editing tools to make changes to the picture (see Chapter 15 for the details).

(17) Tap Camera. You move back into the Camera app and can take more photos.

Taking Panoramic Photos

The Camera app can take panoramic photos by capturing a series of images as you pan the camera across a scene, and then "stitching" those images together into one panoramic image. To take a panoramic photo, perform the following steps:

1. Open the Camera app.

2. Swipe on the selection bar until PANO is selected. On the screen, you see a bar representing the entire image that contains a smaller box representing the current part of the image that will be captured.

3. Tap the Shutter button. The app begins capturing the image.

Current position in the image

The shaded bar indicates the total possible area that can be included in the image

Move iPhone continuously when taking a Panorama.

PHOTO SQUARE PANO

4 Slowly sweep the iPhone to the right while keeping the arrow centered on the line on the screen (if you move the phone too fast, you see a message on the screen telling you to slow down). The better you keep the tip of the arrow aligned with the line, the more consistent the centerline of the resulting image will be.

5 When you've moved to the "end" of the image you are capturing or the limit of what you can capture in the photo, tap the Shutter button. You move back to the starting point and the panoramic photo is created. You can tap the image's thumbnail to view, delete, or edit it.

Taking Telephoto Photos (iPhone 7 Plus Only)

The iPhone 7 Plus has a Zoom button just above the Shutter button; it's initially labeled with 1x. Tap this to use the telephoto lens to go to 2x zoom using optical zoom, which means you get the same quality of photo as you do with the wide-angle lens. When you drag across this button, you can increase the zoom using software zoom up to 10x.

1 On the Home screen, tap Camera.

2 Swipe right or left (up or down if the phone is horizontal) on the selection bar until PHOTO is in the center and in yellow.

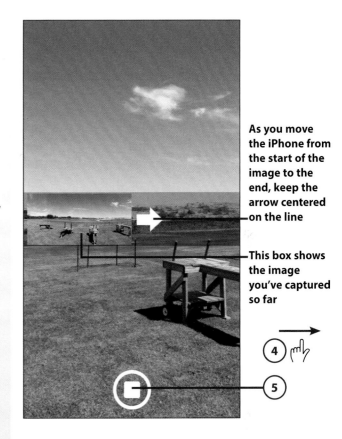

As you move the iPhone from the start of the image to the end, keep the arrow centered on the line

This box shows the image you've captured so far

3 Tap the Telephoto Zoom button. It becomes 2x, and the image you see is magnified to a 2x optical zoom level.

4 Touch and hold on the Telephoto Zoom button. The Telephoto Zoom slider appears.

5 Drag the slider to the right to increase the level of zoom or to the left to decrease it. When you are at the level of zoom you want, lift your finger off the screen. The current level of magnification is shown in the Telephoto Zoom button.

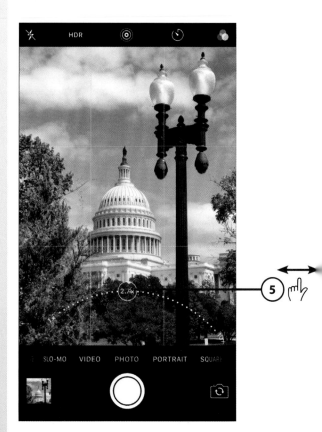

6 Finish taking the photo (see "Taking Photos" earlier in this chapter for details).

Current zoom level

Taking Portrait Photos (iPhone 7 Plus Only)

You can use the Camera app to capture Portrait photos, like so:

1 On the Home screen, tap Camera.

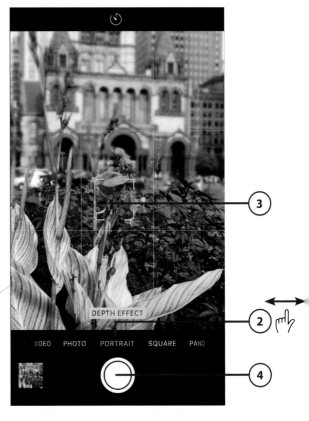

2 Swipe right or left (up or down if the phone is horizontal) on the selection bar until PORTRAIT is in the center and in yellow. The Portrait focus box appears on the screen along with the DEPTH EFFECT box.

3 Tap on the screen where you want the image to be focused.

4 Take the photo. The area inside the focus box is in sharp focus, and the image outside the box is in a soft blur.

A Word of Thanks

Jason Rich, author of *iPad and iPhone Tips and Tricks*, 6th Edition, was extremely helpful in providing information and figures to cover the iPhone 7 Plus camera features. Thanks to Jason for his help! You should check out his book, which provides lots of timesaving shortcuts and shows you how to enhance your efficiency and productivity with iPads and iPhones.

Image in soft blur

Image in sharp focus

Taking Video

You can capture video as easily as you can still images. Here's how.

1. Move into the Camera app by tapping its icon on the Home screen (not shown in the figure).

2. To capture horizontal video, rotate the iPhone so that it's horizontal; of course, you can use either orientation to take video just as you can with any other video camera.

3. Swipe on the selection bar until VIDEO is selected.

4. Choose the back-facing or front-facing camera, configure the flash, or zoom in, just like setting up a still image. (The Self-timer, Grid, and HDR mode are not available when taking video.)

5. Tap on the screen where you want to focus.

6. If needed, adjust the exposure by sliding the "sun" icon up or down just like a still photo (not shown on the figure).

7. Tap the Shutter button to start recording. You hear the start/stop recording tone and the app starts capturing video; you see the timer on the screen showing how long you've been recording.

Length of video

(9)

(8)

(8) Take still images while you take video by tapping the white Shutter button.

(9) Stop recording by tapping the red Shutter button again. Also, like still images, you can then tap the video's thumbnail to preview it. You can use the Photos app's video tools to view or edit the clip. (These tasks are explained in Chapter 15.)

Taking Photos and Video from the Lock Screen

Because it is likely to be with you constantly, your iPhone is a great camera of opportunity. You can use its Quick Access feature to quickly take photos when your iPhone is asleep/locked. Here's how:

(1) When the iPhone is locked, press the Sleep/Wake button, touch the Touch ID/Home button, or lift your phone up (if you have a model that supports the Raise to Wake feature and it is enabled). The Lock screen appears.

(2) Swipe to the left. The Camera app opens.

3 Use the Camera app to take the photo or video as described in the previous tasks. You can only view the most recent photos or videos you captured from within the Camera app when your iPhone is locked; you have to unlock the phone to work with the rest of your photos.

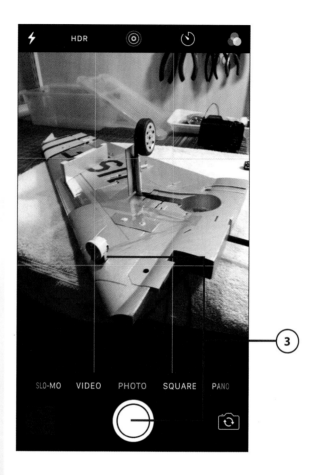

Taking Photos and Video from the Control Center

You can get to the camera quickly using the Control Center, too.

1 Swipe up from the bottom of the screen to open the Control Center.

2 Tap the Camera button. The Camera app opens.

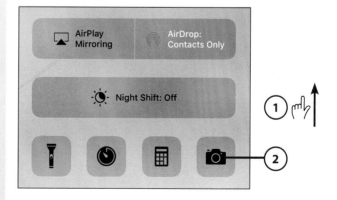

3   Use the Camera app to take photos or video as you've learned in the previous tasks.

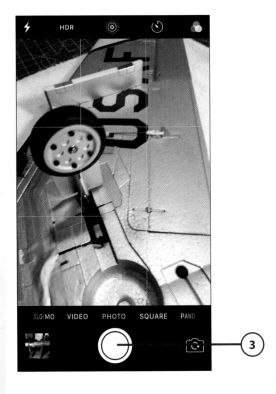

Taking Photos with Quick Actions (Models with 3D Touch)

On iPhone 6s/6s Plus and later models, the Quick Access menu offers a selection of photos and video commands that you can choose right from a Home screen.

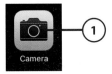

1   Tap and hold on the Camera icon until the Quick Actions menu opens.

2   Tap the type of photo or video you want to take. The Camera app opens and is set up for the type you selected.

3   Use the Camera app to capture the photo or video (not shown).

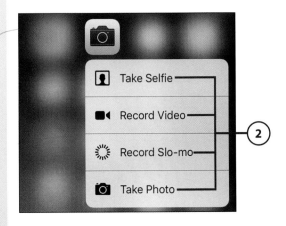

>>>Go Further

MORE ON TAKING PHOTOS AND VIDEO

The Camera app enables you to do all sorts of interesting and fun things with photos and video. Following are some additional pointers that help you make the most of this great app:

- **Set once**—You need to set the Flash, HDR, and other options only when you want to change the current settings because these settings are retained even after you move out of the Camera app and back into it.

- **HDR**—The High Dynamic Range (HDR) feature causes the iPhone to take three shots of each image, with each shot having a different exposure level. It then combines the three images into one higher-quality image. HDR works best for photos that don't have motion and where there is good lighting. (You can't use the iPhone's flash with HDR images.) Also, HDR photos take longer to capture.

  When the Keep Normal Photo switch in the Photos & Camera Settings is on (green), you see two versions of each HDR photo in the Photos app: One is the HDR version, and the other is the normal version. If you prefer the HDR versions, set the Keep Normal Photo switch to off (white) so that your photos don't use as much space on your iPhone, and you don't have twice as many photos to deal with.

- **Location**—The first time you use the Camera app, you are prompted to decide whether you allow it to use Location Services. If you allow the Camera app to use Location Services, the app uses the iPhone's GPS to tag the location where photos and video were captured. Some apps can use this information, such as the Photos app on your iPhone, to locate your photos on maps, find photos by their locations, and so on.

- **Sensitivity**—The iPhone's camera is sensitive to movement, so if your hand moves while you are taking a photo, it's likely to be blurry. Sometimes, part of the image will be in focus and part of it isn't, so be sure to check the view before you capture a photo. This is especially true when you zoom in. If you are getting blurry photos, the problem is probably your hand moving while you are taking them. Of course, because it's digital, you can take as many photos as you need to get it right; delete the rejects as you take them and use the Photos app to periodically review and delete photos you don't want to keep (see Chapter 15), so you don't have to waste storage room or clutter up your photo library with photos you don't want to keep. This is less of a problem with the iPhone 7 and 7 Plus because of their built-in image stabilization.

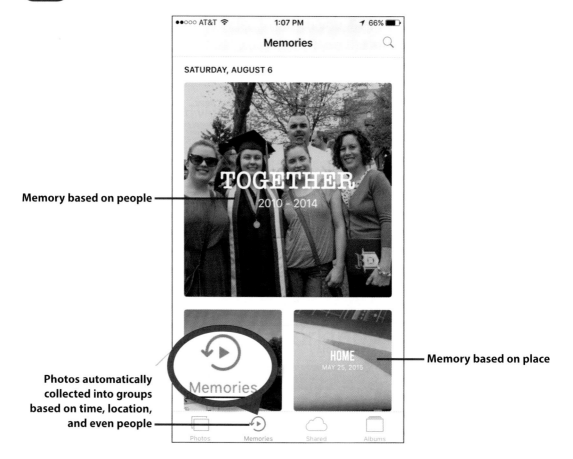

Memory based on people

Photos automatically collected into groups based on time, location, and even people

Memory based on place

The Memories source builds collections of photos for you automatically. These collections can be based on a number of factors, such as time, location, holiday, and even people. You can view the photos in a memory individually, and the app builds slideshows automatically to make viewing your photos more interesting.

Shared shows photos you are sharing with other people and photos other people are sharing with you. For each group of photos being shared, you see the name of the group and who is sharing it (you, for photos you are sharing, or the name of the person sharing with you). When you tap a shared group, you see the photos it contains and can work with them. (Working with photo sharing is covered in detail in "Using iCloud with Your Photos" later in this chapter.)

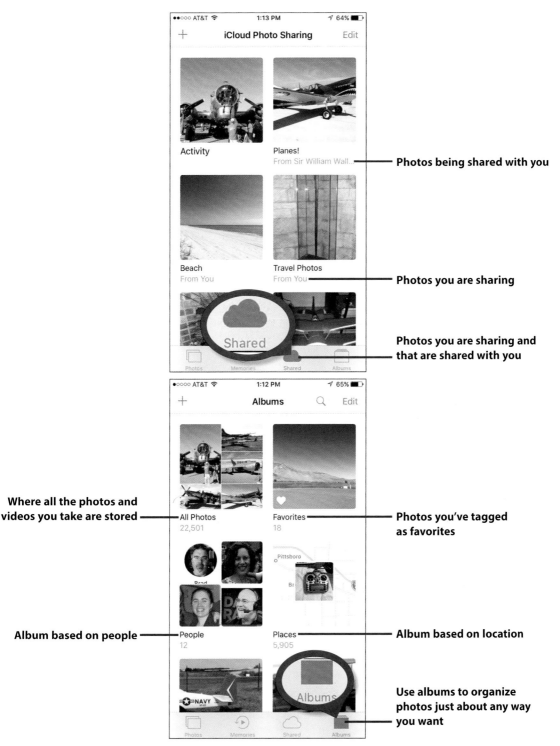

Photos being shared with you

Photos you are sharing

Photos you are sharing and that are shared with you

Where all the photos and videos you take are stored

Photos you've tagged as favorites

Album based on people

Album based on location

Use albums to organize photos just about any way you want

Albums allow you to organize your photos in a number of ways. Following are some of the albums or types of albums you might see:

- **All Photos or Camera Roll**—When you see the All Photos album, you have the iCloud Photo Library enabled so that you can use this album to see all the photos in your library. When this is not enabled, you see Camera Roll instead. When you use the iCloud Photo Library, all the photos that you've taken or downloaded (such as from an email) on the iPhone or other devices that are using the same iCloud account are stored here. If you don't use the iCloud Photo Library, the Camera Roll album contains photos and videos you've taken with the iPhone's camera or saved from other apps, such as attachments to email in Mail.

- **Favorites**—This folder contains images you have tagged as a favorite by tapping its heart button.

- **People**—This folder contains images based on the people in them (people are identified by the iPhone's facial recognition software).

- **Places**—This groups photos by the location at which they were captured.

- **Videos**—Videos you record are collected in this folder.

- **Selfies**—Photos you take with the front-facing camera are stored here.

- **Panoramas, Slo-mo, Time-lapse, Bursts, and Screenshots**—These folders contain photos and videos of the types for which they are named.

- **My Albums**—In this section, you see albums you create to manually organize photos. You can create albums for any reason and determine which photos are stored within them.

Your Albums May Vary

Some apps, such as Instagram, might add their own albums to the Albums tab.

Although each of these sources looks a bit different, the steps to browse them to find the photos you want to work with are similar for most of these sources (the Memories source is a bit different and is covered separately); this example shows using the Photos source to browse for photos:

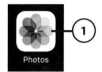

1 On the Home screen, tap Photos.

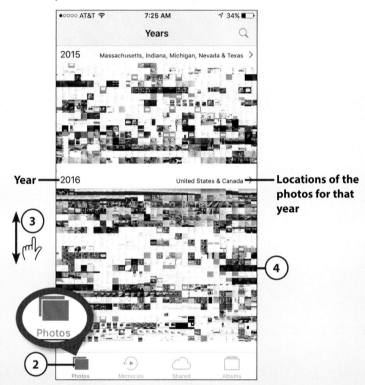

2 Tap Photos. On the Years screen, you see photos collected by the year in which they were taken. Next to the year, you see a summary of the various locations where the photos were taken.

Start at the Beginning

If the title at the top of the screen isn't "Years," tap the back button located in the upper-left corner of the screen until it is.

---

3 Swipe up and down the screen to browse all the years.

4 Tap the thumbnails in the year that contains photos you want to work with. You move to the Collections screen that groups the selected year's photos based on locations and time periods.

Memories

If you want to jump directly to memories for the photos, tap a group's heading, such as the locations for a group of photos. You move into the Memory view of those photos (covered later in this chapter).

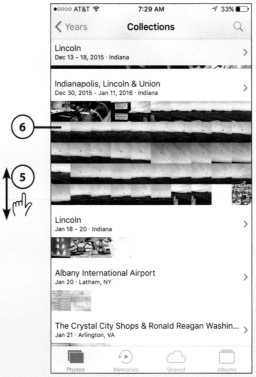

(5) Swipe up and down the screen to browse all the collections in the year you selected.

(6) Tap the collection that contains photos you want to see. Doing so opens the Moments screen, which breaks out the photos in the collection by location and date.

(7) Swipe up and down the screen to browse all the moments in the collection you selected.

(8) Tap a photo to view it.

(9) You're ready to view the photos in detail as described in the task "Viewing Photos Individually" later in this chapter.

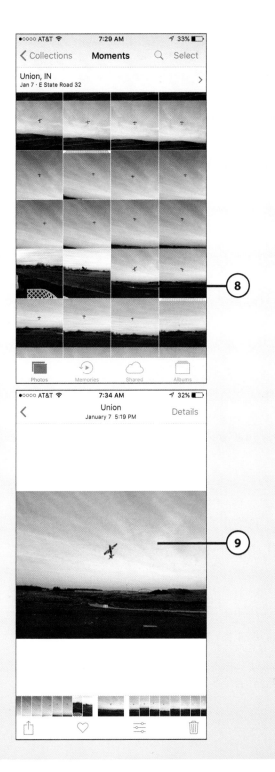

Go Back

You can move back to the screens from where you came by tapping the back button, which is always located in the upper-left corner of the screen; this button is named with the screen it takes you back to. To choose a different source, you might have to tap the back button a time or two as the Photos, Memories, Shared, and Albums buttons at the bottom of the screen are only visible on some screens.

Finding Photos to Work With by Searching

Browsing photos can be a fun way to find photos, but at times you might want to get to specific photos more efficiently. The Search tool enables you to quickly find photos based on their time, date, location, and even content.

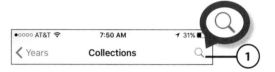

1. Continuing in the Photos app, tap the magnifying glass, which is available on many of the app's screens. The Search bar opens.

2. Type your search term. This can be any information associated with your photos. As you type, collections of photos that match your search criteria are listed under the Search bar. The more specific you make your search term, the smaller the set of photos that will be found.

3. Swipe up and down the screen to browse all the results.

4. Tap the results you want to explore.

5 Swipe up and down the screen to browse the results to find the photo you want.

6 Tap a photo to view it.

7 View the photos in the group (covered in the next section).

8 Tap the back button to return to the search results.

9 Tap the Search button to return to the Search screen.

(10) To change the search, tap in the Search bar and replace the current search term.

(11) Tap Cancel to exit the search.

Viewing Photos Individually

The Photos app enables you to view your photos individually. Here's how:

(1) Using the skills you learned in the previous tasks, open the group of photos that you want to view.

Orientation Doesn't Matter

Zooming, unzooming, and browsing photos works in the same way whether you hold your iPhone horizontally or vertically.

---

(2) Swipe up and down to browse all the photos in the group.

(3) Tap the photo you want to view. The photo display screen appears.

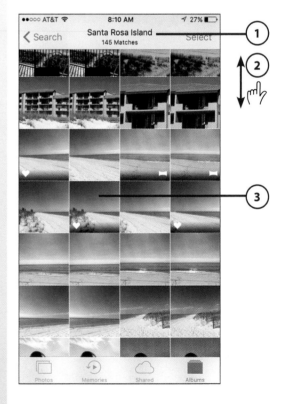

4 If it is a Live Photo, tap and hold on the screen to see the photo's motion.

5 To see the photo without the app's toolbars, tap the screen. The toolbars are hidden.

6 Rotate the phone horizontally if you are viewing a horizontal photo.

7 Unpinch or double-tap on the photo to zoom in.

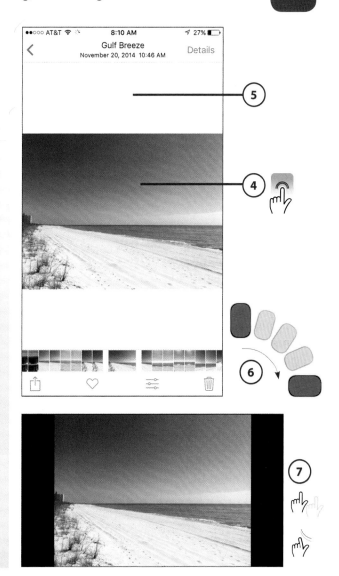

It's Not All Good

How Do I Know It's a Live Photo?

There's currently no way to tell if a photo is a Live Photo or not; there isn't even a Live Photos album as you might expect. (Refer to Chapter 14 for more information on what a Live Photo is.) The only way to tell if a photo is a Live Photo is to tap and hold on a photo to see (you must be using an iPhone 6s or later to be able to view a Live Photo). Hopefully, Apple will add some sort of icon to Live Photos so you know if a photo is a Live Photo without trying it.

Using 3D Touch with Photos

You can use 3D Touch (iPhone 6s and later models) to preview and open photos as follows:

(1) Browse a collection of photos in the Photos app.

(2) Tap and hold on a photo in which you are interested. A Peek of that photo appears.

(3) To open the photo, press down slightly harder until it pops open and use the steps in the previous task to view it. (If you pop the photo open, skip the rest of these steps.)

(4) To see actions you can perform on the photo preview, swipe up the image.

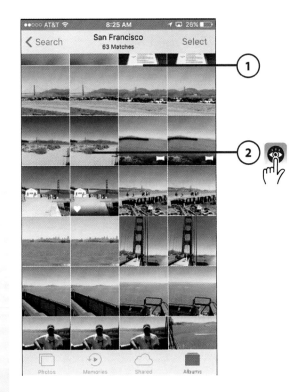

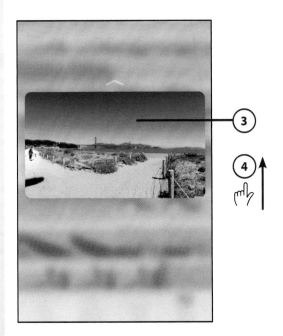

(5) Tap the action you want to perform, such as Favorite, to tag the photo as a favorite.

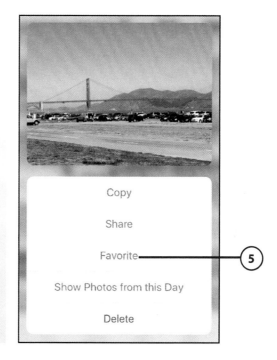

Copy

Share

Favorite————————(5)

Show Photos from this Day

Delete

Working with Memories

New! The Memories feature automatically creates collections of photos for you to view in a number of ways. You can view them in a slideshow, individually, by selecting places, by selecting people, and so on. This feature provides lots of options and at times can be a very interesting way to view photos, because you might be surprised by some of the photos included in a particular memory.

There are a number of ways to access memories, including: tapping the Memories button on the Photo app's Dock at the bottom of the screen; tapping a heading for a group of photos when viewing years, collections, or moments; or tapping a Related item on a photo's Details page.

When you access a memory (no matter how you arrived), you see different options depending on the content of that memory. These can include:

- **Slideshow**—The photos collected in a memory play in a slideshow that plays using a theme, which has effects and a soundtrack. You can change the theme and length of the slideshow, and you can also edit it.

- **Photos**—All memories enable you to view the photos they contain just like photos stored in other places.

- **People**—If the photos in a memory include people, the app identifies those people by facial recognition and enables you to view other photos containing those people or groups of people.

- **Groups & People**—If the photos in a memory include people that are in consisten groupings, you can use these groups to view photos containing those groupings.

- **Places**—You can use the Places tool to view the photos in a memory on a map. You can click on locations on the map where photos were taken to view those photos.

- **Related**—This section of a memory presents other memories that are somehow related to the one you are viewing. This relationship can be based or location, people, and so on.

The Photos app creates memories for you dynamically, meaning they change over time as the photos in your library change. You can save memories that you want to keep as they are. Otherwise, the memories you see change as you take more photos or edit photos you have. This keeps memories a fresh and interesting way to view your photo.

Following are examples of different ways to access memories:

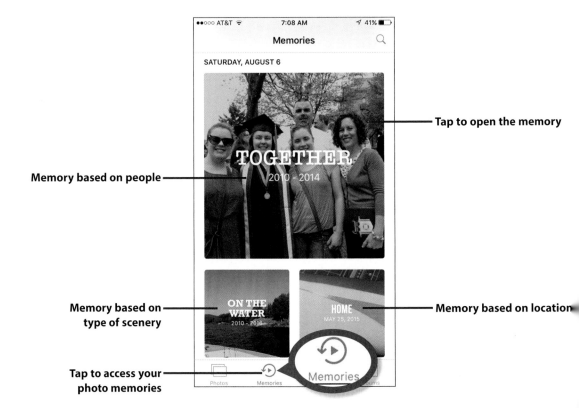

Tap to open the memory

Memory based on people

Memory based on type of scenery

Memory based on location

Tap to access your photo memories

- **Memories button**—When you tap the Memories button on the Photo app's Dock, you see the Memories screen that contains the current memories the app has created and those you have saved. Tap a memory to open it.

Memory slideshow ——

Photos in the memory ——

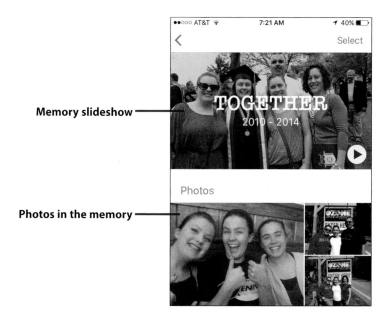

On the memory's screen, you see different tools for viewing its photos, as described in the previous list, depending on the content of the memory. For example, if there aren't any people in the photos, there won't be a People section.

Tap to access a memory based on this group of photos ——

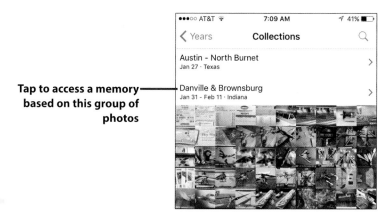

Memory containing
photos in the
selected group

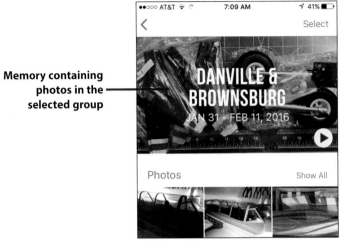

- **The heading of group of photos**—As you learned earlier, the Photos app collects photos based on the time and location at which they were taken. As you browse these groups, you can tap on a group's heading to view the photos it contains in a memory.

You can work with memories in a similar way no matter how you open them or what kind of photos they contain. Following are examples showing how to use several of the sections you see in memories.

Watching and Changing a Memory's Slideshow

All memories have slideshows that you can watch using the following steps:

1. Open a memory using an option described previously. Slideshows appear at the top of a memory's screen.

2. Tap the Play button. The slideshow begins to play. If some of the photos in the slideshow aren't currently stored on your iPhone, there might be a pause while they are downloaded (you see the Downloading status on the opening screen while this is done).

3 Watch the slideshow; to view the slideshow in landscape orientation, rotate the iPhone. As the slideshow plays, you see effects applied to the photos; videos included in the memory also play.

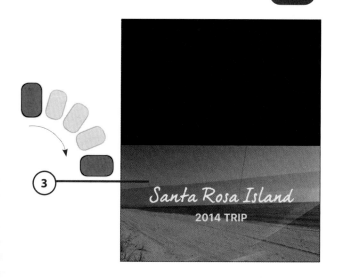

4 Tap the screen to reveal the slideshow controls.

5 To pause the slideshow, tap the Pause button. (When paused, this becomes the Play button that you can tap to resume the slideshow.)

6 Swipe to the right or left on the theme bar to change the slideshow's theme. As you change the theme you might see changes on the screen, such as a different font for the title.

7 Swipe to the right or left on the duration bar to change the slideshow's length. As you make changes, you see the slideshow's current length just above the theme bar.

8 Swipe to the left or right on the thumbnails at the bottom of the screen to move back or forward, respectively.

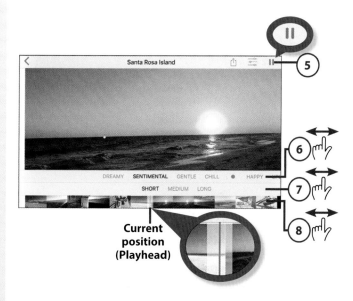

Current position (Playhead)

9 To restart the slideshow with the new settings, tap the Play button.

10 Tap the Adjust button to make manual changes to the slideshow (see the Go Further sidebar "Make Your Own Memories" for more information).

11 Tap the Share button and use the resulting menu to share the memory via AirDrop or an app; you can also save it to your iCloud Drive or Dropbox.

12 Tap the back button to return to the memory.

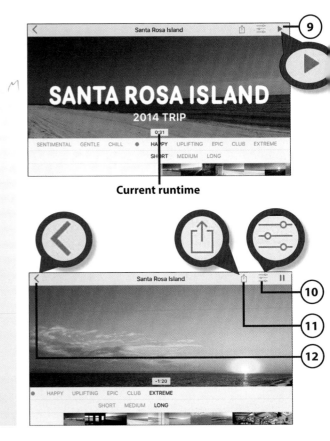

Current runtime

>>>Go Further
MAKE YOUR OWN MEMORIES

You can edit a slideshow to change how it plays. Tap the Adjust button. Tap Title to change the slideshow's name and title style. Tap Music to change its soundtrack; you can choose None to remove the soundtrack; Soundtracks to use one of the default soundtracks; or My Music to use music in your iTunes Music Library. Tap Duration to set the slideshow's playing time. Tap Photos & Videos to manually select the photos that are included. Tap Done to save your slideshow. When you play the slideshow, the options you selected are used. You can return to your version of the slideshow by choosing Custom on the Theme bar.

Viewing a Memory's Photos

You can view the photos contained in a memory using the following steps:

① Open a memory using an option described previously.

② Swipe up the screen until you see the Photos section. Here you see the photos in the memory.

Show All, Tell All

If the memory has lots of photos, you might see only a summary view of them on the Photos section. Tap Show All to see all the photos. Tap Summary to return to the summary view.

---

③ Swipe up and down the photos section to see all the photos the memory contains.

④ Tap a photo to view it.

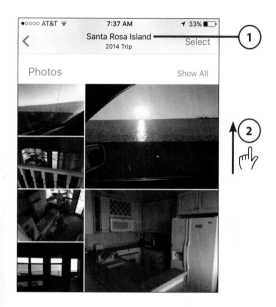

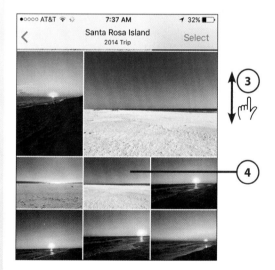

5 Use the techniques you learned in "Viewing Photos Individually" earlier in the chapter to work with the photos in the memory.

6 Tap the back button to return to the memory.

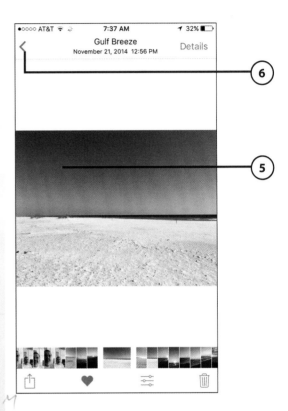

Viewing a Memory's Photos by Place

You can choose the photos in a memory to view based on the location using the Places section.

1 Open a memory using an option described previously.

2 Swipe up the screen until you see the Places section.

3 Tap a place. The map expands to fill the screen and you see more locations associated with photos in the memory.

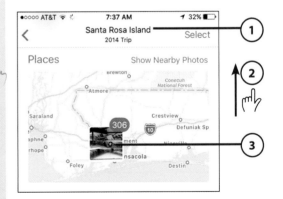

Nearby Photos

Tap Show Nearby Photos to show other photos that were taken near the locations that you are viewing on the map, but that are not currently included in the memory. Tap Hide Nearby Photos to hide those photos again.

4 Unpinch your fingers on the screen to zoom in to reveal more detailed locations.

5 Swipe around the screen to move around the map.

6 Tap a location to see the photos associated with it.

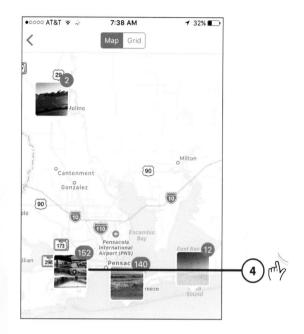

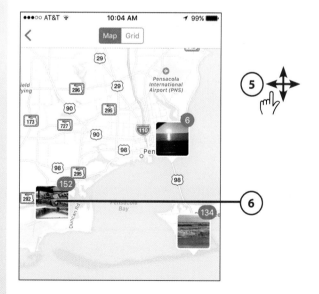

(7) Swipe up and down the screen to browse the photos taken at the location.

(8) Tap a photo to view it.

(9) Use the techniques covered in "Viewing Photos Individually" earlier in the chapter to work with the photos in the memory.

(10) Tap the back button to return to the place.

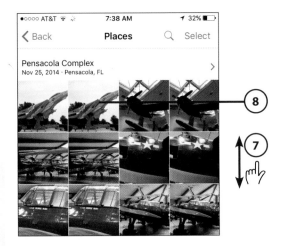

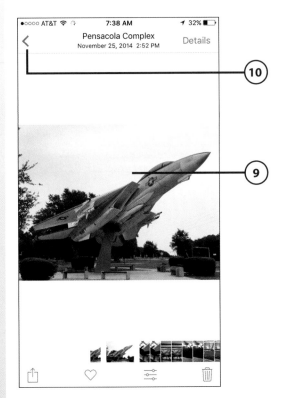

11 Tap the Back button to return to the map.

12 Tap other locations to view their photos.

13 Tap the back button to return to the memory.

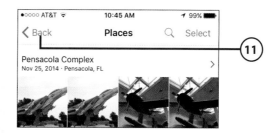

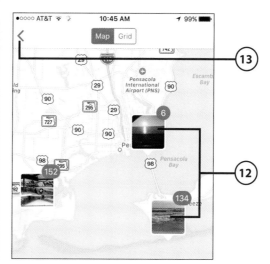

>>>Go Further
MAKING THE MOST OF YOUR MEMORIES

Here are a few more ways to make the most of your memories:

- To view memories based on people or groups of people, tap the person or group in the Groups & People or People section; you see a memory focused on the person or group you selected. You can confirm more photos of a person by tapping Confirm Additional Photos. You see more photos that might contain that person. Tap Yes to confirm it is the same person or No if it isn't. Any photos you confirm are added to that person's memory.

- Tap a memory in the Related section to see a memory that is related to the current one, such as one with photos containing the same people or in the same locations.

- Tap Add to Favorite Memories to add a memory you are viewing to the Favorite Memories album. Tap Remove from Favorite Memories to remove the memory from the Favorite Memories album.

- Tap Add to Memories to add a memory to the Memory screen. For example, when you are viewing a related memory and want to be able to get back to it quickly, tap Add to Memories. That memory appears on the Memory screen.

- Tap Delete Memory and then confirm you want to delete a memory by tapping Delete Memory again; the memory is deleted. When you delete a memory, only the memory is deleted; the photos that were in that memory remain in your photo library. (However, if you delete a photo from within a memory, that photo is deleted from your photo library, too.)

>>>Go Further
ROLL YOUR OWN SLIDESHOWS

The Memories feature creates slideshows that include effects and soundtracks for you automatically. However, you can create your own slideshows manually. View a photo in a collection that you want to view as a slideshow. Tap the Share button. Tap Slideshow. The slideshow plays. Tap the screen to show the slideshow controls. Tap Options to configure the slideshow, such as to choose music for it. When you're done watching a slideshow, tap Done.

Working with Burst Mode Photos

When you use the Burst mode to take photos, the Camera app rapidly takes a series of photos. (Typically, you use Burst mode to capture motion, where the action is happening too quickly to be able to frame and take individual photos.) You can review the photos taken in Burst mode and save any you want to keep as favorites; your favorites become separate photos just like those you take one at a time. Here's how:

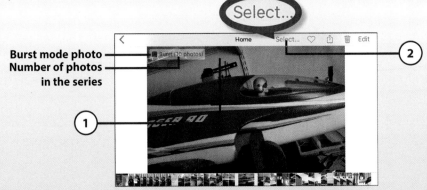

Burst mode photo
Number of photos
in the series

1 View a Burst mode photo. Burst mode photos are indicated by the word Burst and the number of photos in the burst. (You can see all of the burst photos on your phone by opening the Bursts album.)

2 Tap Select. The burst is expanded. At the bottom of the screen, you see thumbnails for the photos in the burst. At the top part of the screen, you see thumbnails of the photos; the photo in the center of the previews is marked with a downward-facing arrow. Photos marked with a dot are "suggested photos," meaning the best ones in the series according to the Photos app.

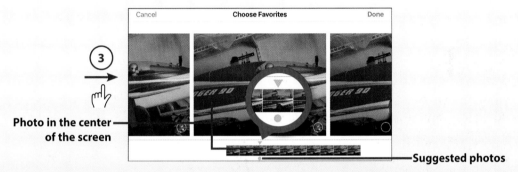

Photo in the center of the screen

Suggested photos

3 Swipe all the way to the right to move to the first photo in the series; swiping on the thumbnails at the bottom flips through them faster.

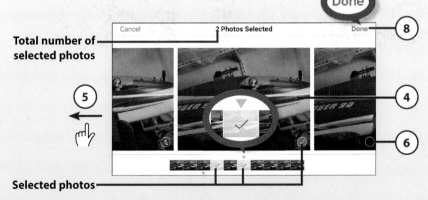

Total number of selected photos

Selected photos

4 Tap a photo that you want to save. It is marked with a check mark.

5 Swipe to the left to move through the series.

6 Tap each photo you want to save.

7 Continue reviewing and selecting photos until you've gone through the entire series.

8 Tap Done.

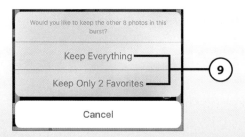

(9) Tap Keep Only *X* Favorites, where *X* is the number of photos you selected, or tap Keep Everything to keep all the photos in the burst. Each photo you keep becomes a separate, individual photo; you can work with these just like photos you take individually.

Burst Mode Photos and Uploads to the Cloud

If the Upload Burst Photos switch on the Photos & Camera Settings screen is set to off, burst photos are not uploaded to the cloud until you go through the steps to select and save photos from a burst. The photos you selected to keep are then uploaded to the cloud just like individual photos you take.

Editing Photos

Even though the iPhone has great photo-taking capabilities, not all the photos you take are perfect from the start. Fortunately, you can use the Photos app to improve your photos. The following tools are available to you:

- **Enhance**—This tool attempts to automatically adjust the colors and other properties of the photos to make them better.

- **Straighten, Rotate, and Crop**—You can rotate your photos to change their orientation and crop out the parts of photos you don't want to keep. You can also have the Photos app do this with the tap of a button.

- **Filters**—You can apply different filters to your photos for artistic or other purposes.

- **Red-eye**—This one helps you remove that certain demon-possessed look from the eyes of people in your photos.

- **Smart Adjustments**—You can adjust the light, color, and even the black-and-white properties of your photos.

- **Markups**—You can add markups, such as redlines, drawings, and magnification to photos.

Enhancing Photos

To improve the quality of a photo, use the Enhance tool.

(1) View the image you want to enhance.

(2) Tap the Adjust button.

(3) Tap the Enhance button. The image is enhanced and the Enhance button turns blue.

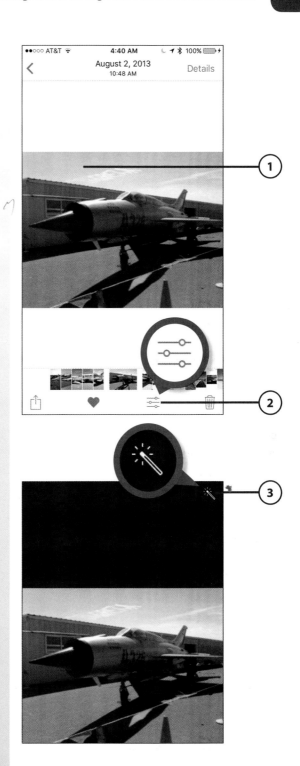

(4) If you don't like the enhancements, tap the Enhance button again to remove the enhancements.

(5) Tap Done to save the enhanced image.

Straightening, Rotating, and Cropping Photos

To change the alignment, position, and part of the image shown, perform the following steps:

(**1**) View the image you want to change.

(**2**) Tap the Adjust button.

(**3**) Tap the Rotate/Crop button. The Photos app attempts to straighten and crop the photo automatically.

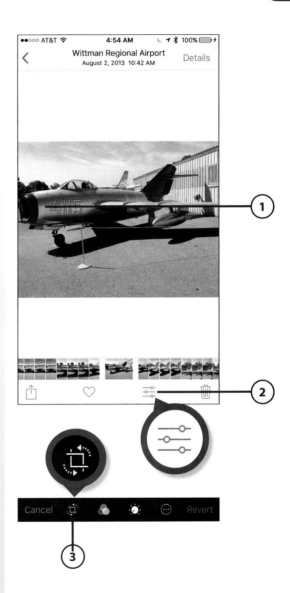

(4) If you are satisfied with how
the photo is straightened and
cropped, tap Done and skip
the rest of these steps. If not,
continue to the next step.

(5) To undo the automatic
straighten and crop, tap RESET.

(6) To rotate the image, tap the
Rotate button. Each time you
tap this button, the image
rotates 90 degrees.

(7) Straighten the image by
dragging the triangle to the left
or right to rotate the image.

(8) When the image is straightened,
lift your finger from the screen.
The dial shows how much
you've rotated the image.

(9) Crop the image proportionally
by tapping the Constrain
button; to crop the image
without staying to a specific
proportion, skip to step 11.

Photo is
straightened
and cropped

10 Tap the proportion with which you want to crop the image. You use this to configure the image for how you intend to display it. For example, if you want to display it on a 16:9 TV, you might want to constrain the cropping to that proportion so the image matches the display device.

11 Drag the corners of the crop box until the part of the image you want to keep is shown in the box.

12 Drag on the image to move it around inside the crop box.

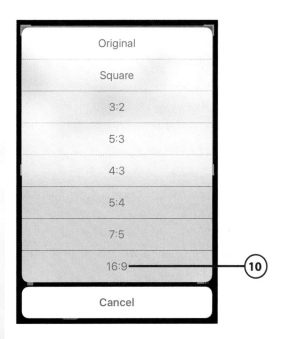

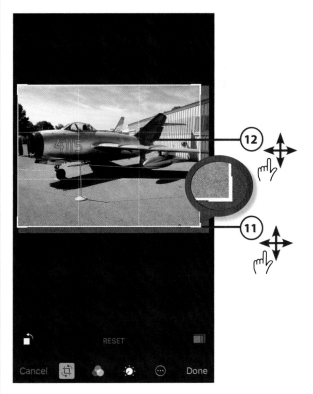

(13) When the image is cropped and positioned as you want it to be, tap Done. The edited image is saved.

More on Straightening and Cropping Photos

To undo changes you've made, tap the RESET button and the photo returns to the state it was in before you started editing it. To have the app automatically straighten and crop the photo again, tap AUTO. To exit the Edit mode without saving your changes, tap Cancel.

Applying Filters to Photos

To apply filters to photos, do the following:

(1) View the image to which you want to apply filters.

(2) Tap the Adjust button.

(3) Tap the Filters button. The palette of filters appears.

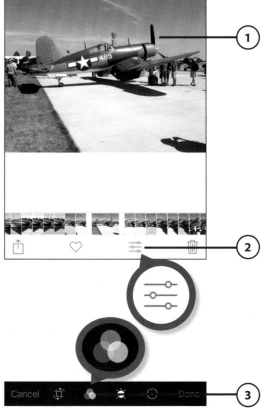

4 Swipe to the left or right on the palette to browse all of the filters.

5 Tap the filter you want to apply. The filter is applied to the image and you see a preview of the image as it will be with the filter; the filter currently applied is highlighted with a blue box. Keep trying filters until the image is what you want it to be.

6 Tap Done. The photo with the filter applied is saved.

Filter currently applied

Undoing What You've Done

To restore a photo to its unedited state, tap Revert, which appears when you edit a photo that you previously edited and saved. At the prompt, tap Revert to Original, and the photo is restored to its "like new" condition.

The original version of photos is saved in your library so you can use the Revert function to go back to the photo as it was originally taken or added to the library, even if you've adjusted it several times.

However, you can't have the adjusted version and the original version displaying in your library at the same time. If you want to be able to have both an adjusted and original version (or multiple adjusted versions of the same photo), make a copy of the original before you alter it. To do this, view the photo, tap the Share button, and tap Duplicate. You can do this as many times as you want. Each copy behaves like a new photo. If you adjust one copy, the original remains available in your library.

Removing Red-Eye from Photos

When you edit a photo with people in it, the Red-eye tool becomes available (if no faces are recognized, this tool is hidden). To remove red-eye, perform the following steps:

1. View an image with people that have red-eye.

2. Tap the Adjust button.

3. Tap the Red-eye button.

4. Zoom in on the eyes from which you want to remove red-eye.

5 Tap each eye containing red-eye. The red in the eyes you tap is removed.

6 Repeat steps 4 and 5 until you've removed all the red-eye.

7 Tap Done to save your changes.

Making Smart Adjustments to Photos

You can edit your photos using the Photos app's Smart Adjustment tools. Using these tools, you can change various characteristics related to light, color, and black-and-white aspects of your photos.

1 View the image you want to adjust.

2 Tap the Adjust button.

3 Tap the Smart Adjust button.

4 Tap the area you want to adjust, such as Color.

Get Straight to the Point

To jump directly to a specific aspect of the area you are adjusting, tap the downward-facing arrow along the right side of the screen. On the resulting menu, tap the aspect you want to adjust. For example, if you open this menu for Color, you tap Saturation, Contrast, or Cast to adjust those factors.

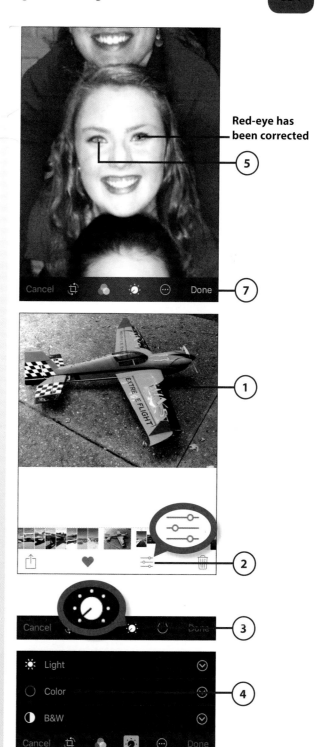

Red-eye has been corrected

5 Swipe to the left or right to change the level of the parameter you are adjusting. As you make changes, you see the results of the change on the image.

6 When you're done adjusting the first attribute you selected, tap the List button.

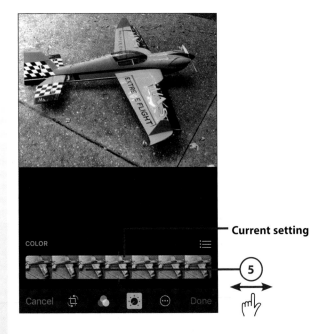

Current setting

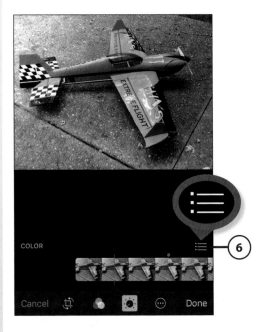

7 Tap one of the options under the attribute you are already working with to adjust it; or tap the downward-facing arrow under one of the other attributes, and then tap the characteristic you want to change.

8 Swipe to the left or right to change the level of the parameter you are adjusting. As you make changes, you see the results of the change on the image.

9 Repeat steps 6 through 8 until you've made all the adjustments you want to make.

10 Tap Done to save the adjusted image.

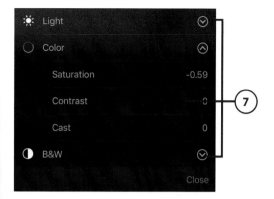

Marking Up Photos

New! You can add markups to photos, including:

- **Draw**—You draw directly on top of photos, such as to indicate areas of interest or highlight something.

- **Magnify**—This tool magnifies a section of an image in a circle that looks kind of like an image you see through a magnifying glass.

- **Add text**—You can use the text tool to add words to an image.

With the draw and text tools, you can choose the format of the markup, such as its color.

The following steps show the magnification and text markup tools; the drawing tool works similarly.

(1) View the image you want to adjust.

(2) Tap the Adjust button.

(3) Tap the Photo Editor tool. The
Photo Editing menu appears.

(4) Tap Markup.

But Wait, There May Be More

The Markup tool is the default photo
editor that comes with the Photos
app. Over time, other photo-editing
tools will become available. When
installed, you see them on the Photo
Editing menu. Tap a tool to use it.
Tap More to configure the photo-
editing tools you have installed—
for example, set a tool's switch to
off (white) to hide it. You can also
change the order in which the tools
are listed on the menu.

---

(5) Tap the Magnify tool. The
magnification circle appears.

(6) Drag the circle over the area of
the image you want to magnify.

(7) To change the size of the area
being magnified, drag the blue
dot away from the center of the
circle to increase the area or
toward the center to decrease the
size of the area.

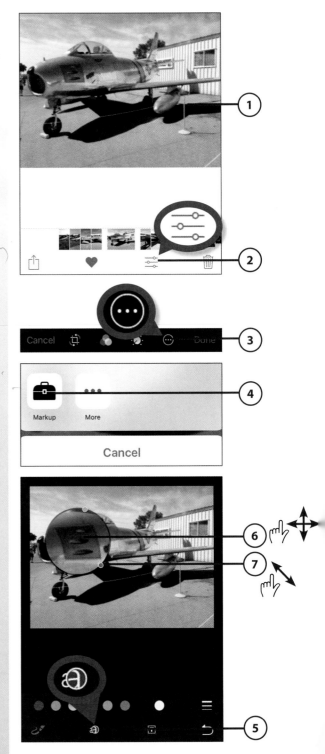

De-magnify

To remove a magnification mark-up, tap it and then tap Delete.

(8) Tap the Text tool to add a text markup. A text box appears.

(9) Drag the text box to be where you want the text to appear.

(10) Double-tap the text box.

(11) Type the text you want to add.

(12) Tap Done.

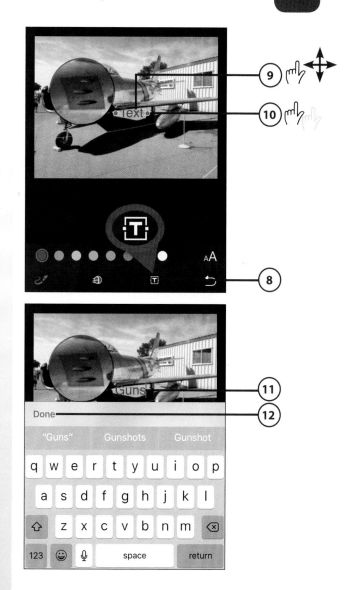

13 Tap Done to save your markups on the photo.

Formatting Markups

Tap one of the colored circles to change the color of the markup you are working with. When you are working with text, tap the format button (AA) to change the text's font, size, and justification. When you are working with a drawing markup, you can use the line format menu to change the thickness of the markup's line.

Working with Photos

Once you have photos on your iPhone, there are a lot of things you can do with them, including

- Emailing one or more photos to one or more people (see the next task).

- Sending a photo via a text message (see Chapter 10, "Sending, Receiving, and Managing Texts and iMessages").

- Sharing photos via AirDrop (see Chapter 3, "Connecting Your iPhone to the Internet, Bluetooth Devices, and iPhones/iPods/iPads").

- Sharing photos with others via iCloud (covered later in this chapter).

- Posting your photos on your Facebook wall or timeline.

- Assigning photos to contacts (see Chapter 7, "Managing Contacts").

- Using photos as wallpaper (see Chapter 6, "Customizing How Your iPhone Looks and Sounds").

- Sharing photos via tweets.
- Printing photos (see Chapter 2, "Using Your iPhone's Core Features").
- Deleting photos (covered later).
- Organizing photos in albums (also covered later).

Copy 'Em

If you select one or more photos and tap the Copy button, the images you selected are copied to the iPhone's clipboard. You can then move into another app and paste them in.

You'll easily be able to accomplish any actions on your own that are not covered in detail here once you've performed a couple of those that are demonstrated in the following tasks.

Individual Versus Groups

Some actions are only available when you are working with an individual photo. For example, you can send only a single photo via Twitter, whereas you can email multiple photos at the same time. Any commands that aren't applicable to the photos that are selected won't appear on the screen.

Sharing Photos via Email

You can email photos via iPhone's Mail application starting from the Photos app.

1. View the source containing one or more images that you want to share.

2. Tap Select.

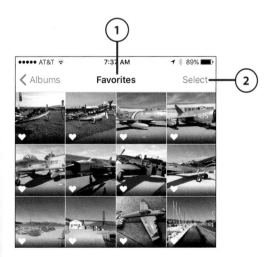

③ Select the photos you want to send by tapping them. When you tap a photo, it is marked with a check mark to show you that it is selected.

④ Tap the Share button.

Too Many?
If the photos you have selected are too much for email, the Mail button won't appear. You need to select fewer photos to attach to the email message.

⑤ Tap Mail. A new email message is created, and the photos are added as attachments.

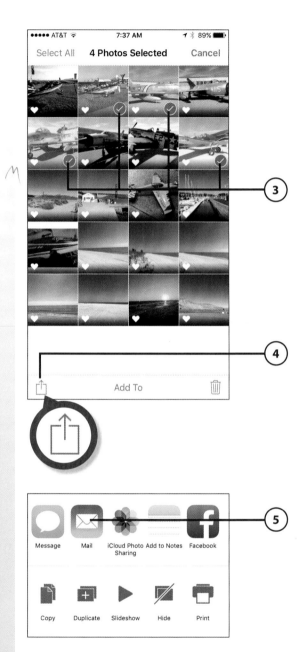

6 Use the email tools to address the email, add a subject, type the body, and send it. (See Chapter 9, "Sending, Receiving, and Managing Email," for detailed information about using your iPhone's email tools.)

7 Tap the size of the images you want to send. Choosing a smaller size makes the files smaller and reduces the quality of the photos. You should generally try to keep the size of emails to 5MB or less to ensure the message makes it to the recipient. (Some email servers block larger messages.) After you send the email, you move back to the photos you were browsing.

Images from Email

As mentioned in Chapter 9, when you save images attached to email that you receive, they are stored in the All Photos or Camera Roll photo album just like photos you take with your iPhone.

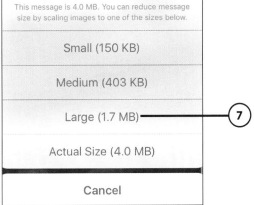

Organizing Photos in a New Album

You can create photo albums and store photos in them to keep your photos organized.

To create a new album, perform these steps:

(1) Move to the Albums screen by tapping Albums on the toolbar.

(2) Tap the Add button (+).

(3) Type the name of the new album.

(4) Tap Save. You're prompted to select photos to add to the new album.

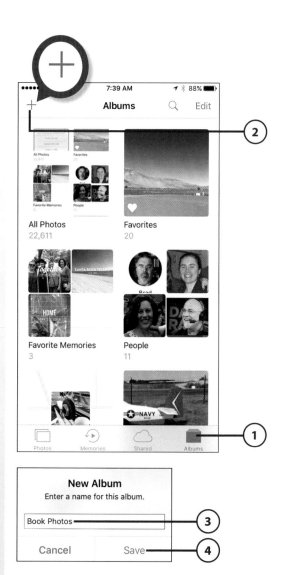

⑤ Move to the source of the photos you want to add to the new album.

⑥ Swipe up and down to browse the source and tap the photos you want to add to the album. They are marked with a check mark to show that they are selected. The number of photos selected is shown at the top of the screen.

⑦ Tap Done. The photos are added to the new album and you move back to the Albums screen. The new album is shown on the list, and you can work with it just like the other albums you see.

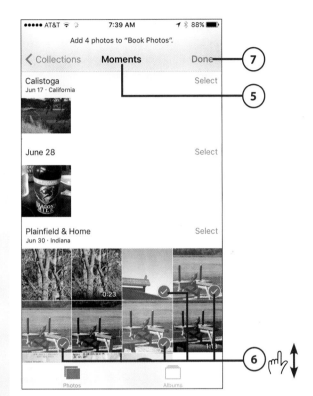

Playing Favorites

To mark any photo or video as a favorite, tap the heart button. It fills in with blue to show you that the item you are viewing is a favorite. Favorites are automatically collected in the Favorites album, so this is an easy way to collect photos and videos you want to be able to easily find again without having to create a new album or even put them in an album. You can unmark a photo or video as a favorite by tapping the heart button again.

Adding Photos to an Existing Album

To add photos to an existing album, follow these steps:

1. Move to the source containing the photos you want to add to an album.

2. Tap Select.

3. Tap the photos you want to add to the album.

4. Tap Add To. You move to the Add to Album screen.

5. Swipe up and down the list to find the album to which you want to add the photos.

6. Tap the album; the selected photos are added to the album. (If an album is grayed out and you can't tap it, that album was not created on the iPhone and so you can't change its contents.)

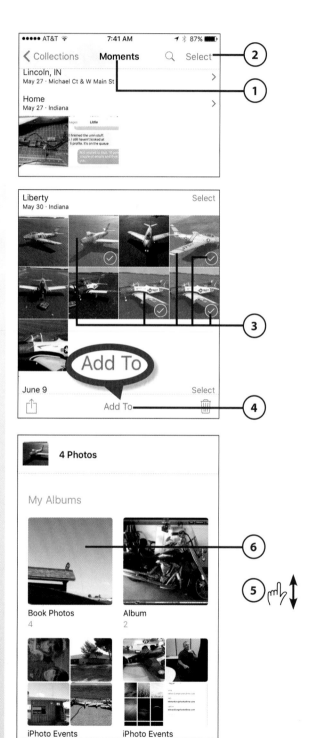

More Album Fun

You can change the order in which albums are listed on the Albums screen. Move to the Albums screen and Tap the Edit button. Drag albums up or down the screen to reposition them. To delete an album that you created in the Photos app, tap its unlock button (red circle with a –) and then tap Delete Album. When you're done making changes to your albums, tap Done.

To remove a photo from an album, view the photo from within the album, tap the Trash Can button, and then tap Remove from Album. Photos you remove from an album remain in your photo library; they are only removed from the album.

Deleting Photos

You can delete photos and videos that you don't want to keep on your iPhone. If you use the iCloud Photo Library, deleting the photos from your phone also deletes them from your photo library and from all the other devices using your library. So, make sure you really don't want photos any more before you delete them.

(1) Open the source containing photos you want to delete.

(2) Tap Select.

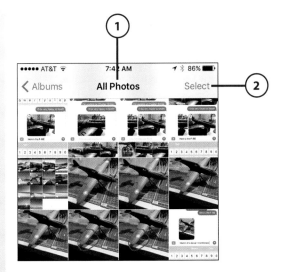

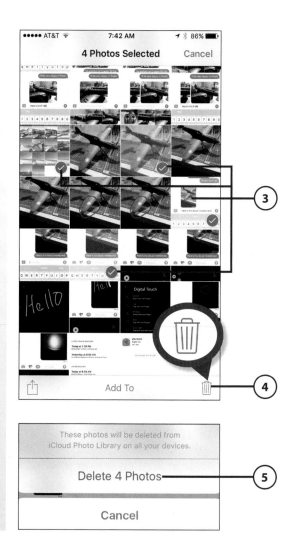

(3) Tap the photos you want to delete. Each item you select is marked with a check mark.

(4) Tap the Trash Can button.

(5) Tap Delete X Photos, where X is the number of photos you selected. The photos you selected are deleted.

Deleting Individual Photos

You can delete individual photos that you are viewing by tapping the Trash Can button, and then tapping Delete Photo.

Viewing, Editing, and Working with Video on Your iPhone

As explained in Chapter 14, you can capture video clips with your iPhone. Once captured, you can view clips on your iPhone, edit them, and share them.

Finding and Watching Videos

Watching videos you've captured with your iPhone is simple.

1. Move to the Albums screen.

2. Tap the Videos album. Video clips display their running time at the bottom of their thumbnails.

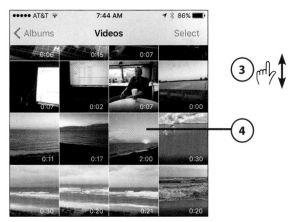

3. Swipe up and down the screen to browse your videos.

4. Tap the video you want to watch.

5. Rotate the phone to change its orientation if necessary.

6. Tap Play. The video plays. After a few moments, the toolbars disappear.

Deleting Video

To remove a video clip from your iPhone, select it, tap the Trash Can button, and then tap Delete Video at the prompt.

7 Tap the video. The toolbars reappear.

8 Pause the video by tapping the Pause button.

9 Jump to a specific point in a video by swiping to the left or right on the thumbnails at the bottom of the screen. When you swipe to the left, you move ahead in the video; when you swipe to the right, you move back in the video.

Watching Slow-Motion and Time-Lapse Video

Watching slow-motion video is just like watching regular speed video except after a few frames, the video slows down until a few frames before the end at which point it speeds up again. Watching time-lapse is similar except the video plays faster instead of slower than real time.

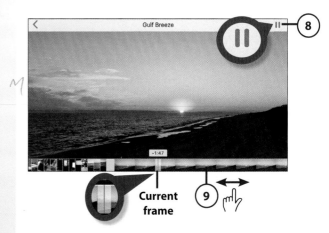

Current frame

Editing Video

You can trim a video clip to remove unwanted parts. Here's how you do it:

1 View the video you want to edit.

2 Tap the Adjust button. If the video isn't stored on your phone, it is downloaded. When that process is complete, you can edit it.

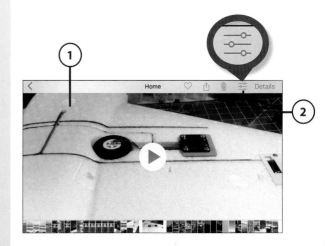

3 Drag the left trim marker to where you want the edited clip to start; the trim marker is the left-facing arrow at the left end of the timeline. If you hold your finger in one place for a few seconds, the thumbnails expand so your placement of the crop marker can be more precise. As soon as you move the trim marker, the part of the clip that is inside the selection is highlighted in the yellow box.

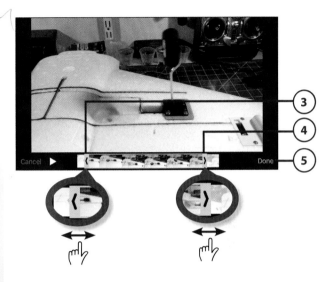

4 Drag the right trim marker to where you want the edited clip to end.

5 Tap Done.

6 Tap Save as New Clip to save the trimmed clip as a new clip or Cancel to leave the clip as it was. When you save it as a new clip, the frames outside the crop markers are removed from the clip and it is added to your library as a new clip.

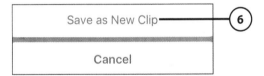

There's an App for That

For more powerful video editing on your iPhone, download the iMovie app. This app provides a much more powerful video editor. You can use themes to design a video, add music, include titles and photos, and much more.

>>>*Go Further*

SHARING VIDEO

There are lots of ways to share your videos. Select the video you want to share. Tap the Share button. Tap how you want to share the video; you can choose to use Messages, Mail, iCloud, iCloud Photo Sharing, YouTube, Facebook, or Vimeo. Follow the onscreen prompts to complete the sharing process. The options available to you might depend on the size of the video; for example, you might not be able to email a large video.

Using iCloud with Your Photos

With iCloud, your devices can automatically upload photos to your iCloud account on the Internet. Other devices can automatically download photos from iCloud, so you have your photos available on all your devices at the same time. Using iCloud with your photos has two sides: a sender and receiver. Your iPhone can be both. Photo applications can also access your photos and download them to your computer automatically.

In addition to backing up your photos and having all your photos available to you, you can also share your photos and videos with others and view photos and videos being shared with you.

Sharing Your Photos

You can share your photos with others by creating a shared album. This is a great way to share photos, because others can subscribe to your shared albums to view and work with the photos you share. When you share photos, you can add them to an album that's already being shared or create a new shared album.

To create a new, empty, shared album, do the following:

(1) Open the Shared source. You see the iCloud Photo Sharing screen that lists the shared albums in which you are currently participating (as either the person sharing them or subscribed to them).

(2) Tap the Add (+) button.

(3) Type the title of the new album.

(4) Tap Next.

(5) Enter or select the email address of the first person with whom you want to share the photos.

(6) Add other recipients until you've added everyone you want to access the photos.

(7) Tap Create. The shared album is created and is ready for you to add photos. The recipients you included in the new album receive notifications that invite them to join the album.

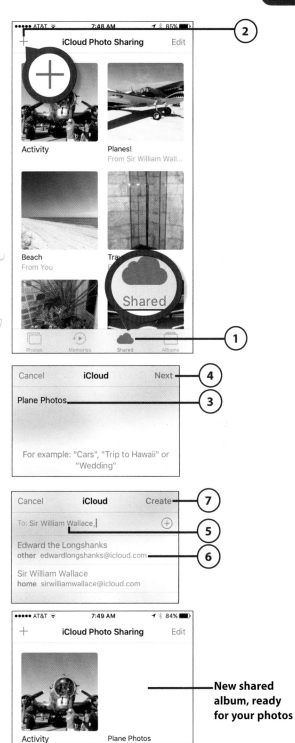

New shared album, ready for your photos

Adding Photos to a Shared Album

To add photos to an album you are sharing, perform the following steps:

(1) Move to the source containing photos you want to add to a shared album.

(2) Tap Select.

(3) Tap the photos you want to share.

(4) Tap the Share button.

(5) Tap iCloud Photo Sharing.

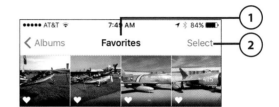

6 Enter your commentary about the photos you are sharing. (Note, this commentary is associated only with the first photo.)

7 Tap Shared Album.

8 Swipe up and down to browse the list of shared albums available.

9 Tap the album to which you want to add the photos.

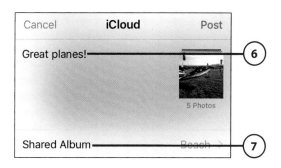

New Shared Album with Photos

You can create a new shared album with the selected photos by tapping New Shared Album.

10 Tap iCloud.

11 Tap Post. The photos you selected are added to the shared album. People who are subscribed to the album receive a notification that photos have been added and can view the new photos along with your commentary.

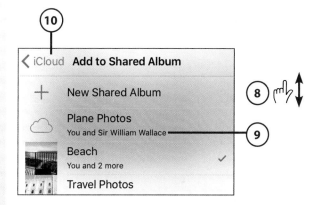

iCloud Account Required

The people with whom you share photos must have an iCloud account.

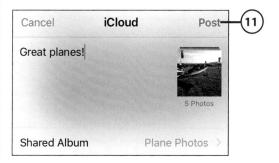

>>>Go Further

MORE ON ICLOUD PHOTO SHARING

Following are a few more pointers to help you use iCloud photo sharing:

- You can add comments to photos you are sharing. Open the shared album and tap the photo to which you want to add comments. Tap Add a comment. Type your comment and tap Send. People with whom you are sharing the photo receive a notification and can read your comments.

- To add more photos to a shared album, open the album and tap the Add (+) button. Use the resulting screen to select the photos you want to add, include commentary, and post the photos.

- To invite people to join a shared album, open the shared album. Tap the People tab at the bottom of the screen and then tap Invite People. Enter the email addresses of the people you want to invite and tap Add.

- You can configure various aspects of a shared album by opening it and tapping the People tab at the bottom of the screen. You can see the status of people you have invited, determine if the people with whom you are sharing the album can post to it, make the album a public website, determine if notifications are sent, or delete the shared album.

Working with Photo Albums Shared with You

You can work with albums people share with you as follows:

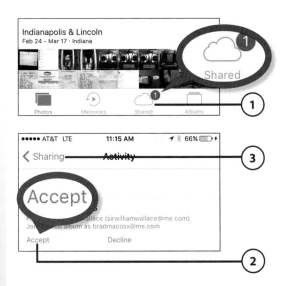

1. Tap the notification you received, or tap the Shared source when you see a badge indicating you have activity.

2. Tap Accept for the shared album you want to join. The shared album becomes available on your Shared tab.

3. Tap Sharing.

4 Tap the new shared album.

5 Tap a photo in the album.

6 Tap Like to indicate you like the photo.

7 Tap Add a comment. (If you previously liked the photo, you see the number of likes for it instead; tap that number to add a comment.)

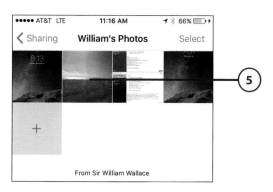

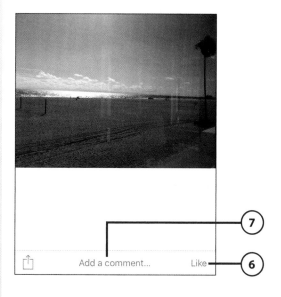

Chapter 15 | Viewing and Editing Photos and Video with the Photos App

8 Type your comment.

9 Tap Send. Your comments are added to the album.

10 Tap the back button.

11 If allowed, tap the Add (+) button and post your own photos to the album you are sharing. This works just like posting to your own albums.

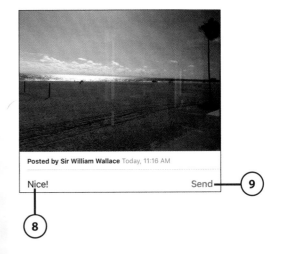

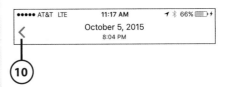

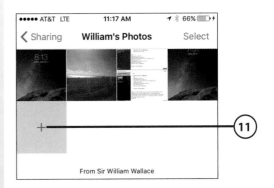

>>>*Go Further*

MORE ON PHOTOS SHARED WITH YOU

When you share other people's photos, keep the following points in mind:

- You can do most of the tasks with shared photos that you can with your own, such as emailing them, using them as wallpaper, and so on.

- To unsubscribe from an album, move to its People screen and tap Unsubscribe and confirm that is what you want to do. The shared album is removed from your iPhone.

- To see the activity associated with albums being shared with you, and those you are sharing, open the Activity Album on the iCloud Photo Sharing screen. You see new postings to the albums, when someone comments, and so on.

Index

U